M000207241

Li Hung-chang and China's Early Modernization

Li Hung-chang at Tientsin. (From Mrs. Archibald Little, *Li Hung-chang: His Life and Time*. London: Cassell, 1903.)

Li Hung-chang and China's Early Modernization

Edited by
Samuel C. Chu &
Kwang-Ching Liu

An East Gate Book

M. E. Sharpe INC
ARMONK, NEW YORK
LONDON, ENGLAND

An East Gate Book

Copyright © 1994 by M. E. Sharpe, Inc.

A shorter version of this study appeared in *Chinese Studies in History*, Vol. 24, Nos. 1 & 2 (fall–winter 1990–91); Vol. 24, No. 4 (summer 1991); and Vol. 25, No. 1 (fall 1991)

Library of Congress Cataloging-in-Publication Data

Li Hung-chang and China's Early Modernization
edited by Samuel C. Chu and Kwang-Ching Liu.
p. cm.
"East Gate Book"
Includes bibliographical references and index.
ISBN 1-56324-242-7(c); ISBN 1-56324-458-6(p)
1. China—History—1861–1912.
2. Li, Hung-chang, 1823–1901.
I. Chu, Samuel C., 1929–
II. Liu, Kwang-Ching, 1921–
DS761.2.L5 1993
951′.035—dc20
93-31417
CIP

Printed in the United States of America

Cover design: Ted Palmer
Cover calligraphy: Li Hung-chang's signature,
in Li's own hand, private collection.

♾

BM (c) 10 9 8 7 6 5 4 3 2 1
BM (p) 10 9 8 7 6 5 4 3 2 1

Contents

Part IV. Li as Diplomat

Part V. Li as Modernizer

Part VI. Conclusion and Bibliography

Photographs:
Li Hung-chang at Tientsin, frontispiece.
Ministers of the Navy Yamen, page 215.
Li Hung-chang in London, 1896, page 215.

Acknowledgments

Most of the papers in this volume were first presented in two panels devoted to Li Hung-chang at the 1987 annual meeting of the Pacific Coast Branch of the American Historical Association (AHA–PCB). At this conference the two panel discussants, Thomas Kennedy and Richard Smith, greatly enriched our efforts. Immediately thereafter Liu presented the Chinese version of his introductory chapter at the conference on the Self-strengthening Movement at the Institute of Modern History, Academia Sinica, in Taiwan, where he benefited from the reactions of the conference participants.

Yuen-sang Leung's chapter was added at the suggestion of Liu, while Chu suggested the inclusion of two of Liu's earlier published articles. While the articles were being published in *Chinese Studies in History,* we asked Thomas Kennedy and Richard Smith if they would like to join us in producing this book version. They responded, and we are fortunate to have their contributions.

In the completion of this book many have inspired and assisted us: our teachers, who first gave us the professional training and acted as role models, and to whom we dedicate this work; our colleagues, our students, and our families and friends. Other scholars who helped us in various ways to improve this study include Joshua Fogel, Guan Jie, James Hsiung, Akira Iriye, Marius Jansen, Bonnie Oh, Qi Qizhang, and C. Martin Wilbur.

Grateful acknowledgments for permission to reprint are hereby tendered to the *Harvard Journal of Asiatic Studies* for chapter 2 (vol. 30 [1970], pp. 5–45), the University of California Press for chapter 3 (*Approaches to Modern Chinese History*, ed. Albert Feuerwerker et al. [1967], pp. 68–104), and the Center for Chinese Studies (Taipei) for chapter 5 (*Chinese Studies*, vol. 4 [1986], pp. 315–31). The Institute of Modern History of the Academia Sinica in Taipei published earlier versions of the Introduction (*Proceedings of the Conference on the Self-strengthening Movement in Late Ch'ing China, 1860–1894* [1988], pp. 1121–33) and the Conclusion (*Newsletter for Modern Chinese History*, no. 6 [1988], pp. 120–35). We are grateful to the Institute for permission to republish the two chapters in their revised form.

Since several of the chapters in this volume have appeared earlier, as editors we have not attempted to adopt uniform style for the entire volume, but have sought only consistency within each chapter.

In the preparation of the manuscript, Marjorie Haffner did the typing of the many drafts, with partial assistance from Janice Gulker. Our thanks to both. Technical and clerical services were also rendered by Constance Berroteran, Xiaoqi Wu, and Cynthia Fowler.

Finally, the co-editors wish to acknowledge the support of Yu-ning Li, editor of *Chinese Studies in History*, who invited us to be guest editors of the special issues devoted to Li Hung-chang, and that of Douglas Merwin, Ana Erlic, Angela Piliouras, and Rita Bernhard of M. E. Sharpe, our publisher. They have improved this work. All remaining errors and imperfections are the responsibilities of the authors and the editors, respectively.

This work is dedicated to the memory of John K. Fairbank and Franklin L. Ho, and to Wing-tsit Chan and C. Martin Wilbur.

Samuel C. Chu
Ohio State University

Kwang-Ching Liu
University of California, Davis

Contributors

Samuel C. Chu, Professor of History
Ohio State University

Thomas L. Kennedy, Professor of History
Washington State University

Key-Hiuk Kim, Professor of History and Director of General Education
Pohang Institute of Science and Technology, Korea

Chi-kong Lai, Lecturer in History
University of New England, Armidale, New South Wales, Australia

Edwin Pak-wah Leung, Professor of Asian Studies
Seton Hall University

Yuen-sang Leung, Associate Professor of History
California State University, Los Angeles

Ming-te Lin, Research Fellow
Institute of Modern History, Academia Sinica

Kwang-Ching Liu, Professor of History Emeritus
University of California, Davis

David P. T. Pong, Professor of History
University of Delaware

Richard J. Smith, Professor of History
Rice University

Chia-chien Wang, Professor of History
National Taiwan Normal University

Coastal China, Korea and Japan

Part I
Introduction

1

The Beginnings of China's Modernization

Kwang-Ching Liu

When did China's modernization begin? The answer to this question depends, of course, on how modernization is defined. Different social sciences (e.g., political science and economics) have defined modernization in different ways. An important series of books on China's modernization as seen in different provinces or groups of provinces has defined modernization as the process leading toward greater social equality, political democratization, and economic liberalization.[1] Such an optimistic and all-embracing definition of modernization is difficult to reject. Scholarship need not be an exercise in universal value judgments, however. In comparative history, it may perhaps be argued that what is essential to modernization is the process of transition from commerce to industry—in other words, industrialization. This essay begins by treating the historically specific concepts of "statecraft" (*ching-shih*) and "self-strengthening" (*tzu-ch'iang*) in the history of nineteenth-century China. It then proceeds to a consideration of major enterprises of nineteenth-century China that introduced steam-driven machines. I believe that a historical survey in this sequence is helpful to understanding modern Chinese history.

Statecraft

In the context of late Ch'ing history, what is the meaning of *ching-shih*—a term many historians have employed and have translated as statecraft? In popular

---

This essay is an expanded version of the first section of the author's Chinese article "Ching-shih, tzu-ch'iang, hsin-hsing ch'i-yeh—Chung-kuo hsien-tai hua ti k'ai-shih" (Statecraft, self-strengthening, and newly arisen enterprise—The beginnings of China's modernization), in *Ch'ing-chi tzu-ch'iang yun-tung yen-t'ao hui lun-wen chi* (Proceedings of the Conference on the Late Ch'ing Self-strengthening Movement) (Taipei: Institute of Modern History, Academia Sinica, 1988), pp. 1121–33. The Chinese version includes an assessment of the successes and failures of the late Ch'ing modernization movement.

usage, the phrase *ching-shih* could simply mean being an official (*tso-kuan*), but in the Chinese intellectual tradition, the phrase means much more than mere bureaucratic experience. The term suggests the ideal of service—service to the state and the people. It implies an idealistic purpose and a concern for practical results as well—concrete and fruitful service to be rendered to state and society by the intellectual.[2]

Wei Yuan (1794–1857) and others of the late Ch'ing period believed that there was a branch of learning as important as the Sung scholarship on metaphysics or the Han learning of the textual study of the classics. This was the learning of statecraft (*ching-shih chih hsüeh*), which calls for facing squarely the practical needs of state and society. Wei Yuan wrote: "Since ancient times, wealth and strength (*fu-ch'iang*) have been achieved without the Kingly Way (*wang-tao*), but the Kingly Way has never been achieved without wealth and strength."[3] Problems of production and finance cannot be avoided; utility and effectiveness must be stressed. Although the study of the classics must continue, the lessons so derived must meet the test of present needs. So must the institutions of government meet practical tests. Wei Yuan, while serving as advisor to Ho Ch'ang-ling (1785–1848)—judicial commissioner of Kiangsu (1824) as well as the financial commissioner there (1825–26)—and to T'ao Chu (1779–1839)—governor of Kiangsu (1825–30) and governor-general of Liangkiang (1830–39)—took part in making plans for shipments of tribute grain by the sea route (instead of relying on the Grand Canal alone) and for the reform of the salt monopoly, making licenses for the salt trade available to some two thousand traders or investors (instead of merely a dozen or so hereditary license-holders). These reforms were both practical and timely. The championing of reforms that were not only desirable but also feasible was the hallmark of the *ching-shih* approach to statecraft.

Pao Shih-ch'en (1775–1855), a statecraft scholar who was Wei Yuan's contemporary, not only was interested in such questions as the tribute rice transport and the salt trade but was also an expert on the Yellow River and knew a great deal about the technical aspects of dredging and dike-building. He was also conversant with agricultural techniques and was the author of an agricultural handbook. As compared with Pao, Wei Yuan was more thoroughly committed to a policy favoring merchant enterprise. He would rely on the resources and the managerial capability of the merchants to help solve the government's problems. "The strength of the officials has been exhausted," he wrote, regarding the problem of transporting tribute grain to North China. "Without the merchants, results cannot be achieved."[4] Wei Yuan was by no means underestimating the role of government, but he felt that allowing merchant wealth to develop would redound to the wealth and power of the state. The state should be benevolent while it becomes wealthy and strong: "The Kingly Way has never been achieved without wealth and strength." Wei Yuan also said: "The latter-day Confucians, because of the distinction made by Mencius between the ways of the King and the Hegemon, would thereafter allocate military and economic matters to the Five Hegemons and would not talk about them. Did they ever realize that to provide for the people and to regulate the taxes are the concerns of the sages, and that Mencius himself had spoken on agriculture, sericulture, forestry, and animal husbandry?"[5]

Given such utilitarian concerns, it was unlikely that scholars of statecraft would be entirely inhospitable to machine technology that would promote the wealth and strength of both the state and the people. In Wei Yuan's case, it was only a small jump from his advocacy of the Kiangsu seagoing junks as carriers of the tribute grain in the 1820s to his interest in Western steamships in the 1840s. Because he believed in making licenses for the salt trade available to some two thousand investors, it was merely consistent that he favored private enterprise. Within two years of the outbreak of the Opium War, Wei published two voluminous works—*Sheng-wu chi* (Imperial military history) and *Hai-kuo t'u-chih* (Illustrated geography of maritime countries). In *Sheng-wu chi*, he presents not only a history of the Ch'ing military campaigns but also proposals regarding fiscal and economic policies that would benefit the people as well as the state. Among his proposals was the encouragement of private enterprise in gold and silver mining. Once "the people are not prohibited" from taking up such enterprise, the government need only establish a bureau and impose a flexible tax of "ten or twenty percent, and the amount of silver produced will be incalculable and tax revenue will be more than the state can spend."[6]

Wei's *Hai-kuo t'u-chih* is a geography of the world based partly on materials collected by Commissioner Lin Tse-hsü in Canton. In an introductory essay on coastal defense, Wei proposed to establish a navy and to build ships and manufacture guns by Western methods—"to learn from the especially strong techniques of the barbarians in order to control them." Wei Yuan was aware of the value of Western technology as applied to production—"all the power of ears, eyes, and intelligence being devoted to usefulness to the people (*min-yung*)."[7] He believed, however, that the Chinese could catch up with the West in this regard and that they were not inferior.

Wei had already drawn a profile of the self-strengthening movement that was to come. Later, in 1876, when Tso Tsung-t'ang (1812–85) wrote an epilogue to a new edition of *Hai-kuo t'u-chih*, he declared that Wei's proposal "is feasible and its outline cannot be improved upon."[8] There was evidently a continuity between early nineteenth-century statecraft thought and the self-strengthening movement.

Self-strengthening

What was the meaning of "self-strengthening"? Whence was the concept derived? In *I-ching* (Book of Changes), there is this famous passage:

> The movement of Heaven is full of power. Thus, the superior man makes himself strong and untiring (*tzu-ch'iang*).

In the biography of Tung Huai (*chin-shih*, 1213) in *Sung-shih* (History of the Sung dynasty), it is recorded that in response to imperial inquiry about frontier affairs, i.e., relations with the Jurchen state in north China, Tung said: "When there is an enemy state beyond [the frontier], the best policy is first to strengthen oneself (*tzu-ch'iang*). Those who have strengthened themselves will be feared by others and will not fear others."[9]

It was in this context of Sino-barbarian relations that the Ch'ien-lung emperor (r. 1736–95), commenting on a passage in a historical work regarding the Sino-barbarian negotiations during the Eastern Han dynasty (A.D. 25–220), wrote: "Those who are able to strengthen themselves, no foreign aggressor dare have designs on. Those who are not able to strengthen themselves will, even if they are exceedingly careful, be taken advantage of by foreign aggressors."[10] In his brief essay on the Opium War and the peace settlement, Wei Yuan extolled the policy he believed Commissioner Lin Tse-hsü had hoped for—that of continuing to trade with the Europeans, except in opium, while China "prepares and strengthens itself" (*tzu-hsiu tzu-ch'iang*).[11]

It was in a similar sense that the phrase "self-strengthening" was employed when, in the aftermath of the Anglo-French occupation of Peking, Prince Kung and Wen-hsiang memorialized the throne in January 1861 and recommended new policies including the establishment of the Tsungli Yamen:

> Your servants have deliberated on and proposed regulations in six articles. The principal aim is to understand the enemy, to watch the frontiers and prevent future disasters. These are, however, superficial measures, falling short of the fundamentals. The policy for the fundamentals is to strengthen ourselves (*tzu-ch'iang*). Among the measures for strengthening ourselves, the foremost is training troops.[12]

In a memorial dated July of the same year, Prince Kung and his colleagues explained that they had "obtained imperial authorization for Tseng Kuo-fan and others to purchase foreign ships and guns and had requested the appointment of a high official to be in charge of training troops in Peking"—all for the purpose of self-strengthening, "so that we will not be controlled by others."[13] This concept of not yielding control to others in China's foreign relations is the traditional meaning of the term that can be traced at least to the Sung dynasty.

In the context of the late Ch'ing period, there was, however, a further implication of the term *tzu-ch'iang*—namely, that it was necessary to adopt Western technology in order to gain leverage in foreign relations. In his letter to the Tsungli Yamen in the spring of 1864, Li Hung-chang wrote:

> The Japanese today are the Wo pirates of the Ming period. They are far away from the Western countries and are close to us. If we can stand our ground, they will be subordinate to us, and we can watch for opportunities to compete with the Westerners. If we have no wherewithal to strengthen ourselves, then

Japan will follow the Westerners and share their sources of profit [at our expense].[14]

In the same letter, Li identifies the source of Western power as technology (chi-i) and recommends that China learn how to manufacture "machines that make machines." In forwarding Li's letter for imperial attention, the Tsungli Yamen summarized its discussion on policy with the governors and governors-general over the past two or three years: "We have found that the way to govern the state lies in self-strengthening, and in the present time and circumstances, the most important matter regarding self-strengthening is to train troops, but the training of troops must be preceded by the manufacture of weapons."[15]

Such was the new policy that emerged in the early T'ung-chih period. The expanded contact with the West after 1860 called for a new category of government activity—this was called "Western affairs" (yang-wu), and both the handling of diplomatic matters and the establishment of arsenals and shipyards were described as "Western affairs."

The scope of self-strengthening and of Western affairs was not confined, however, to building ships and making guns. There were at least some provincial officials who saw the approach of European technology as applicable to nonmilitary matters. In September 1865, when Li Hung-chang memorialized the throne to recommend the establishment of the Kiangnan Arsenal, he expressed the hope that the arsenal would eventually produce machines useful to agriculture and industry—"farming and weaving implements, printing and pottery-making equipment." Li predicted that within a few decades, the Chinese would be able to master Western technology and that "among the wealthy farmers and merchants, there will inevitably be those who follow the example of Western machine manufacturing for their own benefit."[16]

In retrospect, such a proposal from Li was putting into practical terms what Wei Yuan had presaged in 1842. Li was responding to the challenge of Western power that he personally witnessed in Shanghai in the early 1860s, when, with the help of Western weapons and even Western commanders, his army successfully fought the Taipings.[17] Yet Li did not depart from the assumptions behind statecraft thought—the defense of legitimate political authority based on Confucian loyalties. In the same memorial that proposed the founding of the Kiangnan Arsenal, Li denied that he was regarding the adoption of technology as more important than other policies of statecraft (ching-kuo chih lueh). Although Li did not use the formula "substance and application" (t'i-yung), he did state explicitly in this context that machine-manufacturing was less important than good government—that technology, like "herbs that cure the symptoms" or "dikes that dam the floods" was indispensable, yet not the most fundamental matter.[18] Such a view was in accord with the statecraft thought of the early nineteenth century that always returned to the defense of the imperial structure and familistic ethics.

In other ways, however, the statecraft of the self-strengthening era went beyond the early nineteenth-century thought. Although Wei Yuan realized the seriousness of the Western challenge to China, he did not address the issue of China's sovereign rights as a nation among nations. Wei was still thinking in terms of a Chinese empire that had somehow to bring barbarians under control. Li Hung-chang had had the experience, however, of residing by the foreign settlement in Shanghai from 1861 to 1863; he realized that the Europeans were not only militarily superior but were also aggressively pushing for commercial expansion, backed not only by military technology but also by diplomatic representation and pressure. More than Wei Yuan, Li recognized the importance of *li-ch'üan* (economic control, lit., prerogative over profit, implying economic sovereignty), a term not to be confused with *ch'üan-li* (rights), a neologism introduced much later. Although Li instinctively identified China with the Ch'ing dynasty, he frequently used the terms *Chung-kuo* or *Chung-t'u* for China, in a sense differentiating the country from the dynasty. Li was aware of China's claims as a sovereign state, even though he was realistic enough to have accepted the treaty system that was already in existence when he came on the scene.

A concept of administrative integrity may be derived from the policies of Li and of the successive Shanghai taotais beginning with Ting Jih-ch'ang (1823–82), the Cantonese whom Li brought to that office in 1864.[19] Li had to face aggressive British officials like Harry Parkes. Between Horatio Nelson Lay and Robert Hart, Li favored Hart as long as the latter acted as a Chinese official. Though he appreciated the effectiveness of the Ever-Victorious Army, he insisted it be disbanded. Li's experience in foreign relations in Kiangsu trained him as a diplomat. For some twenty-five years in Chihli, beginning in 1870, he was a virtual foreign minister, to whom representatives of the powers brought their problems.

Diplomatic history is a complex field and is not easily summarized. Li's performance as a maker of China's foreign policy has yet to be fully reappraised. It may be assumed that Li had a consistent goal beginning in the 1860s—that of preserving China's territorial and administrative integrity as much as possible under the treaty system. It was also his aim to protect Korea from foreign domination.[20] Li realized that diplomatic success ultimately depended on a country's military and economic strength. It was Li's fate—and China's—to confront an exceptionally successful country, Japan. Li realized Japan's challenge perhaps as early as the 1860s, certainly by the early 1870s, when he negotiated China's earliest treaties with Japan. Yet Li was destined to see China fall increasingly behind, despite his efforts at self-strengthening. As Professor Wang Chia-chien expresses it, in reference to the weaknesses of the Chinese navy on the eve of the Sino-Japanese War: "Li was a loyal official, but he was responsible for many pressing matters, including diplomatic relations and defense both on land and on the high seas, not to mention his domestic duty of being the governor-general of Chihli and actually the leader among governors and governors-general. With political problems arising daily, he was too busy to pay more than peripheral attention to the Peiyang Navy." Professor Wang concludes:

> Li's task was far more difficult than one can imagine today, for he faced the multiple tasks of seeking funds from the government in Peking and persuading other provincial officials to cooperate, while warding off a constant stream of criticism from several sources. The weakness of the central government in Peking is well known. The Ch'ing government, as a whole, saddled Li with many obstacles. It was riddled with bureaucratic abuses, provincialism, and factional infighting. The Peiyang Navy itself suffered from inadequate organization and obsolete equipment. Under the circumstances, Li's naval efforts should be judged not against an impossible ideal but rather within the entire context of the internal situation at the time.[21]

The rise of enterprise

Li obviously failed to win or avert the Sino-Japanese War. Yet his was a record of pioneership; scholars have yet to do justice to his efforts in state-building, which included not only military measures but also economic policies. In 1872–73, when Li founded the China Merchants' Steam Navigation Company, his purpose was not simply to have steamships carry the tribute grain to North China but to compete with the steamships in the carrying trade that hitherto had only been engaged in by foreign firms. Li was aware that Chinese merchants at the treaty ports often invested their capital in Western enterprises and it was his policy to provide government protection to Chinese merchants who would compete with foreign enterprises. Li hoped that the Chinese steamship company would "start a trend in this country, so that economic control (*li-ch'üan*) will be gradually restored."[22] A similar purpose was in the background of Li's plans regarding mining and the cotton textile mills. In supporting the plans for coal and iron mining in Chihli and elsewhere from the mid-1870s on, Li had in mind the large imports of coal and iron that constituted a financial drain on the country. Li also was aware of the fact that coal and iron mines were the basis of England's industrial success:

> China's gold, silver, coal, and iron deposits are superior to those of the Western countries. However, we are as yet unenlightened (*feng-ch'i wei-k'ai*), our treasures are hidden and not yet developed, our sources of wealth are gradually drying up every day. Every year we pay out large sums to buy coal and iron from other countries—this is a major drain on our resources.[23]

In 1882 when Li memorialized for imperial approval of the Shanghai cotton textile mill, he stressed the importance of wealth as a basis for national power. Li believed that without developing the manufacturing industry by adopting Western technology, it would be impossible to foster national strength:

It has occurred to your servitor that regarding the state of power in ancient and modern times, it is necessary to be wealthy first before a country can be strong. It is especially when the people's life is affluent that the foundations of the state can be firmly established. The other countries are all using machines for manufacturing, enabling them to save a great deal in their costs as compared with the Chinese products of manual labor. The foreign products are lower in price, and their markets are increasingly enlarged. It is clear that unless we gradually try to imitate their methods of manufacturing and to develop transport and sales ourselves, we will not be able to share their control over wealth.[24]

Scholars have not yet fully realized that Li, like Wei Yuan, looked to the merchants to supply the capital as well as the managerial talent for the state-sponsored enterprises. In 1872, when the China Merchants' Steam Navigation Company was founded, and in 1877, when the Kaiping mines were started, Li counted on a group of Cantonese comprador-merchants, led by T'ang T'ing-shu (Tong King-sing) and Hsü Jun, to undertake responsibility for the enterprises. Li's original formula for *kuan-tu shang-pan* (government-supervised merchant enterprise) called for the merchants to undertake complete responsibility for organizing capital and management, although they were to receive government loans at a low rate of interest. The initial regulations of the China Merchants' Company stated that although the government should retain control, "profit and loss are the merchants' responsibility and do not involve the government."[25] Li's policy was to rely on the treaty-port merchants to bear the risk as well as perform the work for the enterprise. Although he did authorize Sheng Hsuan-huai to promote coal and iron mines in Hupei, he was skeptical as to whether Sheng was equal to the task. As late as 1882, Li made the following comment on a petition from Sheng Hsuan-huai, referring to the Krupp family of German industrial history:

The Krupps started by melting iron in three thatched huts and were extremely able. Taotai Sheng Hsuan-huai and others will surely not be able to follow in their footsteps. The China Merchants' started with four old steamships for the carriage of tribute rice as an experiment. Although the company has gradually expanded, it has as yet been unable to restore our control over profit (*li-ch'üan*). Yet the Hupei bureau [of iron and coal mines] cannot be compared with the China Merchants'.[26]

This and other sources indicate that until 1884, Li had greater trust in Tong King-sing and other Cantonese comprador-merchants than in such officials as Sheng.

It must also be emphasized that the modernization efforts under Li's aegis were not without success. China Merchants' did start with four old ships, but with fresh merchant capital and government loans, nine new ships were acquired over the next three years, and the company's fleet competed vigorously in the carrying trade in Chinese waters. In early 1877, thanks to government loans, it purchased the entire fleet of the American-managed Russell and Company and added sixteen ships to its roster. In 1877, China Merchants' owned a total of twenty-nine steamships, while its two rivals, Jardine, Matheson and Company and Butterfield and Swire, operated six and five steamships, respectively.[27] The China Merchants' Company was to dominate the carrying trade in Chinese waters for some years, even after 1885, when Tong King-sing and Hsü Jun were no longer its managers and Sheng Hsuan-huai was appointed its director-general (tu-pan).

The Kaiping mines continued to be managed by Tong King-sing and his Cantonese colleagues until Tong's death in 1892. In that year, when China imported 300,000 tons of coal, Kaiping's production was already 187,000 tons, meeting all the needs of the port of Tientsin and beyond. A short railway from Kaiping to the nearby waterway was extended in 1888 to Tientsin and eventually to Peking. While the China Merchants' Company often had difficulties with foreign captains and engineers who worked on its vessels, Tong King-sing, in his management of the Kaiping mines, enjoyed the imaginative service as well as the admiration of the British engineers and foremen that he employed.[28]

In the background of the innovations introduced by the kuan-tu shang-pan enterprises were the hustle and bustle of the treaty-port commerce and the international market for European-trained technical personnel. But the transfer of modern technology that occurred in such enterprises owed much, of course, to Li Hung-chang's vision and political support, which made them possible in the first place.

Li's conviction in the early 1870s was that China had encountered "the greatest change in its situation" in three thousand years: China was now encountering foreign aggression not just from the inland frontiers but from the seacoast, not from nomads that were less civilized but from nations across the seas commanding formidable military and economic power. Li continued to foster his own position in the imperial bureaucracy, to be sure; he had to protect his political rear. But his life goal was not simply personal success. Nor was he simply an advocate of "Chinese learning for fundamental structure and Western learning for practical use"—the phrase formulated by Chang Chih-tung in his famous treatise of 1898. As underscored in a recent study by Li Kuo-ch'i, Li actually devoted very little effort to Chinese learning as such; his patronage of old-style academies of learning was unenthusiastic and pro forma; his heart really lay in what he, as early as 1862, had jokingly termed "changing Chinese ways through barbarian ways" (yung-i pien-Hsia).[29]

It must again be emphasized that especially from 1870 on, while he always kept in mind the intricacies of politics in Peking, Li, as a national official, had taken upon himself the responsibility for China's foreign relations as well as military preparedness. Li had, moreover, taken the lead in promoting economic enterprises of the industrial age. His vision for the part to be played by merchants in his original formula for the kuan-tu shang-pan enterprises was perhaps comparable to the observation made by the statecraft scholar Wei Yuan, as early as the 1830s, that "the strength of the officials has been exhausted; without the merchants, results cannot be achieved."[30] The *kuan-tu shang-pan* enterprises deserve to be further studied. There were enough cases of comparative success in the record of China's late-nineteenth-century modernization to justify their being considered as precursors of the considerable economic development in the China of the early twentieth century.

In addition to pioneering in the promotion of industrialization, Li's statecraft included the advocacy of reform, what he himself described at times as *pien-fa* (change of institutions). As is discussed in chapter 2, Li proposed to the Tsungli Yamen in 1864 that a special category be created in the civil-service examination system so that scholars (*shih*) interested in Western technology would devote their lives and work to "machines that make machines."[31] In addition, as is discussed in chapter 3, Li, in a memorial to the throne of December 1874, attacked the examination system that required the all-but-useless skills of the eight-legged essay and calligraphy. He proposed that a Bureau of Western Learning (Yang-hsüeh chü) be created in each of the provinces involved in coastal defense, where scholars who devoted their careers to such learning would be accorded official status identical to that earned through the civil-service examinations.[32] In order not to provoke further criticism and jeopardize his own political position, as well as the innovative projects he had worked hard to establish, Li did not push the reform of the civil-service examination. He continued to use such personal influence as was at his disposal to provide rewards and incentives to personnel willing to work for Western Affairs projects.[33] In February 1875, he wrote in a letter to Liu Ping-chang, a former commander of the Anhwei Army, now governor of Kiangsi:

> That the eight-legged essays and the small regular-style calligraphy are of no value to current affairs; this is what we already know. . . . Recently, many plans have been proposed regarding the adjustment of the examination system; they have all been rejected by the Board [in Peking]. I have merely made the initial proposal; it is up to those in power to wake up [lit., to examine themselves forcefully] and to choose a policy. To those who continue to be blind and would not be enlightened, I have already spoken—there is no point in refuting them.[34]

There are many such passages in Li's extant letters that would illuminate the policies and problems in China's nineteenth-century modernization. Research on Li's role in the statecraft and reform of the late Ch'ing period has barely begun.

Notes

1. Reference to the series entitled *Chung-kuo hsien-tai hua ti ch'ü-yü yen-chiu* (Regional studies of China's modernization, 1860–1916), published by the Institute of Mod-

ern History, Academia Sinica, Taipei: Su Yun-feng, *Hu-pei sheng* (1981); Chang Yü-fa, *Shan-tung sheng* (1982); Li Kuo-ch'i, *Min-Che-T'ai ti-ch'ü* (Fukien-Chekiang-Taiwan region) (1982); Chang P'eng-yuan, *Hu-nan sheng* (1982); Wang Shu-huai, *Chiang-su sheng* (1984).

2. This discussion on early nineteenth-century statecraft thought is based on my articles "Shih-chiu shih-chi ch'u-chi Chung-kuo chih-shih fen-tzu: Pao Shih-ch'en yü Wei Yuan" (Early nineteenth-century Chinese intellectuals: Pao Shih-ch'en and Wei Yuan), in *Chung-yang yen-chiu yuan kuo-chi han-hsueh hui-i lun-wen chi* (Collected papers of the International Conference on Sinology, Academia Sinica) (Taipei, 1981), *Li-shih k'ao-ku tsu* (History and archaeology section), vol. 2, 995–1007; and "Wei Yuan chih che-hsueh yü ching-shih ssu-hsiang" (Wei Yuan's philosophy and statecraft thought), in *Chin-tai Chung-kuo ching-shih ssu-hsiang yen-t'ao hui lun-wen chi* (Collected papers from the Conference on Statecraft Thought in Modern China) (Taipei: Institute of Modern History, Academia Sinica, 1984), 359–90.

3. Cited in Liu, "Wei Yuan chih che-hsueh," 372–73.

4. *Wei Yuan chi* (Collected writings of Wei Yuan) (Beijing: Chung-hua, 1976), vol. 1, 411.

5. Cited in Liu, "Wei Yuan chih che-hsueh," 372–73.

6. Ibid., 369.

7. Ibid., 370.

8. See Wang Chia-chien, *Wei Yuan nien-p'u* (Chronological biography of Wei Yuan) (Taipei: Institute of Modern History, Academia Sinica, 1967), 96.

9. For the quotation from Tung Huai, see *Sung-shih* (History of the Sung dynasty), chüan 414.

10. *Yü-p'i li-tai t'ung-chien chi-lan* (Imperial commentaries on collected abstracts from the *Comprehensive Mirror for Aid in Government*) (lithographed edition, 1904), 22:54b.

11. *Wei Yuan chi*, 187.

12. Cited in Chiang T'ing-fu (T. F. Tsiang), *Chung-kuo wai-chiao shih tzu-liao chi-yao* (Selected materials for the history of China's foreign relations), vol. 1, 1934 (Taipei reprint: Commercial Press, 1959), 351–52.

13. Ibid., 352–53.

14. Ibid., 365–66.

15. Ibid., 363–64.

16. Li Hung-chang, *Li Wen-chung kung ch'üan-chi* (The complete works of Li Hung-chang) (Nanking, 1905; hereafter *LWCK*), *Tsou-kao* (*Memorials*), 9:34b; see below, chapters 2 and 3.

17. See also Richard J. Smith, *Mercenaries and Mandarins: The Ever-Victorious Army in Nineteenth-Century China* (Millwood, N.Y.: KTO Press, 1978).

18. See below, chapter 2.

19. See below, chapter 5; also Lü Shih-ch'iang, *Ting Jih-ch'ang yü tzu-ch'iang yun-tung* (Ting Jih-ch'ang and the Self-strengthening Movement) (Taipei: Academia Sinica, 1972).

20. See below, chapters 7–9.

21. See below, chapter 12.

22. See below, chapters 3 and 11.

23. *LWCK Memorials*, 40:41.

24. Ibid., 43:43–44.

25. *LWCK, I-shu han-kao* (Letters to the Tsungli Yamen) 1:39b–40; see below, chapter 11.

26. *Sheng Hsuan-huai tang-an tzu-liao* (Materials from the Sheng Hsuan-huai ar-

chives): *Hupei k'ai-ts'ai mei-t'ieh tsung-chü; Ching-men K'uang-wu chü* (Hupei bureau of coal and iron mines; Ching-men mining bureau) (Shanghai: Jen-min, 1981), 456; see also 51–53, 244, 370.

27. See my article, "British-Chinese Steamship Rivalry in China, 1873–85," in *The Economic Development of China and Japan*, ed. C. D. Cowan (London: Allen & Unwin, 1964), 49–78. See also below, chapter 11.

28. Ellsworth C. Carlson, *The Kaiping Mines, 1877–1912*, 2d ed. (Cambridge, Mass.: Harvard University, East Asian Research Center, 1971); see the brief summary in my article, "A Chinese Entrepreneur," in *The Thistle and the Jade: A Celebration of 150 Years of Jardine, Matheson & Co.*, ed. Maggie Keswick (London: Octopus Books, 1982), 103–27; 266–68.

29. Li Kuo-ch'i, "T'ung-chih nien-chien Li Hung-chang ying-pien t'u-hsin ssu-hsiang" (Li Hung-chang's ideas regarding adjusting to change by innovation during the T'ung-chih period, 1862–74), *Chung-yang yen-chiu yuan ti-erh-chieh Kuo-chi Han-hsüeh hui-i lun-wen* (Paper for the Second International Conference on Sinology) (Taipei: Academia Sinica, December 1986).

30. See above, note 4.

31. See below, 33–34.

32. See below, 65–66.

33. See below, chapter 5.

34. *LWCK Letters*, 15.4.

Part II
The Rise of Li Hung-chang

2

The Confucian as Patriot and Pragmatist: Li Hung-chang's Formative Years, 1823–1866

Kwang-Ching Liu

Anyone acquainted with nineteenth-century Chinese history must be impressed by the complacency with which the bulk of the Chinese scholar-officials greeted China's unprecedented external crisis. There was, to be sure, ample resentment among the Chinese who came to be aware of the facts of Western encroachment. But even among those who were so aware, cultural conditioning made them slow in arriving at ideas of innovation and reform that were necessary for coping with the new challenge. By contrast, the Japanese developed a sense of crisis as soon as they were apprised of Western power. The Japanese, besides being of warrior background, were open-minded enough so that even their long and rigid self-training in Confucianism did not prevent them from seeking new ways to meet the challenge of the West.

Although the attitude of most Chinese scholar-officials toward this challenge must be described as inert, if not resentful, there were Chinese who saw the crisis and who were realistic enough to see that change was required to meet the new situation. There were, in fact, stirrings within the scholar-official world during the mid-nineteenth century. Although the Chinese upper class of the Ch'ing period was notoriously confined by its excessive literary training and pedantic habits, there were many holders of high literary degrees who became involved in military affairs after the Taiping Rebellion had broken out. The success of their war against the rebels testified to their pragmatism as well as their ability. It would have been surprising if some of these men, given the opportunity to learn of the aggressive nature of the West's power, had not responded with a sense of urgency and realism.

Li Hung-chang (1823–1901) was one such man. Coming from a literati background, he proved his practical ability in military and administrative work during the Taiping Rebellion, but in 1862, when he went to Shanghai to become the governor of Kiangsu, leading the war against the rebels there, he came face to face, for the first time in his life, with the threat of Western power and aggression. His remarkably pragmatic qualities, as well as his unusual opportunity to become closely acquainted with Western weapons and Western military men, put him in a unique position to respond to the West. The fact that he was an eminent official made it possible for him to bring to the court's attention proposals for innovation and reform. Beginning in 1862, he was for more than three decades the foremost champion of China's self-strengthening (tzu-ch'iang), a policy calling for the development of China's military and financial power, primarily through the adoption of Western technology, so as to enable her to cope with future aggression. For his work in the period when he served as the governor-general of Chihli and as imperial commissioner of trade and foreign relations in North China (1870–95), he was often described by contemporary writers as the Itō Hirobumi of China and even as the "Bismarck of the East"[1]— not only for his part in the conduct of Ch'ing diplomacy, but also for his pursuit of state power through a military buildup and through industrialization.

Although aspects of Li's career have been given monographic treatment,[2] there is as yet no study on the origins and nature of the new policies Li came to advocate—how such policy proposals arose and how they differed from the pattern of traditional Chinese statecraft. The essay that follows will attempt to fill this gap in our knowledge by a survey of Li's formative years as a statesman— his early career as a successful literatus turned military stategist and the crucial years between 1862 and 1866 when, as the civil and military administrator in Kiangsu, he emerged as the boldest advocate of innovation and reform in the China of that time. The story should remind us of the flexibility within the Confucian tradition—the fact that a man with the top literary degree could with apparent ease move into the role of a patriotic champion of military and educational reform. But it should also be apparent from this study that the reforms Li advocated were limited in nature—that Li could not be an Itō or a Bismarck because the very pragmatism that enabled the young Chinese statesman to recognize the need for new policies also prompted him to compromise with the existing military and administrative practices that were, in the long run, inconsistent with his aims. Although the policies that Li advocated were far-reaching for the China of his time and are of great significance to any study of China's tortuous history of modernization, the compromises that Li made were in no way modern in spirit, even though they represented in fact a derogation of Confucian principles.

In a review of Li Hung-chang's early career,[3] it should be emphasized that his training and connections fell very much within the traditional pattern. He was born in 1823 into an upper-class family in Lu-chou (Ho-fei) in Anhwei Province. Both his grandfather and his great-grandfather held low degrees through purchase, and the family is known to have seen indigent days during Li's youth.

However, Li's father, Li Wen-an, passed the examinations and won the *chin-shih* degree in 1838, and he became an official in Peking, rising to a department director (*lang-chung*) of the Board of Punishments in the early 1850s.[4] Li himself moved through the examination system rapidly and with distinction. He won the provincial *chü-jen* degree at twenty-one and, three years later, in 1847, won the *chin-shih* degree. He was chosen Bachelor (*shu chi-shih*) of the Hanlin Academy and, in 1851, was promoted to a compiler (*pien-hsiu*) of the academy.[5] Li was thus a highly successful literatus when he was in his twenties, well launched on an official career.

Beginning in about 1843, Li formed a disciple-teacher relationship with Tseng Kuo-fan, who was a *chin-shih* classmate of Li's father and was then living in Peking. Tseng later wrote that he had recognized Li's talents as early as 1845,[6] but it should be noted that Li was not a man of scholarly bent, which Tseng was. Despite the fact that Li is supposed to have studied under Tseng, in Li's early writings, which his descendants published in a collection, we find no trace of any interest in either the "Han learning" or the "Sung learning," both of which Tseng was much immersed in at that time. In fact, we find no trace in Li's early writings of any interest in administrative statecraft (*ching-shih chih hsüeh*), to which Tseng was also devoted. Those of Li's early writings that are preserved[7] consist chiefly of two types: poetry and poetic prose of the *fu* genre. The poems deal mainly with the stereotypical themes of friendship or of longing for his parents. If there is anything unusual in them, it is perhaps the occasionally eloquent expression of passion for success, for official rank and glory. Li's poetic prose, written in the florid style common to its genre, shows his great skill in the manipulation of the language and his intimate knowledge of the classics and other literature. The subjects dealt with are all of a conventional nature. Besides paying the usual tributes to nature, Li dwelt on such themes as "literature as the vehicle for truth" (*wen-i tsai-tao*), and on the moral training appropriate for a monarch. One detects in Li's early poetry and prose a muscular quality, a competent hand that achieved technical perfection untroubled by any deep thought. Li himself has told us that "in my twenties I had some aspirations toward scholarship."[8] But, at least as far as his extant early writings show, he was not a man of scholarly bent. Like many literati produced by the China of the past, he was highly trained in the classics and in essay writing but was, at heart, a man of action.

In any case, Li soon showed that he preferred action to the pursuit of literature or scholarship. The Taiping Rebellion gave him the opportunity. In the spring of 1853, he returned to his native province of Anhwei, as assistant to Lü Hsien-chi, a vice president of the Board of Works and an Anhwei man, who was sent by the throne to that province to help organize local defense against the Taipings. We have no knowledge of Li's motives in joining Lü and returning to Anhwei, except for what Li wrote in his poems about his anxiety to serve the dynasty and defend his native place.[9] At all events, we find him embarking on a military and administrative career. Even before Lü Hsien-chi died in late 1853, Li was given independent military assignments by the governor of Anhwei, Li Chia-tuan. As early as June 1853, the erstwhile Hanlin compiler had under his command one thousand men, presumably men he himself recruited from local militia and other forces. In August, Li's troops won their first victory against the Taipings near Ch'ao-hsien, in northern Anhwei. Li seems to have built an immediate reputation with the small army he commanded, for we find Tseng Kuo-fan, with whom Li kept in touch through these years, writing him from Hunan in late 1853: "I heard that the temporary force (*yung*) under your command is very vigorous and well disciplined."[10]

For the next three years, Li was engaged in military work in the general area of Anhwei as battlefield commander and as strategic adviser to the governor of the province. In early 1854, Li's father, Wen-an, also ordered by the court to return to the province, organized local armies in nearby Lin-huai, but the father and son seem to have worked independently at first. The younger Li had by then entered the service of the new governor of Anhwei, Fu-chi (a Manchu who happened to have been Li's examiner during his *chin-shih* trials in 1847). Fu-chi's memorials of 1854–55 indicate that Li was one of the commanders he most relied on and that Li often personally led his forces in seizing rebel-held towns, advancing with the troops to the town-walls.[11] In early 1855, joined by his father, Li played a key part in the Ch'ing offensive against Lu-chou, the Lis' native place. In July, just after his father's death, Li had to interrupt his mourning to help Fu-chi repulse a severe Taiping attack. He was allowed to resume mourning for only one hundred days and, upon his return, he worked in the governor's military secretariat (*ying-wu ch'u*) and also helped to direct a fleet of war junks on Lake Ch'ao. In 1856, he played a large part in the planning of several land battles that culminated in the recovery of Ch'ao-hsien.[12]

Although materials on Li's life in the years 1853–56 are scant, there is no doubt that he did engage in organizing and commanding troops, as well as doing staff work for Fu-chi. Li received his award in official ranks. In 1854, he gained the title of honorary prefect (*chih-fu hsien*). In 1855, he was promoted to candidate for circuit intendant (*chi-ming tao-fu*) and, in 1856, after the victory at Ch'ao-hsien, he was awarded the honorary title of provincial judicial commissioner.[13]

At the end of 1856, Li asked for leave to bury his father and to complete the proper mourning period. In early 1859, a few months after Fu-chi had resigned from the Anhwei governorship, Li responded to an invitation from Tseng Kuo-fan, then the chief commander against the Taipings in Kiangsi and southern Anhwei, to enter Tseng's service.[14] Li was a member of Tseng's personal staff (*mu-fu*) for more than three years, and from the frequent mention of Li in letters from Tseng and others, it is possible to observe the new capacities that Li, then in his late thirties, had developed, as well as some of his personal traits.

There is little doubt that Tseng considered Li one of his disciples and, moreover, trusted his ability. Li became one of Tseng's personal assistants as soon as he arrived at the latter's headquarters in Kiangsi. He was asked by Tseng to make plans for the recruitment of new troops and, in June 1859, Tseng asked Li to assist his brother Tseng Kuo-ch'üan, in directing the attack on the Taiping stronghold in Chingtechen (which was recovered from the rebels a month later). Li made inspection trips and presented recommendations with a view to improving the effectiveness of the Hunan Army. Tseng so trusted Li's judgment that he made him his chief secretary (wen-an) thereafter. From about August 1859 to November 1860, Tseng relied on Li for the drafting of his letters and memorials.[15] Tseng was convinced, at least by 1860, that Li was qualified to be a provincial administrator as well as a principal military commander. In the summer of 1860, when Tseng planned to expand his forces to northern Kiangsu, he recommended Li to the throne for the post of Liang-Huai salt commissioner, to be stationed in Yang-chou, where Li was to raise funds and also organize a naval force for campaigns in the Lower Yangtze.[16] The appointment was not approved by the throne, however, and Li continued to serve as Tseng's secretary.

From remarks made by Tseng and others, it seems that Li gave the impression in this period of being a man of ambition and character. He was more than six feet tall and had a distinguished appearance. Tseng Kuo-fan described him as possessing "a disciplined vigor, great talents, and a fine mind for detail," while Hu Lin-i, whom Li met on a trip to Hupei, was struck by Li's physiognomy and felt that he was "predestined for great success."[17] If Tseng was mildly critical of Li, it was because of the latter's great self-esteem and obvious aspirations for higher government position. Once when Li was on a trip, Tseng wrote to him expressing faith that Li was destined to be a "a good instrument for setting in order and providing relief to the state" (k'uang-chi ling-ch'i), but cautioning him affectionately that the opportunity for high office is a matter of fate, not to be brought about by human effort. To this, Li responded that he had been endeavoring "to keep to that which is my due and to acknowledge fate" (shou-fen chih-ming).[18] Despite his rather apparent ambition, Li impressed the officials who met him at that time as a man of principles. In November 1860, when Li left Tseng's service over a disagreement they had had concerning whether Li Yüan-tu, one of Tseng's commanders as well as a friend of Li's, should be recommended to the throne for censure because of a military defeat that was not his fault, Tseng did not resent Li's action. Li went to live in Nanchang, the capital of Kiangsi, where he soon began to do errands for Tseng, acting as liaison between Tseng and the acting governor of Kiangsi. Tseng repeatedly urged Li to rejoin his secretariat and, in July 1861, some two months before Tseng's major victory over the Taipings at Anking, Li returned to his service as his principal secretary responsible for drafting letters and memorials.[19]

Li was soon to be given one of the most crucial assignments of the anti-Taiping war. Shanghai, the major center of trade and revenue, was then threatened by the resurgent forces of the Taipings, and the throne urged Tseng to take steps to protect that city, as well as Chinkiang. In November 1861, Tseng received representations from a delegation of prominent gentry of Kiangsu residing in Shanghai, begging him to send troops there. Because there were no available troops to send, Tseng, who had for some time been distressed by the declining morale and discipline of the Hunan Army, asked Li to go to northern Anhwei, the area around Li's native Lu-chou, to recruit a new army and bring it to Anking for training.

Capitalizing on his familiarity with some of the militia leaders (*lien-chang*) of the area who had cooperated with the government forces since the mid-1850s, Li was able to recruit five or six leaders and, through them, some 3,500 men. These, together with 2,000 men detailed from the newer units of the Hunan Army, formed the initial Anhwei Army (*Huai-chün*), patterned in its organization after the Hunan Army. At first, the plan was to send the new army by land to Chinkiang. But in March 1862, the gentry at Shanghai sent seven steamships, hired from a British firm, to Anking to carry the new forces down the Yangtze to Shanghai. Tseng made the decision to send Li there, and Li, with the first contingents of the Anhwei Army, was in Shanghai by early April. At Tseng's recommendation, the throne, on April 25, appointed Li acting governor of Kiangsu, and he was made governor of Kiangsu in December of that year.[20]

Li's phenomenal rise in the Ch'ing officialdom was made possible by the extraordinary circumstances created by the Taiping Rebellion, as well as his own recognized aptitude for the military and administrative work required by the situation. But the existing evidence does not indicate that he had departed from the Confucian norms up to this point in his career. The three years that Li spent in the service of Fu-chi must have made him worldly in the ways of the Ch'ing bureaucracy. His association with this Manchu governor, as well as his work with the uncouth and self-seeking militia leaders of northern Anhwei, may have introduced an element of cynicism into his thinking.[21] But there is no reason to believe that in his general outlook he had departed significantly from the pattern set by Tseng Kuo-fan and other T'ung-chih officials. The sixty-odd poems that have been preserved which Li wrote between 1856 and 1860 are on such themes as impatience with the unending turmoil and rebellion, grief for his departed father and for friends who had died fighting the rebels, and the beauty of nature observed in moments between arduous assignments. Although Li himself left no political writings during this period, there is no reason to believe that his ideas on statecraft would not have harmonized with those of Tseng Kuo-fan, many of whose memorials and letters written in the period from 1859 to 1861 Li had drafted.[22] In Shanghai, however, Li was confronted by a situation that Tseng had not had to face. In an atmosphere of crisis, he responded to the challenge of the West as well as to the peculiar military and administrative problems of his new post. Li was struck by the evidence of foreign aggression toward China, as well as by the power of the West, and realist though he was, he developed a new patriotism.

From Li's letters to Tseng Kuo-fan and other colleagues (which have been fully preserved for the period after he came to Kiangsu), it is evident that Li became conscious of the West's challenge to China almost from the moment he set foot in Shanghai after his voyage on a British steamship down the Yangtze through territory held by the Taipings. Up to this time, there is no indication that Li had given much thought to, or indeed was well informed on, China's external crisis. The Anglo-French War, which saw the allied occupation of Peking in the fall of 1860, was never touched upon in his poems. Although new-style "Western muskets" (yang-ch'iang) imported from Hong Kong or Shanghai are known to have been used by some of the Ch'ing armies against the Taipings,[23] neither Tseng nor Li had realized the implications of modern Western weapons. In Shanghai, Li was suddenly confronted by this challenge. Shanghai, in early 1862, was being defended by some three thousand British, British-Indian, and French troops, in addition to a Chinese army of some three thousand men equipped with rifles and howitzers and officered by Western volunteers under the command of the American, Frederick Townsend Ward—a force that had been organized origi-nally in 1860 as a band of foreign mercenaries hired by local Chinese gentry and merchants, but which had grown and changed and was recognized by imperial decree in March 1862 and given the title of the Ever-Victorious Army.[24] Having arrived in Shanghai, Li found himself hemmed in on all sides by these forces and discovered, moreover, that they were all superior to his own, if only because of their awesome weapons. On April 30, three weeks after Li's arrival, we find him reporting to Tseng on a recent victory that the British and French had won over the Taipings on the strength of their firearms and artillery: "The rifles and cannon of several thousand foreign troops are fired at the same time, and what-ever is in the way is immediately destroyed. The shells that explode [before] touching the ground (lo-ti k'ai hua) are indeed a device of the gods!"[25] Such weaponry had profoundly impressed the Chinese officials in Shanghai before Li. The policy of Hsüeh Huan, Li's predecessor as governor, and his chief adviser Wu Hsü, the provincial financial commissioner as well as the Shanghai taotai, had indeed been to beseech and encourage the British and French to assume more responsibility for the defense of Shanghai.[26] Unlike Hsüeh and Wu, how-ever, Li reacted to the situation with defiance. He was determined to maintain the standing of his own forces, without allowing them to be made dependent on the Europeans or even on the Chinese force commanded by Ward. It was in this context that Li first used the term self-strengthening (tzu-ch'iang), meaning the building up of the fighting capacity of his own troops as opposed to foreign or foreign-officered forces.

As early as April 23, Li had written Tseng that he planned to employ his troops in one sector of the defense line around Shanghai and "to strive for self-strengthening and not to mix with foreigners."[27] In the succeeding weeks and months, Li made a great effort to improve the fighting quality of his troops by judiciously selecting the commanders under whom the various positions were to be held, by equipping the forces with Western arms, and by requiring fresh training and drill. By June 1862, one of Li's commanders, Ch'eng Hsüeh-ch'i, had organized a Foreign Arms Platoon (yang-ch'iang tui) with a hundred rifles; by September, the various units of the Anhwei Army had acquired a total of a thousand rifles. In May 1863, when this army, absorbing new recruits from Anhwei, as well as the surrendered Taipings, had grown to forty thousand men, it was equipped with a total of more than ten thousand rifles and a number of cannon using thirty-six-pound shells.[28] Meanwhile, Li's Anhwei Army was winning important battles on its own. Li availed himself of help from the Ever-Victorious Army, in conjunction with which his forces sometimes fought. Beginning in July 1862, he even encouraged the plan of the Ever-Victorious Army starting on a water-borne expedition to attack the Taiping capital of Nanking, an idea that was never realized. But Li saw to it that the Ever-Victorious Army was effectively under Chinese control as well as strategic direction.[29] Li was determined to prevent the Europeans from expanding their direct military role. Referring to the British and French forces in Shanghai, Li wrote to Tseng in August 1862: "No matter how urgent our military situation, I would not request that they send forth columns to help us. . . . [To ask them to do so] would not only be humiliating, but would make them more arrogant."[30] In October 1862, Li did accept Vice Admiral James Hope's suggestion that the British and French forces take part in the attack on Chia-ting, but Li insisted that these forces were to remain within the thirty-mile radius of the Shanghai foreign settlement, of which Chia-ting was the outer limit.[31]

In retrospect, Li's efforts to arm his forces with Western weapons made a vital contribution to the Ch'ing suppression of the Taipings. The effectiveness of the Anhwei Army helped the defense of Shanghai and made a westward offensive possible. A large number of the Taipings' best forces (some of which had also acquired Western rifles) were tied down, while the tax revenue of the commercially rich Shanghai area was invaluable to Tseng's forces up the Yangtze as well as to the Anhwei Army itself.[32] There was, however, a further reason why Li wanted to do his utmost to improve the weapons of his forces, for he was faced with possible political consequences of the Western intervention in the war against the Taipings. His headquarters situated near the foreign settlement, Li became keenly aware of the license and power the foreigners were enjoying in Shanghai and was particularly resentful that the Chinese, not only the merchants but also officials like Wu Hsü, had come to admire foreigners and submit willingly to their wishes. In early August 1862, he wrote to Tso Tsung-t'ang: "Although Shanghai is on our population register and on our map, the hearts of the officials and the people have long since gone over to the foreigners, as if unaware that the Chinese [themselves] can still manage affairs and that the Chinese troops can still fight."[33] Li strongly suspected that the British and French had territorial designs on China in the areas adjacent to Shanghai and Ningpo. In mid-August, Li wrote Tseng Kuo-fan that local Western-language newspapers (which were translated for him regularly) had published the proposal that all of Shanghai, not just the foreign settlement, should be placed under Western control when the Taiping threat receded. "In my official communication to the Tsungli Yamen," Li reported to Tseng, "I had said earlier that it was difficult to guarantee that some day [the foreigners] would not occupy [Shanghai]. . . . We are treading on frost over ice; there is indeed a hidden danger."[34]

Li's letters of 1862–63 show that a new patriotism was growing in him, one distinguished from the traditional Chinese pride in the celestial dynasty and in the inherited culture. He had to deal constantly with European consuls and naval and military men; he could not but be aware that the world was made up of contenders of varying strength and that the West was superior to China in power and technology. Li continued, of course, to identify the Ch'ing dynasty with China, as he would do throughout his life. But when he used the phrase *Chung-kuo* (the middle kingdom) or *Chung-t'u* (the middle land), which he frequently did, he was undoubtedly thinking not just of the dynasty but also of China's land and people. Referring to the situation in Ningpo, which was being defended by the British and French forces, Li wrote Tseng in late September 1862 that it was necessary to send strong Chinese forces to that port, to "remove" the influence of the Cantonese merchants who were collaborating with the Europeans, "so that the control of the Westerners can gradually be removed (*yang-jen chih ch'üan k'o chien fen*) and the city prevented from eventually turning into a foreign land."[35] Li wrote repeatedly in his letters that the future role of the Europeans in China "depends on the strength of China's armies," and that if China should fail to strengthen herself, "the calamity for the future is unthinkable."[36]

If his new experiences had thus generated in him a sense of China's external challenges, what then were the measures that, in Li's view, China had to take, beyond equipping the Anhwei Army with Western weapons? Before discussing this question, however, we need to look at the other exigencies to which his pragmatic faculties responded. As Tseng's assistant, Li was well acquainted with the system that the elder statesman had developed for the administration of armies and revenue.[37] But certain concrete situations that Li faced in his new post, concerning armies and the tax-collecting machinery, compelled him to accept administrative methods that were at variance with those employed by Tseng. The expedients to which Li resorted, not always consistent with Confucian principles, were, as we shall see, to have the effect of compromising his proposals for innovation and reform.

In military matters, Li's urgent task, beyond the acquisition of Western arms, was to organize and expand the Anhwei Army so that, in addition to defending Shanghai, it could mount an offensive toward Soochow, a strategy destined to contribute greatly to the war against the Taipings.[38] Li's was a difficult task, however, for the Anhwei Army, being hastily brought together from a variety of sources, presented thorny problems of command and discipline. Superficially, the Anhwei Army was patterned exactly after Tseng's Hunan Army. The recruitment of the troops, as well as responsibility for them, was entrusted to the small number of commanders (*t'ung-ling*) who supervised the battalion officers (*ying kuan*), each of the latter being in charge of about five hundred men. The troops were supposed to have received training identical with that of the Hunan Army, whose "battalion regulations" (*ying-chih* and *ying-kuei*) were adopted for them.[39] But the components of the Anhwei Army were far more mixed than those of the Hunan Army. The latter, formed in 1852 in a comparatively peaceful area of Hunan, was led largely by men of scholarly background, at least 24 percent of the battalion officers and eight of thirteen commanders being literary candidates. The troops of the Hunan Army, moreover, were made up predominantly of farmers, although some had had experience as local militiamen.[40] The Anhwei Army, on the other hand, was made up principally of two types of forces: (1) hard-boiled irregular forces of the northern Anhwei area that had seen war and turmoil for nearly a decade, and (2) recently formed Hunan Army units led by nonliterati officers. Although among the Anhwei Army's nine earliest commanders, two were holders of literary degrees—a *chü-jen* and a *sheng-yüan*—the remaining seven were less cultivated men. Among the seven, three were leaders of irregular forces in northern Anhwei as of 1861 and four were nonliterati officers of the Hunan Army and other forces (although one of the four men could boast a military *chü-jen* degree).[41] The more boisterous of Li's commanders proved to be the more battleworthy—Liu Ming-ch'uan and Chou Sheng-po who, as "local bosses" of the Western villages (*Hsi-hsiang*) near Lu-chou, had been fighting rebels intermittently ever since 1853; Ch'eng Hsüeh-ch'i, a former Taiping who had surrendered to the Hunan Army and become one of its officers; and Kuo Sung-lin, an illiterate Hunan Army officer who seems to have started life as a carpenter. The soldiers that came from the area of the backward Western villages, especially, because of their strong clannish organization, made cohesive fighting units.[42] But perhaps it is not surprising that ideological training, which was the hallmark of the Hunan Army, could not be easily maintained with the Anhwei Army. The desire for plunder and profit became the chief motivation of most of Li's battalions, good fighters though the men might be.

Li's method was to transform these forces, as best he could, with the Hunan Army system. The troops were paid regularly, and songs with the theme of "love the people" were chanted daily.[43] But under the exigency of having to replenish and expand his forces quickly, he had to allow the fresh recruits from northern Anhwei to form new battalions without going through the proper training. Li invited at least one more degree-holder to be a commander, Liu Ping-chang, a Hanlin compiler whom Li had known for a long time. But for the pressing and expanding campaigns, he had to depend increasingly on the doughty Liu Ming-ch'uan (one of the "local bosses" from the Western villages), the brilliant tactician, Ch'eng Hsüeh-ch'i (the former Taiping), and the courageous but corrupt Kuo Sung-lin (the former carpenter who, according to one report, brought along five concubines during one military expedition).[44] In Li's letters to his commanders, he frequently urged them to discipline the troops and to restrain them from disturbing the populace. Li told a friend that he adopted as his own motto "not to wish for money nor be afraid of death," so as to set an example for his commanders. Li himself often visited the front on horseback during battles, and his personal bravery even won the praise of Western observers.[45] But, plainly, he had to close an eye to the pecuniary habits of his commanders and officers. When Tseng Kuo-fan wrote to him regarding unfavorable reports about the Anhwei Army's discipline, Li merely replied that he was doing his best to exhort the commanders by correspondence and that he would soon leave on an inspection tour.[46]

In the matter of raising revenue, which was as urgent a task as planning military campaigns, Li faced a similar need to compromise with existing conditions. This can be seen most strikingly in Li's methods regarding the administration of the likin, a tax instituted in the early years of the Taiping Rebellion, which had long been levied at particularly high rates in the commercially wealthy Shanghai area. When Li first arrived in April 1862, the likin collection system in eastern Kiangsu was controlled by the notoriously corrupt Wu Hsü, who was the provincial financial commissioner as well as the Shanghai taotai. Wu had been raising 100,000 to 200,000 taels of likin per month and, according to Li's report to Tseng Kuo-fan, was known to have embezzled as much as 40 percent of the portion of the revenue that was expended by him for military purposes.[47] Li aimed to remove Wu from office, as soon as the latter's services, particularly as liaison man between Li and the Ever-Victorious Army, could be dispensed with. Wu was actually removed in late 1862. To replace him as the principal financial administrator in the Shanghai area, Li had solicited the services of Kuo Sung-tao, the famous Hunan scholar-official. Kuo declined the offer, however, and instead took up the post of Grain Intendant of Soochow and Sung-chiang under Li (and, later on, that of Salt Commissioner at Yang-chou). Li eventually arranged to have as the Shanghai taotai Huang Fang, a former acting magistrate of Shanghai, who knew the local conditions and who was recommended to Li by Tseng Kuo-ch'üan.[48] Some scholars have cited these moves by Li as the principal evidence of his building up a personal "bureaucratic machine" in Kiangsu. Actually, the change of personnel was necessary and desirable under the circumstances, and there is no evidence that either Kuo or Huang belonged to the inner circle among Li's subordinates.[49] In any case, Li instituted financial reforms in Shanghai before and after Wu Hsü's removal. Hsüeh Shu-t'ang, a chin-shih from Honan and a former prefect of Ch'ang-chou, Kiangsu, whom Li described to Tseng as an "earnest and incorruptible" man, and Wang Ta-ching, a Chekiang chü-jen, who had experience doing military staff work in northern Anhwei and whom Li regarded as a man "of great integrity," were appointed in July 1862 as commissioners of the General Likin Bureau of the Shanghai area, and prominent members of the gentry, including Feng Kuei-fen, accepted appointments at the bureau.[50] For the post of Financial Commissioner of Kiangsu, Li's nominee was Liu Hsün-kao, formerly judicial commissioner of the province, who had had the reputation of being "unpretentious and loving the people."[51]

Although Li did attempt to bring what he described as "superior men" (chüntzu)[52] into the Kiangsu financial administration, in practice, however, he had to compromise with the vested interests that had grown up in the likin collection system. Li aimed to do away with "embezzlement and concealment on the part of the [likin-bureau's] deputies" and he dismissed many men from the collecting offices.[53] But he found that he had to retain, for example, such a notorious agent as Chin Hung-pao, because he had such local connections and had developed such special expertise as to have become indispensable. As Li explained in a letter to Tseng: "Chin Hung-pao is wily and cruel. [But] his special charge, the Bureau of Commodity Levies, has been bringing in seventy or eighty thousand taels monthly. His responsibility is great and it is difficult to find a replacement. I hope that his talents and intelligence may be channeled in the direction of the generally changing attitude here."[54] In the two years after July 1862, Li instituted many new kinds of likin and increased the rates generally, and as towns and trade routes were recovered from the Taipings, new likin stations were established. The monthly revenue from likin collected by Li's administration rose to 200,000 taels in the fall of 1862 and increased steadily through 1863.[55] This revenue made possible the expansion of the Anhwei Army as well as Li's regular remittances to Tseng Kuo-fan's forces. But as the likin levies and stations multiplied, the abuses in the collection system also increased, as some Kiangsu gentry members eventually complained.[56]

Did Li become the head of a system of organized corruption, with the intention of gaining profits for himself? In view of the funds that he came to control, rumors about his amassing a large fortune were inevitable. Li himself wrote to a friend: "I am the son of a poor man with the reputation of suddenly possessing immense wealth."[57] Li's letters show, however, that he was always pressed for funds, not only to meet the growing military needs in the area under his charge, but also to send aid to the armies of the Tseng brothers, in the form of munitions as well as silver ingots (delivered by government-owned steamers).[58] It does not seem that Li had a personal stake in the Anhwei Army's plundering. In the confidential letter Li wrote to P'an Ting-hsin, an Anhwei Army commander of literary background who had been his friend since the 1840s, we find Li repeatedly exhorting P'an to get his men to refrain from "disturbing the populace"; there is never any hint of a financial arrangement between the two men.[59] So far, we have found no information about Li's relationship with his likin collectors, except that Hsüeh Shu-t'ang, his appointee as head of the bureau, was an official in Kiangsu whom Li had met only in 1862. However, of the ten officials known to have served as staff members of the Kiangsu likin administration in this period, five were from Li's native province, Anhwei.[60] After the Taiping War had ended, Yin Chao-yung, a prominent member of the Kiangsu gentry who was then serving as an official in Peking and was a partisan of the conservative Grand Secretary Wo-jen, memorialized the throne and accused Li's likin system of being staffed by "relatives of officials, *mu-fu* members, visiting literati (*yu-k'e*), and undesirable members of the gentry."[61] Whether Li himself was as corrupt as some of his likin collectors undoubtedly were is still a moot point. But he was at fault, in any case, for not attempting a more thorough reorganization of the likin collection system or of the Anhwei Army. Given the circumstances, Li probably had no alternative. But his acceptance of the existing realities was to have an important bearing on his concepts of the policies China needed.

Involved as he was in the immediate tasks of organizing campaigns and raising revenue, Li found time to bring forward numerous proposals regarding the general policy of the state. Like other scholar-officials of the T'ung-chih period, Li paid attention to the rehabilitation of the agricultural economy and the reassertion of the inherited principles of government. But his most distinctive contribution lay in his proposals designed to enhance the state's "wealth and strength" (*fu-ch'iang*), increasingly concerned as he was with China's external crisis. Several of Li's proposals—regarding both traditional problems of administration and "self-strengthening"—were influenced by Feng Kuei-fen (1809–74), the eminent statecraft scholar whom Li brought into his *mu-fu*. But Li did not accept all of Feng's ideas, and the emphasis he gave to the proposals was his own.

Li did not neglect the relief and rehabilitation of the war-torn areas. In the winter of 1862–63, after a series of victories west of Shanghai, he established a Relief and Rehabilitation Bureau (*Shan-hou fu-hsü chü*), to provide rice and cash to destitute farmers in the recovered areas. Officials were instructed to collect donations from the gentry for immediate relief, as well as for seeds and farming and weaving implements that were to be distributed. The provincial government's annual expenditure for this purpose was reported to be "several hundred thousand strings of cash," but local officials and gentry were counted on to do more.[62] Li also proposed to the throne the remission and reduction of the land taxes. Remission was limited to the first year after each prefecture was recovered, and due to his military needs and the court's demands for rice for Peking, in areas not directly affected by the war, such as the Chiang-pei region north of the Yangtze, Li even imposed new taxes in the form of "donations" or "acreage levies" (*mou-chüan*) upon the landowners.[63] But in June 1863, Li did recommend to the throne that the grain tribute quotas from the particularly heavily taxed Soochow, Sung-chiang, and T'ai-ts'ang areas should be reduced permanently. This major proposal followed the precedent of tax-rate reductions proposed by Hu Lin-i and others in several Yangtze provinces; it had the blessing of Tseng Kuo-fan who attached his name to Li's memorial of June 1863. But the memorial was largely the work of Feng Kuei-fen and of Liu Hsün-kao, the Kiangsu financial commissioner.[64] Liu actually was less ambitious than Feng and wanted only to reduce the official rates of the land or grain tribute taxes without tampering with the surtaxes (fou-shou), which Feng wanted to have abolished entirely. Li, however, favored Feng's plan, at least to the extent of putting before the throne the principle of abolishing the surtaxes, although he suggested that the details be worked out later. Li also followed Feng's advice and bitterly attacked, in a supplementary memorial, the system prevailing in Kiangsu under which the rates of land and grain tribute taxes applicable to the large landlords were sometimes only one-fourth of those applied to the peasant households. Once the principles Li suggested were approved by the throne, he established a bureau in August 1863 to work out the concrete plans, with Feng Kuei-fen as a leading bureau commissioner.[65]

From time to time over the next two years, Li attended to this bureau's work personally. When the final memorial embodying suggested new rates was presented to the throne in 1865, he again stressed that the tax differentiation between the "big and small households" should be corrected, and he proposed that at least the traditional surtaxes should be reduced.[66] In early 1865, Li launched a major project to invite emigrants from other areas to settle in the particularly devastated Ch'ang-chou prefecture. Li's longtime friend, Ch'en Nai, once, like Li himself, a protégé of Tseng Kuo-fan, played a leading role in this work and, within a few months' time, more than a million mou of land were said to have been brought under cultivation.[67]

Although Li did what was proper regarding the relief of the agricultural economy, it is doubtful that he put equal emphasis on the major policy of the T'ung-chih period, the reassertion of the principle that men of moral attainment as well as ability should be selected for official posts. In Li's letters of 1862–63, we find statements such as the following: "The civil government needs reform. We should regard as our responsibility the revival of talent and the recovery of good customs."[68] But as areas were won back from the Taipings and Li had occasion to recommend men for the local government posts, he seems to have emphasized the candidates' abilities rather than their moral qualities. A circuit intendant was criticized by Li as amply "good and kindly but not sufficiently astute." An acting prefect whom Li himself had brought to office was discovered by Li to be "superior in virtue rather than in ability" and was asked to leave at the end of one term of service.[69] Li aimed at finding men who were "earnest and unpretentious, industrious and able, and who had shown results in the past."[70] But his chief concern with the prefects and hsien magistrates under him seems to have been their ability to produce revenue, especially by exacting donations from wealthy members of the gentry for military expenditures. Li had no love for the country gentry as a whole. He berated the "bad gentry" (tiao-lieh shen-tung) who shifted the burden of government levies to the "indigent people"; he realized that "most of the big households are resisting [taxes] and are in arrears."[71] In his memorials on tax reform in Kiangsu, mentioned above, he not only suggested that the preferential tax rates of "big households" should be abolished but proposed also that gentry members who either did not meet their tax requirements or engaged in a practice known as *pao-lan* (assuming responsibility for tax payment for the less influential landowners, for a financial consideration) should be punished regardless of academic or official standing.[72] These were important proposals, but, on the other hand, it does not seem that Li was concerned with the basic local-government situation that lay behind such practices. In Li's letters and memorials, one fails to find any discussion of the abuse of power by the yamen clerks or of the fact that many prefects and *hsien* magistrates at this time won their offices through purchase—problems that greatly worried Feng Kuei-fen and others.[73]

Like other T'ung-chih officials, Li promoted the recovery of the examination system. In 1864, he recommended to the throne the creation of a new examination center at Soochow, and in the following year, he proposed an increased quota for preliminary degrees in Shanghai and the adjacent areas. In 1865, he served as the supervising examiner (*chien-lin*) in the first provincial examination held at recovered Nanking.[74] While Li performed these acts in the line of duty, it seems from his letters that he had no great enthusiasm for the propagation of Confucian learning. He does not appear to have done much to promote the republishing of the inherited literature; in 1864 to 1865, as far as is known, he was responsible for the revival of only two academies (*shu-yüan*), both in Soochow.[75] Li's letters of this period hardly ever refer to bookish or cultural subjects; the values he had once attached to literature and scholarship must have been somewhat altered. After 1861, he apparently stopped writing poetry. He also gave up his former hobby of collecting good brushes for his calligraphy.[76]

While Li was not a central figure of the T'ung-chih reign's Confucian revival, he made a signal contribution in another direction, the advocacy of new policies aimed at the building up of China's power to enable her to cope with the challenge from abroad. Li continued to be irked by evidence of Western aggressiveness. He had difficulties with Ward's successors, particularly Henry Burgevine and even with the comparatively cooperative Charles George Gordon. Li was aware that the Ever-Victorious Army, though under Chinese direction, was ultimately under heavy British influence.[77] He was greatly incensed in the summer of 1863 when Horatio Nelson Lay demanded absolute control over the naval fleet he purchased for China, and Li strongly suspected that when the British General W. G. Brown requested, in October 1863, that the British troops participate in the offensive toward Soochow, he was motivated by a desire for the extension of the foreigner's privileges in the interior.[78] Li had been appointed by the throne as the acting commissioner of trade (*t'ung-shang ta-ch'en*) in March 1863. He was aware of the increased activities of the Western merchants and shipowners not only in Shanghai but also in the recently opened Yangtze ports. Although he came to realize, at least by the spring of 1863, that the Europeans were primarily interested in commerce and had no immediate plans to occupy Chinese territory, he was convinced that this situation could change at any time.[79] Li began to use the phrase "self-strengthening" in this long-range context. To a former teacher, then a high official in Peking, Li wrote in April 1863: "Ever since [foreign] trade began on the Yangtze River, the economic control (li-ch'üan) of China has fallen into the hands of the foreigners. The abuses which we cannot check are multifarious. . . . If we could strengthen ourselves, perhaps the foreigners would not recklessly covet us. Otherwise, the calamity for the future is unthinkable." In early November 1863, at the time General Brown requested that British troops be sent in the offensive against Soochow and when the question of H. N. Lay's flotilla was still not settled, Li wrote to a friend then in retirement in Fukien: "While our present trouble is with the internal rebel, the long-range trouble is with the Western people. Great as the Chinese state (Hua-hsia) is, she has been so weakened that she has come to this pass!"[80]

Soon after his arrival in Shanghai, as we have seen, Li had arranged for some units of the Anhwei Army to buy and use Western weapons. He also hired foreign instructors, including the officers of the Ever-Victorious Army, to drill his troops and to teach the Chinese the use of artillery.[81] He soon became convinced, however, that the Chinese themselves should take steps to acquire what was believed to be the chief basis of Western power, the armament industry. As early as September 1862, Li asked F. T. Ward to recommend to him foreign workers who could instruct the Chinese in the manufacture of cannon shells.[82] Meanwhile, in his letters to Tseng, he urged the latter to hire foreign workmen and to adopt new techniques in the arsenal at Anking, where a group of talented Chinese engineers had gathered, making old-fashioned firearms—gingalls and matchlocks of the type the Chinese were already making during the Opium War.[83] Part of Li's motive was simply to insure the supply of ammunition and weapons that he had been purchasing at exorbitant prices, but there is no doubt that he was also thinking in terms of a long-range policy of self-strengthening. In February 1863, describing the visits he had made to the British and French warships, Li wrote Tseng: "Of course I would not dare to subscribe to heterodoxy (hsieh-chiao) to benefit ourselves, but I am deeply ashamed that Chinese military equipment is far inferior to that of foreign countries."[84] In May, Li wrote Tseng of the world history that he had learned since coming to Shanghai, the fact that the strength of a country in a world of international rivalry depended on modern arms. "In the past, neither Russia nor Japan was versed in artillery techniques; they therefore became increasingly weaker states. Because their monarchs and officials humbled themselves and sought the secret skills of the British and the French, they have gradually learned to make, as well as use, firearms, cannon, and steamships. They can therefore rival Britain and France. If China would pay attention to these matters, then we would be able to stand on our own feet a hundred years from now and even long after."[85] Later in the same month, when Li learned that H. N. Lay was putting pressure on the Tsungli Yamen to have his fleet accepted on his terms, Li exclaimed in a letter to Tseng: "I only hope that the evil influence of the rebels can be quickly subdued, and that we can devote ourselves to the study and pursuit of Western weapons. Once China possesses two things, mortars ($k'ai-hua\ ta-p'ao$) and steamships, Westerners will have to keep their hands off!''[86]

Li himself took steps to establish arsenals in Shanghai. He planned to buy ''cannon-forging'' machinery from Hong Kong and to hire foreign mechanics. He had difficulty getting suitable foreign personnel; nonetheless, he founded two small arsenals in Shanghai with Chinese workmen, and he asked Ting Jih-ch'ang, a Chinese official with some experience supervising the manufacture of munitions in Kwangtung, to come to Shanghai to head one of the new plants. Later, in 1863, Li established a third arsenal in Sung-chiang, near Shanghai, under Halliday Macartney, a medical officer of the Ever-Victorious Army, who impressed Li with the shells and percussion caps he produced.[87] Li was overjoyed when, in late 1863, Tseng Kuo-fan's Chinese engineers convinced Tseng that Yung Wing, an American-educated Chinese then engaging in business in Shanghai, should be sent to the United States to purchase machinery that could, in turn, be used to make the machines needed by Chinese arsenals. Li arranged for the funds for Yung Wing's trip and congratulated Tseng, saying that this move marked ''the beginning of self-strengthening on our coasts.''[88]

While Li was anxious to have Western machines introduced into China, he also realized that complex knowledge and skills lay behind the machines. While Li himself had only a general notion of Western science,[89] he came to believe—and he had the audacity to bring the idea to the attention of the Tsungli Yamen—that a drastic change needed to be made in the government's personnel policy before China could compete with the West in the matter of armaments. In March 1863, when he recommended to the throne that new foreign-language schools be established in Shanghai and Canton, he proposed that the schools should not only aim at the training of interpreters useful in diplomatic negotiations—such was the aim of the T'ung-wen Kuan established by the Tsungli Yamen in 1862—but should go further and train Chinese youths in mathematics and sciences in the hope that they could some day unlock the secrets of Western technology. ''That which the foreigners are good at, such as mathematical studies, the principles of science ($ko\text{-}chih$), and the techniques of manufacturing and astronomy, have all been written up in books. . . . Can the Chinese be inferior to the Westerners in ingenuity and intelligence? If there are men well versed in the Western language and one person can teach another, then all the skillful techniques of steamships and firearms can be gradually mastered.''[90]

Li's vision did not stop with such a training program, however. A year later, when the Chinese engineers and workmen at his small arsenals in Shanghai further disappointed him, he became persuaded that to enable China to produce good engineers and craftsmen, it was necessary to have a large number of talented scholars devote themselves to technology, and that this aim could be accomplished only when the examination system itself was modified. In a letter to the Tsungli Yamen written in the spring of 1864,[91] Li argued eloquently that in order to enable China to cope with the intimidation and encroachment of Western powers, it was absolutely necessary to do what Tokugawa Japan was doing—to acquire machines that made machines and to have young men of distinguished lineage devote themselves to industrial work. If Japan, which was a puny state beyond the seas, could change her policy in time, should not China also change her policies? The trouble with the Chinese, Li pointed out, was that the literati were "immersed in the time-honored practice of essay writing and of doing calligraphy in small and regular characters"; few scholars cared to do manual work and pursue matters of technique (i). This situation could only be changed, Li felt, if the throne itself decided to encourage technology. Li proposed that a new category ($k'o$) be created within the examination system for candidates who specialized in technology "If the scholars should regard this [new] category of the examination as their lifelong goal by which to achieve wealth, rank, and honor," Li wrote, "then their techniques will be perfected and talents will foregather." Both this letter and Li's memorial of 1863 on the foreign-language schools bear the marks of Feng Kuei-fen's influence; very similar ideas can be found in Feng's essays written in 1861.[92] But the letters undoubtedly represented Li's own convictions. Li did not go as far as Feng did in identifying the proposed new examination category as "Western learning" ($hsi\text{-}hsüeh$), but Li did state unequivocally in referring to the Western countries that the Chinese should "learn their methods ($shih\ ch'i\text{-}fa$) without having always to use their men." Li pointed out that works on military technology available in Chinese, such as Ting Kung-ch'en's $Yen\text{-}p'ao\ t'u\text{-}shuo$ (Illustrated treatise on gunnery, 1841), were superficial and unreliable, and he praised the Japanese for sending youths to Western countries to acquire new knowledge. Li pointed out that what he was proposing involved the "reform of institutions" ($pien\text{-}fa$), but he pleaded that the seriousness of the situation demanded such a drastic course.

Li proved to be too bold for the Tsungli Yamen, however. A year before, the latter had supported Li's suggestion of teaching sciences and mathematics at the foreign-language schools to be established in Shanghai and Canton. But the yamen did not endorse Li's new proposal concerning the examination system, although Prince Kung and his colleagues did append Li's letter to one of their memorials to the throne.[93]

If Li's pragmatic turn of mind led him to recommend radical reform of the examination system, did he apply the same attitude to other aspects of the Ch'ing system that were also unsatisfactory? As we have seen, despite his proposal to the throne for the equalization of tax burdens between the large gentry households and the peasant families, Li did not give much thought to the basic problems of local government, such as the sale of offices and the abuses of the yamen clerks. In two areas immediately related to his aim of building up the state's wealth and strength, the military system and economic policy, Li did visualize certain general reforms, but it must be emphasized that, in both cases, his vision was severely circumscribed by what he considered feasible.

Although Li did not admire all that he saw of the Western forces in Shanghai, they did persuade him of one great merit of the European system, namely, the small size of the armies made possible by the quality of their weapons. As Li wrote Tseng Kuo-fan in May 1863, "With a maximum of ten thousand men, the Western armies can enter into major battles."[94] The advantage of a small and effective army was obvious, for with reduced costs, the troops could be paid well and morale could be maintained, whereas even the Hunan and Anhwei armies, which were small by Chinese standards, were constantly plagued by problems of financing and consequently of morale and discipline. Even as the Taipings were being defeated, the Hunan Army, its rich plunder notwithstanding, suffered from large-scale desertions, and Li found it increasingly difficult to maintain the discipline of the Anhwei Army. In August 1864, when Tseng Kuo-fan, immediately after Nanking was recovered, took steps to demobilize the Hunan Army, Li recommended to the throne that the Anhwei Army, which numbered by then some seventy thousand men, should be reduced to thirty thousand men, including twenty-two thousand men equipped with rifles and artillery, to be used for "coastal defense."[95] But if the Anhwei Army, which was of comparatively high quality, required reduction and improvement, should not the Green Standard armies, which constituted the bulk of the dynasty's regular forces, also be reduced in number while being trained in the use of new weapons? Li considered it impolitic to make such a recommendation directly to the throne or to the Tsungli Yamen; instead, he wrote in October 1864 to two officials in Peking who were in a position to suggest new policies—Ch'en T'ing-ching, a censor friend of Li's, and Hsüeh Huan, former governor of Kiangsu, then serving as a minister of the Tsungli Yamen. Li warned of the possibility of renewed Western aggression and suggested again that the situation called for the "reform of institutions" (pien-fa), specifically, a complete reorganization of the Green Standard armies and the replacement of the old-fashioned water force with a new navy. "The conditions of the present and the past are not the same," Li wrote Ch'en, the censor, "how can we be confined to the established ways of our ancestors? It will be necessary to do away with all of the tired and weak troops in order to provide ample rations and pay; to abandon bows and arrows and to specialize and excel in firearms . . . to select able commanders; to drill industriously, and to train with perseverance. . . ."[96] Taking up Li's suggestion, Ch'en did memorialize the throne, recommending reform of the Green Standard Army and of the provincial water forces. But as Li had perhaps anticipated, the throne did not act on Ch'en's proposal beyond referring it to Tseng and Li for their consideration![97]

Without doubt, Li was genuinely convinced of the need for an empire-wide military reform, although it may be suggested that in writing to his Peking friends, he was probably also trying to convey to the court the idea that his own Anhwei Army, which had the status of yung-ying or "nonregular battalions," could still serve a useful purpose now that the Taiping Rebellion had been suppressed.[98] In any event, Li's model for the reorganized regular forces of the empire was none other than the Anhwei Army itself. Beginning in 1862, the Anhwei Army had adopted Western weapons and drill techniques (and soon it even adopted English command words transliterated into Chinese, such as *fa-wei ma-ch'i* for "forward march").[99] But the army's original scheme of organization remained unchanged. Even though, in the summer of 1864, Li seriously considered disbanding the inferior units of the army, there is no evidence that he had in mind any organizational overhaul for the thirty thousand men to be retained. Li's plans for reducing his forces were not in fact realized. He was urged by Tseng to maintain the strength of his forces for the war against the Nien rebels, and during the few months beginning in November 1864, the Anhwei Army was ordered by the throne to service in Anhwei, Hupei, Honan, Shantung, and Chihli, against the Niens, and in Fukien, against the Taiping remnants. By June 1865, when Li went to Nanking to become the acting governor-general of Liangkiang (replacing Tseng, who had taken charge of operations against the Niens), it appears that he had disbanded only about ten thousand men of his forces; of the remaining sixty thousand men, fewer than twenty thousand remained in Kiangsu.[100]

Whatever hope Li had had regarding an empire-wide military reform had plainly to be abandoned. Writing to Tseng, he lamented the fact that "the financial resources of the provinces are being exhausted, while worthless troops and officers are being supported for no purpose."[101] Li persevered in his effort to introduce Western military technology into China. Beginning in September 1864, Li, who relied in this matter on the advice of Ting Jih-ch'ang, the Shanghai taotai after June 1864, discussed with the Tsungli Yamen the plan for a large arsenal in Shanghai that could make machines and build ships as well as manufacture munitions.[102] In the spring of 1865, the Tsungli Yamen consulted Li about the possibility of sending officers and men of the Banner forces abroad to learn arsenal techniques. Li wrote the yamen that he had long considered sending students to Western countries "to inquire into the sources of their technology and manufacturing,"[103] but since few Manchus or Chinese had had the necessary preparation in mathematics and in such sciences as mechanics, it would be best to have men trained first in a Chinese arsenal, where they could be introduced to these subjects. In the summer of 1865, Ting Jih-ch'ang arranged to buy the waterfront "machine shop" of an American firm in Shanghai, and there was founded the famous Kiangnan Arsenal, which incorporated the two small arsenals Li had previously established in Shanghai, as well as the machinery that Yung Wing bought in the United States, which arrived the following year. Reporting to the throne in a memorial dated September 1865, Li referred to the censor Ch'en T'ing-ching's memorial on the Ch'ing army's need for Western weapons and argued that "machine manufacturing" was urgently needed to meet China's external crisis. Now that the arsenal was founded, Li wrote, "we must hope for continuous growth in the future. The techniques at which the foreigners excel will thus become those at which we excel. Thus, we will not seem inferior by comparison, and by being prepared, we shall be free of calamity."[104] While the muskets and small howitzers produced by the arsenal were immediately useful to the Anhwei Army's campaign against the Niens, plans were also made to build steamships and to train young men (including Manchus of the Banner forces detached for that purpose) in Western science and technology.[105]

Although Li's principal concern during his Kiangsu years was military, he also realized that the military prowess of any state depended partly on the economy. In his letters of 1862–65, we find him using such traditional phrases as *li-ch'üan* (economic control) and *fu-ch'iang* (wealth and strength) in the context of China's new international situation.[106] Li was incensed by the fact that Chinese merchants in Shanghai—"most of them reside in the Yangkingpang [area] and in the foreign firms"—could successfully ignore government requests for donations to meet military needs, and that "British and French consuls come forward to offer obstruction and to protect them."[107] We have seen that Li often lamented the fact that the economic and indeed the administrative control of Shanghai and Ningpo was in Western hands. Li did, of course, collect large likin revenue from the foreign-trade merchandise, but the financial difficulties that the Ch'ing armies continued to experience and the utter ruin of war-torn Kiangsu, in contrast to the prosperity of the Shanghai foreign settlement, all convinced him that China was inferior to the West in material matters. In late 1863, he wrote to a friend that China's problem in the future was "not so much military weakness (*jo*) as poverty (*p'in*)."[108]

For the moment, however, there was no feasible economic program that he could propose, except one regarding Chinese shipping between the treaty ports. As early as July 1862, as the acting governor of Kiangsu, Li had to consider measures for the protection of the Kiangsu seagoing junks (*sha-ch'uan*), which had declined because of the competition of Western vessels in the bean trade from the North China ports of Newchwang and Chefoo. Particularly in view of the fact that these junks were to be relied on for the resumption of tribute-rice shipments from Shanghai to Peking, Li recommended to the throne that the original treaty provision barring foreign vessels from the bean trade in these ports be restored. This proved impossible, however, since the Tsungli Yamen found it necessary to give in to the British on the matter. In the spring of 1865, Li found that the best he could do was to seek imperial approval for tax concessions to the junk owners to enable them to survive.[109] But it had also occurred to him by this time that, in the long run, Chinese shipowners could only compete with the foreigners if they abandoned the junks and operated Western sailing vessels and steamships. Li also realized that many Chinese merchants of the treaty ports had actually been investing in Western-style ships under foreign registry; it was better to have them cease this surreptitious complicity with the foreigners. In October 1864, Li accepted the proposal of Ting Jih-ch'ang that the Tsungli Yamen's approval should be sought for a change in the Ch'ing regulations regarding shipping, to enable the Chinese merchants to own Western-style vessels legally. As Ting stressed in his petition to Li, if Chinese merchants at several ports could own twenty or thirty steamships and a hundred or so Western sailing vessels, properly registered with the government, the ships not only could be used as military transports in time of war, but could provide a basis for Chinese competition with Western firms in China, perhaps eventually inducing the latter to withdraw from Chinese waters. Such a fleet, Ting wrote, "not only will add to our prestige and power, but will take away the economic control (li-ch'üan) [now in the hands of the foreigners]." Li submitted Ting's proposal to the Tsungli Yamen, adding himself that "the foreigners of different countries not only gather in the seaports but have penetrated deep into the Yangtze River; they look down upon China and we cannot fight them merely with words."[110] The proposal was approved by the Tsungli Yamen, although due to the delay occasioned by consultations with the officials in other coastal provinces, the regulations permitting Chinese merchants to own foreign-style ships were not promulgated until 1867.[111]

While Li's patriotism thus enabled him to have a measure of sympathy for the Chinese merchants, there was nevertheless one anticommercial policy to which he firmly adhered, namely, the continuation of the likin taxes. For inimical as the likin was to commerce, he saw no other sources of revenue available that would meet China's continuing military needs, even after the rebellions were suppressed. Even if agricultural production could be revived in most provinces, there was still the question of whether the yield of the land tax could be significantly increased. In 1863, Li's administration, following the suggestion of Feng Kuei-fen, conducted an experimental land survey in a small area of eastern Kiangsu. Owing to lack of support from the local officials and gentry, however, the survey showed a taxable land area even smaller than that in the original books![112] Li was convinced that the likin was indispensable to any plans for China's self-strengthening, and he rationalized, without pointing out the inconsistency with his aim of building a wealthy and prosperous China, by saying that "since ancient times, the increase of land tax has been considered tyranny, but taxing commerce has never been regarded as bad policy."[113] Li did envision, however, that the introduction of machines could eventually bring greater wealth for the country. In the same memorial in which he defended the likin, submitted in 1865 in response to an attack by prominent members of the Kiangsu gentry on the excessive likin levies under Li's administration, Li begged the throne to consider the fact that Western nations were all "seeking to excel in wealth and strength (fu-ch'iang)," while the Chinese scholar-officials, "accustomed to doing stylized examination essays" and "congratulating themselves on their classical scholarship," were indifferent to the more vital matters.[114] In his memorial seeking imperial approval for the creation of the Kiangnan Arsenal, submitted in September 1865, Li expressed the hope that the arsenal would eventually produce machines useful to agriculture and industry—"farming and weaving implements and printing and pottery-making equipment." Li also predicted that in a few decades' time, the Chinese would have mastered Western technology, while "among the wealthy farmers and merchants, there will inevitably be men who follow the example of Western machine manufacturing for their own benefit."[115] These ideas were pursued by Li later, in the 1870s, when his great interest was to encourage the working of mines with Western machines—as he put it, "to rely on the treasures of the earth to finance the defense of the seacoast."[116]

The years we have reviewed saw the rise of Li Hung-chang from an aspiring candidate for the literary examinations to an individual in a position of prominence and power. But did he, in this formative period of his career, remain within the usual mode of a Confucian literatus-statesman? We have suggested that despite his early success in the examinations, Li was essentially a man of action. In any case, beginning in 1853 (when he was thirty), he had abandoned the more pedantic pursuits for military and administrative work. There were undoubtedly in Chinese history men with a personality similar to Li's, and it was not unknown for a literatus to become a military commander, as indeed so many officials of the Hsien-feng and T'ung-chih periods did. Evidence suggests that Li was ambitious and determined to achieve rank and glory; he was also keenly conscious of the value of money, whether or not he was personally corrupt. But in these respects, too, he was not unusual. There were many Confucian officials who worked for personal advancement and power, while no less earnestly performing their duties. In the years we have surveyed, there cannot be any doubt that Li was loyally serving the dynasty's cause, and proof abounds that his ambitions for himself did not preclude his being faithful and solicitous toward his friends.[117]

But whether Li departed from the Confucian mode of personal conduct or not, it is plain that he was, during this period, gradually moving away from the inherited cultural values, and that, moreover, his proposals for state policy can no longer be described as falling within the norm of Confucian statecraft.

Li's reaction against literature and scholarship must have begun in the mid-1850s. But it was, we may conclude, the sense of China's external crisis, a sense he gained after his arrival in Shanghai in 1862, that resulted in his acceptance of certain new values. We may describe his concern for China—his Chung-kuo or Chung-t'u—as "Confucian patriotism." While he was solicitous of the security and independence of the land and the people, he was not conscious of any conflict between his loyalty to the reigning dynasty—which to a Confucian was the loftiest of sentiments—and his concern for China as a country. Li's patriotism was strong enough, in any case, to modify his concepts of what he desired. In the years that he had to deal continuously with the threats from Gordon, Horatio Nelson Lay, and Harry Parkes,[118] pursuits relevant to China's "wealth and strength" became increasingly more important to him than the study of literature and classics and, indeed by implication, more important than moral cultivation itself. It may perhaps be argued that such pursuits, involving as they did amoral, collective goals and the channeling of scholars' energies into specialization in technology, were not completely foreign to China's complex tradition, as there had always been a strain of realism in Confucianism and, after all, the Chinese had not always neglected technology. But it cannot be denied that these latter elements were merely peripheral to the dominant ideology of the past, whereas with Li, they had become matters of central concern.

The innovations proposed by Li must seem modest to students accustomed to European statesmanship of the mid-nineteenth century or to the ferment of ideas in Bakumatsu Japan. Li's ideas fall short, in any case, of a general program of modernization. But it must be emphasized that Li did not merely promote the modern armament industry; he also envisioned the competition of Chinese merchants with Western firms. Moreover, Li was the first high Ch'ing official to advocate teaching Western mathematics and sciences in government schools, and he even recommended a new category in the civil service examination for men who specialized in the techniques of machine manufacturing. Although proposals for modifying the civil service examinations to make them more practical were not lacking in Chinese history, Li and his advisor, Feng Kuei-fen, were the first to suggest that knowledge that originated with an alien people—in other words, the barbarians—should be a criterion for the selection of government personnel.[119] Li and Feng were making a startling departure from the cultural egocentrism that had characterized Chinese history from the beginning, and particularly since the Sung dynasty.

While Li's proposals were audacious in certain respects, they were plainly inadequate in others. Despite the fact that he showed a degree of cultural open-mindedness, he never questioned the Confucian sociopolitical order—which still commanded his loyalty and was in any case the source of his personal success and power.[120] There is evidence that Li did not always side with the interest of the country gentry. In his anxiety to get larger revenue for the government, he did not hesitate to recommend that large and influential landowners be made to bear their share of the tax burden. Yet, on other issues of local government and justice, Li seems to have had fewer ideas for reform than many contemporary T'ung-chih scholar-officials. Moreover, Li's very success in his war against the Taipings seems to have restricted his vision of change. Despite his hope that other forces of the empire might follow the example of the Anhwei Army, he saw no way to correct the weaknesses of the Anhwei Army itself; and he saw in the likin collection system, infested as it was with abuses, a dependable source of state revenue. While Li was willing to modify Chinese culture so as to introduce Western technology, his proposals for reform were plainly not comprehensive; in fact, they were limited to certain adjustments in educational and personnel policy, in the size and training of the armed forces, and in the regulations concerning merchants. Despite his patriotism, Li did not seem to have the moral feeling that would make him more concerned with the basic questions of administrative and political reform. But, on the other hand, was he not also being realistic, given the degenerate yet intractable conditions of the Ch'ing government and the society in his time?

Notes

1. See, for example, Mesny's *Chinese Miscellany*, March 19, 1896, 516; Liang Ch'i-ch'ao, *Li Hung-chang* (in Chinese) (n.p., 1902), 140–43; J. O. P. Bland, *Li Hung-chang* (New York, 1917), 283. The late Professor Mary C. Wright provided valuable comments on a draft of this article. Its writing was made possible by a Guggenheim Fellowship in the spring of 1969.

2. The following are some of the significant studies with Li as the central figure: Ono Shinji, "Ri Kō-shō no tōjō—Waigun no seiritsu o megutte" (The emergence of Li Hung-chang—centering on the establishment of the Anhwei Army), *Tōyōshi kenkyū* 16.2 (1957), 1–28; "Waigun no kihonteki seikaku o megutte" (On the fundamental character of the Anhwei Army), *Rekishigaku kenkyū*, no. 245 (1960), 22–38; Stanley Spector, *Li Hung-chang and the Huai Army: A Study in Nineteenth-Century Chinese Regionalism* (Seattle, 1964); John L. Rawlinson, *China's Struggle for Naval Development, 1839–95* (Cambridge, Mass., 1967); Wang Erh-min, *Huai-chün chih* (A history of the Anhwei Army) (Taipei, 1967); Kenneth E. Folsom, *Friends, Guests, and Colleagues: The Mu-fu System in the Late Ch'ing Period* (Berkeley, 1968). This list should also include all significant works on China's modernization and on her diplomatic relations, 1862–1901—too numerous to cite here.

3. On Li's career from 1853 to 1861, I have been guided in my research by Erh-min Wang's *Huai-chün chih* (see note 2). I am also grateful to Mr. Wang for an illuminating discussion in March 1969 on some points of interpretation. A useful reference on Li's life is Tou Tsung-i (T. I. Dow), *Li Hung-chang nien-(jih-)p'u* (A biographical chronicle of Li Hung-chang) (Hong Kong, 1968).

4. *Hsü-hsiu Lu-chou fu-chih* (The gazetteer of Lu-chou prefecture, new edition) (1885), 58.1b; Li Hung-chang, *Li Wen-chung kung i-chi* (Writings of the late Li Hung-chang; hereafter cited as *I-chi*) in *Ho-fei Li-shih san-shih i-chi* (Writings left by three generations of the Lis of Hofei), comp. Li Kuo-chieh (1905), 4.3.

5. Li Hung-chang, *Li Wen-chung kung ch'üan-chi* (Complete papers of Li Hung-chang; hereafter cited as *LWCK*) (Nanking, 1905), *Chüan-shou* (hereafter cited as *Introductory Volume*), 12.

6. Tseng Kuo-fan, *Tseng Wen-cheng kung ch'üan-chi* (Complete papers of Tseng Kuo-fan; hereafter cited as *TWCK*) (1876), *Shu-tsa* (hereafter cited as *Letters*), 3.7b. On Tseng's own scholarly interests in this period, see Han-yin Chen Shen, "Tseng Kuo-fan in Peking, 1840–52; His Ideas on Statecraft and Reform," *JAS* 27 (1967), 61–80.

7. These were published in Li, *I-chi* and constituted most of the 214 double pages.

8. *LWCK, P'eng-liao han-kao* (Letters to friends and colleagues; hereafter cited as *Letters*), 4.21b.

9. *Chiao-p'ing Yüeh-fei fang-lüeh* (Military record of the suppression of the Taipings) (1872), 26.3b; Li, *I-chi*, 4.4b, 5b–6b.

10. *Chiao-p'ing Yüeh-fei fang-lüeh*, 38.15; 42.31; 60.6b; *Anhwei t'ung-chih* (The gazetteer of Anhwei) (1877), 102.12–13, 19; *TWCK Letters*, 3.24b.

11. *Hsü-hsiu Lu-chou fu-chih*, 22.7, 9b; 96.1b–3; *Chiao-p'ing Yüeh-fei fang-lüeh*, 79–30b; 106.39; 116.19b–21; 120.3.

12. *Hsü-hsiu Lu-chou fu-chih*, 22.11b; 96.3.

13. *LWCK Introductory Volume*, 12.

14. *Hsü-hsiu Lu-chou fu-chih*, 22.15; Hsüeh Fu-ch'eng's famous account of how Li joined Tseng's *mu-fu* has been proven apocryphal. See Wang, *Huai-chün chih*, 42–43, note 11.

15. *TWCK Letters*, 4.41, 44; 5.3, 13b, 17, 19, 25b; 9.16b; Wang, *Huai-chün chih*, 44–45, notes 25 and 31.

16. *TWCK Tsou-kao* (hereafter cited as *Memorials*), 14.24b–26.

17. *TWCK Letters*, 5.19; Hu Lin-i, *Hu Wen-chung kung i-chi* (Papers of the late Hu Lin-i) (1875), 73.28.

18. *TWCK Letters*, 5.19; a second letter of Tseng and Li's replies are quoted in Wang, *Huai-chün chih*, 44, note 24.

19. Hu, *I-chi*, 76.10; *TWCK Letters*, 7.31, 40; 8.31b; Wang, *Huai-chün chih*, 45, notes 30–31.

20. *Chiao-p'ing Yüeh-fei fang-lüeh*, 281.18–20; *TWCK Memorials*, 18.41; *LWCK Letters*, 1.7b; *LWCK Memorials*, 1.1; 2.45; Wang, *Huai-chün chih*, 57–67.

21. According to the son of one of the Anhwei Army commanders, Li, in his later life, often quoted Fu-chi's remark that "one should always treat people as if their hearts are degenerate." Liu T'i-chih, *I-tz'u lu* (A record of strange words) (n.p., n.d., Taipei reprint, 1968), 2.10.

22. Tseng wrote to Kuo Sung-tao in 1860: "Everything here is managed by the two of us, myself and Shao-ch'üan [Li Hung-chang]." In the early summer of 1861, when Li was in Nanchang, Tseng urged him to return to his service: "I have not written a memorial for fifty days; please come quickly to help me." Wang, *Huai-chün chih*, 44–45, notes 26 and 31.

23. Although "Western muskets" had been used in the 1850s by several Ch'ing armies, including those of Ho-ch'un and Chang Kuo-liang, Tseng Kuo-fan's forces did not use them to any great extent before 1862. Even then Tseng was not enthusiastic, since he believed that the secret of military victory "lies in men and not in weapons" and that, moreover, the old-fashioned "mountain-spitting guns" (*p'i shan p'ao*) were effective enough. *TWCK Chia-shu* (Family letters), 8.34b–35, 39b–40, 46b; *LWCK Letters*, 2.26b; Wang, *Huai-chün chih*, 194, 205–206.

24. See Richard Joseph Smith, *Mercenaries and Mandarins: The Ever-Victorious Army in Nineteenth-Century China* (Millwood, N.Y., 1978).

25. *LWCK Letters*, 1.20b. See also 1.13, 28; 2.46b–47.

26. Materials on the Shanghai United Defense Bureau (Hui-fang chü), collected by Chao Lieh-wen, in *T'ai-p'ing t'ien-kuo shih-liao ts'ung-pien chien-chi* (Selections from a collection of historical materials on the Taiping Heavenly Kingdom), *T'ai-p'ing t'ien-kuo li-shih po-wu kuan*, ed. (Shanghai, 1963), VI, 165–73; *Wu Hsü tang-an chung ti T'ai-p'ing t'ien-kuo shih-liao hsüan-chi* (Selections from historical materials concerning the Taiping Heavenly Kingdom in Wu Hsü's archives, hereafter cited as *Wu Hsü Archives*), Ching-wu and Chung-ting, eds. (Peking, 1958), 46–50, 64, 67–68, 71–73, 101–105; Feng Kuei-fen, *Hsien-chih t'ang kao* (Collected essays of the Hall of Manifest Aspirations) (1876), 4.19–21; *LWCK Letters*, 1.10,17b.

27. *LWCK Letters*, 1.15; see also 1.26.

28. Ibid., 1.31, 58; 2.26b; 3.22, 29b, 43b; 4.4b; Li Hung-chang, *Li Hung-chang chih P'an Ting-hsin shu-cha* (Letters from Li Hung-chang to P'an Ting-hsin, hereafter cited as *Li Letters to P'an*), Nien Tzu-min, ed. (Peking, 1960), 4–6.

29. See the illuminating discussion in Smith, *Mercenaries and Mandarins*. Before January 1863, the Ever-Victorious Army was under the control of Wu Hsü and his associate Yang Fang (Taki). But Li, as governor, issued directions through Wu. (See *Wu Hsü Archives*, 106–21; 174–75; 189–92.) By June 1862, Ward, through his Chinese colleagues, was reporting to Li about his campaigns, and Li gave him directions regarding the use of his contingent. Beginning at least in August, Li was in frequent personal contact with Ward. (*LWCK Letters*, 1.30b, 41, 46b, 53b–54b, 56b, 61, 63.) After the Ever-Victorious Army was reorganized in January–March 1863, Li assumed personal control over the army's finances and over its munitions procurement; a Chinese officer (Li Heng-sung) was associated with Charles George Gordon as co-commander, and Chinese officers took charge of the payment for the troops. Although it was agreed that any expedition of the

Ever-Victorious Army away from the thirty-mile radius of Shanghai would need the concurrence of the British and the French authorities, Gordon, who was under Li Hung-chang's command, generally went along with the latter's strategic plans, despite the occasional friction between the two men. (*Wu Hsü Archives*, 135–41; *LWCK Letters*, 2.41b–42, 46; 3.8b, 10, 16, 22b, 29.)

30. *LWCK Letters*, 1.52. See also 1.26, 29, 31, 33, 39, 43, 50–54, 58; 2.2b–3, 5, 20, 22, 41b, 42b, 46, 50. Although the policy of the British government in London was to restrict British involvement to the thirty-mile radius of the foreign settlement, General Charles Stavely, who was in charge of the British army in Shanghai in 1862, was desirous of a larger role for the British and made such proposals to his government. In the summer and fall of 1862, it was believed in Shanghai that the British planned to send large reinforcements from India to fight the Taipings—a rumor that originated with the British consul in Tientsin and was made much of by the Tsungli Yamen. See *LWCK Memorials* 1.38–39; *Letters*, 1.36, 57; *Wu Hsü Archives*, 236–37; Smith, *Mercenaries and Mandarins*.

31. *LWCK Letters* 2.8b–9, 12b–13. Several times in 1862, Li rejected the suggestion of the British and the French that large contingents of the Anhwei Army be trained and officered by them. At the insistent request of Vice Admiral Hope, Li did consent, in the early summer of 1862, to have a thousand of Hsüeh Huan's worthless troops trained by the British, and he also had to allow six hundred local troops to be trained by the French. But Li pleaded with the Tsungli Yamen not to support the expansion of this arrangement, lest the Europeans "gradually encroach upon the control [of the Chinese army]" (*chien ch'in ch'i ch'üan*). Li saw to it that the 1,600 men trained by the British and the French were retained in Shanghai and did not participate in the campaigns. *LWCK Letters*, 1.39; 2.38; 3.17; *Hai-fang tang* (Archives on coastal defense, hereafter cited as *HFT*), *Kou-mai ch'uan-p'ao* (Procurement of ships and guns, hereafter cited as *Ships and Guns*) (Taipei, 1957), 1, 188; Wang, *Huai-chün chih*, 195.

32. *LWCK Letters*, 1–43b, 58, 62b; 2.16, 39b; 3.15b, 24.

33. *LWCK Letters*, 1.44; see also 1.17b, 43, 49.

34. *LWCK Letters*, 1.46b; see also 1.22, 52. The Chinese translation that Li saw was made for him by the United Defense Bureau (*Hui-fang chü*) on August 11, 1862, and is preserved in *Wu Hsü Archives*, 233. The statement was ascribed in the translation to European defense authorities in Shanghai. Cf. *North-China Herald*, August 7, 1862, 123, in which was published a letter from Edward Cunningham and other members of the Defense Committee of the Shanghai Municipal Council, recommending, among other things, a future government of Shanghai, with power in the hands of the property-owners but under the "protectorate" of foreign powers, "incorporating the city, its suburbs, and the tract of country immediately surrounding."

35. *LWCK Letters*, 2.3; see also 2.6, 13b.

36. Ibid., 2.3, 21b, 31b; 3.12b–13, 34b.

37. That Li was acquainted with problems of financial administration, as well as military affairs, is indicated by the fact that in September 1861, he helped to draft a set of regulations concerning the "reduction of conversion rates for the land tax and the grain tribute," applicable to Kiangsi Province. *TWCK Letters*, 9.16b.

38. *LWCK Letters*, 3.1, 3b, 16, 20b, 22b, 25, 26–27, 40b, 42; 4.4b.

39. *Li Letters to P'an*, p. 1; *LWCK Letters*, 1.21b; Wang, *Huai-chün chih*, 75–87, 191–93.

40. Lo Erh-kang, *Hsiang-chün hsin-chih* (A new history of the Hunan Army) (Changsha, 1939), 55–65, 81–82.

41. *LWCK Letters*, 1.7b. The nine earliest commanders were: Chang Yü-ch'un (military *chü-jen*, former Anhwei militia leader who became a Hunan Army officer in the

1850s), Liu Ming-ch'uan (Anhwei militia leader), Chou Sheng-po (Anhwei militia leader), P'an Ting-hsin (civil *chü-jen* and Anhwei militia leader), Chang Shu-sheng (civil *sheng-yüan* and Anhwei militia leader), Wu Ch'ang-ch'ing (Anhwei militia leader), Ch'eng Hsüeh-ch'i (Anhwei native and former Taiping officer), Kuo Sung-lin (Hunan native and Hunan Army officer), Yang Ting-hsün (Szechwan native and officer of the T'ing Army under Pao Ch'ao). Wang, *Huai-chün chih*, 117–19, 140–77.

42. *LWCK Letters*, 1.28, 35, 43b, 55; Ono Shinji, "Waigun no kikonteki seikaku," 27–30.

43. *LWCK Letters*, 1.12, 18b, 21b. The Anhwei Army adopted the Hunan Army's monthly pay schedule. Although the former's practice was to pay nine times a year, while the latter in its best days paid twelve times a year, in the period from 1852 to 1864 the Anhwei Army on the whole paid more regularly than did the Hunan Army. See Wang, *Huai-chün chih*, 14–15, note 20; 269–70.

44. *LWCK Letters*, 1.37, 47, 55; 2.22; 3.14, 20, 29b, 35; *Li Letters to P'an*, 13; Wang, *Huai-chün chih*, 232, note 20.

45. *LWCK Letters*, 1.33; 2.22; *North-China Herald*, November 15, 1862, 182. The quotation is from *LWCK Letters*, 2.35.

46. *LWCK Letters*, 3.17; 4.19; 6.16b; Wang, *Huai-chün chih*, 221–24.

47. *LWCK Letters*, 1.33, 37, 39b, 48b–49, 56, 57b; *Memorials*, 2.41b; Lo Yü-tung, *Chung-kuo li-chin shih* (The history of the likin of China) (Shanghai, 1936), 230ff.

48. *LWCK Letters*, 1.15b, 21, 56; 2.11, 23, 36; Kuo Sung-tao *Yang-chih shu-wu wen-chi* (Kuo Sung-tao's essays), 1892, 10.15b, 19–21. Ying Pao-shih, a Chekiang man in Wu Hsü's administration, remained to assist Huang Fang. Later, in March 1864, Huang resigned because of illness and Ying acted as the Shanghai taotai until June 1864, when the post went to Ting Jih-ch'ang, who emerged as Li's most trusted subordinate in Shanghai. See *LWCK Letters*, 5.5b, 6b, 18.

49. Cf. Spector, *Li Hung-chang*, 60–67.

50. *LWCK Letters*, 1.15b, 16, 18b, 37; *Memorials*, 1.23, 2.41, 9.74. It appears that Hsüeh, rather than Wang, had the actual responsibility in likin affairs. See *LWCK Letters*, 1.37, 4.30b; *Memorials*, 5.46b. Hsüeh Shu-t'ang was sometimes referred to as Hsüeh Shu-ch'ang.

51. *LWCK Letters*, 1.15b, 18b; 2.17, 23; *Ch'ing-shih* (History of the Ch'ing dynasty) (Taipei, 1961), VI, 4893.

52. *LWCK Letters*, 2.31, 36; 3.42b.

53. *LWCK Letters*, 1.39b; 2.11b; 3.2.

54. *LWCK Letters*, 1.40; *Memorials*, 2.41–42.

55. *LWCK Letters*, 2.11b, 48b; 3.9b, 11b, 18b; 4.4; *Memorials*, 9.2b–4b.

56. See below, note 61. Aside from the likin, the most important financial source for military operations in eastern Kiangsu was the maritime customs revenue for Shanghai. Forty percent of this revenue went to pay the indemnities to Britain and France for the Arrow War, and beginning in 1861, the remainder was authorized by the throne for Kiangsu military needs. In 1862, the amount after deducting the 40 percent was 100,000 to 140,000 taels per month, but in 1863, because some duties formerly collected at Shanghai were now levied at the new customhouses at Hankow and Kiukiang, the amount available to the Kiangsu administration declined to between 70,000 and 120,000 taels per month. As arranged in July 1862, the funds from the customs were used mainly for the Ever-Victorious Army, for the United Defense Bureau in Shanghai, and for the military needs of Chinkiang. See *LWCK Letters*, 1.37, 59b; 3.30b; 4.14b; *Memorials*, 1.33–34, 55.

57. *LWCK Letters*, 3.2b; 4.4b. Cf. Spector, *Li Hung-chang and the Huai Army*, 115.

58. *LWCK Letters*, 1.40, 43, 58b; 2.14, 23b, 39; 3.4b, 9, 18b, 24–25, 33, 35b; 4.4, 12. In addition to munitions, Li sent to the Tseng brothers at least 130,000 taels in 1862, and

beginning in March 1863, regularly more than 30,000 taels per month. See Wang, *Huai-chün chih*, 247–48.

59. *Li Letters to P'an*, 2–23, especially 2, 7, 8, 20–21. These letters were discovered by the Chinese Communist historians and published in 1960 as evidence of Li's cruelty toward the Taipings and his "collusion with the imperialists." See preface.

60. *LWCK Letters*, 1–15b; for a letter from Li to Hsüeh on likin matters dated January 1864, see 4.30b–31; Wang, *Huai-chün chih*, 315–24.

61. *Ta-Ch'ing li-ch'ao shih-lu* (Veritable records of successive reigns of the great Ch'ing) (Tokyo, 1937–38), T'ung-chih, 139.54–55; *LWCK Memorials*, 9.1b. Yin Chao-yung, *Yin P'u-ching shih-lang tzu-hsü nien-p'u* (Autobiographical chronicle of Vice President Yin P'u-ching) (n.p., n.d., Taipei reprint, 1968), 53–54.

62. *LWCK Memorials*, 3.44–45; 9.5b.

63. *LWCK Letters*, 3.30; 4.14, 16. See *Memorials*, 3.44; on the court's order to have rice shipped to Peking by commercial contract before the normal grain tribute could be resumed, see 3.28–32.

64. *LWCK Memorials*, 3.56–63. Kuo Sung-tao, as the grain intendant, also participated in the initial deliberations. See Feng, *Hsien-chih t'ang kao*, 4.6–9.

65. *LWCK Letters*, 3.27, 35b, 37b, 40; *Memorials*, 3.64–65.

66. *LWCK Letters*, 4.10, 11, 26b; 5.1b, 8, 12, 36; 6.4b–5, 9b–10; *Memorials*, 8.60–66. The final memorial was delayed due to Liu Hsün-kao's opposition to Feng Kuei-fen's idea that more substantial tax reduction should be pursued; Li and Tseng found it necessary to accept some of Liu's views. See Feng, *Hsien-chih t'ang kao*, 4.9; 5.7–15; Hsia Nai, "T'ai-p'ing t'ien-kuo ko-ming ch'ien-hou Ch'ang-chiang ko-sheng chih t'ien-fu wen-t'i" (The land tax problem of the Yangtze provinces before and after the Taiping Rebellion), *CHHP* 10 (1935), 461–63.

67. *LWCK Letters*, 5.32b, 40; 6.6; *Memorials*, 9.6.

68. *LWCK Letters*, 3.4b.

69. *LWCK Letters*, 3.9b; 5.8b. Cf. Wang, *Huai-chün chih*, 327–31.

70. *LWCK Letters*, 5.32b.

71. Ibid., 4.16; 6.10b.

72. *LWCK Memorials*, 3.64; 8.66.

73. Mary C. Wright, *The Last Stand of Chinese Conservatism: The T'ung-chih Restoration, 1862–1874* (Stanford, 1957), 85–90, 93–94; Feng Kuei-fen, *Chiao-pin-lu k'ang-i* (Straightforward words from the Lodge of Early Chou Studies) (1898 ed.), 1.15–18, 20–22.

74. *LWCK Letters*, 5.15b, 33–37, 39; 6.27; *Memorials*, 7.44–45; Li, *I-chi*, 5.1–3; Feng, *Hsien-chih t'ang kao*, 3.9–10; Wright, *The Last Stand*, 81.

75. These were Tzu-yang shu-yüan (Academy of Purple Light), which specialized in the Four Books and the examination essays, and Cheng-i shu-yüan (Academy of Correct Relationships), headed by Feng Kuei-fen and devoted to "the useful study of classics and history." Li, *I-chi*, 5.4–6; Feng, *Hsien-chih t'ang kao*, 3.11–12.

76. *LWCK Letters*, 3.21.

77. *LWCK Letters*, 2.7b, 20b, 41b, 42b; 3.6, 10, 13b, 17, 29.

78. *LWCK Letters*, 3.17, 18, 19b, 29, 34b, 37; 4.5, 8b, 22b, 23b–24; *Memorials*, 4.32–33.

79. *LWCK Letters*, 3.3b, 34b.

80. *LWCK Letters*, 3.12b–13;4.17.

81. *Li Letters to P'an*, 3–4; *LWCK Letters*, 3.16b, 43b; Wang, *Huai-chün chih*, 197–200.

82. *LWCK Letters*, 1.54. Reporting his talks with Ward to Tseng, Li remarked that learning to make Western munitions would be "of benefit both to military affairs and to the general situation of foreign-trade relations [*t'ung-shang ta-chü*]."

83. Tseng's engineers had made a crude steam engine in July 1862 and had assembled a small steam launch in January 1863. But apparently it was not until the latter date that the Anking Arsenal began experimenting with the manufacture of copper percussion caps or of shrapnel. (See Gideon Chen, *Tseng Kuo-fan: Pioneer Promoter of the Steamship in China* [Peiping, 1935], 24, 40–41.) In December 1862, Li wrote Tseng about Li Shan-lan, the outstanding Chinese mathematician of the time, who had written a book on the manufacture of firearms in 1858 and had been making shrapnel for Li. Li also sent Tseng a foreign workman recommended by Li Shan-lan as being "well-versed in munition making." Tseng did not hire this foreigner, but he soon invited Li Shan-lan to Anking, and through the latter, also secured the services of Chang Ssu-kuei, a Ningpo man who had knowledge of steamships and munitions. *LWCK Letters*, 2.39; Wang P'ing, *Hsi-fang li-suan hsüeh chih shu-ju* (The introduction of Western astronomical and mathematical sciences into China) (Taipei, 1966), 188–90.

84. *LWCK Letters*, 2.47; Ssu-yü Teng and John K. Fairbank, *China's Response to the West: A Documentary Survey, 1839–1923* (Cambridge, Mass., 1954), 69.

85. *LWCK Letters*, 3.17.

86. Ibid., 3.19b.

87. Ibid., 3.16b; *Memorials*, 4,44; *Ch'ou-pan i-wu shih-mo* (Complete record of our management of barbarian affairs; hereafter cited as *IWSM*) (Peiping, 1930), T'ung-chih, 25.4–7; Demetrius C. Boulger, *The Life of Sir Halliday Macartney* (London and New York, 1908), 79.

88. Chen, *Tseng Kuo-fan*, 43–44; *LWCK Letters*, 4.29.

89. See below, note 103. Li's advisor, Feng Kuei-fen, was interested in traditional Chinese mathematics and since 1860–61 had come to believe that the West not only surpassed China in geographical knowledge but had actually achieved "the ultimate truth in the investigation of things" (*ko-wu chih-li*) through the development of mathematics, mechanics, and chemistry. (Feng, *Chiao-pin lu k'ang-i*, 2.37b.) Li also had contact with Li Shan-lan, who had collaborated in the 1850s with British missionaries in translating works in mathematics, physics, and astronomy into Chinese. (Wang P'ing, *Hsi-fang li-suan hsüeh*, 165; 176.)

90. *LWCK Memorials*, 3.12b; Feng, *Hsien-chih t'ang kao*, 10.20; Teng and Fairbank, *China's Response*, 74–75.

91. *IWSM*, T'ung-chih, 25.4–10; the last part of the letter has been translated in Teng and Fairbank, *China's Response*, 70–72.

92. Feng, *Chiao-pin lu k'ang-i*, 2.38–39, 42–43.

93. *IWSM*, T'ung-chih, 25.1–4. It was not until three years later, in early 1867, that the yamen itself proposed to the throne that the Peking T'ung-wen Kuan's curriculum should be broadened to include mathematics and sciences and that holders of high degrees, including Hanlin scholars, should be encouraged to enroll in the program. See Knight Biggerstaff, *The Earliest Modern Government Schools in China* (Ithaca, 1961), 108–21.

94. *LWCK Letters*, 3.16b. See also 2.46b.

95. As early as March 1864, Li had mentioned the desirability of reducing the Anhwei Army's size in his letters to friends. In October 1864, Li informed Shen Pao-chen and Wu T'ang, in addition to Tseng Kuo-fan, that he intended to disband the Anhwei Army's weaker units and reduce the force to thirty thousand men. *LWCK Letters*, 5.7b, 10b–11, 32, 32b, 35b; *Memorials*, 7.29; cf. Wang, *Huai-chün chih* 345–48. The seventy thousand figure for the Anhwei Army included the so-called Huai-Yang water force.

96. *LWCK Letters*, 5.34–35.

97. *Ta-Ch'ing li-ch'ao shih-lu*, T'ung-chih, 122.39b–40.

98. Cf. Wang, *Huai-chün chih*, 349–50. Ten days before he wrote to Ch'en and Hsüeh, Li had written to Shen Pao-chen, governor of Kiangsi, on October 1: "The

military system is of particular importance to the general policy of the state. If we should confine ourselves to the effectiveness achieved for the moment and be satisfied, there will be no end to our trouble." On October 2, Li wrote to Wu T'ang, director-general of grain transport: "If the weak armies are disbanded and the support for the strong ones is increased, the country will not have to worry about either the lack of revenue or the lack of military strength." *LWCK Letters*, 5.32 and 32b.

99. Smith, *Mercenaries and Mandarins*; Wang, *Huai-chün chih*, 197–200.

100. *LWCK Letters*, 6.3b, 6, 13, 24; *Memorials*, 7.48, 50, 60–61; 8.14–16, 21, 52; Wang, *Huai-chün chih*, 346–48; 351–52.

101. *LWCK Letters*, 6.23b.

102. *HFT Chi-ch'i chü* [hereafter cited as *Arsenals*], 1, 3–21.

103. Ibid., 13. Li pointed out to the yamen that although the "new technology" (*hsin-fa*) of the West had evolved only since the early eighteenth century, behind it lay several centuries of development in mathematics and mechanics (*li-i* or *chung-hsüeh*). Mathematics, which involved principles that "transcend that which is physical," was the foundation of mechanics. Ibid., 16–17.

104. *LWCK Memorials*, 9.31–32, 35b.

105. See Thomas Larew Kennedy, *The Arms of Kiangnan: Modernization in the Chinese Ordnance Industry, 1860–1895* (Boulder, 1978), chapter 2. Li personally kept a close watch in 1865–66 over the arsenal's production; see a vivid communication from Li to the arsenal's managers, preserved in *Chiang-nan chih-tsao-chü chi* (Record of the Kiangnan Arsenal), comp. Wei Yün-kung (Shanghai, 1905), 3.58–59; also *LWCK Letters*, 6.42.

106. *Li-ch'üan* is a traditional phrase referring to control over revenue as well as merchants' activities, but Li began to use it in the context of Western encroachment in these fields. (See *LWCK Letters*, 2.6; 3.12b; 5, 15b, 35.) Li often used the phrase *fu-ch'iang* in reference to the government's solvency and ability to maintain order; but at least by 1865, he was employing the term in reference to China's need to cope with her external crisis. (*Letters*, 1.19b, 36b; 6.34b, 37b; *Memorials*, 9.6 and 6b.)

107. *LWCK Letters*, 5.14; see also 1.49, 57b; 3.15, 18b–19; 4.15; 5.13.

108. *LWCK Letters*, 4.22; see also 2.48b; 4.17b; 5.5, 7b, 9b, 10b.

109. *LWCK Memorials*, 1.40–41; 7.36–39; 8.30–31; 9.67–68; *Letters*, 5.35.

110. *HFT Arsenals*, 1, 3–5; see also *Ships and Guns*, III, 809–10.

111. *HFT Ships and Guns*, III, 811–81. Robert Hart played a key role in urging the Tsungli Yamen to act and in preparing the draft of the regulations. See also Stanley F. Wright, *Hart and the Chinese Customs* (Belfast, 1950), 403.

112. *LWCK Memorials*, 9.9; Feng, *Hsien-chih t'ang kao*, 4.10–11; 5.16–19.

113. *LWCK Letters*, 6.45. Li also wrote in 1865: "The farmlands are lying in waste, and it is difficult to collect the land tax and the grain tribute. Since regular revenue is insufficient for the support of the troops, it is necessary to have likin supply the military needs. Rather than hurt the farmers, it is better to hurt the merchants; this at least is in accordance with the ancient idea of emphasizing the fundamental and deprecating the subsidiary (*chung-pen i-mo*)." (6.37b; see also 6.27b.)

114. *LWCK Memorials*, 9.6 and 6b.

115. *LWCK Memorials*, 9.34b.

116. *LWCK Letters*, 16.20; see also chapter 2 in this issue.

117. This theme has been persuasively presented in Folsom, *Friends, Guests, and Colleagues.*

118. For Li's contacts with Parkes, who was the British consul in Shanghai in 1864, see *LWCK Letters*, 5.16, 24.

119. Wei Yüan (1794–1857) had suggested in his book *Hai-kuo t'u-chih* (Illustrated

gazetteer of maritime countries, 1844) that a special examination be instituted in two provinces in South China for the selection of naval personnel, and that the ability to make Western ships and guns be made the criterion for one of the naval degrees. Wei's idea of Western technology was vague, however, and his proposal did not involve alteration of the existing civil service examinations. Cf. Wang Chia-chien, *Wei Yüan tui hsi-fang ti jen-shih chi ch'i hai-fang ssu-hsiang* (Wei Yüan's knowledge of the West and his ideas on coastal defense) (Taipei, 1964), 82.

120. In his memorial on the founding of the Kiangnan Arsenal, Li offered an apology for his proposal regarding the introduction of Western machines. He praised the Chinese governmental institutions of the past. "That good government has been achieved, the state preserved, and the great heritage secured from harm cannot be without reason. Your servant does not take the narrow view that the only way to convert danger into security or to pass from weakness to strength lies in the imitation and use of machines. Yet, in statecraft one may distinguish the whole and the part, the fundamental and the subsidiary. When illness is acute, the immediate causes must be dealt with, not that such prescriptions will serve as general tonics toward recovery; and when floods are high, the dikes must be mended, not that it is unnecessary to plan conservancy or to regulate farming." *LWCK Memorials*, 9.35.

3

Li Hung-chang in Chihli: The Emergence of a Policy, 1870–1875

Kwang-Ching Liu

The year 1870, which saw the unification of Germany and the consolidation of a revolution from above in Japan, saw a major event in China—the appointment of Li Hung-chang (1823–1901) as governor-general of Chihli and as imperial commissioner for the Northern Ports. Even while he was absorbed in the task of suppressing internal rebellion in the 1860s, Li had been the foremost advocate of "self-strengthening" (*tzu-ch'iang*)—the policy of building up China's military potential, chiefly by adopting Western technology, so as to meet the challenge of external aggression.[1] In his new position of influence, close to Peking, Li worked to continue and expand this policy.

A reassessment of the self-strengthening movement must include an inquiry into its ideological implications. Did men like Li (there were very few of them) aim merely at the adoption of Western technology, or did they also propose reform? Did they modify the Confucian emphasis on moral government, which relied chiefly on virtue and culture as the sources of power? Inquiry must also be made into the complex factors that frustrated the success of the movement—the institutional and intellectual milieu, and the weakness of the new military and economic forces that had arisen after a generation of contact with the West. But, first, it is necessary to consider the political context. Was the self-strengthening movement initiated by the central government or by the provinces? Was it a matter of sporadic efforts by a governor-general here, by a governor there, or was it a part of Ch'ing national policy?

The self-strengthening movement began in the early Tung-chih period, originating chiefly in the provinces but enjoying the strong support of the court. It was Li Hung-chang who first proposed the teaching of mathematics and the sciences at a government "interpreter's college," and who founded China's earliest modern arsenals; it was Tso Tsung-t'ang who planned a large shipbuilding program. Li and Tso were stoutly backed, however, by the Tsungli Yamen at a time when Prince Kung was at the height of his power and when Wen-hsiang was still in good health. The development of "regionalism"—the administrative leeway that the governors-general and governors enjoyed regarding the temporary imperial armies (*yung*) and the likin—did not handicap the cooperation between Peking and the provinces in the new projects.

In 1870, a new page was turned in the history of the self-strengthening movement. Li Hung-chang, in moving so close to Peking, became in effect a metropolitan official. Li performed many central government functions in the fields of diplomacy and military planning, and he made an attempt to coordinate self-strengthening efforts not only in Chihli but in other parts of the empire. It remained to be seen, however, whether, on the one hand, Li—and, for that matter, Prince Kung and Wen-hsiang (before his death in 1876)—would continue to have an effective voice in the councils around the throne, and whether, on the other hand, the measures they proposed could be carried out in the provinces, particularly in the militarily and financially vital area of the lower Yangtze.

This chapter presents aspects of Li's first five years in Tientsin—his functions in the imperial government, his ideas regarding self-strengthening, and the manner in which his proposals were received in Peking and in the provinces. As a senior official who had occupied key positions during the campaigns for the suppression of the Taipings and the Niens, Li had formed many friendships among governors-general, governors, and lesser officials. As the acknowledged but untitled leader of the Anhwei Army, Li also developed a degree of influence in provinces where units of that army were stationed.[2] But in the last analysis, it was the specific imperial sanction for each of Li's proposals, as well as his position as imperial commissioner, that accounted for his role as coordinator of policy. In the early 1870s, we find him taking remarkable initiative in shaping policy, and for a time it appeared that his programs might, at least in part, be carried out on a national scale.

Li's central government functions

It was a crisis in China's foreign relations that brought Li to Chihli. Under pressure of the harsh French demands that followed the Tientsin Massacre of June 21, the court on July 26 ordered Li, who had been engaged in operations against the Moslem rebels in Shensi, to move his forces to Chihli and join the twenty-eight battalions of the Anhwei Army (Huai-chün) previously brought there by Tseng Kuo-fan. A month later, on August 29, when Li and an army of about twenty-five thousand men arrived at the border of Chihli, he was appointed its governor-general, replacing the ailing Tseng.[3] It was the court's wish that the Anhwei Army, which had proved so effective in fighting the Taipings and the Niens, should now be used for the defense of the metropolitan province against possible invaders.

For one who thinks in terms of twentieth-century Chinese politics it is possible to imagine Li as a proto-warlord, henceforth dominating the area where the capital was situated. This is completely misleading, for although Li's role as leader of the Anhwei Army certainly accounted for his being brought to Chihli, the Anhwei Army itself was by this time an integral part of the dynasty's armed forces. While its status continued to be that of $yung$, a temporary imperial army, Peking had control over the appointment of its higher officers and over its finances. The commanders ($t'ung-ling$) of the Anhwei Army, although normally recommended by Li, were appointed by imperial edict and all had the title of general-in-chief ($t'i-tu$) or brigade general ($tsung-ping$) under the Green Standard system. The subordinate officers, although chosen by the commanders, were also given the titles of Green Standard officers by the Board of War—colonel ($fu-chiang$), lieutenant-colonel ($ts'an-chiang$), and the rest, usually in an "expectant" ($hou-pu$) capacity.[4] There is no question that the troops and officers of the Anhwei Army regarded themselves as serving the dynasty. It was, moreover, from imperially authorized sources that the Anhwei Army was financed—the maritime customs of Shanghai and Hankow, the likin from Kiangsu and Kiangsi, and, in smaller amounts, the treasuries of Liangkiang, Hupei, Chekiang, Shantung, Szechuan, and Shansi. While Li enjoyed close personal relationships with the governors-general of Liangkiang (Tseng) and of Hukuang (Li Han-chang) and was friendly with several governors, the court had the authority and influence to see that the funds were continued or withheld and, indeed, to replace the governors-general or the governors.[5] Ever since 1864, units of the Anhwei Army had been frequently moved by imperial edict from one province to another. In summoning Anhwei troops to Chihli, the throne was merely calling upon the services of one of its best forces.

On the other hand, thanks to his role as the leader of the Anhwei Army, Li gained a trusted position near the capital itself and was relied on to perform duties that belonged to a central government official. On November 12, 1870, less than three months after his designation as governor-general, he was given the further appointment of imperial commissioner ($ch'in-ch'ai ta-ch'en$), vested with duties even broader than those of the former commissioner of trade for the three Northern Ports ($san-k'ou t'ung-shang ta-ch'en$).[6] Li was instructed to reside at the strategic port of Tientsin and not at the provincial capital of Paoting. The edict stipulated that Li was to go to Paoting only in the winter months when the port of Tientsin was closed; it was not until December 1871 that he first visited Paoting. Beginning in 1872, he also went to Peking about once a year for audiences with the throne and consultation with the ministers. Li's letters of 1872–75 mention his discussions with Prince Kung, Wen-hsiang, Shen Kuei-fen, Pao-yun, and Li Hung-tsao—all five being grand councillors and, except for the last, ministers of the Tsungli Yamen.[7]

Li was responsible, of course, for Chihli provincial affairs. The provincial treasurer at Paoting was authorized to act for him on routine petitions, but important matters were brought to his yamen at Tientsin.[8] Among provincial matters to which Li gave his personal attention was internal policing, for which he used the so-called Trained Troops (*lien-chün*), an army of about six thousand men selected from the Green Standard forces by previous governors-general.[9] Among questions of civil administration brought up by Li in memorials to the throne were local government finance (particularly the question of how to reduce the burden on *chou* and *hsien* magistrates), the province's financial obligations to Peking, the salt monopoly, and the transmission of tribute rice to T'ung-chou. Li's most pressing and difficult provincial problems, however, were those created by the breaches in the dikes of the Yung-ting River. Northern Chihli saw one of its worst floods of the century in the summer of 1871, followed by a more moderate one in 1873. It was Li's responsibility to raise funds for relief and to revive agriculture in the areas affected. He also had to supervise repairs on the dikes—work that was to continue for several years.[10]

Meanwhile, Li was increasingly involved in his duties as imperial commissioner. These entailed, first of all, the supervision of foreign trade at the ports of Tientsin, Chefoo, and Newchwang through the superintendents of customs at the three ports—the one at Tientsin being a new post created at Li's recommendation.[11] But Li was also relied on by the Tsungli Yamen in questions concerning foreign trade in the empire as a whole. The Yamen often asked Li to study the proposals made to it by Robert Hart—for example, the latter's draft regulations, submitted in the spring of 1872, concerning the customs declaration form, the re-export certificate, and the transit pass. On his authority as imperial commissioner, Li sent "instructions by letter" (*cha-ch'ih*) to the superintendents of customs at Tientsin, Shanghai, and Hankow for their comments. Li added his own ideas and recommended to the Yamen that revisions be made in Hart's draft to make it more difficult for Chinese merchants to evade duties and likin. The final draft was worked out at Tientsin between Li and Hart.[12]

As imperial commissioner, Li had the responsibility of dealing with foreign representatives on local issues—for example, ironing out the final details of the Sino-French settlement regarding the Tientsin Massacre and determining the Russian and British claims.[13] Moreover, Li's diplomatic activities soon included national issues that the Tsungli Yamen considered would be more convenient for Li to handle at Tientsin. Further, the Yamen frequently sought Li's advice on policy and sometimes would entrust policy making to him.

The first important national issue Li handled was the treaty with Japan. As early as October 1870, after his first meeting with the Japanese representative who came to China to request a treaty, Li advised the Yamen that it was in the Ch'ing interest to form such ties. Li was impressed by Japan's comparative success in dealing with the West (for example, the ability to manage maritime customs without employing foreigners and to regulate missionary activity) and by the large funds that Japan was reported to have raised for arsenals and steamships. Li felt that China should befriend Japan, perhaps even send officials to reside in that country, with a view to preventing her from siding with the Western nations. On the Yamen's recommendation, the throne entrusted Li and Tseng Kuo-fan, who was the commissioner of trade for the Southern Ports, with the responsibility of formulating a policy for the treaty. Subsequently, Li was given full powers for the negotiations. The talks took place in the summer of 1871, China being represented by two officials of lower rank under Li's supervision. Eight months later, when the Japanese representative came to China to demand changes in the draft of the treaty, negotiations were again held at Tientsin. In May 1873, Li was the plenipotentiary who exchanged the ratified texts with the Japanese foreign minister, who had come to Tientsin for the purpose. Li discussed various matters with him, including China's concern about Korea.[14]

Similarly, Li was given the authority to meet with the representative of Peru who requested a treaty in October 1873. Through the intermittent negotiations that lasted until June 1874, Li's objective was to have the Peruvian representative accept a Chinese mission to investigate the conditions of Chinese labor in that country. The upshot was the Yung Wing mission to Peru in August 1874.[15]

Beginning in 1872, the Yamen often enlisted Li's assistance in vital matters with which the Yamen itself was dealing. In September of that year, when the Russian and German ministers were passing through Tientsin, Li took the opportunity to discuss with them, on the Yamen's behalf, aspects of the "audience question." In April 1873, when Li himself was in Peking, he supported the compromise solution that was proposed by Wen-hsiang against those who insisted on kowtow. Li's intervention is said to have been important among the factors that "smoothed away all difficulties," resulting in the modified ceremony adopted at the audience held on June 14.[16]

In May and June of 1874, during the crisis that had been created when the Japanese landed troops on Taiwan seeking redress for shipwrecked Ryūkyū sailors murdered by the aborigines, Li participated in efforts to resolve the problem. Li advised the Yamen on the military measures that would strengthen China's hand in the negotiations—"to prepare for war secretly so that peace may be achieved quickly and endure."[17] When the Japanese minister to China arrived in June 1874, the Yamen hoped that he could remain at Tientsin to negotiate with Li. However, he proceeded immediately to Peking, as did Ōkubo, the special commissioner who came in August. A settlement calling on China to pay 500,000 taels to Japan was reached on October 31, with Sir Thomas Wade acting as intermediary. Meanwhile, however, Li had been actively seeking the mediation of Benjamin P. Avery, the new American minister who had just come from Japan and was then in Tientsin.[18]

If Li was serving as a central government official in his diplomatic activities, the same may be said of his role in the Ch'ing government's military planning—despite the fact that he played but little part in the great Ch'ing military achievement of the period, namely, the suppression of the Moslem rebels in Kansu in 1873 and the reconquest of Sinkiang that followed three years later. It was Li, however, upon whom the court relied for the defense of the capital area and for coordination of military preparations in the coastal and Yangtze provinces. It has been stated above that as the Chihli governor-general, Li had control over the six thousand Trained Troops used primarily for local policing. As imperial commissioner, he had the further duty of supervising the coastal defense of the metropolitan area, including the safeguarding of the Taku estuary and points halfway between Tientsin and Peking.[19] Similar responsibility was formerly borne by the Mongol prince Seng-k'o-lin-ch'in, who was imperial commissioner during the crisis of 1857–60, and by the Manchu grandee Ch'ung-hou between 1861 and 1870, when he served as commissioner of trade for the three Northern Ports. Ch'ung-hou had built fortifications in the Taku area and had organized the Western Arms and Cannon Corps (yang ch'iang-p'ao tui), which grew to 3,200 men, under the command of the Tientsin brigade general.[20] Li was authorized to take charge of the forts and the corps, although his predecessors as governor-general, including Tseng Kuo-fan, were never given this authority. In November 1870, Li appointed Lo Jung-kuang, the famous Anhwei Army artillery officer, as the Taku regiment colonel in charge of the forts. The Anhwei Army's best artillery, as well as new cannon built at the Nanking Arsenal, were brought to Taku, and new Krupp guns were ordered. Li put the Foreign Arms and Cannon Corps through retraining, particularly in the Anhwei Army's favorite technique of constructing fortified encampments.[21]

In November 1870, the court directed that the twenty-eight battalions (about fourteen thousand men) of the Anhwei Army originally under Liu Ming-ch'uan be moved from Chihli to join the nine battalions of the Anhwei Army that Li had left in Shensi. At Li's recommendation, ten battalions of the Anhwei Army under Kuo Sung-lin also went to Shensi and Kuo himself was to bring ten battalions to Hupei, to help guard against the secret societies of the Hunan-Hupei area. However, two battalions of Liu's best troops were retained at Paoting, together with two battalions of the Anhwei Army cavalry. Two battalions of Li's personal guards were stationed at Tientsin. In addition, twenty-three battalions (about 11,500 men) under Chou Sheng-ch'uan were stationed in the area south of Tientsin, particularly at Ma-ch'ang, a base that Chou was to build up. In 1873, Chou's troops were used to construct a fortified town between Taku and Tientsin, and later they were put to work repairing dikes and reclaiming salt marshes for farmland. But they were also drilled and given training in the latest types of rifles and artillery. Li described them as a "mobile force for the defense of the metropolitan territory."[22]

Due chiefly to Li's relationship with the Anhwei Army, he also participated at times in the court's military planning for other parts of the empire. His role was passive with regard to the northwest. In 1870–72, he sent two contingents of a thousand men each from the Trained Troops of Chihli to Urga, to help guard against possible Russian encroachment on Outer Mongolia.[23] On September 1, 1871, apprised of the Russian occupation of Ili, the court ordered Liu Ming-ch'uan, who had requested a leave of absence due to illness, to take his forces from Shensi to Kansu and thence to Sinkiang. Liu again pleaded illness, and on September 21, the court revised its orders, requiring him only to advance to Su-chou in Kansu. Although Li was not convinced of the value of Sinkiang in China's total strategic picture, he wrote Liu urging him to comply. Without consulting Li, however, Liu once more begged the throne for a leave and recommended that Ts'ao K'e-chung, a general not of Anhwei Army background, replace him and lead his forces to attack Su-chou. The request was granted. Ts'ao was summoned to Peking for an audience in November 1871 and was appointed to the command. Li pledged himself to support Ts'ao with Anhwei Army funds but recommended that only twenty-two of Liu's thirty-seven battalions be transferred to him.[24] In August 1872, mutiny occurred in certain units of Ts'ao's forces; the throne referred the matter to Li, who recommended that Liu Sheng-tsao, Liu Ming-ch'uan's nephew and a former Anhwei Army officer, should take over. Liu Sheng-tsao came to Tientsin for consultations with Li and was given the appointment by the throne. Li had hoped to suggest that Liu move all the Anhwei forces in Shensi back to the coastal area, but the twenty-two battalions were retained in Shensi at the request of its governor.[25]

Li's own conviction was that the coast, particularly with a restless Japan quickly arming, was far more in need of protection. Ever since the end of the Nien Rebellion, eight battalions of the Anhwei Army, under Wu Ch'ang-ch'ing, had been stationed at several points in Kiangsu; at Li's recommendation, the throne, in November 1870, approved their remaining there. These forces were under the direction of Tseng Kuo-fan, the governor-general of Liangkiang, but Li often wrote to him to make suggestions on such subjects as the training needed by the artillery corps or the strategic places where troops should be quartered. Tseng, on his part, would inform Li when he ordered the transfer of units from one location to another. In November 1871, when the Anhwei Army in Shensi was transferred to Ts'ao K'e-chung's command, Li took the opportunity to recommend to the throne that fifteen of the thirty-seven battalions be moved to Hsü-chou in northern Kiangsu. In approving the idea, the throne directed that these battalions (led by an Anhwei Army officer named T'ang Ting-k'uei) be put at the disposal of Tseng.[26] After Tseng died in March 1872, Li continued to advise his successors in the Liangkiang post on military affairs—including the organization of a small navy with gunboats built by the Kiangnan Arsenal. Though Tseng's successors were free to direct the Anhwei Army in Kiangsu, they developed the practice of informing Li of their decisions whenever units were reassigned to new locations.[27]

In the summer of 1874, during the crisis created by the Japanese invasion of Taiwan, Li extended his concern to the Fukien-Taiwan area. It was upon Li's advice that the Tsungli Yamen recommended to the throne that Shen Pao-chen, the director-general of the Foochow Navy Yard, be appointed imperial commissioner for the defense of Taiwan. In June, Li suggested to Shen and to the Yamen that thirteen battalions (6,500 men) of the Anhwei Army at Hsü-chou, under T'ang Ting-k'uei, be dispatched to Taiwan to be put under Shen's control. This was approved by the throne in late July, as was Li's further recommendation that the twenty-two battalions of the Anhwei Army in Shensi be transferred to Kiangsu and Shantung, to meet the contingency of a Sino-Japanese conflict.[28]

Meanwhile, Li kept in touch by correspondence with Shen, with Li Tsung-hsi, the governor-general of Liangkiang, and with Chang Shu-sheng, the governor of Kiangsu, arranging to ship munitions from Kiangsu and Chihli to Taiwan. On July 13, Li was instructed by the throne to "make a general plan for the entire situation" and to "deliberate jointly" (hui-shang) with officials in the provinces concerned regarding defense preparations.[29] Li advised Shen that clashes with the Japanese were to be avoided, while preparations for war must be hastened. Li arranged to have three ships of the China Merchants' Steam Navigation Company and three Foochow-built steamships transport the troops in Kiangsu to Taiwan. Because the six vessels had to make three voyages to complete the shipping of 6,500 men, the last contingents did not reach their destination until October, although the first arrived in mid-August. Li corresponded with officials in Fukien and in Liangkiang on defense measures. Alarmed by rumors of Japanese intentions, Li Tsung-hsi and Chang Shu-sheng requested that the twenty-two battalions of the Anhwei Army from Shensi come to southern Kiangsu. Li decided, however, that only five should go there, and that the remaining seventeen (including five cavalry battalions) should be stationed at Chi-ning, Shantung, where they could easily be moved either north or south. Li assured his colleagues that even should there be war, given the resources of the Japanese, action was not likely to spread to the coast for a few months. There was time, therefore, to plan coastal fortifications carefully and to order foreign-made guns and rifles.[30] It is difficult to say whether these defense efforts had any actual bearing on Japan's accepting a peaceful settlement in late October. But Li had clearly emerged during the episode as the coordinator of Ch'ing military preparations on Taiwan and on the coast.

The crisis also revealed that Li depended on the throne's support for the continued financing of the Anhwei Army. Beginning in 1872, such provinces as Shantung, Chekiang, Szechuan, and Shansi had been reducing their annual contributions (hsieh-hsiang) to the Anhwei Army, if not defaulting entirely, due to Peking's pressure on them to supply funds for other purposes. In 1872, the Anhwei Army still received large sums from the Shanghai and Hankow maritime customs and from Liangkiang sources (especially from Kiangsu likin and Kiangsi salt likin), but in the eighteen months following January 29, 1873, the annual average received from Kiangsu likin (which was the largest single source of Anhwei Army funds) dropped from 1,000,019 taels to 873,332.[31] There was danger that the trend might continue, for we find Li frequently writing to the governor of Kiangsu and governor-general of Liangkiang, urging them to see that payments were made promptly. Li had to remind these officials that the appropriations were backed by the throne itself. He warned Li Tsung-hsi not to withhold the Anhwei Army funds "so that I do not have to appeal to the throne." To Chang Shu-sheng, who had formerly been an Anhwei Army commander but whose interests were now not necessarily identical with its interests, Li wrote bluntly: "I will certainly fight for the funds. Let me swear it by smearing my mouth with blood."[32] On at least one occasion, Li actually did appeal to the throne regarding the Anhwei Army appropriations. He requested in a memorial dated September 1, 1874, that Szechuan Province be instructed to pay its arrears of more that 200,000 taels. In his letters to the governor-general of Szechuan and others, Li stressed that the Anhwei Army was in the service of the state and should be supported by it.[33]

Self-strengthening—the emergence of a policy

Li's service to the state was not limited to diplomatic work or to advising the throne on the use of the Anhwei Army. As he himself conceived it, his role in the dynasty's military planning should include the enhancement of China's military capability—which alone could ensure peaceful relations with the powers. Li assumed that the aim of the Western maritime powers in China was commerce and not aggrandizement. Nevertheless, he feared that an occasion might arise when one or more powers would use force. Moreover, a real threat existed in an increasingly powerful Japan. "It is only when we can strengthen ourselves every moment," Li exhorted his colleagues, "that peace can be maintained and trouble prevented."[34]

Li found that he had both to redefine and expand his program for self-strengthening. Although his primary objective continued to be the building up of an armament industry, experience had shown that arsenals and shipyards were by no means easy to operate. Moreover, there were constant innovations in these fields in Western countries, and it was impossible to catch up quickly. To meet China's needs for some time to come, it was necessary to purchase the latest types of foreign-made weapons and to create a navy of foreign-built ships. Li further realized that the capacity of Chinese arsenals and shipyards had been severely restricted by lack of competent personnel and of revenue—the two Chinese words both pronounced ts'ai.[35] While seeking a gradual expansion of the armament industry, it was necessary to support new programs of personnel training and to devise means for enlarging the income of the state.

How, then, could the state best encourage technical personnel or increase its revenue? Although perhaps he was aware that they were not all feasible, Li nevertheless advocated certain institutional reforms that he had been considering since the mid-1860s. The Taiwan crisis and the discussion on coastal defense that followed gave him the opportunity to present his views to the throne, along with his proposal for a fundamental change in the dynasty's strategic concept: to abandon the plans for reconquering Sinkiang and, instead, to concentrate the available resources on defense and self-strengthening programs on the coast.

Although Li could usually count on the court's approval of his conduct of diplomacy or his advice regarding the disposition of the Anhwei Army, it was not as easy to persuade the throne to accept self-strengthening measures involving innovation. The Tsungli Yamen enthusiastically supported some of Li's recommendations, but it was either indifferent or unable to give support to others. There was, moreover, the need for coordinated efforts at the provincial level. After Tseng Kuo-fan's death in 1872, Li increasingly felt the need for allies in Liangkiang and other parts of south China, and we find him using his influence on the court to see that such men as Shen Pao-chen and Ting Jih-ch'ang were appointed to key posts.

Li's efforts up to November 1874

Since the mid-1860s, four modern arsenals had been founded, two of them shipyards as well: the Nanking Arsenal (moved from Soochow to that city in 1865), the Kiangnan Arsenal in Shanghai (founded in 1865), the Foochow Navy Yard (1866), and the Tientsin Arsenal (1867). Except for the Nanking Arsenal, which was financed by Anhwei Army funds,[36] all had been authorized by imperial edict. The Nanking and the Kiangnan arsenals had been founded by Li himself, but he was disappointed by the results. The Nanking plant, which was operated by the Scotsman Halliday Macartney, could produce bronze cannon as well as percussion caps and shells. The Kiangnan Arsenal, a much larger establishment, had spent about 2,500,000 taels in five years, principally from the Shanghai maritime customs revenue. Although it did contribute to the Anhwei Army's campaign against the Niens with muskets and carbines, bronze cannon, percussion caps, and shells, it was not until about 1868 that it succeeded for the first time in producing a rifle—the outdated muzzle-loading type.[37] Li regarded the Kiangnan and Nanking arsenals as no more than "the first step." Between 1867 and 1870, the shipyard attached to the Kiangnan Arsenal constructed four small steamships, described by Li as "neither merchant steamers, nor warships," and as "useful for warfare on the river but not at sea."[38]

One of Li's earliest acts in Chihli was to expand the Tientsin Arsenal, founded by Ch'ung-hou three years before. Li recommended to the throne that a former manager of the Kiangnan Arsenal be appointed its head and that its equipment be increased. Because Li was, at that juncture, planning to equip his army in Chihli with foreign-made breechloading rifles and Krupp guns, he decided that the best contribution the Tientsin Arsenal could make was to supply the ammunition required by these weapons. Between 1871 and 1874, the arsenal received nearly a million taels allocated by the throne from the maritime customs revenue of Tientsin and Chefoo. Three new plants were added to the one originally in existence, so that by 1874 more than a ton of powder was produced daily, as well as a large quantity of cartridges and shells. Li also planned, however, to manufacture the breechloading rifle itself. Machinery for the production of rifles of the Remington type was ordered and installed in 1874–75.[39]

Li hoped that the Kiangnan Arsenal, with its larger plant, could devote greater resources to the manufacture of rifles and ordnance. Although the Kiangnan Arsenal was controlled by the governor-general of Liangkiang, Li often discussed its affairs in his letters to Tseng Kuo-fan. Twice in 1871, Li urged Tseng to check the accuracy of the boastful reports made by Feng Chün-kuang, its chief manager, and to give greater authority to Hsü Shou, the famous mathematician and engineer in the arsenal's service. Li sometimes communicated directly with these managers. It was presumably on his advice that the arsenal acquired additional machinery in 1871 for rifles of the Remington type, some 4,200 of which were produced before the end of 1873.[40] After Tseng died in March 1872, Li continued to advise his successors regarding the arsenal. He urged that, in addition to breechloading rifles and bronze cannon, it should manufacture cast-iron cannon and torpedoes. The first cast-iron cannon was produced in February 1874. During 1871 to 1874, 2,000 rifles and 1,100 carbines produced by Kiangnan were sent to Chihli, but the bulk of its products were assigned to the various armies of the Liangkiang area.[41]

Because the Nanking Arsenal was financed with Anhwei Army funds, Li retained control over its personnel and policies. There was at least one occasion, in 1873, when an order for the change of the arsenal's Chinese director was issued by Li (presumably in his capacity as imperial commissioner for the Northern Ports), although he acted with the written concurrence of Li Tsung-hsi, the governor-general of Liangkiang. Until 1874, the bronze mortars built by Macartney were for the exclusive use of the coastal fortifications at Chihli. Beginning in early 1874, however, Li Tsung-hsi ordered the arsenal to make guns and various kinds of ammunition needed by the forces in Kiangsu.[42]

Li's concern for the Chinese armament industry also extended to Fukien. Late in 1871, the Foochow Navy Yard was attacked by a subchancellor of the Grand Secretariat as wasteful and ineffective. This official, Sung Chin, recommended to the throne that the shipbuilding programs at both Foochow and Shanghai be discontinued. Following instructions from the throne to give his views, Li joined Tso Tsung-t'ang and Shen Pao-chen, the founder and director of the Foochow Navy Yard, in defending it. Li's memorial of June 20, 1872, made the famous statement that China was encountering "the greatest change of situation (*pien-chü*) in three thousand years." Because Western military power was based on rifles, cannon, and steamships, China must master the secrets of such equipment so as to ensure her long-term survival. Li warned that Japan was ahead of China in these matters and was "viewing China in a threatening manner." Supporting a suggestion made earlier by the Tsungli Yamen, Li proposed that the Foochow and Shanghai shipyards might build freighters as well as gunboats and make the former available for purchase or hire by Chinese merchants. Li added a proposal of his own involving reform of institutions. Because the government-built gunboats could be used for coastal and river patrol by the coast and Yangze provinces, should they not be financed by the appropriations from the provinces devoted to the old-style navy? Li suggested that the court should issue an edict to the effect that the construction of war junks be discontinued altogether.[43] He was greatly disappointed when this last proposal was not supported by the Tsungli Yamen, although at its recommendation the throne decided to continue shipbuilding at Foochow and Shanghai.[44]

Li attached great importance to the Foochow Navy Yard and its training programs and took it upon himself to assist Shen Pao-chen's work. Li had formed the opinion by 1872 that Shen (who happened to be a *chin-shih* classmate of Li) was one of the very few high officials of the time who had a clear understanding of what self-strengthening required. Several times Li used his influence with Li Ho-nien, governor-general of Fukien and Chekiang, to persuade the latter not to obstruct Shen's work. In May 1874, during a visit to Peking, Li spoke on Shen Pao-chen's behalf with Shen Kuei-fen, grand councilor and president of the Board of War (who also happened to be a *chin-shih* classmate) and obtained his promise and that of Prince Kung that they would make favorable recommendations on Shen's future requests about the financing of the Foochow yard.[45]

Li realized, more acutely than he had in the early T'ung-chih period, that successful operation of arsenals and shipyards depended on trained technical personnel. The school Li founded in 1863, the Shanghai T'ung-wen Kuan (which was combined with a new translator's school of the Kiangnan Arsenal in 1867 and renamed Kuang Fang-yen Kuan), had been giving instruction in English, mathematics, and science to classes of about forty students still in their teens. But few outstanding graduates had been produced; the results, as in the case of the Peking T'ung-wen Kuan, were disappointing.[46] In 1864, Li had suggested to the Tsungli Yamen that a new category ($k'o$) be created under the examination system to accommodate men who specialized in technology. The little interest that the Shanghai and Peking schools had aroused among the literati convinced Li that only such a change could provide the incentive for the pursuit of "Western learning."[47]

Li supported a proposal to send Chinese youths to the United States for their education. He was persuaded that a prolonged period of study abroad was the best way to train Chinese who, upon their return to China, could become instructors in the Shanghai and Peking schools or serve in the arsenals and shipyards. The proposal originated with Yung Wing and Ch'en Lan-pin and was brought to the court's attention in a memorial from Tseng Kuo-fan in October 1870. However, Tseng merely mentioned the idea casually in connection with another matter, and Li, in a letter dated December 13, 1870, urged him to draft concrete plans to be submitted to the court. "It can never be expected," Li wrote, "that the matter be initiated by the court."[48] Li also suggested that the draft regulations include a provision that the students be awarded *chien-sheng* status before going abroad and that upon their return they be assigned official ranks, after being given an examination by the Tsungli Yamen. Li was later satisfied that the regulations merely promised official positions for the returning students. In August 1871, he joined Tseng in submitting a memorial to the throne on the subject, after having corresponded with the Tsungli Yamen and obtained its concurrence, particularly on the proposal that 1,200,000 taels be allocated over a twenty-year period from the Shanghai maritime customs revenue.[49] As authorized by an imperial edict, a bureau was established in Shanghai in 1872 to select students, and the first group of thirty left Shanghai that summer, to be followed by a similar number annually for three years. The boys selected were between eleven and sixteen *sui*. A tutor went along to teach them Chinese subjects, but each student was to spend fifteen years abroad, traveling during the last two years. Because the authorized plan was based on a joint memorial from Tseng and Li, it was considered to be under the supervision of the two commissioners at Nanking and Tientsin. The officials in charge in the United States reported to Li and to the governor-general of Liangkiang.[50]

In June 1871, Li had briefly considered sending students to Britain also. His more urgent problem, however, was to find mature personnel in China who could serve at once in managerial or technical capacities in the arsenals, the shipyards, or the customs administration. Li often wrote to colleagues in other provinces inviting nominations of such personnel.[51] In January 1874, when Shen Pao-chen consulted him about a plan to send the graduates of the Foochow Navy Yard School to Britain and France, Li responded with enthusiasm. He wrote to the Yamen about the plan and brought it to Prince Kung's attention when he was in Peking in May 1874. Li also considered sending the sons of the Tientsin Arsenal's Chinese technicians to Germany for study.[52] The Taiwan crisis intervened, and it was not until 1876 that further action was taken.

Li was increasingly convinced that Western technology could be used to augment the wealth of the Ch'ing state as well as its military strength. In Kiangsu, in the early T'ung-chih period, he had been impressed by the successful invasion of the carrying trade in Chinese waters by Western steamships, although at that time he was anxious to protect the seagoing junks that carried the tribute rice to Chihli. As early as 1864, Li had proposed to the Tsungli Yamen that Chinese merchants be permitted to own and operate steamships and foreign-style sailing vessels, in competition with Western ships.[53] In the two years after he came to Tientsin, a series of events prompted him to make immediate plans for a Chinese steamship company. During the flood and famine in Chihli in 1871, he deeply resented the exorbitant rates foreign ships demanded for the transport of relief grain. New breaches of the Yellow River dikes that winter convinced him that the Grand Canal was to become useless. He was against investing enormous sums to restore the former course of the Yellow River so as to improve the Grand Canal's navigability. He saw in a fleet of Chinese-owned coastal steamships the solution to the ancient problem of how to carry tribute rice from the south to the north.[54] It was at this juncture that the Tsungli Yamen suggested that ships built by the Foochow Navy Yard might be hired out to Chinese merchants. Li was asked by the Yamen to make arrangements to this end, and through the summer of 1872 we find him corresponding on the subject with such officials as the superintendent of customs at Shanghai and the head of the Liangkiang administration's new naval fleet (which consisted chiefly of Kiangnan-built ships).[55]

Li found that the Foochow- and Shanghai-built ships were not suitable for the freighting trade, as they were costly to operate and drew too much water for some harbors. Following the advice of Chu Ch'i-ang, a Chekiang official in charge of the junk transport of that province's tribute rice, Li decided that the best plan was for a group of Chinese merchants to buy foreign-built steamships and to operate them for the general carrying trade as well as for the transport of tribute rice; presumably Chinese-built ships could be added to the fleet later. Li approved Chu's plan to establish a bureau (chü) in Shanghai and to "invite merchants" (chao-shang) to operate steamships. It was understood that the enterprise was to be "supervised by the government and undertaken by the merchants" (kuan-tu shang-pan). Li arranged a loan of 136,000 taels to the enterprise from Chihli military funds, making it clear, however, that "profits and losses are entirely the responsibility of the merchants and do not involve the government."[56] While the availability of government appropriations for tribute rice transport made the project particularly feasible, Li undoubtedly regarded it as part of a general policy for China's self-strengthening. "The use of the steamship for the transport of tribute rice is but a minor consideration," Li wrote the governor of Kiangsu in December 1872. "The project will open up new prospects for the dignity of the state (kuo-t'i), for commerce, for revenue, for military strength—for the China of centuries to come." Li was also interested in reports of Japan's effort to develop commercial shipping. He wrote in early January to an official whom he had recommended to be a secretary of the Tsungli Yamen: "We let other people move about at will in Chinese waters. Why do we deny the Chinese merchants alone a foothold? Even Japan has sixty or seventy [merchant] steamships of her own; we alone do not have any. How does this look?"[57]

To obtain the tribute rice cargo for the steamships, Li had to enlist the cooperation of officials in the lower Yangtze area. Siding with the vested interests of the junk owners, the Kiangsu officials initially opposed Li's plan. In October 1871, Shen Ping-ch'eng, the superintendent of customs at Shanghai, and Feng Chün-kuang, the head of the Kiangnan Arsenal, joined in a petition of protest to Ho Ching, the governor-general of Liangkiang, and their views were supported by Chang Shu-sheng, the Kiangsu governor. Invoking Peking's authority, Li reminded Ho that the proposed steamship company eventually would purchase and hire Chinese-built ships and was in line with the Tsungli Yamen's original proposal that had been approved by the throne in June 1872; it was therefore a matter with which Ho, as acting commissioner of trade for the Southern Ports, should be properly concerned. To governor Chang, Li exploded: "I have worked together with you for nearly twenty years. Did you ever see anything that I was determined to do discontinued because of unjustified criticism?"[58] Ho and Chang eventually allowed 20 percent of the Kiangsu tribute rice to be shipped annually by steamer. Together with a similar quota from Chekiang, this assured the new enterprise an annual tribute rice freight of 200,000 piculs, or a payment of 112,000 taels. In December, Li memorialized to request imperial sanction of the entire plan. The memorial was approved on December 26, and on January 14, the Bureau for Inviting Merchants to Operate Steamships (Lun-ch'uan chao-shang chü; known in English as the China Merchants' Steam Navigation Company) was inaugurated in Shanghai.[59] Because it was on the basis of Li's memorial that the project was approved, the Bureau was regarded as under the jurisdiction of the imperial commissioner for the Northern Ports. Li retained firm control of its personnel and policies. In July 1873, when two Cantonese compradors, Tong King-sing and Hsü Jun, became the directors (tsung-pan) of the new company, it was Li who issued the appointment. Li found it necessary, however, to appeal to the Kiangsu governor and the Liangkiang governor-general to help by giving the enterprise larger tribute-rice consignments and by providing it with loans from provincial funds. Thanks to such assistance, as well as to the efforts of its ex-comprador managers, the company's fleet grew to thirteen ships (8,546 net tons) by 1875 and services were developed on the Yangtze River and on several coastal routes.[60]

The purpose of the Chinese merchant steamers, as Li told the Tsungli Yamen, was to compete with foreign enterprise and restore China's "control of profit" (li-ch'üan).[61] But Li was particularly intrigued by the possibility of opening up a new source of revenue to the state by working mines with Western methods. Early in 1868, when he was still involved in the war against the Niens, Li had proposed in connection with the question of treaty revision that foreign engineers be allowed to work Chinese coal and iron mines. After coming to Chihli, Li became increasingly convinced that the use of pumps and other machines in mining pits not only would provide the Chinese arsenals and shipyards with vital materials and fuel but would profit the state financially. Li was also aware of the fact that the Japanese had been working their mines with Western techniques. In his memorial of June 20, 1872, concerning the Foochow shipyard, he proposed projects "supervised by the government and undertaken by merchants" to work mines with machinery. He also recommended using Western foundry techniques to produce cast iron and steel. Li emphasized that coal and iron could be marketed for profit and were "of great importance to the policy of enriching the state and strengthening military power."[62]

Li was disappointed when the Tsungli Yamen, while favoring the continuation of the Foochow shipyard, failed to make a recommendation to the throne regarding mining projects. He wrote Wang K'ai-t'ai, the governor of Fukien, that the failure indicated that the Yamen thought only of the present and not the future: "What will become of us a few decades hence?"[63] On his own initiative, Li encouraged Feng Chün-kuang, the director of the Kiangnan Arsenal, and others to make plans for working coal and iron mines at Tz'u-chou, in southern Chihli. In 1874, an English merchant, James Henderson, was sent to Britain to buy machinery and hire workmen.[64] Li was not, however, merely concerned with the opportunities for such projects in Chihli. He wrote the governor of Shansi, Pao Yüan-shen, in November 1873, urging him to open up the rich mineral deposits of that province with new methods. "The earth is not stingy with its treasure," Li wrote, "but few in China are aware of this truth; please give this matter your attention and do not worry all the time about poverty." Early in 1874, Li asked Li Tsung-hsi, the governor-general of Liangkiang, to try to persuade Liu K'un-i, the governor of Kiangsi, to introduce machinery in the coal fields at Lo-p'ing, Kiangsi. Liu refused. In August 1874, at the very height of the Taiwan crisis, Li advised Shen Pao-chen to try to work the mines of that island. Assisted by H. E. Hobson, the commissioner of customs at Tamsui, Shen made arrangements for a coal mine near Keelung in 1875.[65]

Li's proposals of December 1874

Since the Tientsin Massacre, the initiative for self-strengthening had come chiefly from Li, with some cooperation from the Tsungli Yamen and from Tseng Kuo-fan and Shen Pao-chen in the provinces. The Taiwan affair further stimulated attention to the problem of military preparedness. On November 5, 1874, the Tsungli Yamen, in which the ailing Wen-hsiang was still the dominant spirit, memorialized on the lessons of the incident. The Yamen lamented that although there had been much talk of self-strengthening since 1860, little had actually been done. The Yamen recommended that governors-general, governors, and the Manchu commanders-in-chief of the coastal and Yangtze provinces be invited to submit their views on the needs of coastal defense (hai-fang) under five headings: military training, weapons, shipbuilding, revenue, and personnel. In a personal memorial submitted a month later, Wen-hsiang (who had risen from his sickbed to take charge of negotiations with the Japanese on the Taiwan incident) reminded the throne that there was a real possibility that Japan, "accustomed to break her word," would allow her rebels at home to seek adventure in China. Wen-hsiang recommended that military preparations on Taiwan be continued and that plans be made immediately to buy ironclads and gunboats from abroad.[66]

Although it was the Yamen that initiated the policy debate in 1874, Li put forth the boldest proposals. "What is urgently needed today is to abandon established notions and seek practical results," he urged in his memorial of December 10.[67] The two essentials for a successful coastal defense program were, in his view, "the change of institutions (pien-fa) and the proper use of personnel (yung-jen)." Li wrote Wen-hsiang that he was aware that not all his proposals could be adopted, but that he had to make them, because "the responsibility is on my shoulders."[68]

Li proposed general military reform for the coastal and Yangtze provinces. In the early T'ung-chih period, when he worked with the British and French forces in Shanghai and with the Ever-Victorious Army, he became convinced that the number of troops in the Chinese armies could be greatly reduced, thereby saving funds that could provide better equipment and pay for selected and efficient units. Soon after he became imperial commissioner in 1870, Li had drawn the throne's attention to the uselessness of the Green Standard Army, including the so-called Trained Troops.[69] He now went further and pleaded that "Rather than having a large number that are useless, it is better to have fewer of high quality." Li proposed that all "weak and exhausted" army units, whether Green Standard, Trained Troops, or *yung* forces, should be disbanded altogether, while the best troops, fewer than a hundred thousand for all the coastal and Yangtze provinces, should be converted into "foreign-arms and cannon corps." Equipped with recent models of rifles and cannon and reinforced by coastal fortifications, the comparatively small number of troops could be relied on at least to defend the two vital areas, Chihli and the lower Yangtze Valley. Li suggested that orders be placed immediately for firearms such as the Martini-Henry and the Snider and for cannon produced by Krupp, Woolwich, Armstrong, and Gatling. China's own arsenals, however, must also be expanded. They must aim at making breechloading rifles and cannon, as well as torpedoes, while further plans could await the development of a steel industry as well as coal and iron mines. The manufacture of powder, cartridges, and shells needed to be expanded and new plants for this purpose should be established at such inland places as Soochow and in the interior provinces.

Li supported Wen-hsiang's proposal for a Chinese naval fleet of foreign-built vessels. Li felt that the navy was not quite as important as the army, but agreed that effective defense required ironclads for the open seas and floating gun-carriages as well as torpedoes for the harbors. He recommended that six ironclads be ordered immediately, two to be stationed in north China (probably at Chefoo and Port Arthur), two close to the Yangtze estuary, and two at Amoy or Canton. In addition, twenty floating gun-carriages should be ordered for use at the various ports. Li suggested that Chinese students should be sent abroad to the shipyards where the vessels were to be built, to learn shipbuilding and navigation techniques. Meanwhile, the building programs at Foochow and Kiangnan yards should be strengthened. Li visualized a Chinese naval fleet consisting eventually of sixty vessels.

To finance the new army and navy, Li suggested, first of all, that revenue be saved by disbanding worthless troops and by discontinuing the construction of war junks. The new army and navy were expected, however, to cost more than ten million taels and additional appropriations had to be arranged. The most reliable source, Li emphasized, was the "four-tenths quota of the maritime customs revenue" (*ssu-ch'eng yang-shui*).[70] This fund had been allocated at some ports for the use of arsenals and for the Anhwei Army, but a considerable portion remained, particularly if the part reserved for the Board of Revenue at Peking was included. Li proposed that some three million taels that had been saved by the Board from this source should also be used for coastal defense. He also suggested that loans could be obtained from foreign firms, to be paid in installments out of the four-tenths quota. Li recommended that likin on imported opium could be raised somewhat, while taxes could be levied on native opium, which he thought might as well be legalized until such time as the drug's importation could be stopped altogether. To ensure larger revenue for coastal defense, Li proposed, for the first time explicitly, that preparations in coastal provinces be accorded priority over the recovery of Sinkiang. He pointed out that Sinkiang had come under Ch'ing rule only in the Ch'ien-lung reign, and that it was very difficult to defend, particularly now that the Moslem chieftains at Kashgar had Russian and British support and the Russians had occupied Ili. Given the limited revenue available, the court would have to make a choice between adequate preparations in the coastal area and the recovery of the "wasteland" in the far northwest. Li would draw the defense line at the Kansu border and guard it with military colonies into which some of the present armies there could be converted, while the Moslem leaders at Ili, Urumchi, and Kashgar might be accorded the status of native chieftains (*t'u-ssu*) or tributaries. Presumably a balance between Russian and British influence would help to ensure stability in Sinkiang. Funds saved by canceling the expedition could be diverted immediately to the coastal provinces.

Undoubtedly with Li in mind, the Tsungli Yamen had proposed in its memorial of November 5, 1874, that there should be a single commander-in-chief (*t'ung-shuai*) in charge of the coastal and Yangtze provinces, and that under him there should be a system of newly chosen generals-in-chief and brigade generals, to be stationed in different provinces. Li regarded the idea as impractical. Given the existing authority of the governors-general and governors in financial and military affairs, a single command for all the provinces concerned was hardly feasible, particularly since the lack of telegraph and railway prevented rapid communication. Moreover, mere "consultation" (*hui-t'ung shang-ch'ou*) between the commander-in-chief and the provinces was not likely to lead to effective action. Li, therefore, favored more than one command for the coastal and Yangtze areas—perhaps three "high officials" (*ta yüan*) exercising supervision over such new projects as the naval fleet. For the supervisory positions in south China, Li recommended Shen Pao-chen and Ting Jih-ch'ang. From Li's correspondence, we know that he had been using his influence with Wen-hsiang and other ministers at court to get Shen appointed as the governor-general of Liangkiang and Ting to a responsible post in south China.[71] Li obviously hoped that with himself at Tientsin and Shen at Nanking, a high degree of coordination could be achieved in carrying out new programs.

While Li was concerned with the immediate financial and political arrangements, he also put forth proposals of long-range significance. He brought up, for the first time directly to the throne, the need for a change in the examination and civil-service systems. Li lamented the continuing apathy among the literati toward Western methods (*yang-fa*) and pointed out that neither the T'ung-wen Kuan type of school nor sending students abroad would arouse sufficient interest if the criteria for the selection and the advancement of officials remained unchanged. Li attacked the literary examinations, which emphasized calligraphy and the eight-legged essay, as "hollow and ornamental." He pleaded that while this kind of examination could not be "abolished immediately," it was necessary to create "another basis (*k'o*) of advancement through government activity concerning Western affairs (*yang-wu*)." Li proposed that a Bureau of Western Learning (Yang-hsüeh chü) be created in each province involved in coastal defense, where science and technology (including such subjects as chemistry, electricity, and gunnery) would be taught by carefully chosen Western instructors, as well as by qualified Chinese, such as those being trained in the United States. Advanced students were to be "tested through performance" and were to be assigned posts in arsenals, shipyards, and the armed forces. Moreover, such personnel were to be allowed opportunities for rapid promotion, comparable to those for persons possessing military merit, and were to be awarded "substantive posts, in the same way as officials who advanced through regular channels." Li predicted such a new personnel policy would result in an appreciable advance in armament making in China in about twenty years.

Li urged the use of Western technology in transport, mining, and manufacturing. He drew the throne's attention to the military and commercial advantages of the railway, and to the military value of the telegraph. Pointing out that British textile imports into China amounted to more than thirty million taels per year and were harmful to Chinese handicrafts, Li suggested that the Chinese themselves should establish machine-operated textile mills. He particularly stressed the opportunity that lay in opening up mines—not only coal and iron but also copper, lead, mercury, and the precious metals. Li compared the failure to exploit such resources to keeping family treasures permanently sealed up while worrying about starvation and cold. He recommended that foreign geologists be invited to prospect the mines in the provinces and that Chinese merchants be encouraged to form companies (*kung-ssu*) to work mines with machines; the government could help the companies with initial loans and thereafter receive 10 or 20 percent of their profits. Li expected the benefits from the mines to be apparent in ten years. He realized that new mining projects were opposed by the gentry and the people on grounds of geomancy and by "incompetent officials" who feared that the concentration of miners might lead to disorderly conduct. Li described such objections as "ridiculous," for the Western nations and Japan were all developing mines: "Why is it that they do not suffer from them but, on the contrary, have achieved wealth and strength (*fu-chiang*) through them?"

Li had thus proposed programs for self-strengthening that were broader and more far-reaching than those presented by him or by others in the 1860s. The question was, of course, whether any or all of the proposals might be accepted. Li received scant help from the governors-general, governors, and Manchu commanders-in-chief who also gave their views on the Tsungli Yamen's original memorial. Stimulated by the recent Taiwan crisis, all the memorialists agreed that the coastal defense needed to be strengthened. But, in the view of the Tsungli Yamen, except for Li and Shen Pao-chen (who also made a strong plea for a navy that included foreign-built ironclads and for the development of mines), none put forward proposals that were "concrete and practical." By early January 1875, replies had been received from twelve officials, in addition to Li and Shen.[72] Although all twelve favored new training for the army, only one suggested that the particularly weak units of the Green Standard forces should be disbanded. Six favored forming a new navy with foreign-built ironclads, but only one or two had useful suggestions on how they were to be financed. All twelve assumed that war was to be carried into Sinkiang; two in particular argued eloquently that the Russian threat to the land frontier posed an even more urgent problem than coastal defense. Four favored making some exception in the rules of civil or military service to place competent men where they were needed, but only two vaguely suggested that Western studies should be encouraged. Four realized the importance of mineral resources, but only one (Li's brother Hanchang) supported without reservation the use of machines in mines. Only one (the governor of Kiangsi, Liu K'un-i) agreed with the Tsungli Yamen that there should be a single commander-in-chief for coastal defense, but he qualified the proposal by suggesting that the generals-in-chief and brigade generals chosen by the commander-in-chief should be under the direction of the governors-general and the governors of the provinces concerned. Three recommended that the command of coastal defense be divided between the two commissioners at Tientsin and Nanking—two mentioned Li by name for the supervisory responsibility in north China.

Decision rested, of course, with the court. A meeting of the ministers was to consider the matter on January 2, but it was postponed due to the T'ung-chih emperor's illness and his death on the twelfth. In late January, Li went to Peking and was summoned three times to audiences with the dowager empresses. He also talked with Wen-hsiang and Li Wen-tsao and urged that Shen Pao-chen be appointed governor-general of Liangkiang, a post that had been vacated by Li Tsung-hsi (who was taken ill) and temporarily filled by Liu K'un-i as acting governor-general. Wen-hsiang arranged to have Robert Hart, who had obtained price quotations on British-built gunboats through his agent in London, go to Tientsin and discuss the details with Li.[73]

While in Peking, Li personally urged the court to reconsider the expedition into Sinkiang, and, according to Li, there were people at court who agreed with him.[74] But due chiefly to reluctance to "abandon territories acquired by an imperial ancestor," the throne abided by its decision (made as early as February 1874) to encourage Tso Tsung-t'ang to proceed. On March 10, Tso was instructed to formulate plans for the expedition, including arrangements for the supply line. On May 3, Tso was appointed imperial commissioner for military operations in Sinkiang.[75] This effort to reconquer the far northwest was bound to cut into the revenue for the proposed coastal defense plans, although as of 1875 it was still uncertain whether Tso or the dynasty would really persevere in the long and arduous task of recovering Kashgar and Ili.

The court did not entirely neglect coastal defense, however. The Taiwan affair was fresh in its memory and in April 1875, the murder of A. R. Margary, an interpreter entering Yunnan from Burma, raised the possibility of a threat from the British. The court was willing to see Li in a position to coordinate military preparations on the coast. On May 30, 1875, Shen Pao-chen was appointed governor-general of Liangkiang and commissioner of trade for the Southern Ports. At the same time, Li was appointed commissioner of coastal defense of north China and Shen, commissioner of coastal defense of south China, both charged with the responsibility of training troops, establishing "bureaus" (meaning, probably, chiefly arsenals), reorganizing taxes, and other tasks necessary to defense. An edict of the same day declared: "Coastal defense is vitally important, and it is urgently necessary to make preparation before trouble comes, so as to strengthen ourselves." The throne noted that ironclads were extremely costly, but authorized Li and Shen to order "one or two to begin with."[76] The Board of Revenue and the Tsungli Yamen subsequently recommended that beginning in August 1875, an annual appropriation of four million taels be made for coastal defense, to be expended by the two commissioners. It was specified that the yearly sum was to come from the "four-tenths quota of the maritime customs revenue" at the coastal ports and from the likin revenue of coastal and Yangtze provinces. Because the Board of Revenue did not want to give up that portion of the four-tenths quota reserved for itself (or the sums it had received in the past from this source), and because the board plainly was not giving coastal defense priority over other imperially sanctioned claims on the four-tenths quota, Li feared that only a fraction of this annual fund would be left for him and Shen. Moreover, Li was certain that with the pressure from Peking to raise large sums (at least two or three million taels annually) for the construction of imperial mausoleums and palaces and with the Sinkiang campaign being given priority, probably only one or two coastal and Yangtze provinces would have any surplus in their likin revenue, which was also relied on by the provinces themselves for their own financial needs. Li foresaw that the four million taels appropriated was to become largely nominal, although he hoped that at least some small portion might be available.[77]

Predictably, the court did not heed Li's counsel concerning the reform of institutions. Admitting the weaknesses of the Green Standard Army, the court, also on May 30, instructed all governors-general and governors concerned with coastal defense to complete, within a year, the reorganization and consolidation of the Green Standard "outposts" (hsün) and to provide the troops with uniform training. No mention was made, however, of disbanding the inferior units. The throne also passed over the proposed "bureaus of Western learning" and the new civil-service category for persons versed in this learning. One of the May 30 edicts states that both proposals had been referred to Prince Li (Shih-to) and to Prince Ch'un (the new child-emperor's father), along with the Tsungli Yamen's recommendation that diplomatic envoys be sent to Japan and the West. While the two princes favored the latter idea, they did not comment on the proposals regarding Western learning. So as to avoid "disagreement," the throne would therefore defer decision on these proposals until the diplomatic missions abroad proved successful! In another edict of the same day, the throne encouraged Li and Shen to recommend to it men who were versed in *yang-wu*, including those qualified to serve as envoys abroad. None of the edicts mentioned Li's proposals regarding railways, telegraphs, and textile mills, but one gave Li and Shen authorization to proceed with the specific mining projects they had mentioned in their memorials—the coal and iron mines in Tz'u-chou, in Chihli, and on Taiwan.[78]

Thus, only a few of the proposals Li put forward were adopted by the throne and, in view of the priority the throne gave to Sinkiang and to the increasing financial needs of the court itself, a major new start in coastal defense and in self-strengthening was hardly to be expected. Yet, it may be said that new ground had been broken in Ch'ing policy. Not being able to compete with the arsenals and shipyards of the West, China, it was decided, would have to acquire Western-made armaments through purchase. In the next few years, a spate of orders came from Tientsin and elsewhere for Remingtons, Sniders, and Krupp and Gatling guns.[79] As early as April 1875, with the Tsungli Yamen's support, Li ordered four gunboats from Armstrong and Co., through Robert Hart's London agent—two 330-ton ships, each carrying a 26.5-ton rifle gun, and two 440-ton ones, each equipped with a 38-ton gun. The ordering of more gunboats and an ironclad was contemplated, pending the availability of funds. It was planned during 1875–76 to send graduates of the Foochow Navy Yard School to Britain and France.[80] Both Li and Shen interpreted the imperial sanction for the mines in Chihli and on Taiwan as general approval for such projects elsewhere. Within the year following May 1875, Li wrote to the governors of Hupei, Kiangsi, Fukien, and Shantung, urging them to work the mines with machines. Coal and iron fields were planned in Kuang-chi and Hsing-kuo, Hupei, in late 1875 under the sponsorship of the commissioners at Tientsin and Nanking as well as the Hupei governor; a similar project was initiated in Kiangsi in 1876, the same year that prospecting was done at K'ai-p'ing, Chihli. During that year, Li and Shen Pao-chen also considered the establishment of a cotton textile mill at Shanghai.[81]

What was particularly gratifying to Li was the fact that at least two like-minded colleagues had been brought, partly on his recommendation, to positions of influence. Shen Pao-chen arrived at his new post in Nanking in November 1875. In September, Ting Jih-ch'ang, on Li's recommendation, had been appointed director-general of the Foochow Navy Yard, and in January 1876, he became governor of Fukien with authority over Taiwan.[82] In Chihli, Li pressed forward with plans of long-range significance—the sending of five young officers of the Anhwei Army to German military academies, further expansion of the Tientsin Arsenal, the establishment of a school of Western sciences in connection with the Arsenal's new plant for manufacturing torpedoes.[83] Similar work was being carried on by Shen and Ting in south China. In early 1877, thirty students of the Foochow Navy Yard School were sent to Europe. Meanwhile, Shen did much to strengthen the Nanking and Kiangnan arsenals, adding to the former a torpedo plant and acquiring for the latter machinery for making cast-iron rifle guns of the Armstrong type, the first of which was produced in 1878. A school was set up at the Nanking Arsenal, and an effort was made to improve the school and the translation department at the Kiangnan Arsenal. Although the plan for a textile mill was found not to be immediately feasible, in late 1876 Shen Pao-chen arranged large loans from the Liangkiang provinces to the China Merchants' Steam Navigation Company, enabling it to buy sixteen ships from the American firm of Russell and Co. and thereby increase its fleet to thirty-one vessels (22,168 net tons).[84] For the first time since Tseng Kuo-fan's death in 1872, Li had an ally at the head of the Liangkiang administration.

We see, therefore, that only a small part of Li's comprehensive program was put into practice. Nevertheless, as compared to its beginnings in the early T'ung-chih period, the self-strengthening movement had certainly expanded. In the new shipping and mining enterprises, the movement had gained another dimension: to the desire for effective armament was added the desire to augment the nation's wealth, again by using Western technology. The plan for a navy of foreign-built vessels represented a realistic appraisal of the capacity of China's new shipyards, as well as an awareness of the urgent need for preparedness. The sending of students to Europe, in the wake of the educational mission to the United States, was a further acknowledgment of the need for technical personnel. Among the high officials there were very few men who, like Li, wanted to see drastic reform in civil-service regulations and in the military system. But under the continued pressure from foreign powers, at least the objective of gaining "wealth and strength" for the state, which Li so eloquently advocated, had won widespread acceptance, if not active support.

With Li as the imperial commissioner at Tientsin, the self-strengthening movement had, moreover, acquired a strategically placed coordinator. It is plain that Li's power was limited. He could get the court to accept only a few of his proposals, and the financial and other resources he needed often lay in provinces beyond his jurisdiction. But it may be said that in the 1870s, Li was at least given a good opportunity to expand his efforts. The Anhwei Army in Chihli and elsewhere enjoyed the throne's support, and imperial approval had been given to his program for the arsenals, for studies abroad, for merchant steamships and mines, and for a new navy. Beginning in 1875, men who had been recommended by Li, Shen Pao-chen and Ting Jih-ch'ang, were in the vital posts in Liangkiang and Fukien and, with sympathetic officials in other provinces, there was at least a chance that self-strengthening might become an empirewide effort. If by "regionalism" is meant the administrative leeway enjoyed by the governors-general and governors over the armies and the likin of the provinces, this trend had continued since the early T'ung-chih period. But the imperial authority over armies and revenue anywhere in the empire was never questioned, and Peking's control over provincial appointments, at least at the higher levels, had not diminished. The court's support was plainly still the key to the success of any new policy. To the extent that Li's recommendations on policy and personnel met with imperial approval, he represented, in effect, a centralizing force on behalf of what he considered an urgent national task.

Notes

1. I have dealt with Li's early advocacy of *tzu-ch'iang* in "The Confucian as Patriot and Pragmatist: Li Hung-chang's Formative Years, 1823–1866" (see chapter 2).

2. See Stanley Spector, *Li Hung-chang and the Huai Army: A Study in Nineteenth-Century Regionalism* (Seattle, 1964).

3. Li Hung-chang, *Li Wen-chung kung ch'üan-chi* (Complete works of Li Hung-chang), 100 *ts'e* (Nanking, 1905; hereafter cited as *LWCK*), *Tsou-kao* (hereafter cited as *Memorials*), 16.34, 48, 50.

4. In 1870, Liu Ming-ch'uan and Kuo Sung-lin had the title of *t'i-tu*, while Wu Ch'ang-ch'ing was a *chi-ming* (designated) *t'i-tu* and Chou Sheng-ch'uan a *tsung-ping*. See, for example, *LWCK Memorials*, 17.6b–7, 12: Chou Sheng-ch'uan, *Chou Wu-chuang kung i-shu* (Works of Chou Sheng-ch'uan), 10 *ts'e* (Nanking, 1905), 2 *hsia*, 1–9.

5. *LWCK Memorials*, 17.8 and 21.30–31.

6. *LWCK Memorials*, 17.10. When Ch'ung-hou was appointed *san-k'ou t'ung-shang ta-ch'en* in 1861, the edict specifically stated that he was not given the title *ch'in-ch'ai*. However, the commissioner of trade for the southern ports (*nan-yang t'ung-shang ta-ch'en*) had been given the title *ch'in-ch'ai* in the early 1860s. Li's office of imperial commissioner at Tientsin was often referred to later as commissioner of trade for the Northern Ports. See *Ch'ou-pan i-wu shih-mo* (The complete account of our management of barbarian affairs), 260 *chüan* (Peiping, 1930; hereafter cited as *IWSM*), Hsien-feng, 72.1b–2; T'ung-chih, 18.25b.

7. *LWCK Memorials*, 18.76 and 19.83. *P'eng-liao han-kao* (hereafter cited as *Letters*), 12.26; 13.3–4, 6b–8, 32b; 15, 16.

8. *LWCK Memorials*, 17.29b and 18.76.

9. *LWCK Memorials*, 19.31b and 20.46. *Letters*, 11.12. For the figures on the Green Standard forces in Chihli, see *Memorials*, 20.39b.

10. *LWCK Memorials*, *chüan* 17–26, especially 17.41–43; 18.88–89, 92–93; 19.5–6, 20–21, 40; 20.10–11b, 67; 21.7–8, 12–13, 51–52; 22.10–11, 39–41; 24.36. *Letters*, 10.33; 11.6b, 13b–18, 20b–23; 12.2, 9–10b; 13.18.

11. *LWCK Memorials*, 17.10, 14.

12. *LWCK, I-shu han-kao* (hereafter cited as *Tsungli Yamen Letters*), 1.32–33b; *Letters*, 12.23b.

13. *LWCK Tsungli Yamen Letters*, 1.2b–8b, 14–15b, 17b–19, 24b–25b; *Memorials*, 18.57.

14. *LWCK Tsungli Yamen Letters*, 1.3b–4, 10–13, 22–24b, 28b–30, 34–35, 40–46,

48b–50. *Memorials,* 17.53–54b; 18.11–13, 28, 36, 42–52b; 19.24, 57–59; 20.73–74b; 21.18–19. Cf. T. F. Tsiang, "Sino-Japanese Diplomatic Relations, 1870–94," *Chinese Social and Political Science Review,* XVII (1933), 4–16.

15. *LWCK Tsungli Yamen Letters,* 1.51–52; 2.1–7, 29b, 31–33, 34–35. *Memorials,* 23.23–25b; 25.24–25.

16. *LWCK Tsungli Yamen Letters,* 1.35b–38; *Letters,* 13.4, 10b; Hosea Ballou Morse, *The International Relations of the Chinese Empire,* 3 vols. (London, 1910–18), II, 267.

17. *LWCK Tsungli Yamen Letters,* 2.34; see also 2.20, 24, 26b–29, 30–31.

18. *LWCK Tsungli Yamen Letters,* 2.35–40, 51b–57. Cf. Tsiang, "Sino-Japanese Diplomatic Relations," pp. 16–34.

19. *LWCK Memorials,* 17.10b.

20. *LWCK Memorials,* 17.50b; 21.40–41. Cf. *IWSM,* T'ung-chih, 10.16; 61.22.

21. *LWCK Letters,* 10.30b, 34b, 35b; 11.5b; 13. 14b. *Memorials,* 17.50b; 18.20, 66, 67b; 20.36–37; 21.40–41.

22. *LWCK Memorials,* 16.42; 17.1, 6b, 12b, 51; 20. 37; 23. 27b. *Letters,* 11.2b. Chou Sheng-ch'uan, *Chou Wu-chuang kung i-shu, chüan-shou,* 32–40.

23. *LWCK Memorials,* 17.27b; 18.32, 63.

24. *Tung-hua hsü-lu* (Continuation of the Tung-hua records) (Taipei reprint, 1963), T'ung-chih, 91.53, 55–56, 61b, 62b; 92.1. *LWCK Letters,* 11.19, 22–25.

25. *LWCK Memorials,* 19.80–82b; 20.16. *Letters,* 12.20, 23; 13.31b. *Tung-hua hsü-lu,* T'ung-chih, 95. 37, 45.

26. *LWCK Memorials,* 17.7. *Letters,* 10.27b, 30b; 11.7b, 12b–13, 23b. *Tung-hua hsü-lu,* T'ung-chih, 92.7.

27. *LWCK Letters,* 12.12b–13, 24; 13.7, 10b–11, 14b, 27b, 31b, 14. 2b. Tseng's successors as governor-general of Liangkiang up to early 1875 were Ho Ching (acting, March-November 1872), Chang Shu-sheng (acting, November 1872–February 1873), and Li Tsung-hsi (February 1873–January 1875).

28. *LWCK Tsungli Yamen Letters,* 2.24b, 34b; *Letters,* 14.6b–7, 9b; *Tung-hua hsü-lu,* T'ung-chih, 98.39b–40.

29. *LWCK Memorials,* 23.28b; *Letters,* 14, 7b, 8, 11, 14b–15, 18b, 19b, 24, 31.

30. *LWCK Letters,* 14.12–13, 16–18, 20b–23.

31. *LWCK Memorials,* 21.30–31b; 25.40–41b; 27.16–17.

32. *LWCK Letters,* 14.16b, 22. See also 13.8.

33. *LWCK Memorials,* 23. 37–38; *Letters,* 14.24b, 26.

34. *LWCK Letters,* 11.10. See 10.22b, 25, 27b–28; 11.6, 21, 27; 12.14; 13.8.

35. *LWCK Letters,* 12.3b; 14.28b, 32.

36. Sun Yü-t'ang, ed., *Chung-kuo chin-tai kung-yeh shih tzu-liao, ti-i-chi, 1840–95 nien* (Materials on the history of modern industry in China, first collection, 1840–95), 2 vols. (Peking, 1957), I, 263; *LWCK Memorials,* 21.31b; *Yang-wu yün-tung* (The Western Affairs Movement), comp. Institute of Modern History, Chinese Academy of Sciences, and Bureau of Ming and Ch'ing Archives, Central Archives, 8 vols. (Shanghai, 1961), IV, 127.

37. Demetrius C. Boulger, *The Life of Sir Halliday Macartney, K.C.M.G.* (London, 1908), 148–50, 177; *North-China Herald,* August 16, 1867; *Chiang-nan chih-tsao-chü chi* (Records of the Kiangnan Arsenal), 11 *chüan,* comp. Wei Yün-kung (Shanghai, 1905), 3. 2, 58; *Chi-ch'i chü* (Arsenals), 2 vols., in *Hai-fang tang* (Files on maritime defense), ed. Kuo T'ing-i et al. (Taiwan, 1957), I, 27–28, 41.

38. *LWCK Letters,* 11.7b, 23b; 13.14b. See also 11.6b, 27b.

39. *LWCK Memorials,* 17.16–17, 36; 20.12–15; 23.19–22; 24.16; 28.1–4.

40. *LWCK Letters,* 10.28; 11.23b, 31b; 12.3. *Chiang-nan chih-tsao-chü chi,* 3.2.

41. *LWCK Letters,* 13.7, 11, 14; 14.38b–39; 15.13b. Sun Yü-t'ang, *Chung-kuo chin-*

tai kung-yeh shih tzu-liao, I, 294, 299; *Chiang-nan chih-tsao-chü chi*, 5.3b–4b.

42. Boulger, *Life of Sir Halliday Macartney*, 188, 198, 209, 212. *LWCK Letters*, 13.11b, 27b; 14.7a, 10. Sun Yü-t'ang, *Chung-kuo chin-tai kung-yeh shih tzu-liao*, I, 327.

43. *IWSM*, T'ung-chih, 84.35; *LWCK Memorials*, 19.44–49.

44. *LWCK Letters*, 12.21, 26b.

45. *LWCK Letters*, 12.25b; 13.2, 13, 28–29, 32b–33.

46. Knight Biggerstaff, *The Earliest Modern Government Schools in China* (Ithaca, 1961), 156–176; *LWCK Letters*, 10.34.

47. *IWSM*, T'ung-chih, 25.9–10b; *LWCK Memorials*, 24.23b; *Letters*, 15.4.

48. *LWCK Letters*, 10.28.

49. *LWCK Letters*, 10.32b; 11.1b, 4b, 7b, 11; 12.3. *Tsungli Yamen Letters*, 1. 19b–22. *Memorials*, 19.7–10. *IWSM*, T'ung-chih, 82.46b–52.

50. *IWSM*, T'ung-chih, 86.13–14b. Hsü Jun, *Hsü Yü-chai tzu-hsü nien-p'u* (Chronological autobiography) (preface dated 1927), 17–23. *LWCK Letters*, 12, 15, 17b; 13.12; 14.1b, 8b–9; 15.12. *Yang-wu yün-tung*, II, 165.

51. *LWCK Tsungli Yamen Letters*, 1.22. *Letters*, 11.12, 31b; 13.6b, 7, 28, 30; 14.31, 38b; 15.14b, 16b.

52. *LWCK Letters*, 13.28b, 32b–33.

53. *Chi-ch'i-chü*, I, 3–5. *LWCK Memorials*, 8.30–31; 9.67–68.

54. *LWCK Letters*, 11.22, 30b; 12.1b–2, 9, 22b; 13.15b, 17b–18, 22, *Memorials*, 22.9–18.

55. *Kou-mai ch'uan-p'ao* (Purchase of ships and weapons), 3 vols., in *Hai-fang tang*, III, 903–910. *LWCK Letters*, 11.31b; 12.2b, 4, 9b.

56. *Kou-mai ch'uan-p'ao*, III, 910–923; *LWCK Tsungli Yamen Letters*, 1.38–40; *Memorials*, 20.32–33b.

57. *LWCK Letters*, 12.31, 34b. See also 12.36b.

58. *LWCK Letters*, 12.28b–29, 30b.

59. *Kou-mai ch'uan-p'ao*, III, 925; *Han-cheng pien* (Section on shipping), 6 vols., in *Chiao-t'ung shih* (History of communications in China), comp. Ministries of Communications and Railroads (Nanking, 1930 ff.), I, 142.

60. Hsü Jun, *Hsü Yü-chai tzu-hsü nien-p'u*, 18. *LWCK Letters*, 13.13b, 23–24; 14.1b–2. Kwang-Ching Liu, "British-Chinese Steamship Rivalry in China, 1873–85," in C. D. Cowan, ed., *Economic Development of China and Japan* (London, 1964), 55–58.

61. *LWCK Tsungli Yamen Letters*, 1.40; *Memorials*, 20.33b.

62. *IWSM*, T'ung-chih, 55.15b–16; Knight Biggerstaff, "The Secret Correspondence of 1867–68: The Views of Leading Chinese Statesmen Regarding the Further Opening of China to Western Influence," *Journal of Modern History*, XXII (1950), 132; *LWCK Memorials*, 19.49b–50.

63. *LWCK Letters*, 12.21, 26b.

64. *LWCK Letters*, 14.30b, 34b; 15.14b. Ellsworth C. Carlson, *The Kaiping Mines, 1877–1912* (Cambridge, Mass., 1957), 7.

65. *LWCK Letters*, 13.21b; 14.2, 19, 30b. *Yang-wu yün-tung*, VII, 70. Morse, *International Relations*, II, 263.

66. *IWSM*, Tung-chih, 98.19–21, 40–42.

67. *LWCK Memorials*, 24.10–25. See also 24.26–28; *Letters*, 15.12–15b.

68. *LWCK Letters*, 14.32; *Tsungli Yamen Letters*, 2.57b–59.

69. *LWCK Letters*, 3.16b–17; 5.28b, 32, 34–35. *Memorials*, 7.29; 17.12.

70. See C. John Stanley, *Late Ch'ing Finance: Hu Kuang-yung as an Innovator* (Cambridge, Mass., 1961), 81–84.

71. *LWCK Memorials*, 12.26; 13.2; 14.32; 15.2b, 6b–7. See also 14.38; 15.17.

72. *IWSM*, T'ung-chih, 98.31–100. 44.

73. *LWCK Letters*, 14.34, 38b–39; 15.1b. *Tung-hua hsü-lu*, T'ung-chih, 100.47–48.

74. *LWCK Letters*, 15.2b. Strangely enough, Prince Ch'un, who had urged a belligerent stand during the crisis created by the Tientsin Massacre, agreed with Li on Sinkiang; see 16.17.

75. *LWCK Letters*, 15.2, 10b; *Ch'ing-chi wai-chiao shih-liao* (Historical materials on foreign relations in the latter part of the Ch'ing dynasty), 243 *chüan* (Peiping, 1932–35), Kuang-hsü, 1, 4–5; *Tung-hua hsü-lu*, T'ung-chih, 98.30, 32; Kuang-hsü, 1.35. Cf. Immanuel C. Y. Hsü, "The Great Policy Debate in China, 1874: Maritime Defense vs. Frontier Defense," *Harvard Journal of Asiatic Studies* XXV (1965), 217–27; Wen-djang Chu, "Tso Tsung-t'ang's Role in the Recovery of Sinkiang," *Tsing Hua Journal of Chinese Studies*, New Series I, no. 3, 136–45.

76. *Tung-hua hsü-lu*, Kuang-hsü. 1.33, 56–57.

77. *LWCK Letters*, 15, 19b, 20b, 21b, 22b, 26b, 30b–31, 33b–35. *Tsungli Yamen Letters*, 3.18; 5.40.

78. *Tung-hua hsü-lu*, Kuang-hsü, 1.56–57. According to Li's information, when the officials at court held a meeting to discuss the proposals on coastal defense, Wen-hsiang was sympathetically inclined toward Li's recommendations on "bureaus of Western learning," railways, telegraph, and mines, but two Chinese officials strongly condemned them, and others at the meeting were indifferent. *LWCK Letters*, 17.13.

79. In a letter to C. Hannen dated October 25, 1875, Robert Hart commented on the Chinese purchase of foreign arms and on the arrangements being made for a modern coal mine on Taiwan: "Forts are bristling all round Tientsin and in many other places, and official talk loves to dwell on the sweet syllables the Chinese mouth makes of the word 'Krupp.' Torpedoes are toys in all the houses, and, as for an eighty-ton gun creating astonishment, the wonder is that thousand-tonners have not yet been devised for the Chinese and sent out in cases, and as numerously, as needles and matches! The big giant is really waking up, but what a time it takes to yawn and rub his eyes!" Quoted in Morse, *International Relations*, II, 163. See also *LWCK Tsungli Yamen Letters*, 3.17–19; Chou Sheng-ch'uan, *Chou Wu-chuang kung i-shu*, *chüan-shou*. 40b.

80. *LWCK Tsungli Yamen Letters*, 3.6–14, 16; 4.26; 5.40b; 6.28–29b. *Letters*, 15.21b, 31, 33b, 36; 16.3, 12, 14b, 21b–22, 26b–27. Stanley F. Wright, *Hart and the Chinese Customs* (Belfast, 1950), 469–74.

81. *LWCK Letters*, 15.14, 16, 22, 24, 27b, 29b–30, 31, 36; 16.3b, 20. *Yang-wu yün-tung*, VII, 103–106, 113.

82. *LWCK Letters*, 15.29, 30b, 33, 35; *Memorials*, 29.1–2; *Tung-hua hsü-lu*, Kuang-hsü, 1.115, 140.

83. *LWCK Letters*, 16.12. *Tsungli Yamen Letters*, 4.39. *Memorials*, 28.1–4; 33.25–29.

84. *LWCK Letters*, 15.35–36b; 16.1b; 3.5b, 7–9, 14b, 22, 24, 31b, 34b–36. *Tsungli Yamen Letters*, 6.37b–38. Shen Pao-chen, *Shen Wen-su kung cheng-shu* (Works of Shen Pao-chen), 8 vols. (1880), *chüan* 6–7. Sun Yü-t'ang, *Chung-kuo chin-tai kung-yeh shih tzu-liao*, I, 282. 299–300, 317–19, 328. *Yang-wu yün-tung*, IV, 37–41. Liu, "British-Chinese Steamship Rivalry," 60.

Part III
Li in the Role of a National Official

4

Li Hung-chang and Shen Pao-chen: The Politics of Modernization

David P. T. Pong

Politics is about power, the exercise of power over human and material resources, and the priority with which these resources are to be acquired, developed, or deployed. In the context of Ch'ing China in the second half of the nineteenth century, politics entails, at least in part, choosing an appropriate solution for preserving the dynasty in the face of internal disorder and Western as well as Japanese imperialism. Questions concerning the necessity of change, the direction of change, and the control and deployment of resources to bring about that change were the central issues of the day.

Beginnings

In the decades beginning with the mid-1850s, a period generally described as the Ch'ing Restoration,[1] these issues can be profitably studied by examining the relationship of two political figures. One was Li Hung-chang; the other, Shen Pao-chen. Born within three years of each other, in 1823 and 1820, respectively, the two enjoyed certain superficial similarities in their early careers. They both earned their metropolitan degree (*chin-shih*) in 1847; Li was placed thirty-ninth and Shen forty-second in the examination. Both earned a place in the Hanlin Academy for further studies (*shu-chi-shih*), and both did well enough in the examinations at the end of the third year (1850) to be appointed Compiler of the Second Class (*pien-hsiu*) in the Hanlin Academy.

After serving in different but comparable capacities as metropolitan officials over the next few years, their career paths diverged. This was largely because of the fact that Li's home province of Anhwei was at this time seriously threatened by rebels. In 1853, Li was ordered by the throne to accompany his father and return to his native province to deal with the Nien and the Taiping rebels. He

79

quickly became a militia (t'uan-lien) organizer. Shen, on the other hand, was allowed to pursue his bureaucratic career further. He was made a Supervisory Censor for the Kiangnan Circuit (Chiang-nan tao chien-ch'a yü-shih) in 1854, with responsibilities over the provinces of Kiangsu and Anhwei.[2]

Thus, from the early fifties on, Li's rise to prominence was largely due to his success as a militia organizer and, after 1858, as Tseng Kuo-fan's personal aide as well. Tseng, his teacher during his student days in Peking and a friend of his father's, remained his patron and friend from this point on. Meanwhile, Shen rose to fame primarily as a local official, first as a prefect (in early 1856) and then as a taotai (1857–59), although he also served Tseng in his campaign headquarters, albeit briefly and informally in early 1856. Without glossing over some of his spectacular feats in organizing local defense, it must be stressed that Shen's reputation at this time was built on his solid performance as a civil administrator. In short, both Li and Shen had excelled in their respective roles. Their talents had soon attracted sufficient attention for their being appointed governors in early 1862: Li became governor for the important province of Kiangsu and Shen for Kiangsi. Li was then thirty-nine years old and Shen forty-two.[3]

Up to this point, the relationship between Li and Shen had been good. After all, they were metropolitan graduates of the same year (t'ung-nien) and, more important, had shared the same examiner (Sun Chiang-ming).[4] Under the Ch'ing, after the examinations were over and the results known, the candidates and their examiner were expected to develop a kind of teacher-disciple relationship.[5] As "disciples" of the same "teacher," Shen and Li could well have developed strong ties. On the other hand, the significance of t'ung-nien associations can be exaggerated. The history of the mid-nineteenth century is full of conflicts among such scholar-officials. But where common interests existed, t'ung-nien relationships could assume great importance.

In the fifties and early sixties, what bonded Shen and Li together more than anything else was their common patron, Tseng Kuo-fan. Although they did not serve under Tseng at the same time, they certainly shared in the esprit de corps that existed among Tseng's protégés. It was this and their t'ung-nien connection that brought them together for a long chat one evening in 1858 when Li, on his way to visit his mother and brother, Han-chang, stopped at Kuang-hsin (northeast Kiangsi), the seat of Shen's taotaiship.[6] Also thanks to these connections, they tended to look after each other's interest when called for. For example, in 1860, Li disputed the severity of Tseng's punishment of a subordinate who was routed by the Taipings. Whereupon, as one story goes, Tseng, in an attempt to rid himself of Li, recommended for the latter a circuit intendancy in Fukien, Shen's home province. At that juncture, Shen, who was in self-imposed retirement at Foochow, tending his aging parents and also training militia, wrote to Li and advised against his accepting the appointment. As Shen put it, the political conditions in Fukien were so oppressive that a man as gifted as Li would find no future there.[7] Whether or not this story is true, Tseng and Li soon patched up their differences, opening the way for Li's ascendance as the leader of the Huai Army and the governor of Kiangsu.[8] As noted above, Shen was made governor of Kiangsi at about the same time.

The two governors

During the three years from early 1862 until the spring of 1865, when Shen once again retired to Foochow, this time to mourn his mother's death, the relationship between him and Li Hung-chang can be viewed from several perspectives. First, there were few direct official transactions between the two men. Rather, their relationship revolved around their individual ties with Tseng Kuo-fan, the undisputed dominant figure in the final phase of the Taiping war. Although both Li and Shen had become powerful officials in their own right, the inescapable fact was that they owed their rise to Tseng who, as governor-general of the Liangkiang provinces (Kiangsu, Anhwei, and Kiangsi), continued to be their superior. Geographically and strategically, they made up the flanks of Tseng's campaign based in southern Anhwei, and they were given very specific and different tasks. Li's task was to defend the key city of Shanghai to the east, in a province largely occupied by rebels, and to channel the wealth of that city to Tseng's headquarters. Shen's job was to maintain the security of Kiangsi to the southwest, a province which, though constantly under threat and never free of rebels, was to serve as Tseng's main source of military funds and protect his recruiting ground and home province of Hunan.[9] In carrying out their charge, Shen and Li were required to deal far more with Tseng than with each other.

But Shen and Li were not equals in this triangular relationship. At first, in early 1862, Shen, though still in mourning, enjoyed much greater prestige nationally. Not only was he the son-in-law of Lin Tse-hsü but he had also proved his mettle as an extraordinarily able and dedicated local official in the province where he now was the governor. Because of his courage, resolution, and willingness to sacrifice his own life to save the prefectural seat of Kuang-hsin in 1856, he had literally become a legend in his own time. During his first self-imposed retirement in 1859–61, he was repeatedly urged to resume an active career, not just by Hu Lin-i and Tseng Kuo-fan and his aides (including Li Hung-chang) but also by such eminent metropolitan officials as Wen-hsiang (senior vice president of the Board of Revenue) and Sung Chin (vice president of the Board of Works). But Shen consistently declined until late 1861 when he agreed to serve Tseng at Anking with the proviso that he would be allowed to visit his parents once a year. Then, on his way to Tseng's camp, Shen received an edict appointing him governor of Kiangsi.[10] For one who had never held an office higher than a taotaiship, the appointment was a big jump up the bureaucratic ladder.

Li Hung-chang, by contrast, had never served as a provincial official before his governorship. There is no doubt that he distinguished himself as a militia leader in Anhwei and as an aide to Tseng Kuo-fan from 1858 on—Tseng particularly valued him as a policymaker and memorial drafter—but he had no proven record as a territorial administrator. Even when Tseng instructed him to raise an Anhwei army, he had no intention of giving Li sole responsibility for defending Shanghai, a role Tseng had reserved for his younger brother, Kuo-ch'üan. It was only after Kuo-ch'üan had declined the assignment—his eyes were set on the plum, the capture of Nanking—that Li's mission was upgraded. Still, the assignment did not call for a territorial appointment. Thus, when Tseng recommended him and Shen for a governorship in January 1862, the throne readily gave Shen the province of Kiangsi but held out on deciding Li's assignment until more than three months later.[11]

Once in place, however, the ties between Shen and Tseng, and those between Li and Tseng, began to change, eventually also altering the relationship between Shen and Li. As noted, Tseng had had specific objectives in mind when he made his moves toward placing Shen in Kiangsi and Li in Kiangsu. In different ways, the job of the new governors was to render him assistance, particularly financial assistance. The degree to which they succeeded was certainly going to affect their relationship with Tseng, and possibly their mutual relationship as well. In the process, personal, political, and ideological factors all came into play.

The preceding analysis has shown that, given Li's career up to early 1862, his appointment to a governorship, compared to Shen's, was more of a surprise. Thus, despite Tseng Kuo-fan's initial reluctance to give him full power (to better protect the interests of his brother, Kuo-ch'üan), Li was more directly and deeply indebted to Tseng for his elevation. We may surmise that Li, who had become somewhat prone to seeking ideological authority beyond Confucianism and had come to think more about power (pa-shu) than the cultivation of the self in public service,[12] would allow this fact to influence his behavior as governor in a substantial way. If our assumption is correct that he felt deeply indebted to Tseng, we may expect a readiness on his part to accommodate Tseng's needs and desires whenever possible. This, in fact, occurred. As a provider of military funds, Li lived up to Tseng's expectations. To be sure, Shanghai was a rich commercial city where large amounts of custom duties and likin were collected, but it was not an inexhaustible source. For as Li's own military operations expanded, Tseng's demand for money also soared. And although Tseng had to apply pressure on Li from time to time, he always secured the funds in the end, and Li, even at the risk of alienating the Shanghai gentry and elite, or receiving a censure from Peking, was willing to oblige.[13] At the same time, Li was careful not to expand his campaigns too much in order not to undercut Tseng's brother's ambition to be the sole conqueror of Nanking.[14] Although we may be judging Li too quickly, it would appear nonetheless that Li the governor was more compliant with Tseng Kuo-fan's wishes than Li the private assistant who, it may be recalled, once objected so strongly to Tseng's impeachment of a subordinate that he temporarily left his service. As he now explained, one had to be accommodating in managing matters of importance.[15]

By contrast, Shen Pao-chen had not been as deeply indebted to Tseng. His service in the latter's campaign headquarters in early 1856 was brief. And when he became a territorial official in northern Kiangsi in the middle of that year, he was first and foremost answerable to the authorities in his own province, although he continued to operate under Tseng on military matters. Under this arrangement, Tseng's influence on him and his career declined. At the same time, Shen's loyalties also became unavoidably divided, and he began to feel the stress of having to serve two masters. Nevertheless, as Shen's reputation as an effective local official rose and as his territory increased in strategic importance, Tseng wanted to make greater use of him. Thus, a year after Shen became a taotai in mid-1857, he was entrusted with the responsibility for providing military supplies for Tseng's troops who were then pressing their way in the direction of the Taiping capital at Nanking.[16] Shen was able to meet most of Tseng's demands but, in doing so, he had incurred the displeasure of his superiors in Kiangsi. He was eventually saved from an increasingly untenable position by the death of his only surviving brother, compelling him to retire in mid-1859 to look after his parents.[17]

If circumstances had saved Shen at that time from an awkward situation, he still could not avoid a similar predicament during his governorship (1862–65). As he saw it, his primary responsibility as governor was the security of the province. A well-governed province was certainly the surest way to restore social order and prevent the kind of discontent that would feed the Taiping cause. A rapid program of rehabilitation would also generate more resources that could both defend the province and help finance Tseng Kuo-fan's campaign.[18] These were objectives to which Tseng heartily subscribed. In fact, it was Tseng who, in 1861, started a tax reduction scheme for Kiangsi with a view toward containing corruption and increasing that province's financial contribution to his military operations.[19] The same considerations were also behind his recommendation of Shen for the governorship. As a dedicated Confucian administrator, Shen could be entrusted with a province; as a former private assistant of his, as well as a protégé, Shen was also expected to be more sympathetic to his financial needs.

In most respects, Shen indeed lived up to Tseng's expectations. He cleaned up the government, ferreted out corrupt or incompetent officials, punished oppressive gentry, promoted able men in government, and looked after the well-being of the common people.[20] He refined Tseng's tax reduction scheme to make it more flexible and feasible, and buttressed it with a centralized budgeting system for the entire province, so that no office would suffer from inadequate funds as a consequence of the tax reform. Liu K'un-i, Shen's successor in 1865, applauded the scheme for having benefited both the government and the people.[21] Over a decade later, in 1878, the conservative ideologue, Huang T'i-fang, praised both Tseng and Shen for their tax policy which, among other benefits, had also reduced official corruption. These two officials, he said, were "just and loyal in serving the empire; they really understand the business of government."[22]

It was Shen and Tseng's hope that the lower tax burden would induce the gentry to "contribute" more to military campaigns, especially Tseng's campaigns. The extent to which they succeeded is uncertain. Whatever fresh "contributions" there were, they went primarily, if not entirely, to the local militia and perhaps also to the several thousand mercenaries (*yung*) that Shen was forced to recruit in late 1862 and early 1863. But, as far as it can be ascertained, little went to Tseng Kuo-fan.[23]

In fact, as the months and years went by, a decreasing amount of financial aid went from Kiangsi to Tseng's camp, and more and more revenues were kept for the defense and rehabilitation of the province. To some degree, Kiangsi's moves to recover some of its resources previously promised to Tseng were necessitated by the fact that Tseng could no longer keep his original pledge to protect Kiangsi. As Tseng pressed toward Nanking, his forces were just too far away. Perhaps an even more important factor in this dispute was Shen's sense of priority that led him to retain an increasingly larger amount of funds for Kiangsi's internal use. As he argued, good government was the most effective prevention against disorder; military suppression was only a cure.[24] Tseng accepted this premise but, given the military emergency, he was not prepared to live with the consequences. A dispute over the disbursement of Kiangsi's financial resources arose, coming to a head in the latter part of 1863. There were many heated exchanges, and Tseng berated Shen for being impertinent in his official capacity and inconsiderate toward his patron and colleague.[25]

The dispute was disturbing enough for many to fear that the Shen-Tseng split would seriously weaken the dynastic cause.[26] Li Hung-chang certainly did not want to see a running feud between the two, one being a friend, the other a patron. As if to underscore the fact that he was an understanding colleague, Li wrote to Li Huan, Kiangsi's treasurer and Shen's right-hand man, saying that the conflict arose only because both men were eager to assume responsibility.[27] The blame should be equally shared, he told Shen: Tseng was too peevish and Shen unnecessarily excessive in his language. But, conscious of his own indebtedness to Tseng, Li reminded Shen of Tseng's patronage.[28] Then, turning to Tseng, Li, thinking that Shen's recent decision to retire was caused by the rupture, urged Tseng to work toward reconciliation so that Shen could be persuaded to stay. The latter, he argued, should not be allowed to withdraw from office at a time when the empire was so desperately in need of capable leaders.[29]

One could vaguely detect a sense of awkwardness on Li's part. And, for as long as Tseng and Shen refused even to write to each other, it would have been difficult for Li to work with Shen if the occasion arose. This standoff continued at least into the late 1860s.[30] In the long run, however, what also prevented Shen and Li from drawing closer to each other were the location and nature of their jobs. In Li's case, the organization of a new army was virtually a condition of his appointment as governor. In war-torn Kiangsu, his responsibilities remained largely military. As his operations expanded, his Huai Army also grew to some seventy thousand strong. Li was obviously not an ordinary governor preoccupied with civil administration.

This leads us to the second perspective from which to view the relationship between Li and Shen: the interaction resulting from their contrasting world views and the different environments in which they operated. What really made Li an unusual leader in the early 1860s was his ability to grasp the situation. Even before the idea of sending him to Shanghai was broached, he recognized that the city held one of the keys to a successful campaign against the Taipings. When he finally left for Shanghai in early 1862, he did so by steamship, the first high official to travel by steamship over a significant distance. As he put it, he was "using barbarian [ways] to change China."[31] Though referring only to his abandonment of the traditional modes of transportation in favor of the steamboat, this terse statement foreshadowed his new approach to building a stronger China.[32]

Once in Shanghai, Li quickly learned and adopted "barbarian ways." By this time there already existed a Sino-foreign defense force, the Ever-Victorious Army, led and drilled by foreign mercenaries, using Western firearms. Fighting alongside this semimodern army, Li, impressed by its equipment and discipline, admitted that he felt a deep sense of shame because of the inferiority of Chinese arms. As he put it, "If one is stationed at Shanghai for some time and yet unable to learn from the foreigners' strengths, there will be many regrets." He therefore called upon his officers to learn with humility.[33] Within six months, a thousand of his troops were given Western guns and trained in their use. In less than a year, China's first field gun units were formed. Li's troops soon became the most modern in China and, in 1863, he set up three small arsenals, one under Halliday Macartney, a doctor detached from the British military forces, and the other two completely managed and operated by Chinese. These arsenals were the forerunners of the Kiangnan Arsenal.[34]

By contrast, Shen's preoccupation was with the civil administration of Kiangsi Province. His military activities were mainly concerned with the reorganization of existing forces, not the creation of a new army. The foreign presence in Kiangsi was also very different in character from that found in Li's province. Trade in the newly opened treaty port, Kiukiang, was limited. The custom duties collected there for the period up to 1864 amounted to less than 5 percent of Kiangsi's total revenue.[35] The conduct of foreign relations in Kiangsi was restricted to the settlement of minor disputes, the suppression of smuggling, and the curtailment of aggressive missionaries and their converts.[36]

Influenced by his anti-British teacher (Lin Ch'ang-i), father-in-law Lin Tsehsü, and such ching-shih scholars as Wei Yüan,[37] Shen was troubled by China's deteriorating international position. China's defeat by the Anglo-French forces in 1860 also deeply affected him.[38] It is not at all surprising that he wanted to enforce the treaties vigorously to curb further Western encroachment. But Shen was not blindly antiforeign. For example, he would not hesitate to use a steamship for river patrol. The steamer, confiscated from American merchants who had violated trade regulations, had a Western captain and an engineer hired from Shanghai.[39] On principle, he also had no objection to either the steamship or the employment of a foreign crew for such purposes as tribute grain transportation as long as the vessels were owned by the Chinese and the crew placed under Chinese control.[40] But, at this early stage of his exposure to Western contraptions, he saw the telegraph and railways essentially as threats to China's administrative and territorial integrity.[41] He had yet to see the possibility of the Chinese harnessing these foreign amenities for their own benefit. At the same time, Li Hung-chang, being constantly pressed by the foreigners' demand for the introduction of these new means of communication, had begun to advocate that, should the pressure become irresistible, the Chinese should meet the challenge by putting up their own lines.[42] Li's was the most advanced view in 1865. Two years later, however, Shen too became convinced of the usefulness of railways and telegraph lines. He was now prepared to permit foreign-built lines as long as popular opposition could be defused.[43] But Shen's change of mind came only after he had left Kiangsi and had become the head of the Foochow Navy Yard, the empire's first full-fledged naval establishment. He had thus become much more familiar with Western technology.

On balance, then, the foreign presence in Kiangsi during Shen's governorship was more troublesome than beneficial. But environmental differences cannot fully explain the contrasting views of Li and Shen toward the West, for much of that can also be attributed to their views about government and politics. As noted earlier, Li had a more modern, though not necessarily superior, understanding of power. He was also more favorably disposed toward the merchant community.[44] For him, "self-strengthening" meant military and economic power. Shen, on the other hand, had a more Confucian, moralistic view about the purpose of government, which was to ensure that both the country's economic interests and the people's livelihoods (*kuo-chi min-sheng*) were duly looked after.[45] At the root of this was the restoration of the social fabric and moral fiber according to the highest Confucian standards. "Self-strengthening" must therefore begin with self-regulation in government (*tzu-chih*, lit. self-government). This included reforming both the administrative practices and structure of the Ch'ing system from the emperor down. Only then, Shen argued, could the Chinese deal with foreign matters (*yang-wu*), adopt Western ideas and technology, and achieve true "self-strengthening."[46] Thus, even as the views of Li and Shen on Western technology began to converge, there remained fundamental philosophical differences between the two men.

Li and Shen in the age of the arsenals and shipyards

In 1866, Tseng Kuo-fan and Li Hung-chang were the only ones who had an arsenal at their disposal. For as long as either of them remained governor-general of Liangkiang, their control over the Kiangnan Arsenal was strong and gave them additional political power vis-à-vis other provincial officials and the central government. This virtual monopoly over the modern defense industry was soon broken with the proposed establishment of a modern naval dockyard by Tso Tsung-t'ang in mid-1866.

Li at first was not opposed to the building of steam-powered warships in China. In 1864, nearly two years before Tso took the initiative to create a navy yard, Li insisted that the Chinese, in order to prevent future insults from the West, must emulate the West and build steamships. "We should first produce wooden steamers, to be followed at a later stage by warships with large guns, so that we can protect our approaches from the sea," he said, and blamed the Chinese scholar-officials for not seeing the light.[47] Yet, in 1872, six years after Tso Tsung-t'ang's Foochow Navy Yard had been launched and was facing unprecedented financial difficulties, he claimed that he had been opposed to the idea of a naval dockyard all along. As he wrote to Tseng Kuo-fan:

> The building of steamers and warships is indeed one way to self-strengthening but, given the political system of China where there exists little unity [of purpose] between the government and the people or between the central government and the provinces, I worry that our efforts, after they had been put in place, cannot produce salutary results. Therefore, in 1866, when Tso Tsung-t'ang proposed the construction of steamships, I dared not go along with his ideas. On the other hand, if we concentrate on making arms and ammunitions, we [not being dependent on broadly based support] are in control of our destiny. And even if we lack naval defense, we are at least prepared on land.[48]

Li then went on to say that, under ideal conditions where money and time were both available, the Chinese might be in a position to challenge the West on land and at sea in about a century. But where money was short and people expected quick results, the shipbuilding policy was ill conceived.

Whether Li, in 1866, was opposed to a modern shipbuilding industry per se or only to one controlled by a political rival is open to question. It should be noted that he and Tseng Kuo-fan were then still engaged in rebel suppression north of the Yangtze. Given his needs at the time, it is understandable that he should have favored the ordnance industry. Moreover, as he had already invested years of energy and resources on arms production for the land forces, the continuation and expansion of that industry was a natural course for him to take. The situation with Tso Tsung-t'ang, however, was different. By 1866, he, as governor-general of Chekiang and Fukien, had already pacified the rebels in the southern coastal provinces; equipping the land forces there with modern weapons seemed less urgent. Tso could look ahead and think of the future—the threat from the seas. Riding on the crest of his successes during the Taiping years, Tso thought he had the power and the prestige to see through an ambitious naval program. It was with great confidence that he launched the Foochow Navy Yard in 1866.[49]

While Li and Tso might have read the situation of the mid-1860s differently, personal rivalry probably fueled their differences. Li had remained loyal to his patron Tseng Kuo-fan whereas Tso had fallen out with Tseng.[50] The reasons for their seeking different paths to modernize the empire's defense could thus be situational and conceptual, as well as political and personal. Among other advantages, the creation of a naval dockyard could give Tso a power base in the postrebellion age. And when Tso was dispatched to deal with the Muslim rebels in the Northwest in late 1866, he picked Shen Pao-chen to be his successor as the director-general of the Foochow Navy Yard. Shen had cooperated closely with Tso during the early 1860s in the war against the Taipings, and he, too, as noted earlier, had become estranged from Tseng at that time. Apart from their being aggrieved for similar reasons, Tso also held Shen's father-in-law, Lin Tse-hsü, in high esteem.[51] In appearance, at least, the bond between them was strong. No wonder people were already talking about the split of the empire's leading officials into competing camps of confederates.[52]

However, to see the history of the self-strengthening movement mainly in terms of personal or factional rivalry is misleading. All the key leaders of the movement had become quite convinced of the need to engage in *yang-wu* long before personal grudges began to sour relationships. More important, it is often overlooked that Li Hung-chang, the archetype of regional leaders of the period, was not and could not afford to be concerned with his own power in isolation. He was politically smart enough to recognize that his own power depended on the survival of the whole *yang-wu* enterprise. Thus, soon after Shen Pao-chen became the head of the Foochow Navy Yard, Li wrote Shen, now regarded as Tso Tsung-t'ang's protégé, a rather warm letter inquiring after the state of the Navy Yard's development. He also gave a few words of advice:

> People may worry about the difficulties in building the ships, I worry more about the proper and effective use of these vessels after they have been built. People may worry about the difficulties in establishing such a pioneering enterprise in China, I worry more about how we can keep what we may achieve in the future and further expand our endeavors.[53]

These were sincere words. Coming from one who confessed his disapproval of the idea of a navy yard, they are revealing. Li then indicated that he would take one of the Foochow steamships after the Nien rebels had been suppressed.

The story of Shen Pao-chen's quarrel with Tseng Kuo-fan and his subsequent close relationship with Tso Tsung-t'ang was well known to officials who lived through the Taiping era. Li Hung-chang was aware of it. Was his letter, then, an attempt to woo Shen back to his and Tseng's camp? Did he want Shen on his side so badly that he was prepared to modify his views on shipbuilding?

If it was Li's intent to wrench Shen away from Tso, he had failed. My study of the history of the Foochow Navy Yard has shown that Shen remained close to Tso Tsung-t'ang. There was much mutual support between the two until 1876. In any event, Li did not really change his view on steamship construction. The real test of his attitude on the matter came in 1872 when the shipbuilding effort came under attack.

By the second part of 1871 the Foochow Navy Yard was experiencing a period of financial difficulties as the cost of maintaining its vessels began to exceed the budget line by an increasing margin.[54] To alleviate its financial burden, the throne ordered the maritime provinces to adopt Foochow ships for their coastal patrol. But the provinces responded with silence.[55] Li Hung-chang, who had earlier intimated to Shen that he would like to acquire a Foochow gunboat, was also hesitant. Li finally came to the Navy Yard's rescue only after the entire shipbuilding effort, including that at the Kiangnan Arsenal, was called into question.

In early 1872 the Foochow Navy Yard had spent the budgeted three million taels for the shipbuilding program, but only six of the projected sixteen vessels had been completed. Taking advantage of its financial difficulties, Sung Chin, a subchancellor of the Grand Secretariat, criticized both the Foochow Navy Yard and the Kiangnan Arsenal for overspending while producing inferior steamships. He suggested that both institutions be closed and their steamers leased to merchants, using the proceeds for repairs and maintenance.[56] Sung's charges sparked off a controversy, lasting a good part of 1872.

Earlier, Li Hung-chang had already noted the huge expenditures consumed by the Foochow Navy Yard. Now, immediately after Sung Chin's memorial, he wrote to his dear friend and governor of Fukien, Wang K'ai-t'ai, indicating his preferred solutions to Foochow's problems. If shipbuilding were to be continued, he said, it was possible to finance it by using the vessels to carry tribute grain or by selling or leasing them to merchants. But, considering the small cargo capacity of the vessels, the merchants might not be forthcoming. The latter might also question the navigational skills of the Chinese crew. Li was therefore prepared for closure. The only trouble, he noted, was that the Foochow Navy Yard was bound by a contract with the foreign engineers, but he thought that the contract could be renegotiated to effect an earlier termination.[57] The closure of the shipbuilding program at Kiangnan, Li implied, would cause no such complications.

Li's earlier objection to spending China's scant resources on steamship building was now reinforced by his political sense for survival. He was willing to meet Sung Chin's demand more than halfway. The future of the shipbuilding effort was further jeopardized in early April 1872 when Wen-yü's response to Sung Chin's charges reached the throne. Wen-yü was the Tartar General of Foochow who had control over the funds collected by the Maritime Customs in that port, monies that funded the Foochow Navy Yard. The Tartar General, however, was at least as interested in lining his pocket as he was in disbursing the custom duties for public endeavors. The inexorable demand for funds by the Navy Yard threatened his interests. It is not surprising that he, too, favored retrenchment and early repatriation of the foreign technicians employed in modern shipbuilding.[58] Motivation aside, Wen-yü was the father-in-law of Prince Kung's eldest son. His word carried considerable weight.[59]

Circumstances, however, prevented Li from pursuing his antisteamship policy. For even before Wen-yü's memorial appeared, Tseng Kuo-fan strongly defended the shipbuilding efforts at Kiangnan and Foochow. While admitting that Chinese-built ships were both expensive and inferior, he maintained that the goal of the shipbuilding policy—to strengthen China's defense—was basically sound. He recognized the financial problem at hand and suggested that the Kiangnan Arsenal, which he had helped to found, switch to constructing cargo ships and to making them available to merchants under favorable terms. Tseng then promised to look into the matter further before memorializing the throne. It was a promise unfulfilled—he died on March 12—but he had made himself clear.[60]

Tseng's position was well known to Li. Much of the machinery Tseng originally acquired for the Kiangnan Arsenal was for shipbuilding. And, given his relationship with the elder statesman, Li had to be rather circumspect. As indicated, Li justified his reservation about shipbuilding by citing political reasons. Already, he pointed out, one governor-general (Wu T'ang) had been dismissed from Foochow, and another (Ying-kuei) was taking a leave of absence because of the difficulties surrounding the Navy Yard. Now, Shen Pao-chen, who was in mourning, was also considering resignation. Meanwhile, Wang K'ai-t'ai, Fukien's governor, had repeatedly sought Li's advice as to the means to deal with the steamship maintenance problem. In short, the Foochow Navy Yard had caused many a political casualty, while the empire's officials, Li observed, were more interested in their own careers than in the fate of the dynasty. Therefore, even if the provincial authorities were changed a hundred times, the same difficulties would remain. Li then pointed out that in China there was a shortage of both human and material resources, each exacerbating the other. By contrast, there was in Japan a strong leadership from above and wholehearted support from below and, consequently, there was no lack of either. So, for as long as there was no unity of purpose in China, the shipbuilding enterprise would continue to cause political disputes. Thus, by way of explanation, Li had apologized to his former patron for his want of enthusiasm for the shipbuilding effort at Kiangnan. But, recognizing Tseng's role as a pioneer promoter of China's shipbuilding effort, he urged Tseng to uphold his views. He then closed the discussion by considering means by which Chinese merchants could cooperate with the government in commercializing the steamships.[61]

Li's equivocal stance and Wen-yü's critical memorial put the Tsungli Yamen in an awkward position. Under the circumstances, it decided to open up the discussion by instructing Li, Shen Pao-chen, and Tso Tsung-t'ang "to go public" and memorialize on the matter.[62] Fully knowing that the last two were deeply committed to naval development, and perhaps sensing as well that Li would be less critical in public, the Yamen's move amounted to a strong effort to save the shipbuilding program.

Both Tso and Shen responded promptly. Needless to say, Tso gave the Foochow Navy Yard his unqualified support. The details of his argument do not concern us here.[63] Shen's memorial was even more forceful.[64] He began by appealing to the patriotic sentiments of those taking part in the debate. The way of "self-strengthening," he said, was not one of aggrandizement; nor was it an expression of expansionist intentions. Its aim was to protect the Chinese Empire and its people. What happened after the Treaty of Nanking was therefore reason enough for continued military and naval preparation. Of course, he could not deny that Chinese-built vessels were inferior but argued that Western shipbuilding too had once had a modest beginning. It was only after decades of development that the Western nations eventually acquired the ability to produce superior steamships. Even then they had to continue learning from each other to keep abreast of the latest technological advances. Therefore, for the Chinese, there was no escape from this long road of naval development.

Shen then justified the overspending at the Foochow Navy Yard by listing its many new facilities, all of which had to be added because the French directors, unable to visualize the magnitude of the undertaking when it was first begun, had miscalculated. Further, if the Navy Yard were to close now, existing ships could not be repaired; if the European staff were dismissed, 700,000 to 800,000 taels would have to be found for their severance pay and repatriation. This was not the way to save money. Besides, if the Chinese terminated the contract at will, no foreigner would trust them in the future.

Finally, Shen firmly rejected the idea of cutting expenses before the Europeans had left. Even after their departure, he insisted, the salary funds should not be channeled elsewhere but used instead to send Chinese students abroad for further studies. Instead of beating a retreat under pressure, Shen urged a more general program of modernization. Taking advantage of the occasion, he reiterated a previous proposal to replace the outdated traditional military examinations with tests on mathematics, which he and some of China's progressive officials considered the foundation of Western science.[65] In addition, to create a truly naval unit out of the Foochow vessels now scattered among the provinces, he proposed a new item of expenditure of five hundred taels a month to bring them back to Foochow periodically for muster.

Confronted with the strong memorials of Tso Tsung-t'ang and Shen Pao-chen, Li Hung-chang now felt compelled to modify his position, at least in public.[66] In his memorial, he argued that the Chinese, in order to defend themselves, must learn from the West to produce better guns and steamships. But the Westerners' present military and naval power took more than a century to achieve. Given time, the Chinese too could produce similar results. This was the objective Tseng Kuo-fan and Tso Tsung-t'ang had in mind when they started their shipbuilding projects, fully aware of the enormity of their undertakings. Increased production, however, would eventually result in lower cost. This was the principle of Western-style manufacture. The experience at the Kiangnan Arsenal, Li claimed, bore this out. He therefore pleaded for greater flexibility and patience in the central government's policy toward the Foochow Navy Yard.

After this plea on behalf of the Navy Yard, Li returned to a position that was more genuinely his own: China stood a much better chance of success if its resources were invested in developing its land forces and harbor defense craft such as small, armor-plated gunboats. Nonetheless, the Powers should not be given free rein on the sea. Means should therefore be found to maintain the additional gunboats the Navy Yard produced—by scrapping the outmoded war junks of the water forces. On their part, the officials in charge at Kiangnan and Foochow should also modify their policy. At Kiangnan, plans were underway to construct merchant ships. Li suggested that Foochow should also adopt a similar policy, alternating between merchantmen and men-of-war.[67]

Li's solution, then, was a compromise between the critics and opponents of the warship industry and its staunch proponents who, incidentally, had also come to accept the necessity of producing some vessels for commercial purposes.[68] But he came to the industry's rescue only reluctantly, after months of canvassing his friends and colleagues and in the face of pressure coming from the strongly worded memorials of Tso Tsung-t'ang and Shen Pao-chen. Besides, the debate sparked off by Sung Chin also raised the possibility of ending the ordnance industry, threatening a major source of his power. Li was certainly not prepared to sacrifice that industry because of his opposition to the shipbuilding program. As I have suggested elsewhere, Li's defense of steamship construction was largely a political move, not an expression of his conviction.[69]

The debate clearly shows that Li's own interests in the ordnance industry could better survive if he also supported someone else's *yang-wu* effort, even if it was a creation of Tso Tsung-t'ang, a political rival. Whatever the motivation, his public support of the Foochow Navy Yard had brought him and Shen closer together, especially after Li's offer to take three Foochow vessels on behalf of his newly founded shipping enterprise, the China Merchants' Steam Navigation Company. And although, at the same time, he had to warn Shen that the Company, still in its infancy, would not have the capacity to absorb more cargo steamers from Foochow,[70] the basis for greater cooperation between the two had been extended.

The opportunity to cement this new relationship came in 1874 when the Japanese invaded Taiwan on the pretext of punishing the aborigines who had massacred a number of shipwrecked Ryūkyūans three years earlier. During the Taiwan crisis, the court at Peking, acting on Li's advice, ordered Shen to take a few ships to Taiwan under the guise of a routine patrol to keep track of Japanese movements.[71] Soon after, Shen was appointed Imperial Commissioner in charge of Maritime Defense and Foreign Affairs in relation to Taiwan. All the military and civil officials of Fukien from the brigade general and the taotai down were placed under his command, as were the steamships of the provinces from Kiangsu to Kwangtung.[72] Armed with these powers, Shen drafted two vessels from Li's Kiangnan Arsenal.[73] Then Li, on his part, offered Shen 6,500 men (thirteen battalions) from his Huai Army for service on Taiwan.[74] In addition, gunpowder from the Tientsin Arsenal as well as guns and rockets from the Nanking Arsenal, both under Li's influence, were also sent to Taiwan. Meanwhile, Shen, in an attempt to make full use of China's modern defense resources without regard to provincial boundaries, also purchased Remington rifles for his troops because, he explained, the Kiangnan Arsenal was in the process of making ammunition for the guns and had the capacity to repair them.[75]

It would be a mistake to think of Li and Shen cooperating only in times of crises. Nor should their relationship be examined only in terms of direct interactions between them. In fact, their relationship can better be understood when seen in the context of an increasing convergence of ideas and interests in defense modernization.

Their ideas on the telegraph have already been mentioned. By 1874, Shen was so eager to see a line erected that he urged Li, who had the territorial powers that he himself lacked, to start a line in Chihli. This was his reasoning:

> The foreigners have telegraphic lines linking Tientsin, Shanghai, and Canton, and yet we have none. When something happens in the West, they all know about it while we remain ignorant. Though this can still be tolerated, how can we accept the fact that news about China is known to them and not to us?[76]

So when it became obvious that China urgently needed a telegraphic line during the Japanese invasion of Taiwan in mid-1874, and when he was given territorial powers, Shen took steps to construct a line from Foochow to Taiwan.

From the latter part of the 1860s on, both Li and Shen also called for numerous reforms that would result in improving China's international position. The convergence of their ideas is best seen in their proposals during the great policy debate of 1874–75, just after the Japanese invasion of Taiwan.

Space does not permit a detailed comparison of their ideas;[77] here we shall focus mainly on the degree of their convergence. First, Li now conceded that more attention should be given to naval development even though he still felt that the army and coastal defense were more important. In response to Ting Jih-ch'ang's proposal for the establishment of three regional fleets—the northern, the central, and the southern—each with its own commander-in-chief and equipped with sixteen gunboats and large warships, Li gave his strong support, insisting that a service of forty-eight vessels represented the barest minimum for the Ch'ing empire.[78] More interesting was his new attitude toward the ironclad: He now agreed with Shen that these heavily armored vessels were necessary for effective defense and recommended that six such warships be ordered immediately for the proposed regional fleets. As for the smaller warships, Li suggested that some be purchased from the West and the rest be constructed at Kiangnan and Foochow.

Second, Shen's proposals for military modernization included many elements dear to Li's heart.[79] He stressed the importance of training field officers and of combining the use of modern weapons with Western-style drill. Furthermore, he believed the army should be strengthened with the formation of artillery units equipped with heavy rifled guns of ten tons or more. The political importance of this last proposal can be realized if one recalls that Li Hung-chang was the father of China's field gun units. Naturally, Shen advocated the continued modernization of China's ordnance industry which was still very much under Li's influence.

Finally, there was strong agreement between Li and Shen regarding the cultivation of what may be called a modernizing elite, the modernization of the examination system, the abolition or reduction in the size of the decrepit traditional land and water forces, and the generation of funds to support modernizing enterprises by developing mechanized mining and the like. In his memorial, Shen gave credit where credit was due. Thus, in his proposal to send graduates of the Foochow Navy Yard School to further studies in Europe, he cited the success of the youths sent by Tseng Kuo-fan and Li Hung-chang to the United States.

There remained, however, fundamental differences between Li and Shen, differences that can be traced back to their philosophical outlooks and political experiences. Shen, for example, would never have tolerated Li's proposal to legalize domestic cultivation of opium as a means for raising revenue. Nor would he have approved the degree of freedom Li gave to the merchants in the search for wealth and power. More important, Shen continued to see defense modernization as an integral part of the Ch'ing polity. There could be no success if the Ch'ing government itself were run irrationally, inefficiently, or wastefully. Successful *yang-wu* could come only with effective domestic reforms. He therefore pressed for streamlining the government, introducing centralized budgeting and administrative specialization in the Six Boards, and even the reeducation of the emperor.[80] And although both he and Li wanted to modernize the education of the traditional elite and wished for a stronger imperial leadership, Li was far less inclined to meddle with the administrative structure and practices internal to the bureaucracy.

Nevertheless, the area of agreement between the two was great. And although several other provincial officials also shared some of their progressive ideas, none could match the breadth and depth of their reform proposals. As the Tsungli Yamen remarked, the memorials of Shen and Li were the most "concrete and practical."[81] As for Li, he found Shen's ideas so agreeable that he wrote a letter praising Shen for his well-formulated proposals.[82] The ground was laid for the next phase of cooperation between the two.

The two governors-general

It goes without saying that China's maritime defense would become more effective if the coastal provinces worked well together. But since the death of Tseng Kuo-fan in March 1872, Li's counterparts in the south—the governors-general of Liangkiang—had been so frequently changed as to prevent meaningful cooperation between the regions. The fact that the occupants of that office were not sympathetic to Li's ideas on defense modernization further compounded the problem. Thus, when the proposal for the establishment of three regional commands for maritime defense appeared in late 1874, Li nominated Shen Pao-chen and Ting Jih-ch'ang for the central and southern regions. Always mindful of the difficulties he had with other provincial authorities in promoting defense modernization, Li hoped that under the new scheme he could work directly with Shen and Ting.[83]

He soon had to change his plan, however, as the Liangkiang governor-generalship became vacant in mid-January 1875. He now lobbied vigorously to have Shen appointed to the position at Nanking,[84] one that would give a friendly colleague both territorial powers and command of the southern half of the empire's defense system. He could not have been happier when the edict of May 30, 1875, came down naming Shen the governor-general of Liangkiang and superintendent of trade for the Southern Ports. The Southern Commissioner also had the responsibility for maritime defense from Kiangsu to Kwangtung.[85]

The vigor and success with which Li engineered Shen's appointment have often been cited as a sign of growing regionalism, on the one hand, and the rising power of Li, on the other.[86] The danger of assigning too much weight to personal factors is obvious. The relationship between Li and Shen, though generally friendly, had not been particularly strong until the Taiwan crisis of 1874 when they cooperated closely. Shen cannot be characterized as Li's man. As Li himself realized, Shen was "a man of great integrity and extraordinary qualities," but he was also "prone to be short-tempered in handling matters not to his liking, and some may also criticize him for his inability to work harmoniously with others."[87] If Shen could challenge the authority of Tseng Kuo-fan, as he did in the early 1860s, he would not be satisfied to be Li's lackey. On the other hand, Li recognized that Shen's experience at the Foochow Navy Yard would be of great service to the empire, and Shen's commitment to maritime defense would complement his.[88] For the opportunity of having a trustworthy partner at Nanking, Li was prepared to cope with a man known for his political independence and stubbornness.

In the area of naval development, Shen proved unexpectedly supportive. At the conclusion of the great policy debate in mid-1875, a Special Maritime Defense Fund of four million taels per annum was created. The money was to be shared by Li and Shen. Eager to see the early formation of a respectable fleet in the north, Shen immediately offered Li his portion of the Fund for as long as it would take to create such a fleet. In Shen's opinion, this fleet should consist of at least two ironclads, six 250-horsepower corvettes, and ten 80-horsepower gunboats.[89] Given the cost involved in creating a fleet of this magnitude, Shen was in fact handing over to Li his share of the Special Fund for a number of years.

Could Shen's magnanimity be interpreted as payment for Li's efforts at securing his governor-generalship? Available evidence indicates otherwise. First of all, although Li's political maneuvers did result in Shen's appointment to the Nanking post, Shen had built up such a reputation as a successful governor in the early 1860s that he was regarded as a likely candidate for a governor-generalship as early as 1867.[90] Li's efforts are historically important only in that they led to a particular appointment at a specific point in time.

Second, Shen was genuinely eager to see the early development of a single, effective fleet under Li. At the time he surrendered his claim to the Special Fund, he realized that the money, coming from a number of provinces and drawn from several sources (likin and maritime customs), would not be delivered in full. If the undersubscribed Special Fund were still to be divided between him and Li, it would take far too long for each to build up an effective fleet.

As it turned out, only 15 percent of the expected amount for the Special Fund was received by Li in the first four months, and income for the Fund remained at this low level in the subsequent periods. Most provinces either claimed that their meager revenues were already overcommitted or that the little revenue they could spare had to be used for local defense projects. Shen was so upset with the situation that he proposed a joint memorial with Li asking the Board of Revenue to curb further inroads into the Special Fund by the provinces. The memorial was never written because Li considered it an exercise in futility.[91]

Although the Special Fund had been handed over to Li, Shen continued to be strongly protective of the money. Thus, in 1876, he strongly opposed the ten-million-tael foreign loan Tso Tsung-t'ang asked him to raise on his behalf to finance the campaign in the Northwest. Tso had tried to raise the loan through Shen rather than his usual agent, Hu Kuang-yung, because Shen had planned a similar loan during the Taiwan crisis.[92] Furthermore, Shen, unlike Li Hung-chang, had not been critical of his Northwest campaign. If Shen, with his new powers, would negotiate the loan for him, opposition from Li and others could be kept under control. Finally, in Tso's thinking, he had been Shen's patron and had once sacrificed his own valuable military funds to support the Foochow Navy Yard in the early 1870s. Surely, this was the time for Shen to repay his debts.

Shen's objection to the loan thus came as a total surprise to Tso. The details of his argument need not be elaborated upon here. Suffice it to say that Shen had always held the position that foreign loans were not a real source of income and should be reserved only for developmental projects, such as the opening up of Taiwan in order to produce profits in the future, not for military campaigns.[93] What remained unsaid was the fact that the amortization of any sizeable loan would further tie down the country's meager resources, especially the customs revenue, which was the main source of the Special Maritime Defense Fund.

Tso won the battle. The throne permitted him to raise half the money he needed from foreign banks. The other half was to come from domestic sources, including two million taels to be drawn from half the customs revenue earmarked for the Special Maritime Defense Fund.[94] Consequently, income for the Special Fund hit a new low.

The disagreement over the loan caused an irreparable split between Shen and Tso, who quickly accused Shen of doing to him what he did to Tseng Kuo-fan in the early 1860s. This time, Tso claimed, Shen had joined Li Hung-chang to gang up on him.[95] The comparison between the present split and the earlier one is misleading, for now Shen was not defending the interest of his own province but a fund for the entire maritime defense effort. More important, the Fund was at this juncture administered by Li, not by Shen.

In fact, Shen continued to be strongly protective of the Special Fund even against Li's wishes. Starting from the autumn of 1877, increasing pressure was brought to bear on Li to send part of the Special Fund for relief in drought-afflicted Shansi, Honan, and Chihli. Shen at once warned him against giving in to this pressure and sacrifice of China's security. "You will live to regret it," he wrote Li.[96] No matter, in the course of the next few months, Li channeled about 700,000 taels from the Fund for famine relief.[97]

Shen also differed with Li over the direction China's naval development should take. As noted, Shen had had a grandiose plan for the early creation of a large fleet, first in the north, then in the south. Throughout the mid-1870s he had been pressing for the purchase of ironclads so that the Chinese would have a naval force adequate to deal with the Japanese on the high seas. Li, on the other hand, favored the modernization of coastal defense. For this reason, he had used the Special Fund to buy and maintain four Armstrong gunboats of the *Staunch* class. Given the small size of the Special Fund, Li's approach was certainly more realistic. Nevertheless, Shen was disappointed with Li's approach to naval development.[98]

Meanwhile, tensions mounted on the international front. In addition to the Japanese forward policy in the Ryūkyūs and Korea and the Spanish threat in the south (over an old shipwreck incident and the coolie trade), there were difficulties arising from the Margary affair and the Woosung Railway. Defense in the south had to be shored up. Completion of the fortification in the Yangtze estuary, begun by Shen's predecessor (Li Tsung-hsi) during the Taiwan crisis, became an urgent matter. And as funds for the project became seriously inadequate, Shen decided, in early 1878, to retrieve from Li the South's share of the Special Maritime Defense Fund.[99]

Li had no objection to Shen's request, for Li had already agreed to use part of the Special Fund for developing Taiwan's defenses, an undertaking proposed by Ting Jih-ch'ang and approved by him and Shen.[100] Therefore, diverting part of that money to the lower Yangtze area did not represent a significant reduction of Li's share of the Special Fund. By transferring half of the Special Fund back to Shen, Li was perhaps hopeful that Shen, who was less vulnerable to conservative attacks, could better protect it from further encroachments. But as the drought in the northern provinces worsened in 1878, even Shen was unable to withstand the mounting demands from critical *ch'ing-i* spokesmen and had to send half his share of the Special Fund for famine relief.[101]

In short, throughout Shen's incumbency, the funds available for defense modernization in the south remained small. He had to come to terms with undertakings of a smaller scale: Ting Jih-ch'ang's projects on Taiwan and the fortification of the Yangtze estuary. By 1877, he was prepared to follow Li Hung-chang's example and settle for the acquisition of some *Staunch* gunboats, vessels much smaller than the ones he envisaged for his "respectable" fleet. Li agreed to order four such vessels on his behalf. In preparation for their arrival, Shen selected captains for them from the graduates of the Foochow Navy Yard School. But when the newer, more economical and powerful gunboats arrived in November 1879, they were delivered to Li at Tientsin. Li, on the pretext that the older *Staunch* gunboats were due for servicing and repairs at the Kiangnan Arsenal, decided that these older boats should stay in the south for Shen's use after maintenance work had been completed. Shen never lived to see the gunboats. He died in December 1879, still pleading for the purchase of ironclads.[102]

Although the management of the Special Maritime Defense Fund was by far the most important ongoing matter that concerned Li and Shen, numerous other issues also required their attention. Limited space permits discussion of only one other example—the management of the Kiangnan Arsenal. However, other arsenals under Li's control or influence will also be touched upon.

Despite Li's removal to Chihli in 1870, the Kiangnan Arsenal remained under his control. But because of the distances involved, his control was not absolute. The inauguration of the maritime defense program in mid-1875 also added a new dimension, for it gave the Southern Commissioner, Shen, control over all arsenals and defense undertakings in the south, although both the Northern and the Southern Commissioners were expected to cooperate in all matters of defense.[103] Mindful of this new arrangement, Li asked Shen to lend his support to the Kiangnan Arsenal soon after Shen took office in late 1875.[104]

Li's plea proved unnecessary. Shen had had an interest in the development of the Kiangnan Arsenal long before he arrived at Nanking. In part this was because the Arsenal was often lumped together with the Foochow Navy Yard as a target of conservative attacks. More important, Shen saw in it an indispensable supplier of modern arms. During the Taiwan crisis, he bought thousands of Remington rifles from Kiangnan, as he did guns and powder from Li's arsenals at Tientsin and Nanking. Shen thus took an active interest in the Kiangnan Arsenal after he was appointed the governor-general of Liangkiang. He inspected its operation and products both in November 1875 and May 1876. When he looked for an additional gunboat for patrolling the Yangtze, he turned first to Kiangnan. Only when the Arsenal was unable to provide a suitable vessel did he turned to the Foochow Navy Yard. In 1878, he stridently defended the Kiangnan Arsenal from pressures to divert parts of its revenue for famine relief.[105]

To a degree, Shen enjoyed some influence on the internal administration of the Kiangnan Arsenal. He played a major role in organizing its vessels into a squadron and upgrading its training. In an attempt to form a navy on an empire-wide scale, he promoted periodic musters of vessels from all parts of the country, thus incorporating the Kiangnan squadron into a larger force. Only one such muster took place under Shen because of the shortage of funds and the reluctance on the part of other provinces to send more ships. The effectiveness of this exercise was further marred by provincial jealousy.[106]

Because of conservative criticism, Shen also attempted to streamline the financial management of the Kiangnan Arsenal. In 1878, he introduced a biannual accounting system for that establishment. He was also consulted by Li Hung-chang on the selection of the Arsenal's director on the death of Feng Chün-kuang in April 1878.[107] Unfortunately, the extent of Shen's influence in this matter is not known.

Throughout the 1870s, Shen was concerned with the general direction of development of the empire's arsenals, the most important of which remained largely under Li's control or influence. He was particularly troubled by the haphazard and uncoordinated manner in which arms were procured or manufactured. In the policy debate of 1874, he called for specialization and coordination among the major arsenals, a call that he and Li repeated in 1878. No results were achieved, however. Because of the shortage of funds, the numerous types of small arms already in use could not be replaced. The arsenals were thus compelled to continue production of munitions and parts for obsolete guns while trying to manufacture more modern ones. Provincial rivalry and competing interests in buying foreign arms further compounded the problem. Attempts by Shen and Li to introduce a centralized system of arms purchasing came to nothing. Specialization and coordination thus remained wishes unfulfilled.

By and large, despite their differences on many issues, Li and Shen were basically in accord as far as arsenals were concerned. Evidence suggests that Shen regarded the arsenals as an integral part of China's defense efforts rather than Li's property. After Shen's death in 1879, the rapport between Li and the southern commissioners deteriorated, to the detriment of the defense effort.

Conclusion

Li Hung-chang was an astute politician. Compared to Shen Pao-chen, he was, in most instances, more pragmatic and realistic. Shen was more inflexible, even to the extent of being stubborn, whether in his views about civil administration or about defense modernization. His advocacy of the ironclad was almost an obsession. Their different experiences during the Taiping years reinforced the divergence in their outlook and approach to government. Li, with his background in military leadership, which required coping with exigencies on the spur of the moment, had to be flexible, willing to overlook matters of principle, and accommodate people and opinions not to his liking. Shen, by contrast, owed his rise largely to sound civil administration. His tendency to handle political matters from the standpoint of classical Confucian moralism stood him in good stead among officials of different ideological persuasions, and guided his public behavior after he became involved in defense modernization. He managed the Foochow Navy Yard with an iron hand, imposing stringent disciplinary standards on his subordinates. Compared to Li, he was far less tolerant of opposition or deviance and could be hard to work with.

Yet, in the face of a declining China in the new international environment, Shen was able to adjust himself to the needs of the time. Despite differences in their approaches, he and Li worked together well in general. To be sure, there were far more differences between the two than what has already been mentioned. They disagreed over the leadership of the European educational mission for graduates of the Foochow Navy Yard School in 1876 and were at odds with each other over the disposal of the Woosung Railway the following year.[108] On foreign relations, such as those concerning Japan over the Ryūkyūs, they held opposing views. But in matters concerning ongoing endeavors, disagreements were kept to a minimum. Their cooperative efforts concerning the management of the Special Maritime Defense Fund and the arsenals are representative examples.

While the need to build a stronger China brought Li and Shen together, the scant resources available for maritime defense modernization made it imperative for them to be mutually supportive. Competing demands for inadequate funds meant that they had to close ranks and protect the little they had, not only against conservatives, vested interests, the throne, and a central government reluctant to change existing spending priorities, but also cost-conscious critics and even fellow *yang-wu* advocates who, like Tso Tsung-t'ang, had a different but no less urgent agenda at hand.

It should be emphasized, however, that the level of cooperation was neither intensive nor extensive. Both the Ch'ing political system and the state ideology discouraged bureaucratic associations that smacked of factionalism. It was not politically feasible, therefore, for Li and Shen to devise or pursue a grand scheme together for China's development. Thus, each modernizing undertaking had to be dealt with individually by the two officials on an ad hoc basis. All they could hope for was a stronger central or imperial leadership. Nowhere is this predicament more clearly seen than in the policy debate of 1874–75 when both Li and Shen separately proposed wide-ranging reforms. But their plans for future development were heavily trimmed by the court. Because of this, a valuable opportunity for a more rapid and systematic modernization of China's defense was thus squandered.

There is no question that in the partnership between the two after the mid-1860s, Li Hung-chang was the more powerful. But he did not always prevail, as in the settlement of the Woosung Railway. Sometimes, Li's policy was adopted simply because of circumstances. Thus, the lack of funds rendered Li's idea of buying the small *Staunch* gunboats eminently more reasonable than Shen's continuing cry for the expensive ironclad. Although Li might not have prevailed on all issues, his influence did expand to the south in the late 1870s. As one with a large following of modernizing administrators, Li was able to place his men in key positions in the south, even as head of the Foochow Navy Yard. It should be noted, however, that there was also a flow of personnel in the reverse direction. But this process took place more gradually: As the number of new naval officers trained under Shen increased, they began to populate the vessels of Kiangnan and the north, a trend that continued beyond Shen's lifetime.[109] In the Kiangnan Arsenal itself, Shen was also able to exert some influence, introducing his own style of management and naval organization to that Arsenal and its squadron. Li did not have a monopoly of power, even on his own "turf."

Liang Ch'i-ch'ao once asserted that practically all major developments in China since 1870 were related to Li Hung-chang.[110] There is no question that Li was a powerful and important man, but an undue emphasis on him, favorable or not, tends to hide more than reveal the nature of Ch'ing politics in the second part of the nineteenth century. An overemphasis on Li, for example, has created the impression that Li was relentless in the pursuit of power, and that his success had brought about the decline of central control. This phenomenon, known as regionalism, is then considered so prevalent in the late Ch'ing as to cause not only the collapse of the dynasty but also the dismemberment of the Chinese polity in postimperial China.[111] Regionalism may be an interesting concept with which to view nineteenth-century Chinese history. But even the power of Li, the archetype of the so-called regional leaders, was highly circumscribed. And despite Liang Ch'i-ch'ao's claim, there is far more to the history of modern China than the history of one man.

This study does not argue that Li was a self-effacing politician. Far from it. But it does point up the limits of his power, the strength of the conservative diehards (of the *ch'ing-i* variety, for instance), and his need to rely on the support of such colleagues as Shen Pao-chen who were not interested in building a greater Li Hung-chang. In the context of this paper, Shen's interest was to strengthen and modernize China's defense. To this end he cooperated as well as disputed with Li. That he also contributed to Li's influence was incidental.

Notes

Abbreviations

HFT   *Hai-fang tang* (Archives on maritime defense), Chung-yang yen-chiu-yüan chin-tai-shih yen-chiu-so (Institute of Modern History, Academia Sinica), comp. Taipei, 1957.

IWSM   *Ch'ing-tai Ch'ou-pan i-wu Shih-mo* (Complete record of the management of barbarian affairs). Peiping, 1930–32.

LWCK   Li Hung-chang, *Li Wen-chung kung ch'üan-chi* (The complete works of Li Hung-chang), Wu Ju-lun, comp. Nanking, 1905.

SWSK   Shen Pao-chen, *Shen Wen-su kung cheng-shu* (The political works of Shen Pao-chen), Wu Yüan-ping, comp. Soochow, 1880.

TWCK   Tseng Kuo-fan, *Tseng Wen-cheng kung ch'üan-chi* (The complete works of Tseng Kuo-fan). Taipei, 1952. (In note 11, the 1888 edition is used.)

YWYT   *Yang-wu yün-tung* (The foreign affairs movement). Chung-kuo k'o-hsüeh-yüan chin-tai-shih yen-chiu-so shih-liao pien-chi-shih (Office of Archival Materials, Institute of Modern History, the Chinese Academy of Social Sciences), 8 vols. Shanghai, 1961.

1. Since the seminal study of Mary C. Wright, several historians have come to think of the dynastic restoration as having started in the mid-1850s, before the T'ung-chih reign (1862–74). For example, Kwang-Ching Liu, stressing the emergence of the new military organization, the *yung-ying* (lit. "brave-battalion"), dates the Restoration back to 1854. While focusing on the rehabilitation of the areas recaptured from the rebels, I date it a year or two later. The Restoration also lasted well beyond the T'ung-chih era. Calling the dynastic Restoration the T'ung-chih Restoration tends to mislead. Mary C. Wright, *The Last Stand of Chinese Conservatism: The T'ung-chih Restoration, 1862–74*, 2d printing (Stanford, 1962) and rev. ed. with new preface (New York, 1965); Kwang-Ching Liu, "The Ch'ing Restoration," in *The Cambridge History of China*, vol. 10, *Late Ch'ing, 1800–1911*, part 1, ed. John K. Fairbank (Cambridge, 1978), 409–90; and David P. T. Pong, "The Vocabulary of Change: Reformist Ideas of the 1860s and 1870s," in *Ideal and Reality: Social and Political Change in Modern China, 1860–1949*, 2d printing, ed. David P. T. Pong and Edmund S. K. Fung (Lanham, 1988), 25–61.

2. Arthur W. Hummel, *Eminent Chinese of the Ch'ing Period*, 2 vols. (Washington, D.C., 1943), I, 464, and II, 642; Li Shou-k'ung, *Li Hung-chang chuan* (A biography of Li Hung-chang) (Taipei, 1978), 4–5; *Ch'ing-shih* (Dynastic history of the Ch'ing), comp. Ch'ing-shih pien-tsuan wei-yüan-hui (Committee for the compilation of the Ch'ing dynastic history) (Taipei, 1961), VI, 4756 and 4769.

3. Li Shou-k'ung, *Li Hung-chang*, 5–42; *Ch'ing-shih*, VI, 4756 and 4769; *Min-Hou hsien-chih* (Gazetteer of Min and Hou-kuan districts, Fukien) (Foochow, 1933), 93:6–7.

4. *LWCK Letters*, 5:37.

5. Lin Ch'ung-yung, *Lin Tse-hsü chuan* (Biography of Lin Tse-hsü) (Taipei, 1967), 42.

6. Wang Erh-min, *Huai-chün chih* (A history of the Huai Army) (Taipei, 1967), 43; Li Shou-k'ung, *Li Hung-chang*, 15.

7. The story, the accuracy of which has been disputed, is based on Kuo Sung-tao's account. The commander punished by Tseng was Li Yüan-tu who had, for some years, shared with Shen the responsibility of defending northeastern Kiangsi, the Kiangsi-Chekiang corridor. Mutual admiration led to Shen marrying his second son to Li's third daughter. Ibid., 29; Shen Yü-ch'ing, *T'ao-yüan chi*, 206–207, 214–15.

8. In 1861, the merchants of Shanghai and the wealthy gentry from the Liangkiang provinces who had taken refuge there became increasingly uneasy about the threats from the Taipings. Delegations were sent to solicit Tseng's help. Tseng's original plan was to despatch his brother, Kuo-ch'üan, to defend that city and to channel some of its resources to support his own campaign. Li Hung-chang's role was to raise an army from his native Anhwei to give added support. But Tseng Kuo-ch'üan demurred as he wished to direct his forces at Nanking and keep the prize of the Taiping capital for himself. Li was thus assigned to Shanghai in his stead. Wang Erh-min, *Huai-chün*, 47–67; Li Shou-k'ung, *Li Hung-chang*, 29–42.

9. David P. T. Pong, "The Income and Military Expenditure of Kiangsi Province in the Last Years (1860–64) of the Taiping Rebellion," *Journal of Asian Studies*, XXVI.1 (November 1966), 49–51; Wang Erh-min, *Huai-chün*, 58–62; Li Shou-k'ung, *Li Hung-chang*, 31–33.

10. David P. T. Pong, Modernization and Politics in China as seen in the Career of Shen Pao-chen (1820–79), Ph.D. thesis, University of London, 1969. See 56–59; *Pa hsien shou-cha* (Letters of eight worthies) (Shanghai, 1935), 9.

11. *TWCK* (1888 ed.), *Memorials*, 15:1–2; Li Shou-k'ung, *Li Hung-chang*, 40–42; in

Chin-tai Chung-kuo shih-shih jih-chih (A chronology of modern Chinese history, 1829–1911), comp. Kuo Ting-yee (Taipei, 1963), 1:387 and 395. In Wang Erh-min's opinion, between the Hsiang (Hunan) Army and the Huai Army, it was natural that Tseng should be partial to the former and give Li Hung-chang only a subordinate role in his original plans. Wang, *Huai-chün*, 59–67.

12. Li Kuo-ch'i, "T'ung-chih nien chien Li Hung-chang ti ying-pien t'u-hsin ssu-hsiang" (Li Hung-chang's ideas for change in the T'ung-chih period), paper presented at The Second International Conference on Sinology, Academia Sinica, Taipei, December 29–31, 1986, 1–6.

13. Wang Erh-min, *Huai-chün*, 239–49.

14. Li Shou-k'ung, *Li Hung-chang*, 105–10.

15. *LWCK Letters*, 1:8b.

16. *TWCK*, III, *Memorials*, 291.

17. Pong, "Modernization and Politics," 54–55.

18. *SWSK*, 1:1b–2, 3, 9–10.

19. Hsia Nai, "T'ai-p'ing t'ien-kuo ch'ien-hou Ch'ang-chiang ko-sheng chih t'ien-fu wen-t'i" (The problem of land levies in the Yangtze provinces around the time of the Taiping Rebellion), *Tsing Hua hsüeh-pao*, 10.2 (April 1935), 409–74 (Reprinted in *Chung-kuo chin-tai-shih lun-tsung*, 2d series, vol. 2, Taipei, 1958). Unless otherwise stated, sources for the tax reform in Kiangsi come from the reprint edition, 146, 165, 171–81.

20. For examples of Shen's civil administration, see *SWSK*, 1:41–42, 52–53b, 55–56, 89a–b, 2:27–29b, 38–41b, 54.

21. *IWSM*, T'ung-chih, 41:47b.

22. *Tao Hsien T'ung Kuang ssu-ch'ao tsou-i* (Memorials from the Tao-kuang, Hsien-feng, T'ung-chih, and Kuang-hsü reigns) (Taipei, 1970), VIII, 3503–3504. On the return of some illegal exactions, see Hsia Nai, "T'ai-p'ing t'ien-kuo," 200.

23. For the sources for this and the next paragraphs, see Pong, "The Income and Military Expenditure of Kiangsi," passim.

24. *SWSK*, 1:52b.

25. Huang Chun, *Hua-sui-jen-sheng an chih-i ch'üan-pien* (The recollections of Huang Chun), ed. Hsü Yen-p'ien and Su T'ung-ping (Hong Kong, 1979), 55–56; *TWCK*, IV, *Memorials*, 634–36.

26. *SWSK*, 2:72a–b; *Ch'ing-shih*, VI, 4834–35.

27. Li Hung-chang to Li Huan, 15 March 1863, in *LWCK Letters*, 3:7.

28. *LWCK Letters*, 6:12b–13b.

29. Li to Tseng, April 4, 1865, in *LWCK Letters*, 6:14a–b.

30. The two refused to correspond even as late as mid-1867. Tseng Kuo-fan, *Tseng Kuo-fan wei-k'an hsin-kao* (The unpublished letters of Tseng Kuo-fan), comp. Chiang Shih-yung (Peking, 1959), 376.

31. *LWCK Letters*, 1:9b.

32. Li Kuo-ch'i, "T'ung-chih nien chien," 17–19.

33. *LWCK Letters*, 2:46b–47b.

34. Wang Erh-min, *Huai-chün chih*, 90–98; Richard J. Smith, "Foreign-Training and China's Self-strengthening: The Case of Feng-huang-shan, 1864–73," *Modern Asian Studies*, 10.2.(1976), 195–223; Thomas L. Kennedy, *The Arms of Kiangnan: Modernization in the Chinese Ordnance Industry, 1860–95* (Boulder, 1978), 34–57.

35. Britten Dean, *China and Great Britain: The Diplomacy of Commercial Relations, 1860–64* (Cambridge, Mass., 1974), 101–102; Pong, "Income and Military Expenditure," 56–57.

36. Paul A. Cohen, *China and Christianity: The Missionary Movement and the*

Growth of Chinese Antiforeignism (Cambridge, Mass., 1963), 88–104, 200.

37. Pong, "Modernization and Politics," 18–20; Lin Ch'ung-yung, "Lin Ching-jen yü ch'i-yüan hsüeh-shu" (Lin P'u-ch'ing's letter of blood begging military help), *Chung-yang yen-chiu-yüan chin-tai-shih yen-chiu-so chi-k'an* (Bulletin of the Institute of Modern History, Academia Sinica), 7 (June 1978), 289.

38. Ko Shih-chün, comp., *Huang-ch'ao ching-shih-wen hsü-pien* (Collection of Ch'ing dynasty writings on statecraft, continued) (Shanghai, 1888), 101:14b–15; Shen K'o, "Hsien Wen-su kung cheng-shu hsü-pien" (The political works of Shen Pao-chen, a supplement) (n.p., 1889), 67–68. This work is unpaginated. Page numbers refer to my handcopied manuscript. I am grateful to Mr. Shen Tsu-hsing of Taipei for the use of this manuscript.

39. *Chung-Mei kuan-hsi shih-liao: T'ung-chih ch'ao* (Documents on Sino-American relations during the T'ung-chih reign), comp. Kuo T'ing-i (Kuo Ting-yee), et al. (Nankang, 1968), 101–103; *HFT*, I, 709–25.

40. *SWSK*, 1:24–26.

41. *HFT*, IV, 10.

42. *HFT*, IV, 6–20.

43. *IWSM*, 53:5a–b; 55:13–14.

44. Li Kuo-ch'i, "T'ung-chih nien chien," 5–6; *IWSM*, 2:36.

45. *SWSK*, 1:24–26. Shen also presented several other objections to the use of steamships that are not pertinent to our present discussion: lack of storage, loading, and unloading facilities at Kiukiang and Tientsin for large quantities of grain shipped at the same time, and the danger of Taiping attacks. The idea of letting foreign merchants ship grain to Peking was not new. Its merits had been discussed by Hsüeh Huan and the Tsungli Yamen in 1861. *IWSM*, Hsien-feng, 71:10b–11, 72:6a–b.

46. *IWSM*, T'ung-chih, 53:26–29b.

47. *LWCK Letters*, 5:34b.

48. Ibid., 12:3–4b.

49. *HFT*, II, 5–9b.

50. Hsiao I-shan, *Ch'ing-tai t'ung-shih* (A general history of the Ch'ing period) (Taipei, 1963), III, 811–12.

51. Gideon Chen, *Tso Tsung T'ang, Pioneer Promoter of the Modern Dockyard and the Woolen Mill in China* (Peking, 1938), 1–4.

52. Chao Lieh-wen, *Neng-ching-chü jih-chi* (The diary of Chao Lieh-wen) (Taipei reprint, 1964), no date, no pagination, see entry for T'ung-chih 6/12/1 (December 26, 1867). This passage is also cited in Tseng Kuo-fan, *Tseng Kuo-fan wei-k'an hsin-kao*, 391.

53. *LWCK Letters*, 8:18b.

54. Pong, "Keeping the Foochow Navy Yard Afloat," 126–28.

55. *HFT*, II, 257, 306, 311–13.

56. Sung's memorial of 23 January 1872. *YWYT*, V, 105–106.

57. *LWCK Letters*, 12:1b–3.

58. *HFT*, II, 330–31; Pong, "Modernization and Politics," 245–46.

59. *The North-China Herald*, June 23, 1877.

60. *HFT*, II, 325–26.

61. *LWCK Letters*, 12:3b–4.

62. *YWYT*, V, 108–109.

63. *IWSM*, T'ung-chih, 86:3b–8. For a representation of Tso's views, see Pong, "Keeping the Foochow Navy Yard Afloat," 137–38.

64. *HFT*, II, 346–50.

65. Pong, "Modernization and Politics," chapter 8.

66. *LWCK Letters*, 12:16b.

67. *HFT*, II, 367–72.

68. *LWCK Letters*, 11:27b, 31b; Tso Tsung-t'ang, *Tso Wen-hsiang kung ch'üan-chi* (The complete works of Tso Tsung-t'ang) (n.p., 1890), *Letters*, 11:54; *YWYT*, V, 456.

69. Pong, "Modernization and Politics," 249–54; Thomas L. Kennedy, "Industrial Metamorphosis in the Self-strengthening Movement: Li Hung-chang and the Kiangnan Shipbuilding Program," *Journal of the Institute of Chinese Studies of the Chinese University of Hong Kong*, IV.1 (1971), 216–17. In the light of Li's favorable views on the modern warship industry expressed in 1864, it can be further suggested that Li's position on the subject was at best ambivalent, depending on the political situation. Whatever his views were in the 1860s and 1870s, he promoted naval expansion on a large scale in the 1880s, despite his earlier belief that China could only entertain such efforts in about a century. The rise of Japan, of course, had a great deal to do with his new approach. See also chapter 12 below.

70. *LWCK Letters*, 13:28a–b.

71. Sophia Su-fei Yen, *Taiwan in China's Foreign Relations, 1836–74* (Hamden, Conn., 1965), 175–212; *T'ung-chih chia-hsü Jih-ping ch'in-T'ai shih-mo* (The complete account of the Japanese invasion of Taiwan in 1874), comp. Research Department of the Bank of Taiwan (Taipei, 1959), I, 1–4; *LWCK Letters*, 13:33. On the international status of the Ryūkyūs, see Yen, *Taiwan*, 157–58; Robert K. Sakai, "The Ryūkyū (Liu-ch'iu) Islands as a Fief of Satsuma," and Ta-tuan Ch'en, "Investiture of Liu-ch'iu Kings in the Ch'ing Period," in *The Chinese World Order*, ed. John K. Fairbank (Cambridge, Mass., 1968), 112–34, 135–63, 311–20.

72. Edict of 29 May 1874 in *T'ung-chih chia-hsü*, I, 7–8.

73. *T'ung-chih chia-hsü*, I, 13–14, 16–18, 24, 46–47, 121; Gabriel Lemaire to Ministère des Affaires Étrangères, 18 June 1874, in *Ministère des Affaires Étrangères, Chine, Dépêches politiques des consuls*, II, 305; Li Hung-chang to Shen, 2 August 1874, in *LWCK Letters*, 14:18a–b. The two Foochow vessels that did not return to meet the crisis were the *Chen-hai* and the *Mei-yün*, which remained at Tientsin and Newchwang, respectively.

74. *LWCK Letters*, 14:6b–7b. Earlier, still ignorant of Li's offer, Shen had requested the throne to send five thousand modern trained troops to be detached from units under Li Hung-chang and Li Tsung-hsi, the northern and southern commissioners, respectively. *T'ung-chih chia-hsü*, I, 46.

75. Shen K'o, "Hsien Wen-su kung," 56–57.

76. *HFT*, II, 504.

77. For a more comprehensive comparison, see David Pong, "Shen Pao-chen and the Great Policy Debate of 1874–75," in *Proceedings of the Conference on the Self-strengthening Movement in Late Ch'ing China, 1860–94* (Taipei: Institute of Modern History, Academia Sinica, 1988), 189–225.

78. On Ting's memorial, see *YWYT*, I, 30–33. On Li's response, see ibid., 40–54, and Liu, chapter 3 above.

79. For Shen's memorial of December 23, 1874, see Shen K'o, "Hsien Wen-su kung," 50–68. A second version of Shen's memorial has been in print for some time. See Ko Shih-chün, *Huang-ch'ao ching-shih-wen hsü-pien*, 101:11b–15. Neither version is complete. Nor does either give the date of the memorial that could be found in the third version in the archives of the Republic of China, Palace Museum, Taipei: "Chün-chi ch'u" (Grand Council archives), no. 118328.

80. Shen had proposed some of these changes in 1867. *IWSM*, T'ung-chih, 53:26–29b; Pong, "The Vocabulary of Change," 37, 43–45, 47–48.

81. Liu, chapter 3 above.

82. *LWCK Letters*, 15:1. Li also intimated to Ting Jih-ch'ang that only Shen's proposals and his own were sound and practical; the rest were devoid of any substance. Ibid., 15:6b.

83. Ibid., 14:34. At the time, Tso Tsung-t'ang's name had also been mentioned, but Li, who had never gotten along with Tso, hinted to Wen-hsiang that he much preferred Shen. Ibid., 14:32a–b.

84. As Kwang-Ching Liu has written, Li had three audiences with the empresses dowager and talked with Wen-hsiang and Li Wen-tsao at Peking in late January 1875, urging that Shen be appointed governor-general of Liangkiang. Liu, chapter 3 above. By early February, Li was confident enough of the success of his scheme that he told Shen that the southern provinces could not have gone to anyone else. *LWCK Letters*, 15:1a–b.

85. *YWYT*, I, 153–55; *LWCK Letters*, 15:15a–b.

86. Stanley Spector, *Li Hung-chang and the Huai Army: A Study in Nineteenth-Century Chinese Regionalism* (Seattle, 1964), 181.

87. *LWCK Letters*, 14:32b.

88. Ibid.

89. *YWYT*, I, 162–65; *SWSK*, 7:28b–29; *LWCK Letters*, 15:30b–31, 33a–b.

90. Chin Liang, comp., *Chin-shih jen-wu chih* (Biographies of late Ch'ing and early Republican figures compiled from extracts from the works of Weng T'ung-ho, Li Tz'u-ming, Wang K'ai-yün, and Yeh Ch'eng-ch'ieh) (Taipei, 1955), 157.

91. *LWCK Letters*, 15:37a–b.

92. On Tso's plan for a foreign loan, see Tso, *Tso Wen-hsiang kung, Memorials*, 47:49–56b and 48:55b.

93. Ko Shih-chün, *Huang-ch'ao ching-shih-wen hsü-pien*, 101:13b; *SWSK*, 6:9–13.

94. Edict, April 3, 1876, in *Ta-Ch'ing li-ch'ao shih-lu* (Veritable records of the successive reigns of the Ch'ing dynasty) (Mukden, 1937), Kuang-hsu, 27:10b–12b.

95. Tso, *Tso Wen-hsiang kung, Letters*, 16:8b.

96. Hsiao I-shan, *Ch'ing-tai t'ung-shih*, III, 928–29.

97. Li Ho-nien's memorial of May 18, 1878 (KH 4.4.17) in Palace Museum, Taipei, "Yüeh-chieh tang," KH 4/4 *chung*; Chuang Chi-fa, "Ch'ing-chi nan-pei-yang hai-fang ching-fei ti ch'ou-ts'o" (Raising funds for maritime defense for the northern and southern regions in the late Ch'ing), *Ta-lu tsa-chih* (Continent magazine), 55 (November 15, 1977), 232.

98. *LWCK Letters*, 17:4a–b, 19b–20, 24b–25, 31b, 33, 35a–b; *YWYT*, II, 369–71, 374–76.

99. *SWSK*, 7:52–53b.

100. *LWCK Letters*, 17:39b–40b; *YWYT*, II, 346–62.

101. *Shih-lu*, Kuang-hsu, 68:21a–b, 69:2b–3, 7b–8, 70:8a–b; *Tao Hsien T'ung Kuang*, VIII, 3421.

102. *LWCK Letters*, 17:12a–b, 18:4; *YWYT*, II, 345–46, 382–83, 406–407, 418–19, and III, 300. For a description of these gunboats, see John L. Rawlinson, *China's Struggle for Naval Development, 1839–95* (Cambridge, Mass., 1967), 69–70, 248–51, and Stanley F. Wright, *Hart and the Chinese Customs* (Belfast, 1950), 467–76.

103. Wang Erh-min, *Ch'ing-chi ping-kung-yeh ti hsing-ch'i* (The rise of the military industry in late Ch'ing) (Nankang, 1963), 79; Kennedy, *The Arms of Kiangnan*, 49.

104. *LWCK Letters*, 15:35a–b.

105. *North-China Herald*, May 20, 1876; *SWSK*, 7:60–61b.

106. Liu K'un-i, *Liu K'un-i i-chi* (Collected works of Liu K'un-i) (Peking, 1959), II, 596–97; *SWSK*, 7:102–103b.

107. *Shih-lu*, Kuang-hsu, 63:5; *YWYT*, IV, 469.

108. On the European educational mission, see *LWCK Letters*, 13:28b–29, 16:12a–b, 21b–22b, 23b–24, 35a–b; *HFT*, II, 502–503b. On the Woosung Railway, see *LWCK Letters*, 17:15a–b; David Pong, "Confucian Patriotism and the Destruction of the

Woosung Railway, 1877," *Modern Asian Studies*, 7.4 (1973), 650–54, 657–59.

109. Lu Fang, "Shih lun Li Hung-chang ti yang-wu huo-tung" (Li Hung-chang's *yang-wu* activities, a preliminary discussion), *Chi-lin ta-hsüeh she-hui k'o-hsüeh lun-ts'ung*, no. 2: *Yang-wu yün-tung t'ao-lun chuan-chi*, 308; Yao Hsi-kuang, "Tung-fang ping-shih chi-lüeh" (A record of military affairs in the Orient), in *Chung-kuo chin-pai-nien shih tzu-liao hsü-pien* (Historical sources for the past hundred years, a supplementary compilation), comp. Tso Shun-sheng (Taipei, 1958), 195–97.

110. Liang Ch'i-ch'ao, *Lun Li Hung-chang* (On Li Hung-chang) (Preface, 1901; reprinted, Taipei, 1965), 1.

111. Spector, *Li Hung-chang*. See, especially, the introduction by Franz Michael (xxi–xliii).

5

The Shanghai-Tientsin Connection: Li Hung-chang's Political Control over Shanghai

Yuen-sang Leung

One of the most important effects of modernization in late Ch'ing China was the emergence of a new horizontal relationship between provincial governments and urban-industrial centers. In the past, regional and provincial leaders seldom consulted each other on administrative affairs. Each province or region was an isolated administrative unit. There were few communication channels between provinces. The governmental transportation-communication network, as exemplified by the postal routes, or *i-tao*, was constructed in a radial pattern focusing on the links between the central government and the provinces rather than on horizontal connections.

The government's traditional emphasis on vertical relationships was accentuated by two factors. First, China's provinces are usually physically divided by natural barriers. Most provincial boundaries fall on mountain ranges, lakes, or rivers. As a result, interregional communication was often more difficult than transport within the intraprovincial structure.[1] The second and perhaps more important factor was political motivation. The Manchu government was deeply suspicious of the expansion of power of the Han Chinese in the provinces. Just as the Law of Avoidance was promulgated to prevent provincialism, so was the design of the postal communication network made to ensure central authority and discourage horizontal alliances.

With the advent of the steamer and the telegraph, the distance and natural barriers became less of an obstacle to communication. Moreover, the new system of foreign relations generated the need for more understanding and cooperation not only between central and local governments but between the provincial governments as well. For instance, Kuo Sung-tao in the 1870s urged China to improve communication between the provinces, saying that the country's defeat during the Arrow War was a result of disunity and lack of cooperation between provincial governments. He pointed out that while Canton was at war, Shanghai was negotiating peace; and when the north was fighting against the foreigners, the southern provinces continued to trade with them.[2]

The most important stimulus for change in interprovincial and interregional relationships, however, was provided by the modernization movement. The mechanical-electrical devices of telegraph lines, railroads, and steamships shortened distances and saved time, but the establishment and management of such innovations required the cooperation of two or more provinces. Other modernization projects such as arsenals, textile factories, steel and iron plants, and mining bureaus, also demanded an improved and extended transportation-communication system for supply and market reasons.

On the other hand, the introduction of modern enterprises generated the problem of cross-provincial control. The lack of governmental regulations in the operation of these new programs made possible greater administrative flexibility and the expansion of power by some provincial leaders. Because of the lack of rules and precedents (wu-li k'o-hsün), several governors and governors-general were allowed to control a number of modernization projects outside their provincial boundaries. The most telling example was Li Hung-chang. He was governor of Kiangsu in the mid-1860s, and it was he who started the modernization movement in Shanghai. During the years 1870–95, as governor-general of Chihli, Li remained one of the most influential figures in the politics of Kiangsu and maintained a strong grip over the control of the Kiangnan Arsenal, the China Merchants' Steam Navigation Company, the Shanghai Cotton Mill, and other modernization bureaus in Shanghai.

Some historians have asserted that the cooperative interprovincial relationship and cross-provincial control signified increasing regional power and weakening central authority.[3] However, others have refuted the "periphery-overpowered-center" thesis by saying that many provincial leaders' cross-provincial control of modernization projects was justifiable on the grounds that they often acted in the interest of the central government.[4]

This chapter is an attempt to examine the new interregional relationship between Chihli and Liangkiang in general and the intercity relationship between Tientsin and Shanghai in particular. In light of the "regionalism versus centralism" controversy, this chapter tries to raise the following questions: Did Li Hung-chang have political control over Shanghai outside his jurisdiction? If he did, was his controlling power a legitimate one?

Intercity transportation and communication

Before the steamship era, the major transportation line between Tientsin and the lower Yangtze valley was the Grand Canal. Almost all government revenues and tribute grains from the south were transported to Tientsin through the Canal by traditional junks. Occasionally, goods and passengers were transported via the

Yellow Sea, usually between Taku and Shanghai. However, the sea route was not a popular line until the middle of the nineteenth century when the Taiping Rebellion disrupted canal transportation. The introduction of steamers, with abiding safety and speed, elevated the importance of the sea route. In the past, it took more than eight days to travel from Shanghai to Tientsin or vice versa; now the steamers reduced the trip to four days. Roads never assumed a dominant role in transportation in the nineteenth century. Even government postal horses took more than ten days to cover the same distance.[5]

The steamship was first introduced on the Yangtze River between Hankow and Shanghai. Then another line was developed in the late 1860s between Shanghai and Ningpo. The Shanghai-Tientsin steamship line in the initial years of steamship enterprise was far less important by comparison. But as time rolled on, the Tientsin-Shanghai line emerged as the most important and the busiest. The growing connection between the two cities can be seen from the data below.[6]

In June of 1873, steamship departures from Shanghai to selected cities were: to Tientsin—9, to Ningpo—24, to Hankow—21. Arrivals that month for Shanghai were: from Tientsin—18, from Ningpo—24, from Hankow—20. A decade later (May 1883) the comparable monthly figures were: to Tientsin—41, to Ningpo—29, to Hankow—34; and from Tientsin—30, from Ningpo—24, from Hankow—30.

To highlight these differences, let us look at the Shanghai-Tientsin traffic alone. In the early 1870s, there were nine steamers leaving Shanghai for Tientsin and eighteen arriving from there within a month. The average number of departures was one in three days and that of arrivals was one in two days. In the next decade, the number of steamers arriving at Shanghai from Tientsin rose to thirty in a month, averaging one per day. In departures, the rate of increase was even greater. The number of departures rose to forty-one in a month, or approximately three departures every two days.

The telegraph lines erected in 1881 established another communication link between the two cities. The line was first built for diplomatic purposes. Li Hung-chang in Tientsin, being saddled with more and more diplomatic duties by the Tsungli Yamen in Peking, was the driving spirit behind the development of the communication system. Pointing out that it was impossible for him to deal with foreigners effectively with a poor transportation-communication system, and complaining that the information flow between Shanghai and Moscow was faster than that between Shanghai and Tientsin, Li urged the central government to adopt his plan of establishing the Imperial Telegraph Administration.

Li's plan was approved and the construction work begun in June 1881. Construction was completed in December of that year. The line not only connected Tientsin with Shanghai but also linked seven cities between them in three provinces: Chihli, Shantung, and Kiangsu.[7]

Personnel transfer between the two cities

The modern transportation-communication network was a visible link between the cities. Yet the Shanghai-Tientsin connection was more than a physical linkage. The modernization movement also facilitated the personnel flow between the two cities. In the post-1860 era, there were many personnel transfers between the Shanghai and Tientsin yamens. Among the Shanghai officials transferred or promoted to positions in Tientsin were Liu Han-fang, Sun Shih-ta, P'an Wei, Liu Ju-i, Wu Yü-fen, Shen Pao-ching, Cheng Tsao-ju, Li Hsing-jui, Hsü Chien-yin, Wang Te-chün, Wu Ts'an-ch'eng, Huang Chien-kuan, Chang I, Chou Fu, Ling Huan, and many others. These officials generally fell into two categories: One group was made up of former military officers of the Huai Army, such as Wu Yü-fen, Liu Han-fang, and Wu Ts'an-ch'eng, and former private aides of Li Hung-chang, such as Ling Huan and Chou Fu.[8] In other words, they were either followers or old friends of Li. Another group consisted mostly of technical personnel, the staff of the Kiangnan Arsenal: Shen Pao-ching, Cheng Tsao-ju, Hsü Chien-yin, and Wang Te-chün, to cite a few examples.[9] All of these personnel transfers and promotions had one thing in common: they were all recommended or arranged by Li Hung-chang.

Needless to say, Li Hung-chang was, like many Chinese officials of the day, a governor-general who saw great importance in interpersonal connections and practiced nepotism. He was said to have paid bribes to eunuchs in the palace and to patronize corruption. He worked hard to place his own men (members of his *mu-fu*, military officers of the Huai Army and other Anhwei natives) in his provincial government and other agencies under his control.[10]

However, favoritism could not explain all the Shanghai-Tientsin personnel transfers. For example, Cheng Tsao-ju was neither a former *mu-fu* member nor an Anhwei man. Li Hung-chang came to know him only through the reports of the Kiangnan Arsenal submitted to him by Shen Pao-ching. Impressed by Cheng's management skills, Li requested that Cheng be transferred to Tientsin in the hope that his expertise in arsenal management could help the development of the newly reorganized Tientsin Arsenal.[11] Other transfers of technical personnel—Shen Pao-ching, Hsü Chien-yin, Wang Te-chün, and so on—can be seen in the same light. As Tientsin gradually became a diplomatic center and an experimental center for modern industries after 1870, the need for *yang-wu* experts also increased immensely. Li Hung-chang expressed this need in a letter to Tseng Kuo-fan in 1871: "None of my staff here have any knowledge of *yang-wu*," he wrote. "It has been a painful experience to draft all memorials and reports of this kind [myself]."[12] It was largely this need arising from modernization and foreign relations that facilitated the personnel flow from Shanghai to Tientsin.

In addition to the regular flow of personnel from Shanghai to Tientsin, transfers of Tientsin officials to Shanghai were also frequent. Many officials who were nominally attached to the Tientsin government carried out their actual administrative duties in Shanghai. In fact, many of the managers of the modernization bureaus such as the China Merchants' Steam Navigation Company (*Chao-shang chü*), the Diplomatic Correspondence Bureau (*Wen-pao chü*), the Shanghai Educational Mission Bureau (*Ch'u-yang hsüeh-sheng Hu-chü*), and the Telegraph Bureau (*Tien-pao chü*) were sent by Li Hung-chang from Tientsin. For instance, the major managers of the China Merchants' Steam Navigation Company in the 1870s and 1880s (T'ang T'ing-shu, Hsü Jun, Chu Ch'i-ang, Chu Ch'i-chao, Sheng Hsuan-huai, and Ma Chien-chung) all had official titles of Chihli Province.

In all, the transportation-communication lines and the personnel exchange between Tientsin and Shanghai in the late nineteenth century suggest a close intercity relationship that did not exist in previous years.

The Shanghai taotais: Li's men?

Did an intercity linkage mean that one city had political control over the other? Or, in this case, did Li Hung-chang in Chihli have political control over Shanghai?

From the outset, Li appeared to have a strong grip on Shanghai's personnel and policies. Stanley Spector and other "regionalist" historians believe that Li controlled the appointment of the Shanghai taotai (the highest local official) during the entire period of self-strengthening. Spector says, "These men [Shanghai taotais during 1863–94] were sources of strength to Li wherever he was. It is clear that they were placed in Liangkiang because Li and Tseng [Kuo-fan] wanted them there. They monopolized the region's wealth for the Li-Tseng Clique."[13] A careful examination of Li's relationship with the taotais and the appointment procedures would cast doubt on Spector's assumption. It is true that most of the occupants of the Shanghai taotai office during this period were, at one time or another, followers of Tseng and Li. However, this does not mean that they always cooperated with Li. For instance, Feng Chün-kuang, one of Li's economic advisers in the 1860s, did not always support Li's policies.[14] Actually, only three of the Shanghai taotais obtained their appointment through Li's recommendation. Ting Jih-ch'ang and Ying Pao-shih were recommended for the taotai post by Li while he was governor of Kiangsu. It was not unusual for a provincial leader to exercise the power of recommendation. After Li left Kiangsu, he used personal influence in the selection process of the Shanghai taotai only once, on behalf of Liu Jui-fen, a former military officer of the Anhwei Army.[15] Li also maintained good relationships with T'u Tsung-ying and Kung Chao-yüan, both Anhwei natives and old friends. But T'u's appointment was suggested by Tseng Kuo-fan, governor-general of Liangkiang, and Kung was recommended by Liu K'un-i, holder of the same office at a later time.

There is no evidence that Li intervened in the appointment process of Feng Chün-kuang, Shen Ping-ch'eng, Shao Yu-lien, and Nieh Ch'i-kuei. Nothing has been found in Li's private writings and the biographies of Shen and Shao to suggest that these men had been acquainted with Li in their earlier years. Not long before Feng's appointment, Li mentioned Feng in a letter to Tseng Kuo-fan: "Cho-ju [Feng] is a man who used to exaggerate things and his actions do not match ideas. In his heart are suspicions and jealousies; he would never have the respect of his colleagues."[16] Nor should Nieh be considered one of Li's men, despite the fact that he was Tseng Kuo-fan's son-in-law and a Hunanese. Spector has wrongly alleged that all Hunanese or Tseng's followers were indiscriminately Li's allies. It is generally known that there were constant struggles among Tseng's *mu-fu* members as well as provincial rivalries between the Hunanese and Anhwei men. In the case of Nieh Ch'i-kuei who was a protégé of Tso Tsung-t'ang, an arch rival of Li, the appointment was made mainly on the strength of a recommendation by his wife's uncle, Tseng Kuo-ch'üan, governor-general of Liangkiang at that time.[17]

Formal political control

The most fundamental element of formal control was the power of appointment. The "regionalist" historians claim that during and after the Taiping Rebellion the military leaders in the provinces had preempted the power of appointment from the center. This power, they believe, included the power of appointing secondary-level administrative officials such as military taotai (*ping-pei tao*), customs taotai (*hai-kuan tao*), and other middle-echelon posts formerly assigned by the central government.[18] It may be correct to say that at the height of the Taiping war, the provincial satraps had more or less a free hand in placing their own men in local and provincial governments.[19] But the central government never relinquished its authority over appointment, approval, and removal, especially over important administrative posts.

Official posts in the provinces during the Ch'ing period could be divided into three categories: the *chien-fang* (dispatched by imperial edict) posts, the *pu-hsüan* (selected by the Six Boards) posts, and the *wai-pu* (appointed by provincial leaders) posts. All high-ranking and significant posts, including governor-generalship, governorship, provincial treasurership, and provincial judgeship, belonged in the *chien-fang* category. Most of the taotai posts, including the Shanghai taotaiship, also belonged in this group. The *pu-hsüan* posts were also controlled by the central government even though the posts in this category were usually of lesser importance. The power of appointment enjoyed by provincial leaders was very limited. They had formal control over only a small number of posts in the *wai-pu* category. In the whole country, only fourteen taotai posts fell into this category. In Kiangsu, only one, namely the Hsü-chou taotai, was a *wai-pu* post. The following is the numerical breakdown of the taotais according to these three categories:[20] *chien-fang* posts—69; *pu-hsüan* posts—14; and *wai-pu* posts—16. Thus, the provincial authorities' power of appointment, in theory, was very limited. Even many administrative posts below the taotai level, such as the prefects, were controlled by the central government.

Actually, the provincial leaders did manage to gain more power of appointment in the mid-nineteenth century. It was reported that all *pu-hsüan* posts were under their control in the 1860s. In 1873, there was a proposal from one of the ministers of the Six Boards to the throne claiming that there was no need for provincial leaders to retain control over the *pu-hsüan* posts after the Taiping Rebellion and that at least half of the posts should be taken back into the hands of Board officials. After some deliberation, a compromise known as "1-*tzu*/ 2-*liu*" was reached in 1881. The solution was that after two appointments by provincial leaders, the Board of Civil Appointment would send one appointee to a *pu-hsüan* post in the province. The ratio was later changed to 1-central/1-province.[21]

These facts suggest that the central government in the post-Taiping era still maintained a strong grip over the appointment of provincial officials, even though provincial leaders enjoyed relatively more power in local militia and in local financing. In the case of selecting candidates for the *chien-fang* posts, the provincial authorities could recommend qualified officials to the Grand Council, but the appointive power rested with the Grand Council and the emperor. The misconception of regional control over the appointment of taotais is probably the result of the following: first, a false identification of the power to recommend with the power to appoint, and, second, the failure to differentiate the three types of taotais. For instance, the Tientsin customs taotai, a post created to handle foreign affairs and external trade in 1870, was a *wai-pu* post. The governor-general of Chihli could appoint anyone to the post, and then would report to the central government. The Tientsin military taotai, however, was not appointed by the governor-general. The selection was made in the Grand Council and the appointment came directly from the emperor, because it was a *chien-fang* post.[22]

In this light, Spector's assumption of cross-provincial control seems questionable, because even the governor-general of Liangkiang did not have the final say over the appointment of the Shanghai taotai.

Li Hung-chang, knowing the administrative system well, did not want to challenge central authority or the power of the governor-general of Liangkiang over the appointment of local officials in Kiangsu. Nor did he want to interfere in another province's affairs. When he was drawn into the entanglement of the Wusung Railway dispute in 1876, he apologized to the Nanking and Shanghai authorities: "This matter [the Wusung Railway dispute] should be handled by the Southern Commissioner. I am only an outsider. The reason for my stepping in is that I saw that the two sides had reached a stalemate and therefore I hope to offer a compromise solution."[23]

Then how can Li's control over the modernization projects in Shanghai be explained? Did he or did he not have the power of appointment over the managerial posts of these bureaus?

He did. Most of the managers and directors of the China Merchants' Steam Navigation Company, the Shanghai Cotton Mill, and the Telegraph Bureau were directly appointed by Li. The main reason for this was that these projects were new to the country and there were no regulations to govern their operations. Moreover, during the initial years of modernization, many provincial leaders did not want to be involved in these new projects. This left Li Hung-chang and some other leaders of self-strengthening room to retain control over the programs outside their own provincial jurisdiction. Li Hung-chang had another good reason to justify his involvement in Shanghai's modernization projects. As the trade superintendent of the Northern Ports or Northern Commissioner, he was responsible for overseeing all *yang-wu* affairs in the north. Because there was an interlocking and interdependent relationship between Shanghai's modern enterprises and the modernization projects in the north, Li's involvement in Shanghai's modernization policies was administratively justifiable.

However, there were strong forces restraining cross-provincial control, even in the unconventional realm of *yang-wu*. First, modernization programs were under the close watch of conservative officials, particularly the censors. Second, when the central government became more receptive to military and economic reform, it also became more anxious to reestablish its power over the operation of these projects. For instance, Chang Chih-tung, governor-general of Hukuang, was impeached by the Grand Council in late 1889 for "not reporting to the Council about additional purchase of machines [for the Canton Textile Bureau]." The Grand Council stated, "From now on, any proposal to start [new projects] and purchase machines and firearms, must first be reported [to the Grand Council]. No action should be taken before [the Council] gives its approval."[24] Moreover, cross-provincial control depended on the cooperation of the leaders of the provinces affected. A provincial leader could not effectively control the modernization projects in another province ruled by his rival or enemy. For example, when Tso Tsung-t'ang was governor-general of Liangkiang, Li's influence over the Kiangnan Arsenal was evidently reduced.[25] Li had the power to appoint directors of the Shanghai Cotton Mill, but Tso, as governor-general of Liangkiang, could remove any manager from this bureau.[26]

Informal political control

Although Li Hung-chang had legitimate power to interfere with the modernization programs in Shanghai, he relied more on the informal system of interpersonal relationships than on formal administrative channels to exert his influence. This interpersonal network included three kinds of connections: fellow provincials (*t'ung-hsiang*), colleagues (*t'ung-liao*), and fellow examination graduates (*t'ung-nien*). All three kinds of connections were valued in the traditional Chinese society, especially in officialdom. To work through these channels was socially acceptable and not considered political corruption. Li was from Anhwei. His *t'ung-hsiang* in Kiangsu and Shanghai included Governor Chang Shu-sheng (1872–74), the Shanghai taotais T'u Tsung-ying (1868–70), Liu Jui-fen (1876–82), and Kung Chao-yuan (1886–89), and Commander of the Yangtze Navy Liu

Ming-ch'uan. In the central government, Wu T'ing-fen and Sun Chia-nai were the two influential Anhwei men during the Kuang-hsü reign. The second kind of relationship included both friends from the Hsiang Army such as Tseng Kuo-fan and P'eng Yü-lin, and former *mu-fu* members like Hsüeh Fu-ch'eng, Ting Jih-ch'ang, and Feng Chün-kuang, to name only a few who were active in the Kiangnan region. The most important connection between Li Hung-chang and Kiangnan, however, was the *t'ung-nien* relationship. Li Hung-chang passed the metropolitan examination in 1847. Two of his fellow graduates in the year 1847 (*Ting-wei t'ung-nien*), Chang Chih-wan and Ho Ching, became governors of Kiangsu in the early 1870s. Three assumed the governor-generalship of Liangkiang: Ma Hsin-i (1867–70), Li Tsung-hsi (1873–74), and Shen Pao-chen (1875–79). Two other graduates of 1847, Shen Kuei-fen and Chang Chih-wan, for years were leading members of the Grand Council.[27]

These three types of relationships made it possible for Li to meddle in Kiangnan's politics especially when Liangkiang was under the rule of Shen Pao-chen and Chang Shu-sheng. Shen, for instance, asked Li more than once for advice and evaluation of the Shanghai officials. Ho Ching also asked for Li's comments on Shanghai personnel.[28]

On the basis of these informal relationships that linked him with the Kiangsu and specifically Shanghai bureaucrats, Li was able to gain strong support from the nonofficial sector, the Shanghai merchants and gentry members. From these socially and commercially powerful groups, he raised funds and selected mana-gerial staff for his modernization projects. When Chihli and other parts of north-ern China were plagued by drought and famine in 1877–78, this private sector organized relief bureaus and contributed money for that purpose. Among Li's supporters were Chou Chen-sheng of Soochow, Kung Ch'ang-ling of Sung-kiang, and Hung Kuang-yeh and Ch'en Hsu-yüan of Shanghai.[29] Many such merchant gentlemen seem to have trusted only Li. When Li withdrew from public service in 1883 because of the death of his mother, the directors of the Soochow-Shanghai relief bureaus and "contribution bureaus" (*chüan-chü*) an-nounced that they would dissolve the bureaus until Li's return to office. The reason appears to have been twofold. First, Li was a shrewd politician who knew how to manipulate opinion and rally support by rewarding his followers with brevet ranks and family honors (*feng-tien*). Chin Yu-ch'ing, a member of the Shanghai gentry who worked hard for the Chihli relief fund-raising bureau in Shanghai, had Li's promise that "he would be given a post, so that he could collect living stipends from the government without working [in later years]."[30] Second, the gentry and merchants supported Li's modernization programs in Shanghai because they had vested interest in the new economic ventures.

In short, Li did have considerable influence in the lower Yangtze valley by means of a modern transportation-communication network and through an infor-mal system of interpersonal connections. The formal political control, however, remained in the center.

Notes

Abbreviations

IWSM   *Ch'ou-pan i-wu shih-mo* (The complete account of the management of barbarian affairs), 260 *chüan*. Peiping, 1930–32.

LWCK   *Li Wen-chung kung chüan-chi* (The complete works of Li Hung-chang), 7 vols., ed. Wu Ju-lin, 165 *chüan*. Taipei reprint, 1962.

NCH   *North China Herald.*

TCHT   *Ta-Ch'ing hui-tien* (Ch'ing statutes).

YWYT   *Yang-wu yün-tung* (The Western Affairs Movement), 8 vols., ed. Chungkuo Shih-hsueh hui. Shanghai, 1958.

1. Diana Lary, *Region and Nation: The Kwangsi Clique in Chinese Politics, 1925–37* (Cambridge, England, 1974), 4; for G. William Skinner's grouping of "physiographic regions" based on a similar idea, see "Regional Urbanization in Nineteenth-Century China," in *The City in Late Imperial China*, ed. Skinner (Stanford, 1977), 211–19. Studies by Skinner on central places support the idea of an intraprovincial commercial and marketing system; see "Cities and the Hierarchy of Local System," in *The City*, ed. Skinner, 281–96.

2. Kuo T'ing-i (Kuo Ting-yee) et al., comps., *Kuo Sung-tao hsien-sheng nien-p'u* (A chronological biography of Kuo Sung-tao) (Taipei, 1975), 529. For more on disunity and provincialism, see Kenneth E. Folsom, *Friends, Guests, and Colleagues: The Mu-Fu System in the Late Ch'ing Period* (Berkeley and Los Angeles, 1968), 160, and *NCH*, December 13 and December 20, 1856.

3. See Stanley Spector, *Li Hung-chang and the Huai Army: A Study of Nineteenth-Century Chinese Regionalism* (Seattle, 1964), especially the introductory article by Franz Michael.

4. Kwang-Ching Liu, "The Limits of Regional Power in the Late Ch'ing Period: A Reappraisal," in *The Tsing Hua Journal of Chinese Studies*, n.s., 10.2 (1974), 207–23; and chapter 3 above. For a brief discussion of the controversy, see Daniel H. Bays, *China Enters the Twentieth Century: Chang Chih-tung and the Issues of a New Age, 1895–1909* (Ann Arbor, 1977), 5.

5. Liu Hsiung-hsiang, "Tsung-li ko-kuo shih-wu ya-men chi ch'i hai-fang chien-she" (The Tsungli Yamen and its efforts in coastal defense) in *Chung-kuo chin-tai-shih lun-ts'ung* (Taipei, 1975), ser. 1, vol. 5, 33–55.

6. Data from *Shen-pao*, for 1873 (June, 30 days) from vol. 5 (Taipei, reprint ed.), and for 1883 (May, 29 days), from vol. 38.

7. On reasons for the establishment of the telegraph, see Liu Hsiung-hsiang, "Tsung-li ko-kuo"; also *Shen-pao* (12.3. 1881), vol. 33, no. 21333.

8. For a brief background of Li's *mu-fu* and former military officers of the Huai Army, see table 17 and table 18 in Spector, *Li Hung-chang and the Huai Army*, 280–96, 301–13.

9. *YWYT*, IV, 170–71.

10. Hu Ssu-ching was the most critical among Li's critics; see Chuang Lien, *Chung-kuo chin-tai-shih shang ti kuan-chien jen-wu* (Key figures in modern Chinese history), 3 vols. (Taipei, 1978), 2:21–22, 72–73.

11. For Li's relationship with Cheng, see *LWCK Letters*, 11:12–12b, 11:23b–24, 15:36b, 18:16b.

12. *LWCK Letters*, 10:31b, also 12:33–33b.

13. Spector, *Li Hung-chang and the Huai Army*, 132–33.

14. Feng differed with Li on the question of how to deal with the Wusung Railway after its purchase. Feng sided with Shen Pao-chen, who wanted to destroy it. For this, Li called both Shen and Feng lackluster reformers. *LWCK Letters*, 18:5b–6. See also chapter 4 above.

15. *LWCK Memorials*, 74:41–43, also *Letters*, 17:3b.

16. *LWCK Letters*, 11:23b–24.

17. Nieh Ch'i-chieh, comp., *Chung-te lao-jen tzu-ting nien-p'u* (Autobiography of Tseng Chi-fen) (Shanghai, 1933), 24, 27. Also see Wellington K. K. Chan, *Merchants, Mandarins, and Modern Enterprises in Late Ch'ing China* (Cambridge, Mass., 1977), 45.

18. Albert Feuerwerker, *Rebellion in Nineteenth-Century China* (Ann Arbor, 1975), 93.

19. This was implied in a Tsungli Yamen memorial in 1864, saying that the posts of Kiukiang, Hankow, Chinkiang, Ningpo, Shanghai, and Tengchow taotais "formerly have been controlled by the governors-general and governors," *IWSM*, T'ung-chih, 24:29b–32. But another memorial in 1870 showed that the situation had changed and the Grand Council had taken back control; see *IWSM*, T'ung-chih, 73:29b–30.

20. Data from *TCHT* (1899), 8:8–10.

21. *Shen-pao* (2.1.1882), vol. 33, 21815.

22. A list of all taotais including the Tientsin customs taotai is given in Appendix B of the author's Ph.D. dissertation, The Shanghai Taotai: The Linkage Man in a Changing Society, 1843–93 (University of California, Santa Barbara, 1980).

23. Li did not want to intervene in Kiangsu affairs, see *LWCK Letters*, 16:13b. Other references also indicate this attitude, 16:20b–21, 17:1b, 18:18.

24. *YWYT*, VII, 503.

25. Lei Lu-ch'ing, *Li Hung-chang nien-p'u* (A chronological biography of Li Hung-chang) (Taipei, 1977) 251, 167, 178.

26. *YWYT*, VII, 464.

27. For a discussion of Li's *t'ung-nien* (Class of 1847), see Chuang Lien, *Chung-kuo chin-tai shih*, vol. 2, 2. T'u Tsung-ying and Ling Huan were also *t'ung-nien* of the provincial examination (*chü-jen*), see *An-hui t'ung-chih* (Provincial gazetteer of Anhwei) (Taipei reprint, 1968), *chüan* 100.

28. *LWCK Letters* (Ho Ching) 11:28b–29, (Shen Pao-chen) 18:18b, 18:21. Note his opening words, "In response to your inquiry regarding Kiangsu personnel . . ." (*ch'eng-hsün Chiang-tso jen-ts'ai . . .*). For more discussion on his relationship with the governor-general of Liangkiang, see Wang Erh-min, *Huai-chün chih* (The Anhwei Army) (Taipei, 1967), 253–54.

29. *Shen-pao*, (8.9.1880), (11.15.1880), also *LWCK Memorials*, 67:7.

30. *LWCK Letters*, 11:16.b.

6

Li Hung-chang's Use of Foreign Military Talent: The Formative Period, 1862–1874

Richard J. Smith

No high-ranking official in nineteenth-century China had more direct and sustained contact with foreigners than did Li Hung-chang. Even the most cursory glance at his memorials, letters, and telegraph messages for the period from 1862 to 1901 reveals that Americans and Europeans loomed large in Li's world of discourse, both official and private. In part, of course, Li's preoccupation with Westerners can be explained by the simple fact of imperialist expansion into Asia during the late Ch'ing period; from the 1840s onward, Chinese officials found it increasingly difficult, if not impossible, to ignore the unsettling presence of foreigners in the Middle Kingdom. But not all Ch'ing bureaucrats responded to the West in the same way, just as not all Westerners responded to Ch'ing officials in the same way. The salient feature of Li's approach was his Janus-like effort to build up China's wealth and power by using the scientific and technological skills of Westerners, yet all the while working to eliminate dependence upon them—or as he put it, to learn Western methods "without always having to use their men."[1] What were the origins of Li's strategy of "barbarian management"? How did his early experiences with foreigners affect his outlook? And how successful was he in the pursuit of his twin goals?

The employment of foreigners was, of course, nothing new in Chinese history. By the mid-nineteenth century, Chinese policymakers could look back on more than two thousand years of precedent in the use of "barbarians" for civil and military purposes. In the early Ch'ing period this tradition included the appointment of Jesuit missionaries as civil officials in the Imperial Board of Astronomy (Ch'in-t'ien chien), the incorporation of Russian soldiers into the dynasty's elite Banner forces, the employment of Dutch troops as "allies" against Cheng Ch'eng-kung, and the periodic use of individual Westerners as mercenaries and military technicians in the Opium War era.[2] But China's mid-nineteenth-century circumstances were unique in at least two fundamental ways. First, imperialism gave Westerners political and economic power in China vastly disproportionate to their numbers; second, Americans and Europeans had far more to offer to China technologically, and perhaps even culturally, than had any barbarians in the past.

When Li Hung-chang became acting governor of Kiangsu in April 1862, it did not take him long to realize both things. The problem was what to do about the situation. In a sense, Li had few choices. The location and timing of his appointment placed him inescapably in the vortex of Sino-foreign relations at the provincial level. As the Taip'ing Rebellion raged seemingly out of control, the throne and local officials had already acted to secure Western assistance against the rebels. In 1860 the foreign powers defended Shanghai against the Taip'ing forces of Li Hsiu-ch'eng, although they simultaneously conducted military operations against the Ch'ing to secure compliance with the Treaty of Tientsin (1858). During 1860–61, negotiations began for the purchase of Western ships and guns, as well as the formal and informal employment of foreign military and naval personnel. By early 1862 not only had the Ch'ing central government committed itself to purchasing a naval force for the Yangtze River to be staffed by British officers (the Lay-Osborn flotilla) but local officials in Kiangsu and Chekiang had also begun to raise Sino-foreign mercenary contingents, such as the Ever-Victorious Army (EVA), to contend with the persistent Taip'ing menace. Meanwhile, the Sino-foreign Inspectorate of Customs, established in 1854 at Shanghai, had become an ever more visible and influential feature of China's civil administration. Despite his claim to Tseng Kuo-fan that he would simply "strive for self-strengthening and not mix with foreigners," Li Hung-chang could not have avoided contact with them even if he had wanted to.[3]

Li Hung-chang and the Ever-Victorious Army

Li quickly sized matters up in 1862. As Professor Kwang-Ching Liu has indicated, the newly appointed acting governor immediately recognized the inevitability of dealing with foreigners and lost no time in trying to gain the upper hand with them. Within two weeks of his arrival at Shanghai, he began to acquire modern Western weapons for his Anhwei Army, having viewed their effectiveness against the Taip'ings firsthand. Employment of Western instructors from the Ever-Victorious Army followed naturally. By late 1862 Li's army had acquired more than a thousand rifles and employed perhaps half a dozen Western instructors from the EVA. Less than a year later, the Anhwei Army had expanded to more than forty thousand men and now boasted more than ten thousand rifles and several large cannon, in addition to about a dozen new foreign drill instructors—most of whom also came from the Ever-Victorious Army.[4]

In the early stages of modernizing his military forces, Li relied heavily on the personal assistance of Frederick T. Ward, the colorful American commander of the Ever-Victorious Army. He used Ward's contacts to acquire guns, ships, and other military supplies, and he sought to win the American commander's friendship in order to ingratiate himself with the foreign powers. In what would become a characteristic feature of Li's approach to foreign relations, he over-estimated American influence, both locally and at the capital. He had, however, a far more realistic grasp of domestic political realities. He saw, for example, that Ward enjoyed a close personal relationship with the corrupt but powerful local taotai, Wu Hsu, and that any effort to undermine the position of one would necessarily provoke the antagonism of the other.[5]

As the first Westerner in modern times to hold official rank in the Ch'ing military hierarchy, Ward presented special problems of responsibility and re-straint. Although the American adventurer had petitioned to become a Chinese subject and had married a Chinese woman (the daughter of his merchant-official patron, Yang Fang), his loyalties were difficult to judge, much less to assure. Although in the early stages of his career as a Chinese officer Ward had estab-lished an extraordinary reputation for bravery and effectiveness against the Taip'ings, reports in March and April by Li's predecessor, Hsueh Huan, that the American commander had not yet shaved his head in the Manchu fashion nor changed to Chinese clothing because he feared the ridicule of other foreigners provoked the throne to issue several anxious edicts on the subject. Li, however, remained relatively unconcerned. Writing to Tseng Kuo-fan in June, he stated that although Ward had not yet shaved his forehead nor paid him a courtesy visit, Li had no time to quarrel with foreigners over such "petty faults."[6]

Significantly, the concerns expressed by Ch'ing officials (including Prince Kung) over Ward's devotion to the imperial cause were not entirely groundless. According to letters written in the summer of 1862 to the American minister, Anson Burlingame, Ward complained vociferously about the "rascally officials" at Shanghai who, he claimed, had robbed him of credit for his accomplishments against the Taip'ings and had withheld some 350,000 taels of payment due him. Significantly, Ward asked Burlingame to "say a word" to Prince Kung "about my people" and remarked "if I had not my foot so deeply in the mire I would throw them all overboard." This last remark is a telling one, for it suggests that by August 1862 Ward had become ensnared in an elaborate web of control spun by local officials. Although claiming to be disgusted with the "lying, swindling, and smuggling" that surrounded him, he had become, in fact, a part of the problem by virtue of his multifarious dealings with the undeniably corrupt Yang Fang and Wu Hsu.[7]

Li was well aware of Ward's involvement in at least some of the illegal activities of Yang and Wu; yet while the American commander remained alive he did not move overtly against either him or them. As a result, Ward continued to work closely with Li, providing advice and assistance in obtaining arms, and cooperating closely with the Anhwei Army in military operations against the Taip'ings. Despite Ward's occasional complaints over the policies and practices of the "Devilish Governor," he and Li seem to have been on generally good terms. The American commander recognized the need for Li's political support, while the Kiangsu governor saw in Ward a strong, fearless, and well-connected Western leader whose weapons were extremely powerful and whose Chinese soldiers were "no different from foreign troops."[8]

Ward's death at the battle of Tz'u-ch'i in late September 1862 brought both opportunities and difficulties to Li. On the one hand, it helped him to undermine the power of Wu Hsu, since the Shanghai taotai had relied heavily on Ward. On the other hand, it deprived the Kiangsu governor of a valuable foreign adviser and brought a raft of administrative problems to his door. These had to do with the politics of replacing Ward as commander of the EVA. Although both the British and the French put forward their own candidates for leadership of the force, Li steadfastly insisted that if a Westerner were to head the Ever-Victorious Army that person would have to be "a man of Ward's stamp, ability, sagacity, and willingness to attach himself to the Chinese cause"—someone who would be entirely under Chinese jurisdiction "as to praise or blame." Peking expressed a similar view, indicating that if foreigners were to lead Chinese troops they had to petition to become Chinese subjects and accept Chinese control as Ward had done.[9]

Ward's right-hand man, Henry A. Burgevine—also an American adventurer—seemed to fit the bill. Like Ward, he was a brave officer who had petitioned to become a Chinese subject, taken a Chinese wife, and devoted himself wholeheartedly to the anti-Taip'ing cause. Unlike Ward, however, he was impetuous, short-tempered, extravagant, unreliable, and difficult to get along with. In early January 1863, after several months of continuous bickering with the Chinese authorities, Burgevine had a particularly serious altercation with Yang Fang over payment of the EVA, during which he struck Yang and took from him forty thousand dollars. Li Hung-chang immediately called for the American commander's dismissal, accusing him of robbery, rebellion, and treason. The Chinese government was reported to have placed a reward of 50,000 taels on his head. After failing to secure reinstatement, Burgevine eventually joined the Taip'ings, only to be captured by the Ch'ing authorities. He "accidentally" drowned in their custody during 1865.[10]

In the meantime, Li Hung-chang found it necessary to appoint two regular British officers to lead the Ever-Victorious Army—first, John Y. Holland of the Royal Navy (on a temporary basis); then, in March 1863, Charles G. Gordon of the Royal Engineers. Brilliant but erratic, Gordon managed to pull the EVA together and once again employ it with effect against the Taip'ings. Like Ward, he worked closely with Li, although he, too, chafed at the Kiangsu governor's administrative practices—most particularly his consistently dilatory payment of the force. In fact, at several points during Gordon's tenure as commander of the Ever-Victorious Army, he and Li had basic disagreements that threatened to undermine their cooperative venture. On at least two occasions, the EVA and the Anhwei Army nearly came to blows.[11]

The most serious altercation between Li and Gordon occurred in late 1863 after the Kiangsu governor had executed several high-ranking Taip'ing leaders who had surrendered the strategic city of Soochow to the Anhwei Army on December 4, having received Gordon's personal guarantee of their safety. This so-called Soochow Incident provoked a huge outcry on the part of Westerners in China. At Shanghai, for example, representatives of the foreign powers denounced Li in a strongly worded public proclamation. Gordon, humiliated and outraged, threatened to restore Soochow to the rebels, attack Li's troops with his foreign-led Ever-Victorious Army, and even join the Taip'ings. The British commander-in-chief, General W. G. Brown, took the Ever-Victorious Army under his own command and directed Gordon to "suspend all active aid to the Imperialist [i.e., Ch'ing] cause," and the British minister, Frederick Bruce, informed the Ch'ing authorities that Gordon could hold no communication with Li Hung-chang "or in any way be under his orders."[12]

The Chinese government, for its part, felt that Li Hung-chang's response to the situation at Soochow had been perfectly appropriate in light of the threatening attitude of the surrendered rebel leaders, and that the foreign powers had no right or reason to become involved in the matter. Thus, although in Li's report of the Soochow affair to the throne he had suggested the possibility of punishment for himself in order to placate the Western authorities, Peking had no such intentions. Commenting simply that "foreigners do not understand the principles involved," the throne shifted the burden of this delicate matter to the Tsungli Yamen.[13]

With passions still high and matters at a diplomatic impasse, Li found a strong foreign supporter in Robert Hart, newly appointed Inspector General (IG) of the Chinese Maritime Customs administration. In Shanghai to settle the accounts of the ill-fated Lay-Osborn flotilla and to take care of other customs-related business at the treaty port, Hart immediately and almost instinctively began to act as a mediator for the Ch'ing government. In so doing, he became, wittingly or otherwise, a valuable ally of Li Hung-chang. Hart would continue to play these dual roles of middleman and advocate for Li, with greater or lesser enthusiasm, throughout his long career in China.[14]

The IG believed from the outset that Gordon should take the field against the Taip'ings rather than remain in garrison. In his view, the first priority was unquestionably the rapid suppression of the rebels. This development would, Hart reasoned, benefit both the foreign powers and the Ch'ing government—not least in the expansion of Sino-foreign trade. Furthermore, despite the EVA's recent problems with pay and discipline, Hart saw the force as a potent weapon in the Ch'ing-Taip'ing struggle. Significantly, he also sought to protect Gordon from "impeachment" by Li Hung-chang for insubordination—a possibility he foresaw based on the Lay-Osborn affair and his own growing experience with the Ch'ing bureaucracy. Finally, Hart genuinely believed, as did Li, that since the Chinese supported the Ever-Victorious Army, they had every right to its services.

Few other foreigners in China shared Hart's view. General Brown, for instance, urged that the Ever-Victorious Army be disbanded immediately, "leaving the Chinese to fight their own battles." On December 19, 1863, the *North-China Herald* editorialized: "We are glad that ... Major Gordon will refrain from farther [*sic*] operations. It is by such means only that the Chinese can be acted on. It is hopeless to appeal to their sense of honour, for they have none; but they are keenly alive to their interests, and, rather than sacrifice these, may accommodate their actions to European principles.... [If Li Hung-chang finds] that the consequence of his conduct has been to deprive him of the all-important aid of the disciplined Chinese contingent [the EVA], he will in [the] future refrain from acts of treachery."[15]

Li greatly resented these foreign insults, but he was also anxious to placate Gordon. He therefore sent Dr. Halliday Macartney, who had also recently entered Li's service as an independent adviser and arsenal supervisor, to see Gordon immediately after the Soochow Incident in an attempt to placate the enraged foreign commander. Gordon, as it developed, vigorously denounced Macartney for interceding on Li's behalf, accusing the well-intentioned Scotsman of conduct unbecoming a British gentleman. Yet soon thereafter Gordon reestablished contact with the Kiangsu governor, presumably on the latter's initiative—despite his own initial outrage and Bruce's unambiguous orders. Why? The answer is simple: Gordon desperately wanted to return to action.

Quite apart from his well-known and insatiable love of battle, the British commander believed that the Ever-Victorious Army would grow increasingly degenerate and difficult to manage if it remained in garrison at K'un-shan. Furthermore, Gordon was quite aware that the Anhwei Army had proven itself capable of achieving military victory in his absence. This raised the unpalatable possibility that he and his vaunted Sino-foreign force might come to be viewed as no longer indispensable to the safety of Shanghai and the suppression of the Taip'ings—a blow to Gordon's ego. Finally, according to General Brown, Gordon had received "direct hints" that Li Hung-chang would dismiss him if he refused to take the field against the Taip'ings. In a letter to the British minister, Bruce, Gordon later claimed: "I know of a certainty that Burgevine meditates a return to the rebels; that there are upwards of 300 Europeans ready to join them, of no character, and that the Footae [Governor Li] will not accept another British officer if I leave the service, and therefore the Government may have some foreigner put in, or else the force put under men of Ward's and Burgevine's stamp, of whose action at times we should never feel certain."[16]

Meanwhile, Hart had been trying on his own to prod Gordon back into Li Hung-chang's service. Although a memorial written by the Kiangsu governor on February 25, 1864, suggests that Li himself initiated a reconciliation with Gordon, using Hart as his intermediary, the IG's journals provide no such indications. An entry for January 18 states simply: "My intention is to endeavor to get Gordon to work again, and to find out all the circumstances connected with the

Footae's action in beheading the Wangs [kings] at Soochow." At this point, Hart was obviously inclined to urge Gordon's return to action regardless of what he might discover about the execution. This was not only because of the IG's views regarding Shanghai's security; it was also because, as he indicated in his private journal, he feared that the Chinese authorities would read Gordon's refusal to fight as evidence of the unmanageability of "an able and reliable" man, who just happened to be a foreigner in the Ch'ing service. As such a person himself, Hart apparently felt that any stigma or doubt that might attach to Gordon might also apply to him. Under these circumstances, issues of personal morality surrendered to the demands of expediency.[17]

In any case, on February 1, after a number of false starts, Hart, Li, and Gordon finally met at Soochow and agreed that the Ever-Victorious Army would take the field following the Chinese New Year. From this point onward, Hart played an integral role in the EVA's affairs. He assisted Gordon in securing prompt and regular pay for his men, and he also detached a member of the customs staff, H. E. Hobson, to serve as an interpreter for the force. In addition, Hart helped Li Hung-chang to improve his tattered image among the foreign ministers in Peking. On February 6, for example, Hart wrote a long letter to Bruce, providing a lengthy and vigorous defense of Li's actions at Soochow. This letter unquestionably enhanced Li's stock in the foreign diplomatic community.[18]

Hart's journal indicates that at this time he also became an adviser to Li, and that the two chatted at length about diplomatic and study missions to Europe, iron and coal mining, foreign steamers, weapons and arsenals, as well as customs matters. These conversations obviously impressed Hart, who lamented later in the year (and in subsequent years as well) that Li—although impetuous, and relatively unconcerned with details—did not hold a position in the Tsungli Yamen. From this time onward, Hart came to consider Li an "ally" in his quest to modernize China; for the next several decades he continually gave Li assistance and advice. But the IG was by no means the only one of Li's foreign advisers during this initial and formative period of the governor's contact with Westerners. Nor was he even the most influential. From all indications, Halliday Macartney, who aspired to occupy a position in nineteenth-century China analogous to that of the Jesuits Adam Schall von Bell and Ferdinand Verbiest in the early Ch'ing, was Li's most valuable adviser. According to Gordon himself, Li and Macartney "talked for hours" about Western inventions, foreign relations, and other matters of vital concern; Gordon acknowledged without apparent jealousy that Macartney had done a great deal for the Chinese in the face of many obstacles. The British commander, however, was less willing to admit the key role Macartney played in the Ever-Victorious Army's internal affairs.[19]

The Ever-Victorious Army played a significant role in the recovery of several major Taip'ing strongholds following its return to action in February 1864, but by May it had become clear to both Li and Gordon that the force had passed its prime. They therefore hastily made plans for its disbandment. In their opinion, the EVA was too expensive, too ineffective, and too "local" in its loyalties to justify further financial support. The Anhwei Army, they both believed, was a superior and sufficient instrument for the protection of Kiangsu Province. But Hart and the British authorities at Shanghai felt that the Sino-foreign contingent should not be disbanded too precipitously, and that at least part of the EVA should be "kept up permanently" as a local defense force and training program. After extensive and sometimes difficult negotiations involving Hart, British Consul Harry Parkes, Gordon, Li, and Li's newly recruited and extremely able assistant, Ting Jih-ch'ang, the various parties reached a compromise whereby about a thousand men from the Ever-Victorious Army would be retained under Gordon's temporary supervision as the nucleus of a foreign training program at Feng-huang-shan, a small town about twenty-five miles southwest of Shanghai.[20]

The early lessons of barbarian management

By the summer of 1864, Li had learned virtually all he needed to know about the advantages and disadvantages of using foreigners in his self-strengthening enterprises. His experience with the Ever-Victorious Army and his contact with foreigners such as Ward, Burgevine, Gordon, Hart, and Macartney—not to mention his frequent and often frustrating negotiations with various Western civil and military authorities—formed the basis for his opinions regarding foreign assistance and the adoption of Western military technology for the next three decades. What exactly did he learn?

Although Li readily perceived the advantages to be gained by utilizing foreign arms, training methods, and personnel, he also recognized the special problems involved in accepting foreign assistance, especially in military affairs. One difficulty was, of course, the danger of inordinate foreign influence. Few Westerners in the Chinese military service were inclined to "turn toward Chinese civilization" (*hsiang-hua*) in the classic pattern. Most foreign officers had no admiration for Chinese culture, and few, Ward and Gordon included, bothered to learn Chinese, just as few Chinese learned a foreign language. Disputes between Western officers and the Chinese occurred frequently. Dressed in semi-Western uniforms and responding to foreign command words, the men of the Ever-Victorious Army and other such contingents were in the minds of most Chinese "counterfeit foreign-devils" (*chia yang-kuei-tzu*)—overpaid, rowdy, unacquainted with Confucian moral instruction, and, in Tseng Kuo-fan's words, "utterly coarse."[21]

The problems created by the Ever-Victorious Army's system of foreign officering went well beyond cultural subversion and the inevitable friction of daily Sino-foreign contact. Independent freebooters like Ward, Burgevine, and their subordinates tended to be arrogant and unmanageable, whereas commanding officers on loan from regular Western military and naval forces, such as Holland and Gordon, invited continual interference from their home governments. Even civilian advisers such as Hart—although a Ch'ing bureaucrat and reportedly "as completely Chinese in his sympathies as the Chinese himself"— created problems for Li. Despite his appreciation for the IG's useful and energetic services, Li occasionally described him as "quite contentious" and wrote that his willingness to exert himself on China's behalf was primarily because he coveted his large salary.[22]

Furthermore, foreigners involved in Chinese military affairs inevitably constituted a security risk. Rumors circulated throughout Ward's lifetime that he planned to dethrone the Manchus; Burgevine actually defected to the Taip'ings in 1863, together with several officers of the Ever-Victorious Army; Gordon threatened to join the rebels and attack the Anhwei Army in the aftermath of the Soochow Incident; and after disbandment of the EVA in 1864, several prominent officers of the force entered the Taip'ing service under Li Shih-hsien.[23]

From the Ch'ing government's standpoint, the exposure of foreigners to the inner workings of the Ch'ing military only increased the possibility of subterfuge. According to some reports, contact with Western officers in the Ever-Victorious Army encouraged certain "anti-Mandarin" tendencies on the part of the Chinese rank-and-file—even though antiforeignism seems to have been by far the more common outcome. Furthermore, Westerners in the Ch'ing military service were clearly in a position to report on Chinese military matters to their home governments. Even Gordon, one of the two foreigners Li admired most, according to Liang Ch'i-ch'ao (the other was U.S. Grant), used his knowledge of the Ch'ing military to advise the British on how best to attack China. Western drill also had its apparent hazards. Thus, in the name of security, Prince Kung inveighed strongly against the use of foreign command words in the training of Chinese troops—although the practice continued.[24]

Another problem with the employment of Western military men, less threatening than frustrating, was the prospect of interference in Chinese military affairs on the part of foreign governments. Motivated by an unclear mixture of altruism and self-interest, the Western powers, particularly France and Great Britain, proved to be especially meddlesome as they competed for increased influence in Chinese military affairs. Military aid became a foreign policy tool. Throughout the 1860s and thereafter, the foreign ministers in Peking made continual demands for Chinese military reform along Western lines, in addition to requesting honors, authority, and other special favors for their respective nations in the Chinese service. At the local level, foreign civil and military officials made thinly veiled threats to advance personal and national interests. The Burgevine affair demonstrated that the lack of official attachment to a foreign government and even Chinese "citizenship" did not preclude the foreign powers from intervening in what was properly a domestic matter, and the Soochow Incident underscored the potential for foreign control of a Chinese military force.[25]

Li Hung-chang understood and lamented all these things, but he also learned that there were ways to handle them. One was by exploiting international rivalries. In early 1863, for instance, he wrote that if the British continued to cause difficulties in pressing for their own commander of the Ever-Victorious Army, the force might simply be placed under France's Tardif de Moidrey or Bonnefoy, both French nationals who had recently been invested with Chinese military rank by Peking. The British could (and did) threaten to withdraw the Ever-Victorious Army's guns if they did not get their way, but they could not be certain that the French would refrain from supplying both officers and artillery to the force if Li chose to look to France for aid. Similarly, after the Soochow massacre, one reason the British did not simply deny further assistance to the Ch'ing out of disgust seems to have been a fear, exploited by Li, that France or another country would gain influence over the Ever-Victorious Army. In April 1864 Bruce wrote to Lord Russell in London: "If we were to withdraw our officers we should thereby do an unfriendly act towards this Government, but we should not prevent foreigners being employed." In the same vein, Gordon noted in May that "refusal of the license to serve [Li Hung-chang] will oblige the Chinese to resort to foreigners not of our nation."[26]

Li also learned how to manipulate individual foreign employees. Based on his experiences with Ward and Burgevine in particular, Li saw only too clearly that traditional signs of barbarian submission, such as the acquisition of Chinese "citizenship," could neither guarantee the loyalty of foreigners nor even assure that they would be subject to Chinese legal jurisdiction.[27] On the other hand, it is true Li could not help but appreciate the cultural transformation of individuals such as Macartney, who took a Chinese wife, and Jean Pennell, a Frenchman who entered Li's military service in 1862.

Pennell was originally attached to Liu Ming-ch'uan's "foreign-artillery battalion" (yang-p'ao ying), and by 1863 he had shaved his forehead, changed to Chinese clothing, and begun acquiring a knowledge of Chinese. Sometime later he married a Chinese woman, and in 1866, after receiving several awards for distinction in battle (including Manchu pa-t'u-lu rank and tsung-ping status), he petitioned to become a Chinese subject and to be registered as a native of Ho-fei (Lu-chou, Anhwei). Li's memorial reporting Pennell's petition was couched in standard world order rhetoric, complete with references to the foreigner's admiration for Chinese customs and the emperor's "cherishing and soothing men from afar." But Li recognized that there was substance to Pennell's petition, unlike those of Ward and Burgevine. Pennell's thorough sinicization allowed him to fit in perfectly with his Chinese peers in the Anhwei Army and facilitated Li's control over him.[28]

Unfortunately for Li, Pennell's cultural sensitivity, like that of Macartney, was rare among Westerners in nineteenth-century China. Recognizing this, the Kiangsu governor adopted a strategy of barbarian management that emphasized concrete inducements over cultural commitments. For more than two thousand years the Chinese had relied heavily on financial rewards as a means of attracting and maintaining the loyalty of foreign employees. Ward's legendary thirst for money conformed closely to a long-standing stereotype of foreigners, and even Gordon seemed, at least in Li's eyes, quite greedy. In fact, however, Gordon disdained monetary rewards, and as a matter of principle he refused a ten-thousand-tael gift from the Ch'ing government in the aftermath of the Soochow Incident.[29]

But while Gordon could not be tempted by material inducements, he, like Ward, wanted desperately to be appreciated. Li therefore played effectively on his ego, continually telling Gordon about the memorials he had written concerning the British commander's achievements in battle and conveying the substance of appreciative edicts in response. He even gave Gordon the impression that the empress dowager, Tz'u-hsi, took a personal interest in the Ever-Victorious Army. Meanwhile, Li's subordinates in the Anhwei Army had other military units kept in constant contact with Gordon, not only sharing information but also sending compliments. Li's praise of Gordon, it should be added, was genuine. Although occasionally disturbed by the latter's impatience, impetuousness, and sudden outbursts of temper, Li's memorials repeatedly commended the foreign commander for his bravery, zeal, obedience, military wisdom, and effective use of Western weapons.[30]

Li employed bureaucratic controls as an institutional complement to self-conscious flattery. From the very outset of Gordon's employment, the Kiangsu governor constantly reminded the British commander, as well as other British officials, both civil and military, that the Ever-Victorious Army was a Ch'ing military force, under Li's own direction. Soon after Gordon's appointment as commander of the force, Li told British Consul Markham that he had recently requested that Gordon be given a Ch'ing military commission as a brigade-general (tsung-ping) so that he could consider him "part of my command." Li had in fact made the same point in his memorial of April 12—although he also had to admit that he was bound to offer Gordon tsung-ping status by the terms of an agreement with the British in mid-January 1863. On April 27, in response to Li's memorial, Peking granted Gordon a temporary commission as brigade-general, charging him with the task of keeping the Ever-Victorious Army under control. Significantly, the edict to the Grand Council did not require the British commander to become a Chinese subject or change to Chinese clothing. Li conveyed the substance of these and related documents to Gordon, leaving him with no illusions about his position. "The Futai considers the force as his own," Gordon wrote in early May, "under an officer who has entered the Chinese Service and has nothing further to say to the British Authorities for the time that he remains in the Chinese Service."[31]

Meanwhile, Li subjected his foreign employees to constant surveillance. The same Ch'ing commanders who sent information and compliments to Gordon also kept a close eye on him. Thus, for example, we find that the Green Standard Colonel Li Heng-sung sent independent reports to Li on Gordon's administrative problems and military movements. Other Ch'ing commanders, including Ch'eng

Hsueh-ch'i of the Anhwei Army, did the same. Meanwhile, civil officials such as the Sung-chiang prefect, Chia I-ch'ien, also filed reports on Gordon's activities.[32] Furthermore, Li had the Anhwei Army to rely on as a potent means of control. By late 1863 it had grown to about sixty thousand men, and although some were trained by foreign officers, none had any loyalty to them—except perhaps to Pennell. Foreign observers often spoke of the large numbers of "excellent troops" under Li's commanders; the *North-China Herald* went so far as to suggest (after the Soochow Incident) that the Ever-Victorious Army would have "a sorry chance" against Ch'eng Hsueh-ch'i's army if the two forces had clashed. Li and his commanders obviously were not anxious for a confrontation but neither did they fear Gordon's troops.[33]

The legacy of foreign assistance in military affairs

Throughout the remainder of Li's illustrious career he continued to avail himself of Western assistance in all realms of self-strengthening. Although a full treatment of this vast topic lies well beyond the reach of this essay, a few examples of Li's approach to the employment of foreigners in military affairs after 1864 may indicate some of the ways in which his experiences during the Taip'ing period conditioned his later outlook and policies.

The foreign-training program at Feng-huang-shan provided Li with an opportunity to implement his policies of barbarian management without the immediate and profound pressures of the Taip'ing Rebellion. He was under no illusions about the camp's origins, however; without British pressure, and Hart's persistent urging, it would never have come into existence. Li knew only too well from his experience with the Ever-Victorious Army that foreign assistance invited foreign interference, and from the very beginning he perceived in Western demands for the expansion of foreign-training programs an attempt to "seize our military authority and squander our financial resources." He was "enraged," therefore, when Consul Harry Parkes demanded that six British officers be appointed to serve as instructors at Feng-huang-shan in the fall of 1864.[34]

Li understood, as did Hart and most other foreign observers, that the retention of a force "officered by Englishmen—whether you style them Military instructors or commanding officers"—would promote rivalry among the other Western powers. But British officials in the vicinity of Shanghai at the time considered the move justifiable, perhaps even essential, in the light of growing French influence in foreign-training programs. On July 29, 1864, for example, Consul Parkes reported to Wade with dismay that there were "probably" more French than British subjects serving the Ch'ing government in a military capacity. This theme of Anglo-French competition, which had emerged prominently in 1862, remained a feature of Western military assistance to the Ch'ing government throughout much of the remainder of the nineteenth century; ironically, some of Hart's own customs employees, notably Prosper Giquel and Eugene de Meritens, proved especially active in promoting French interests against the British.[35]

The training program at Feng-huang-shan began auspiciously enough. By mid-August, only a month or so after the camp had been established, Gordon could already write of the "great progress" he had made with the troops in manual, platoon, and gun drill. "It is," he wrote, "much easier than I supposed it would be." But the energetic British commander also found the mere instruction of troops to be "very tedious," requiring "a great deal more patience than I have." He decided, therefore, to return to Great Britain. His announced departure, in turn, provided impetus for negotiations between the Chinese and British over the future of Feng-huang-shan. Gordon himself expressed satisfaction with the program, feeling that it should continue "to assimilate the men as much as possible to the Imperialists [i.e., the Chinese military] with respect to . . . dress, pay and discipline." Gordon acknowledged that under Li Hung-chang there had been no cause for complaint regarding the program at Feng-huang-shan, but he believed that an understanding should be reached with the Chinese authorities that would place the camp on a more permanent footing in the event of Li's transfer.[36]

The outcome of extended negotiations between Parkes and Ting Jih-ch'ang was a thirteen-point agreement, arranged on November 12, that satisfied both parties. Although Li Hung-chang had to accept Lieutenant Jebb of the 67th Regiment as head drillmaster replacing Gordon, he succeeded in making Feng-huang-shan a Chinese institution in fact as well as name. According to the terms of the agreement, a Chinese commander (t'ung-ling) would assume responsibility for all matters of promotion and dismissal, camp discipline, payment, rations, and other major aspects of military administration. Jebb and his foreign drillmasters were responsible only for instruction and drill. With P'an Ting-hsin, a local Anhwei Army officer, as t'ung-ling and Ting Jih-ch'ang as taotai (later financial commissioner of Kiangsu and eventually governor of the province), Li could be reasonably sure of Chinese control over affairs at Feng-huang-shan. Hart's journal entry of November 9, 1864, indicates that although initially the Chinese authorities considered the camp to be a "sop" to foreigners, Li Hung-chang now fully supported it. According to his account, "3,000 men and 60 gunboats, in all a force of 4,500 men, are to be regularized, under Pwan Fantae [Finance Commissioner P'an Ting-hsin]."[37]

Several months later, in May 1865, Hart revisited Feng-huang-shan and reported favorably on the program. According to the IG, the nine hundred Chinese soldiers directly under Yü Tsai-pang and Yuan Chiu-kao of the Anhwei Army "drilled remarkably well, the instructors interfering but little." Although Jebb told Hart that periodic interference by Parkes had "done harm" to the program and discouraged P'an Ting-hsin from more active involvement at Feng-huang-shan, he "could not complain of anything done by the Chinese, or left undone with regard to the Camp."[38]

When Jebb received his transfer back to England the next month, however, it raised the troublesome issue of who would succeed him. Parkes naturally felt that the new British commander-in-chief, General Guy, should name a successor; but Ting Jih-ch'ang, with Li's tacit support, cleverly bypassed regular channels to secure the appointment of William Winstanley, a former British officer who had also served in the Ever-Victorious Army. In justifying this move, Ting emphasized that Gordon had recommended Winstanley in a letter from home, and he took special pains to point out that Winstanley's lack of official connections with the British government would be an advantage. The British authorities at Shanghai protested Ting's coup vociferously, but to no avail. At Peking, Thomas Wade affirmed China's right to appoint a successor to Jebb, asking only that the Chinese inform him of their final selection.[39]

For the next several years, the routine at Feng-huang-shan proceeded much as it had under Gordon and Jebb: Commands were given in Chinese rather than English; Chinese officials supervised the basic administration of the camp; An-hwei Army officers occupied the military posts of *t'ung-ling* and *ying-kuan* (battalion commander); and customs revenue sustained the camp. But by 1873, after nearly a decade of operation and the expenditure of nearly a million and a half taels, the training program had degenerated beyond any hope of redemption. As early as 1869, the *North-China Herald* described it as a collection of "quondam rebels, opium smokers and idlers." Ting Jih-ch'ang, now governor of Kiangsu, expressed a similar view, writing that the troops at the camp were inadequately trained, riddled with corruption, extravagant, unclean, and poorly led. Most of the middle-grade officers smoked opium, and he described the two Chinese battalion commanders at Feng-huang-shan as listless and "slippery." Ting considered the whole program to have "form without substance."[40]

Winstanley, too, complained vehemently about the situation, but bound by the 1864 agreement, he and his foreign associates were "powerless to correct domestic abuses." British officials in Shanghai, and Winstanley himself, tried unsuccessfully to expand the foreign role at Feng-huang. The Chinese felt that foreign meddling in camp affairs was already too pronounced. In mid-1873 the Feng-huang-shan program was abruptly terminated, to the intense displeasure of local British officials and the extreme satisfaction of the Ch'ing authorities. Too much attention on the part of Westerners had not compensated for neglect on the part of the Chinese. Indeed, the two tendencies had a complementary effect in hastening the decline of the program.

The failure of Feng-huang-shan reflected the failure of foreign-training programs generally in the T'ung-chih period (1862–74). Lacking central government direction and support, these programs lasted only as long as the enthusiasm or tenure of their local sponsors. Most programs withered and died well before Feng-huang-shan.[41] Yet in the absence of a regular institutional means of producing a modern, Western-trained Chinese officer corps, Ch'ing officials, including Li Hung-chang, continued to use foreigners to train their troops.[42] Li, however, approached the matter of using Western talent from two directions. One was naturally the familiar strategy of employing Westerners in China on an ad hoc basis, according to immediate needs. The other, more complex in conception and execution, was to send Chinese abroad for exposure to Western military influences.

After Li became governor-general of Chihli in 1870, he found that he could now draw on an ever-widening circle of foreign contacts in the pursuit of both approaches. In part, this development can be explained by his own rapidly expanding domestic network of progressively minded protégés, such as Ting Jih-ch'ang, who not only acquired increasing power and prestige within the Ch'ing bureaucracy but also enjoyed good standing among foreigners in China. His greater access to foreign talent can also be attributed to the maturation of his long-standing friendship with Robert Hart, who allowed Western employees from the maritime customs administration to serve Li (and other Chinese officials) in various modernizing enterprises. Yet another explanation for his success is that in Tientsin—as both governor-general of the metropolitan province and commissioner for the three northern ports—Li became, in effect, a central government official, in a position to attempt the coordination of China's diplomacy, military defense, and self-strengthening projects. Few foreign representatives on their way to Peking could afford to pass up an opportunity to visit Li, sound out his views, and press their own pet projects.[43]

One distinguished foreign visitor to China in the mid-1870s was the American general Emory Upton, who called on Li and inspected the Anhwei Army as part of his grand military tour of Asia. According to Li, the two men talked about the idea of establishing a Chinese military academy, but nothing came of the discussion. Although Li's writings at the time indicate a clear awareness of the value of such a step, apparently the need was not considered sufficiently great to justify the cost of establishing a full-fledged military academy on Chinese soil. During the same period, Li also inquired into the possibility of placing a few Chinese cadets at West Point—presumably a small-scale version of the famous educational mission of civilians sent to the United States in 1872. Again nothing materialized—this time for political reasons. In 1876, however, Li was able to send seven of his Anhwei Army officers to Germany to learn "the art of war," accompanied by one of Li's best drill instructors, a man named Lehmayer.[44]

The Germans, with a newly formed East Asian squadron and an eye to the establishment of a German territorial foothold in China, were only too happy to oblige Li. Although Hart continued to work unceasingly for the advancement of British interests, his zeal was now matched by Krupp and the Reich, who made considerable efforts through the use of such means as subsidies to prospective instructors, to ease the way for Germans to serve the Chinese. German military men flocked to Li's standard, including the influential adviser and sometime field officer, Constantin von Hanneken, who entered Li's service as an aide-de-camp in 1879.[45]

Meanwhile, some of the students sent by Li had returned to the Anhwei Army. The experience of one of them, Cha Lien-piao, is illuminating. Cha served in Chou Sheng-ch'uan's ten-thousand-strong Sheng-chün—perhaps the best detachment of the Anhwei Army in all of China up to the time of Chou's death in 1885. Convinced of the value of Western training and drill from long exposure to foreign instructors in Li's force (dating from the Taip'ing period), Chou lamented the fact that the spirit of foreign drill had not more fully permeated the Anhwei Army. Hoping to remedy the situation and appreciative of Cha's contributions to the overall efficiency of the Sheng-chün, Chou urged Li to "break the rules" by giving Cha a salary increase in order to reward and encourage him. Significantly, however, Chou did not recommend him for high-level promotion within the Green Standard system—a reward that most *yung-ying* officers especially esteemed. Although Chou's voluminous writings repeatedly emphasize the importance of Western-style drill, it is apparent that Chou himself was not prepared—for whatever reason—to request maximum rewards for those who mastered it.[46] How much more of a problem must this have been in other, less progressive military forces?

We can also see in the Sheng-chün a certain hostility to foreigners and foreign influences reminiscent of both the Ever-Victorious Army and foreign-training programs of the T'ung-chih period, such as Feng-huang-shan. Although foreign meddling in this particular unit of the Anhwei Army seems to have been minimal, and although Chou took pains to point out that his foreign-trained officers were trusted by their men, it is clear that the acceptance of foreign influences within Li's army was far less than complete. In the words of one well-informed observer of the Anhwei Army, "to be smart [in Western drill] is to be like a hated foreigner and to lose caste." This attitude, together with an inherited distaste for active involvement in drill, undoubtedly compromised the military effectiveness of the Anhwei Army's officer corps.[47]

To bring the Anhwei Army more in line with Western practice, Chou suggested shortly before his death the establishment of a foreign-style military academy (*wu-pei yuan*). Apparently fearful of upsetting vested interests within the Anhwei Army, Chou emphasized that it would "not be necessary to teach many commanders." He did, however, encourage Li to establish an office (*kung-so*) as soon as possible to provide systematic instruction for Chinese soldiers under German supervision.[48] The immediate incentive was threefold: the military demands of the Sino-French conflict; the support of other Anhwei Army commanders; and the presence of a core group of capable German instructors.

Interestingly enough, Gordon had suggested a similar step in 1880, when he returned to China to assist Li Hung-chang in the midst of the so-called Ili crisis that threatened war with Russia. Li's effort to use Gordon at this time, like his employment of the eccentric British commander during the Taip'ing period, illustrates once again the deficiencies of China's ad hoc approach to military reform and the use of foreign talent. Correspondence between Li and Gordon in 1869 foreshadowed the latter's return to China eleven years later. At that time, British subjects were permitted to serve the Chinese in peacetime but not in war.

This stipulation reportedly discouraged Hart from a grand scheme to employ about a hundred British subjects as instructors for a Chinese army of ten thousand men. It did not, however, deter Gordon. As soon as he arrived in Tientsin, he told Li Hung-chang that he would fight for China if Russia attacked; when Li asked if Gordon would be able to act independently of the British government, the latter responded: "I have already resigned my commission. England is unable to control me."[49]

Impressed by Gordon's personal loyalty and "love for China," Li Hung-chang wrote to the Tsungli Yamen: "Since Gordon has stated that he is no longer a British officer, the British minister cannot control him. Nor is he worried about Russian jealousy. With a view toward utilizing foreign talents [*Ch'u-ts'ai Chin-yung*], I ought to keep him here and discuss with him all relevant matters, so as to be benefitted by his experience and knowledge." He went on to say: "Gordon is loyal and sincere at heart, unmoved by venal considerations [. . .] In spite of his distinguished reputation, he is still frugal and diligent as before, and I find him most congenial. He will do his utmost to help us in case of an emergency."[50]

But Gordon's advice, that China should not go to war to uphold China's "dignity," was most unpopular in Peking. Even Li, who greatly admired Gordon's devotion to the Middle Kingdom, felt that his foreign friend had lost touch with Chinese realities, was too susceptible to "idle talk," and was too indecisive. Hart wrote to his London agent: "Much as I like and respect him, I must say he is 'not all there.' " The height of Gordon's irrationality was his attempt to persuade Li Hung-chang to "march on Peking, and assume charge as Guardian of the Emperor." Li had no such plans, of course, but the foreign press abounded with rumors that he and Gordon were conspiring to oust the Manchus. Troubled by these rumors, and frustrated by Chinese and Western policymakers, Gordon decided that he should leave. "If I stayed," he wrote in the latter part of August, "it would be bad for China, because it would vex the American, French, and German governments, who would want to send their officers. Besides I am not wanted."[51]

This unfortunate pattern of recourse to foreign assistance repeated itself throughout the 1880s and into the 1890s. Foreign instructors kept Li Hung-chang's troops abreast of new developments in Western military science; but they, like their counterparts in the Tung-chih period, could not make fundamental changes in the Anhwei Army, much less the Chinese military as a whole. As the *Chinese Times* observed in early 1887, "It is true that foreign officers have been employed [in various parts of China], and that they have taught the Chinese recruits a great deal of drill. . . . But reforms have not penetrated to the essential factors in a campaign, the handling of troops, the transport, commissariat, medical staff, etc., without which a drilled army is as much a loose rabble as if they had no drill."[52] Chinese observers came to similar conclusions. Western-trained armies, such as Li Hung-chang's, had the ability to cope with poorly armed internal rebels, but they were not up to the challenge of foreign aggression.

Furthermore, the rising external threat after 1874, together with the related growth of Chinese antiforeignism, complicated the process of obtaining and systematically using the foreign military assistance that China continued to require. As a means to check foreign incursions, the employment of Westerners had increasingly obvious limitations, not the least of which was that one or the other Western power was usually the enemy. The *Economist* pointedly remarked during the Ili crisis that if the Chinese were to organize an army officered by Europeans, "it could not possibly be used for any general attack upon the [foreign] settlements."[53] And even Gordon, who loyally counseled the Chinese on how to defend themselves against foreign aggression in 1880, also advised the British on how best to attack China.[54] In the end, national self-interest seems to have animated even the most altruistic-sounding of foreign reform proposals.[55]

Throughout the remainder of the nineteenth century, foreign rivalries continued to encourage intrigue, "wire-pulling," and increased foreign pressure on Chinese officials. At the same time, ironically, neutrality laws and other legal obstacles hindered the free employment of Western military men. There was, moreover, growing resentment over the employment of foreign officers and instructors in Chinese armies.[56] All these problems had emerged in the Taip'ing period, but they became increasingly difficult to solve as time wore on. It is therefore particularly surprising that as late as 1895 there were still some individuals—Chinese as well as foreigners—who advocated for China a military model that closely resembled the force led by Ward and Gordon some thirty years before. Although one ambitious plan to build a foreign-officered Chinese army under von Hanneken fell through, Chang Chih-tung's Self-Strengthening Army (Tzu-ch'iang chün), which used Germans as brigade, battalion, and company officers until Chinese officers could be trained to replace them, suffered from virtually all the flaws of the EVA: unqualified and disorderly foreign officers, Sino-foreign friction, and, ultimately, Western intervention.[57]

In short, as the nineteenth century drew to a close, Li Hung-chang and like-minded individuals had still not solved the basic problems brought on by using foreign assistance. Despite more than three decades of painful but potentially instructive experience, Chinese policy regarding the employment of Westerners in military affairs remained much the same as it had been during the Taip'ing period. Westerners were still employed by Li Hung-chang and others as advisers, instructors, and even officers; but Peking made no real attempt to coordinate or supervise their modernizing efforts. Arms, training, and even the language of instruction varied greatly from army to army and place to place. Like the foreign-training programs of the T'ung-chih period, the few Chinese military academies founded in the 1880s and 1890s depended primarily on local sponsorship and irregular financing, and the officers they produced were too few in number for China's needs.[58]

Conclusion

Odd as it may seem, there was no real contradiction between Li's substantial and sustained use of foreign employees and his expressed desire to eliminate reliance on them. His own writings and the testimony of his associates, both foreign and Chinese, indicate clearly that he genuinely despised the idea of depending on Westerners for assistance—particularly in military affairs. Even his good friend Hart took Li to task for his particular brand of antiforeignism. In a fascinating and somewhat ironic journal entry dated November 25, 1874, Hart recounts a visit from one of Li's foreign affairs experts (*yang-wu wei-yuan*) by the name of Hsu—the son of a former president of the Board of Works who, two years before, had been sent to Japan for six months "to watch things on Li's behalf." In the course of their conversation, Hart extended compliments to the governor-general on his efforts to promote change and pointedly remarked on Li's "great friendship" with William Pethick, who had become one of Li's most useful and trusted employees. Then, in the same breath, the IG complained to Hsu that Li did not "fully understand foreign affairs" since he was opposed to "more contact with foreigners."[59]

The problem was not, of course, Li's bigotry. As I have tried to indicate, certain kinds of Chinese antiforeignism indeed hindered China's modernizing efforts; but Li himself was not blindly xenophobic. His attempt to build a modern, Western-trained officer corps obviously did not fail because he refused to employ large numbers of foreigners, or because his Western employees were generally unwilling to become Chinese "citizens" or to accept Chinese culture. Nor was it because prior to 1895 the vast majority of Chinese subjects—including the officers and men of Li's Anhwei Army—lacked the kind of enthusiasm for foreign things that made possible the tidal wave of Westernization that washed over Meiji Japan in the 1870s.[60] To be sure, such enthusiasm would obviously have helped ease the way in China for foreign-inspired military reform, but it was unthinkable in the nineteenth century.

Even the stubborn persistence of Confucian "orthodoxy" does not satisfactorily explain Li's difficulties in the realm of military affairs. Conservative critics of his modernizing projects, including foreign-training programs, could always complain that reformers were "using [the ways of the barbarians] to transform China [*yung-i pien-Hsia*]"; but the throne's lack of enthusiasm for military reform along Western lines cannot be explained in terms of ideology alone. In the first place, we should remember that little if anything in the way of Confucian learning had ever been expected of regular Ch'ing military officers in the first place. Paradoxically, it was in the innovative *yung-ying* mercenary armies, about which the throne had extremely mixed feelings, rather than the Green Standard and Banner forces of the empire, that the inculcation of Confucian virtues received special stress. Even "pragmatic" officials such as Li Hung-chang continually emphasized the importance of instilling orthodox Confucian values in

Chinese soldiers—not only in *yung-ying* forces, but also in the new-style military academies of the 1880s and 1890s. Surely Li's officers in the Anhwei Army were no less "Confucian" than their Green Standard and Banner counterparts.[61]

Viewed from the perspective of foreign training, the major stumbling block to effective military reform in China seems to have been the Ch'ing central government's unwillingness to promote meaningful institutional change. This attitude stemmed not only from the long-standing administrative principle of fragmented military responsibility but also from the lack of a sustained sense of crisis. As the Tsungli Yamen wrote in the early 1870s, "When something happens, we hurriedly plan to make up our deficiencies; but after the incident, we again indulge in pleasure and amusements."[62] The temporary use of foreign-officered contingents such as the Ever-Victorious Army, like the temporary support of foreign-training programs such as the camp at Feng-huang-shan, was perfectly consistent with Peking's ad hoc and localized approach to the management of military affairs. But in the long run it ran counter to China's needs: The very success of such temporary expedients in contending with immediate problems stifled the reform impulse that Westerners expected them to spark.

Fearful of upsetting vested interests at all levels of society, and conscious of its increasingly precarious administrative position, the Manchu throne resisted fundamental institutional change until after the debacle of 1895. Although traditionalism and antiforeignism remained powerful forces in China, they might have been overcome had the Ch'ing government provided substantial rewards for the acquisition of new military and other technical skills—such as prestigious examination degrees and coveted bureaucratic appointments. It is true, of course, that under the best of circumstances reform would have been agonizingly slow. State revenues were extremely meager, and Peking's fears over foreign meddling in Chinese military affairs were not entirely unfounded. But it is also evident that the Manchus, as alien rulers and the self-appointed protectors of Chinese tradition, had no desire to establish a systematic, centralized program of modern military education in China—particularly when it became apparent that Western arms and training could not be confined to the traditional Banner and Green Standard forces of the empire.[63]

Ironically, had the Manchus undertaken meaningful, centralized reform during the 1860s and 1870s, when anti-Manchu sentiment was no longer a political problem and imperialist pressure was minimal, the dynasty might have been able to build a Meiji-style system of military education and eventually dispense with foreign instructors altogether, as did Japan.[64] Instead, the Ch'ing government, by stages, alienated patriotic Chinese and disappointed the foreign powers by its failure to build a modern, Western-style military force capable of doing more than simply keeping a lid on internal rebellion. Most ironic of all, in seeking foreign talent after the Sino-Japanese War, the Chinese turned to the one-time "dwarf bandits" of Japan, who began training large numbers of Chinese soldiers in modern military methods, both at home and abroad. This new education, and the nationalism that inspired it, had revolutionary consequences.

Notes

Abbreviations

BPP   *British Parliamentary Papers.*

IWSM   *Ch'ing-tai ch'ou-pan i-wu shih-mo* (Complete record of the management of barbarian affairs), Peiping, 1930; TC (T'ung-chih period).

LWCK   Li Hung-chang, *Li Wen-chung kung ch'üan-chi* (The complete works of Li Hung-chang), Wu Ju-lun, comp. Nanking, 1905.
        Memorials (tsou-kao)
        Letters (p'eng-liao han-kao)
        Letters to the Tsungli Yamen (I-shu han-kao)

NCH   *North-China Herald.*

TPTKSL *T'ai-p'ing t'ien-kuo shih-liao* (Historical materials on the Taiping Heavenly Kingdom), Tien Yü-ch'ing et al., comps. Peking, 1950.

WCSL   *Ch'ing-chi wai-chiao shih-liao* (Historical materials concerning foreign relations in the late Ch'ing period), Wang Yen-wei and Wang Liang, comps. Peiping, 1932–35.

WHTA   *Wu Hsu tang-an chung ti T'ai-p'ing t'ien-kuo shih-liao hsuan-chi* (Selections of historical materials concerning the Taiping Heavenly Kingdom in Wu Hsu's archives), Ching Wu and Chung Ting, eds. Peking, 1958.

YWYT   *Yang-wu yün-tung* (The foreign affairs movement), Chung-kuo k'o-hsüeh yüan chin-tai-shih yen-chiu-so, ed. (1961)

1. *IWSM,* TC 25: 10 (June 2, 1864). See also Kwang-Ching Liu, "The Confucian as Patriot and Pragmatist: Li Hung-chang's Formative Years, 1823–1866," *Harvard Journal of Asiatic Studies* 30 (1970); chapter 2, this volume. I would like to acknowledge here not only Professor Liu's many outstanding contributions to the field of Chinese history but also my profound debt of gratitude to him as both a teacher and a colleague.

2. See Richard J. Smith, "The Employment of Foreign Military Talent: Chinese Tradition and Late Ch'ing Practice," *Journal of the Hong Kong Branch of the Royal Asiatic Society* 15 (1975).

3. For background, consult Richard J. Smith, *Mercenaries and Mandarins: The Ever-Victorious Army in Nineteenth Century China* (Millwood, N.Y., Kraus-Thomson Ltd., 1978), chapter 3; see also Richard J. Smith et al., eds, *Robert Hart and China's Early Modernization: His Journals, 1863–1866* (Cambridge, Mass.: Harvard University Press, 1991).

4. Liu, "The Confucian as Patriot and Pragmatist," pp. 16ff.

5. Smith, *Mercenaries and Mandarins,* pp. 28–40, 54–57, and 83–91, passim. The most recent account of Ward's exploits, which uses Chinese-language materials from the F. T. Ward Collection at Yale University to document his close relationship with Wu Hsu, is Caleb Carr, *The Devil Soldier* (New York: Random House, 1992).

6. *LWCK Letters,* 1:29, Li to Tseng Kuo-fan (June 3, 1862). Cf. Smith, *Mercenaries and Mandarins,* pp. 75–78.

7. See note 5 above; see also note 32 below.

8. See *LWCK Letters,* 1:30b, Li to Tseng Kuo-fan (June 7, 1862); ibid., 1:39, Li to Tseng Kuo-fan (July 21, 1862); ibid., 1:43, Li to Tseng Kuo-fan (August 3, 1862); ibid., 1:54a–b, Li to Tseng Kuo-fan (September 8, 1862).

9. *IWSM,* TC 9:4 (October 8, 1862), and ibid., 9:13b (October 11, 1862). Cf. *WHTA,* pp. 112, 137.

10. On Burgevine, consult Smith, *Mercenaries and Mandarins,* pp. 108–14, 120–22.

11. For details on Gordon's administration of the EVA, see ibid., chapters 7 and 8.

12. Smith et al., eds, *Robert Hart and China's Early Modernization: His Journals, 1863–1866,* pp. 33–44, 47–79, passim. For opinions by both Chinese and Westerners, see Lei Lu-ch'ing, *Li Hung-chang hsin-chuan* (A new biography of Li Hung-chang) (Taipei, Wen-hai, 1983), 1:159–62.

13. See *IWSM,* TC 22:9–10b (December 23, 1863), and ibid. 22:17b (January 6, 1864).

14. The evidence can be found in Smith et al., eds, *Robert Hart and China's Early Modernization: His Journals, 1863–1866,* and John K. Fairbank et al., eds., *The I.G. in Peking: Letters of Robert Hart, Chinese Maritime Customs, 1868–1907* (Cambridge, Mass.: Harvard University Press, 1975), two volumes.

15. *North-China Herald,* December 19, 1863. Cf. *LWCK,* Letters, 4:29–30, Li to Tseng Kuo-fan (January 13, 1864).

16. See Smith, *Mercenaries and Mandarins,* pp. 146–48, 160–61.

17. On Hart's role in the Soochow affair, see Smith et al., eds, *Robert Hart and China's Early Modernization,* chapters 1 and 2, passim.

18. Ibid., pp. 41–42 includes several passages from this letter.

19. On Macartney's role, consult the Gordon Papers, British Library, Ad. Mss. 52,386. This collection contains a large number of Macartney's letters to Gordon, many of which are undated. See also *LWCK Memorials,* 7:34 (October 3, 1864), ibid., 10:38a–b (September 28, 1866), etc.; Demetrius Boulger, *The Life of Sir Halliday Macartney* (London: J. Lane, 1908), passim.

20. See Jonathan Ocko, *Bureaucratic Reform in Provincial China: Ting Jih-ch'ang in Restoration Kiangsu, 1867–1870* (Cambridge, Mass., and London: Harvard University Press, 1983), pp. 18–20.

21. Cited in William J. Hail, *Tseng Kuo-fan and the Taiping Rebellion* (New Haven: Yale University Press, 1927), p. 260. See also Smith, *Mercenaries and Mandarins,* pp. 88, 98–102, 154.

22. *IWSM,* TC 55:8 (December 31, 1867).

23. Smith, *Mercenaries and Mandarins,* pp. 54–56, 111–14, 145–48, 159, 162, 181.

24. Ibid., p. 181; see also *YWYT* 3:510. Cf. *LWCK Letters,* 2:37b–38 (Li to Tseng Kuo-fan, December 22, 1862, and *LWCK Memorials,* 20:46 (January 17, 1873).

25. On the theme of foreign competition and meddling, see Smith, *Mercenaries and Mandarins,* pp. 58–60, 67–71, 102–105, 107–12, 178–82; Steven Leibo, *Transferring Technology to China: Prosper Giquel and the Self-Strengthening Movement* (Berkeley: Center for Chinese Studies, 1985), pp. 72–73, 84–87; Steven Leibo, ed., *A Journal of the Chinese Civil War 1864* (Honolulu: University of Hawaii Press, 1985), pp. 26ff., esp. p. 39.

26. Smith, *Mercenaries and Mandarins,* pp. 151–55.

27. *IWSM,* TC 10:46a–b, 49b–50 (December 6, 1862). For a discussion of Li's efforts to manipulate Ward, Burgevine, and Gordon, consult Smith, *Mercenaries and Mandarins,* pp. 54–58, 105–106, 115–17, 153–60, 164–67.

28. *YWYT* 3:479–80. On Macartney, see Boulger, *Sir Halliday Macartney,* pp. 140–41; see also *IWSM,* TC 44:20a–b (October 7, 1866).

29. *TPTK,* pp. 357–58; *IWSM,* TC 22:18–19 (January 16, 1864).

30. See, for example, *LWCK Letters*, 3:8a–b, Li to Tseng Kuo-fan (March 28, 1863); ibid., 3:10a–b, Li to Tseng Kuo-fan (April 3, 1863); ibid., 3:14, Li to Tseng Kuo-fan (April 27, 1863); ibid., 3:16–17, Li to Tseng Kuo-fan (June 15, 1863); *TPTK*, pp. 299–438 reproduces a great many letters to Gordon from Li Hung-chang and Li's subordinates. See also the translated Chinese documents in the Gordon Papers, British Library, Orig. Mss. 2338.

31. Gordon Papers, British Library, Ad. Mss. 52,393, "Views Respecting the Sung-keong Force," May 5, 1863. Cf. *TPTK*, pp. 309–10, and *IWSM*, TC 15:10b–11 (April 27, 1863).

32. See, for example, the communications in *TPTK*, pp. 313–14, 318, 321–22, 326. The precedent had been established in the Ward period, as various documents in the Ward Collection at Yale University indicate. See Misc. Mss. Coll. Ms. Gr. 352.

33. *North-China Herald*, June 18, 1864; *LWCK Letters*, 4:24, Li to Tseng Kuo-fan, December 24, 1863. For a recent analysis of one of Li's leading military commanders, see Chang Yen-chung, *Liu Ming-ch'uan ts'an-yü p'ing Wu chiao Nien chan-i chih t'an-t'ao* (An inquiry into the military contributions of Liu Ming-ch'uan in pacifying Kiangsu and destroying the Nien) (Taipei: Wen Shih Che, 1986).

34. *IWSM*, TC 25:27a–b (June 14, 1864). See also Hart's account of his conversation with Li on the subject in Smith et al., eds, *Robert Hart and China's Early Modernization*, p. 262.

35. See note 25 above.

36. For a general overview of the project, consult Richard J. Smith, "Foreign-Training and China's Self-Strengthening: The Case of Feng-huang-shan, 1864–1873," *Modern Asian Studies* 10.1 (1976).

37. Smith et al., eds, *Robert Hart and China's Early Modernization*, p. 230.

38. Ibid., pp. 260–61.

39. See the discussion in Smith, "Foreign-Training and China's Self-Strengthening," pp. 203ff.

40. Ting Jih-ch'ang, *Fu Wu kung-tu* (Official papers of the governor of Kiangsu) (Canton, 1877), 50:7b–8; cf. *North-China Herald*, October 2, 1869.

41. See Smith, "Foreign-Training and China's Self-Strengthening," pp. 210–15.

42. The documentation on this subject is vast. See *YWYT*, vol. 3, passim. Li's writings contain many references to his use of foreigners to train Chinese military forces. See, for example, *LWCK Memorials*, 20:46a–b (January 17, 1873). Cf. Hart's journal entry for October 15, 1867, in which Hart reports that Li is critical of Tso Tsung-t'ang for employing too many foreigners at the Foochow Shipyard. Robert Hart Collection, Queen's University Library, Belfast, Northern Ireland. See also note 59 below.

43. On Hart's support, see ibid., February 16, 1867, where the Inspector General (IG) describes Li as "my ally." Li's use of foreigners in his various modernizing projects after 1870 is discussed in Kwang-Ching Liu, "Li Hung-chang in Chihli: The Emergence of a Policy, 1870–1875," chapter 3 in this volume, Albert Feuerwerker et al., *Approaches to Modern Chinese History* (Berkeley, University of California Press, 1967); see also Kenneth Folsom, *Friends, Guests and Colleagues: The Mu-fu System in the Late Ch'ing Period* (Berkeley: University of California Press, 1968), passim.

44. I have discussed these efforts in "The Reform of Military Education in Late Ch'ing China, 1842–1895," *Journal of the North China Branch of the Royal Asiatic Society* 18 (1978), p. 22.

45. On von Hanneken, see John Rawlinson, *China's Struggle for Naval Development, 1839–1895* (Cambridge, Mass.: Harvard University Press, 1967), pp. 147, 175, 178–80, 183, 186–87, 198.

46. Kwang-Ching Liu and Richard J. Smith, "The Military Challenge: The Northwest

and the Coast," in John K. Fairbank and Denis Twitchett, eds., *The Cambridge History of China* 11.2 (Cambridge: Cambridge University Press, 1980), pp. 244–46.

47. Smith, "The Reform of Military Education in Late Ch'ing China," p. 23.

48. Chou Sheng-ch'uan, *Chou Wu-chung-kung i-shu* (Writings of the late Chou Sheng-ch'uan) (Nanking, 1905), 1.4:33b–34; see also ibid., 1.1.2.:41b–42.

49. *LWCK*, Letters to the Tsungli Yamen, 2:14 (July 21, 1880). For background, consult Immanuel C. Y. Hsü, "Gordon in China, 1880," *Pacific Historical Review* 33.2 (May 1964).

50. Hsü, "Gordon in China," pp. 157–58.

51. Ibid., p. 163.

52. *Chinese Times*, January 29, 1887; see also ibid., February 19, 1887.

53. Cited in the *North-China Herald*, June 29, 1880.

54. Mark Bell, *China* (Simla, Government Central Branch Press, 1884), 2:104.

55. In a highly confidential dispatch to the British Foreign Secretary (Granville), dated July 25, 1880, the British Minister to China, Thomas Wade, wrote that one important reason for being "specially concerned" with the well being of the Foreign Inspectorate of Customs under Hart was that, "unless I am greatly mistaken ... [it provides] for every measure of precaution against her [China's] acquisition of a fleet or her organization of an army." In other words, Wade wanted China to remain dependent on British advice and assistance, offered through the medium of the Foreign Inspectorate. See Great Britain, Public Record Office, F.O. 418/1/242, Wade to Granville. I am grateful to an anonymous reader of the manuscript version of *Robert Hart and China's Early Modernization* for this citation.

56. Smith, *Mercenaries and Mandarins*, pp. 180–81, 190.

57. Ralph Powell, *The Rise of Chinese Military Power, 1895–1912* (Princeton, N.J.: Princeton University Press, 1955), pp. 60–68.

58. Ibid., pp. 106–107; see also Liu and Smith, "The Military Challenge," pp. 268–73; Smith, Foreign-Training and China's Self-Strengthening," pp. 220–23; Smith, *Mercenaries and Mandarins*, p. 192; Smith, "The Reform of Military Education in Late Ch'ing China," pp. 25–29.

59. Journal entry of November 25, 1874, in the Robert Hart Collection, Queen's University Library, Belfast, Northern Ireland. Cf. note 42 above.

60. See Richard J. Smith, "Reflections on the Comparative Study of Modernization in China and Japan," *Journal of the Hong Kong Branch of the Royal Asiatic Society*, 16 (1976); see also Smith et al., eds., *Robert Hart and China's Early Modernization*, p. 293.

61. Traditional values were, however, undermined in some of the new military academies. See, for example, Wang Chia-chien, "Pei-yang wu-pei hsueh-t'ang ti ch'uang-she chi ch'i ying-hsiang" (The Peiyang Military Academy: Its creation and influence), *Kuo-li T'ai-wan shih-fan ta-hsueh li-shih hsueh-pao* (April 1976), pp. 9, 11–12, 19–20, and notes.

62. Cited in S. Y. Teng and John K. Fairbank, eds., *China's Response to the West: A Documentary Survey, 1839–1923* (New York: Atheneum, 1969), p. 119.

63. Smith, *Mercenaries and Mandarins*, pp. 192–94; Smith, "The Reform of Military Education in Late Ch'ing China," pp. 32–33; Smith, "Foreign-Training and China's Self-Strengthening," pp. 220–23. On the high costs of employing foreigners in military affairs, see, for example, Thomas L. Kennedy, *The Arms of Kiangnan: Modernization in the Chinese Ordnance Industry, 1860–1895* (Boulder, Colo.: Westview Press, 1978), esp. p. 155.

64. See Ernst Presseisen, *Before Aggression: Europeans Prepare the Japanese Army* (Tucson: University of Arizona Press, 1964); see also Noboru Umetani, "Foreign Nationals Employed in Japan during the Years of Modernization," *East Asian Cultural Studies* 10.1 (March 1971).

Part IV
Li as Diplomat

7

The Aims of Li Hung-chang's Policies toward Japan and Korea, 1870–1882

Key-Hiuk Kim

On August 29, 1870, Li Hung-chang, who had been brought to Chihli along with twenty-five thousand men of the Anhwei Army to deal with the Sino-French crisis touched off by the Tientsin Massacre of the preceding June, was appointed governor-general of Chihli, replacing the ailing Tseng Kuo-fan. Less than three months later, on November 12, he was given an additional appointment as imperial commissioner of trade for the Northern Ports. Li was instructed to reside in Tientsin, going to the provincial capital of Pao-ting only in the winter months when the port of Tientsin was closed. In addition, Li remained the untitled commander of the Anhwei Army, which was at this time responsible for, among other things, the defense of the metropolitan region. He was also to function as the unofficial central coordinator for the self-strengthening activities from his key position within the Ch'ing government.[1] In these multiple capacities, Li played the leading role in the conduct of Ch'ing foreign policy for a quarter of a century. In particular, he was in charge of policies toward Japan and Korea, the two eastern neighbors whose relations with China presented the most vexing of all the external problems Li faced during his long career.

It is neither practical nor perhaps feasible to deal adequately in a single chapter with Li Hung-chang's foreign policy during the entire period in which he was actively and closely involved in the conduct of Ch'ing foreign relations. This chapter, therefore, will examine the period from the early 1870s through the early 1880s, focusing attention exclusively on his policies toward Japan and Korea. Rather than treating his policies toward these countries separately, they will be discussed together as an integrated whole.

145

Li's pre-1870 view of Japan

Li's interest in Japan and Korea predated his personal involvement in Japanese and Korean affairs, which began immediately after his appointment as governor-general of Chihli in 1870. It was his interest in Western weapons during the campaign against the Taipings that first attracted Li's attention to what Japan—and Russia—were doing to learn and adopt Western science and technology for military self-strengthening. In May 1863, Li wrote a letter to Tseng Kuo-fan from Shanghai, where he had been sent to direct operations against the Taipings. Impressed by the effectiveness of Western artillery, Li told his mentor: "In the past, neither Russia nor Japan was versed in artillery techniques; they therefore became increasingly weak. However, because their monarchs and officials humbled themselves and sought the secret skills of the British and the French, they have gradually learned to make, as well as use, firearms, cannon, and steamships. They therefore can rival Britain and France."[2] In a letter to the Tsungli Yamen in the spring of 1864, Li again praised Japan's energetic efforts at military self-strengthening. He coupled his praise with a warning to China. Recalling that the contemporary Japanese were descendants of the Japanese pirates of the Ming period, he predicted that the Japanese would attach themselves to China if China stood on its own and maintained its independence, but would turn to the West if China failed to maintain its independence. Li stressed that if China were to cope successfully with the Western threat, it was absolutely necessary to do what Japan was doing—to acquire machine-making tools and have young men of distinguished lineage devote themselves to industrial work. To provide the needed incentive, Li proposed the creation of a new category within the existing government examination system for candidates who specialized in technology.[3] His proposal was rejected by the conservative Manchu court.

In a period when it was common for Ch'ing officials and literati to view Japan with disdain and prejudice and regard it chiefly as a potential source of trouble for China, Li did not express, at least not outwardly, such views or feelings. Instead, he praised Japan as a model for China to emulate in military self-strengthening. Although it is not likely that Li fully trusted the Japanese, he seems to have entertained some vague hope for Sino-Japanese cooperation in China's struggle against Western aggression.

As for Korea, there is little in his voluminous writings that provides clear indications of, or direct clues to, what Li's attitude was toward the peninsular kingdom in this period. Li had no reason to question Korea's loyalty as China's closest and most important tributary. His strategic concept for the defense of China, in which Korea occupied a vital position, was yet to be developed.

Checking Japanese-Western collaboration, 1870–1874

Li's quarter-century stewardship of Chinese foreign policy toward Japan began in the fall of 1870 when Yanagiwara Sakimitsu, a Japanese foreign ministry official, arrived in Tientsin on a mission to sound out Chinese authorities on the feasibility of a treaty between the two countries. When informed of Yanagiwara's mission, the Tsungli Yamen at first decided to reject the Japanese request, for it feared an undesirable effect that a treaty with Japan might have on China's relations with tributary states, such as Korea and Vietnam. In distress, Yanagiwara appealed for assistance to Li and Tseng Kuo-fan, both of whom were in Tientsin at that time.

Li had been told earlier by Yanagiwara that Japan was not happy because it had been forced to trade with Great Britain, France, and the United States, and these countries had taken advantage of Japan. But Japan could not resist these powers alone and wished to cooperate with China. Whether or not he completely believed Yanagiwara, Li did not question his word. Regarding a treaty with Japan as not only inevitable but even desirable, Li wrote the Tsungli Yamen urging it to accept the Japanese request.[4] In response to the Japanese envoy's new appeal for help, after the Yamen's rejection of his request, Li wrote the Yamen again, arguing that it was not right for China to deny a treaty to a close neighbor like Japan when it already had treaties with many Western nations. Should Japan approach China again through the good offices of Britain or France, he pointed out, China would have no choice but to accommodate. Not only would this hurt Chinese authority and prestige, he warned, but it might turn Japan into an enemy of China and an ally of the West. He emphasized that China should ally itself with Japan and never allow Japan to become a Western base of aggression against China.[5] Li had, as yet, no way of knowing the attitudes and intentions of the contemporary Meiji Japanese leaders, who were aligning their country, psychologically as well as diplomatically, with the Western powers.[6] At Li's intervention, the Yamen reversed its earlier decision and memorialized the throne to request that Li be put in charge of preparations for the treaty negotiations with Japan, which were expected to begin the following spring.

In pursuit of his aim, Li showed himself willing to speak on behalf of the Japanese and to give them the benefit of the doubt, although it is unlikely that he personally ever fully trusted them. In December 1870, the proposed treaty with Japan was attacked by Ying-han, the ultraconservative governor of Anhwei, who, recalling Japanese piracy during the Ming period, questioned Japan's motives in seeking a treaty from China when the latter was in the grip of the crisis touched off by the Tientsin Massacre. Ying-han also feared that a treaty with Japan might encourage tributaries, such as Korea and Vietnam, to seek the same treatment and privilege.[7] In a memorial to the throne in January 1871, Li noted that during the years following the events of 1860–61, when Kiangsu and Chekiang lay enfeebled by Taiping attack and the Westerners were threatening China, Japan did not take advantage of the situation to demand a treaty from China. This shows, he argued, that Japan was submissive of its own accord. As for the Japanese piracy during the Ming period, Li said that it had originated from the Ming prohibition of trade. Noting Japan's successful efforts in military self-strengthening through the adoption of Western technology, Li again warned that if rejected by China, Japan would surely ally itself with the West, whereas it would become useful to China if handled properly. He repeated his earlier proposal that after signing a treaty with Japan, China station diplomatic and consular officials in Japan, to promote Sino-Japanese cooperation and check Japanese moves against China.[8]

While willing to accommodate the Japanese, Li was certainly not blind to their intentions and deeds. He was vigilant against Japan's aggressive designs on Korea. Early in 1871, when it was reported that Japanese warships might accompany the forthcoming American naval expedition to Korea, which Washington was sending to ascertain the fate of the *General Sherman* (an American merchant ship destroyed after it had ventured into Korean inland waters in 1866), Li became concerned over the possibility of secret collaboration between Japan and the United States against Korea. In a letter to the Tsungli Yamen on the matter, he expressed fear that Japan might become an immediate threat to Korea and that, alone, the latter would not be able to resist that threat.[9]

The negotiations that led to the signing of the Sino-Japanese treaty of amity in September 1871, for which Li served as chief Chinese negotiator, provided him with the first opportunity to take concrete steps toward achieving his foreign policy goal of checking Japan's aggressive designs on Korea and of preventing Japanese-Western collaboration against China. His pragmatism made Li willing to grant Japan a status equal with China in international diplomacy—a major concession and an unprecedented departure from traditional Ch'ing practice in the conduct of interstate relations with East Asian states and peoples. On the other hand, Li was uncompromising in his demand for what he considered to be of vital interest to China. Overcoming strong and protracted Japanese objections, he succeeded in including in the treaty a pledge of nonaggression against each other's "states and territories" (*pang-t'u*) and a guarantee of mutual assistance in the event of a conflict between either of the contracting parties and a third power. Without so specifying, the phrase "states and territories" was inserted by Li to protect Korea from Japanese encroachment. The mutual assistance clause was his device for preventing the Japanese from allying themselves with the Western powers.[10]

Many Western observers charged that the treaty represented a Sino-Japanese military alliance against the West.[11] Their professed desire for cooperation with China notwithstanding, this was far from the intentions of the Japanese leaders. Nor was it Li's intention. Although it is possible that earlier he may have entertained vague hopes for some form of cooperation with the Japanese, Li was too realistic to hold such a view for very long. His objective was more limited and specific. In accordance with his perception of Korea's strategic importance, which he considered more vital to the defense of the Ch'ing state than China's own southern coastal provinces, Li wanted to use the treaty as a tool to protect Korea and China's strategic interests, as well as its traditional suzerainty in the peninsular kingdom, from Japanese and Russian encroachment, and to prevent Japan from turning against China in alliance with the West.[12]

During the years following the signing of the treaty, Li's policy was put to a severe test by the actions of the Japanese government. Unhappy because China did not grant them the same privileges and special rights in China as those enjoyed by the Western treaty powers under the unequal treaties, the Japanese tried, though unsuccessfully, to revise the new treaty even before it was ratified. Specifically, they wanted to delete the mutual assistance clause to avoid "Western suspicion." In addition, they wished to add a most-favored-nation clause so that Japan could achieve legal parity with the Western treaty powers and practical advantages accruing therefrom in China. For this and other reasons, it was not until the end of April 1873 that the treaty was formally ratified.[13] Almost immediately, however, two events occurred that should have dispelled any delusion Li may have had of Sino-Japanese cooperation in a common struggle against the West: Japan's *sei-Kan* controversy of 1873 and its Taiwan expedition of 1874.[14] Although the former did not immediately lead to Japanese military action against Korea, it clearly demonstrated Japan's arrogant attitude and aggressive ambitions toward its peninsular neighbor. The latter event created a serious international crisis that could have escalated into a major military conflict between China and Japan. That it did not do so was owing, to a considerable degree, to the caution exercised by Li and the restraint that he counseled.

The Taiwan expedition had its genesis in the murders, in December 1871, of shipwrecked sailors from Liu-ch'iu by the aborigines of southern Taiwan. Disregarding Liu-ch'iu's dual status as a tributary of China and a feudatory of the defunct Japanese feudal domain of Satsuma, the Tokyo government unilaterally put the tiny archipelagic kingdom under exclusive Japanese control in 1873. In the name of avenging the murdered sailors—whom it claimed as Japanese subjects—it launched an expedition the following April, without formally notifying China. Taken by surprise, Li was incredulous when he heard the news of the expedition. In a letter to the Tsungli Yamen in late April, he expressed the view that, having just suppressed a rebellion led by ex-state councilor Eto Shimpei, who had been ousted from the government for his advocacy of military action against Korea during the *sei-Kan* controversy, Japan would not be capable of a distant campaign at that time. If Japan wanted to use military force, Li said, it would most likely be against Korea rather than the Taiwan aborigines, for Eto staged his rebellion after his demand for a Korean expedition had been rejected.[15] In another letter to the Yamen in early June, Li counseled caution, saying that once hostilities commenced, events might occur that no one could anticipate.[16]

During the ensuing crisis, Li functioned as the unofficial coordinator of China's defense efforts. He advised the Tsungli Yamen on the military measures that would strengthen China's hand in negotiating a settlement. To facilitate defense preparations on the coast and in Taiwan, he worked closely with the governors and governors-general of the coastal provinces concerned, including Shen Pao-chen, director-general of the Foochow Navy Yard, who was given the additional appointment of imperial commissioner for the defense of Taiwan on Li's recommendation through the Tsungli Yamen.[17] Although Li repeatedly urged the Yamen to take a firm stand against the Japanese in the negotiations, his aim was to seek a peaceful diplomatic settlement, not a military confrontation. He advised the Yamen to "make its peaceful intentions clear, while preparing for war secretly so that peace may be achieved quickly and be lasting." He suggested to Shen that "clashes with the Japanese were to be avoided, while preparations for war must be hastened."[18] When he learned that Japanese commissioner Ōkubo Toshimichi would soon arrive in Peking to negotiate a settlement, Li advised the Tsungli Yamen to treat him with courtesy. He went so far as to argue that as far as the case of the murdered Liu-ch'iuan sailors was concerned, China was at least partly at fault, because Chinese authorities in Fukien failed to conduct a serious investigation of the case for three years. He urged the Yamen to make a monetary settlement, both from a humanitarian standpoint for the murdered sailors and in consideration of the hardships endured by the members of the Japanese expedition.[19]

Li's firm and yet conciliatory position stemmed, no doubt, from his pragmatism and his belief that the Ch'ing army and navy at this time were no match for those of Japan. But it was, most of all, in accord with his foreign policy aimed at preventing Japanese-Western collaboration against China. He no longer deluded himself with any hope for Sino-Japanese cooperation in meeting the Western challenge, but he wished at least to avoid a complete Sino-Japanese rupture or alienation when China remained militarily weak. The final settlement, signed in Peking at the end of October 1874, reflected the realism, moderation, and restraint that characterized Li's foreign policy toward Japan.

The search for a new strategy, 1875–1879

When he was first put in charge of Ch'ing foreign policy toward Japan in late 1870, Li began with basic goodwill toward the Japanese and praise for their success in military strengthening. Although he was not sanguine of active Japanese cooperation or collaboration with China, Li at least wished to prevent Japan from turning against China in alliance or collaboration with the West. Although he did not regard Japan, in itself, as hostile or a threat to China, he believed that a Japan controlled or allied with a major Western power would be a serious threat to the security of the Ch'ing state.

Subsequently, as his contact with the Japanese began to increase, Li came to think that their courteous and respectful exterior concealed a calculating and crafty nature.[20] A series of Japanese actions—the claim of exclusive jurisdiction over Liu-ch'iu, the *sei-Kan* controversy, and the Taiwan expedition—starkly revealed Japan's expansionist ambitions toward its neighbors. In particular, Li regarded every Japanese act of aggression anywhere as a prelude to future Japanese aggression against Korea. He was convinced that a Japanese-controlled Korea would be a mortal threat to the Ch'ing imperial homeland of Manchuria.[21] As the Taiwan expedition fully revealed, Japan alone had become a threat, regardless of whether it was allied with a Western power. Li apparently believed that this rendered his policy of merely checking Japanese-Western collaboration too passive and inadequate. The situation clearly called for a new policy.

Li appears to have begun his search for a new policy in the period immediately following the settlement of the Taiwan crisis. Specifically, Li's aim was to protect Korea and China's strategic position, as well as its traditional suzerainty there, from the growing Japanese military threat. This coincided with the celebrated policy debate between the proponents of maritime defense and those of Inner Asian frontier defense within the top leadership of the Ch'ing government. Leading the former, Li, who had for years been calling for the construction of a Western-style navy to meet the new challenge facing China, forcefully argued for a large-scale naval expansion and modernization program. Representing the latter, Tso Tsung-t'ang eloquently advocated a strategy that would, for the moment, give priority to Inner Asian frontier defense. Although not a few officials recognized the growing Japanese threat and the concomitant importance of maritime defense, Li's position represented an unprecedented departure from the traditional Ch'ing strategy that had historically assigned priority to the Inner Asian frontier. There was also the compelling fact that all of Sinkiang was at this time in the hands of the Muslim rebels, with the strategic Ili area under Russian occupation. The decisive voice in determining the outcome of the debate was perhaps that of Wen-hsiang, the influential and respected Manchu statesman, who warned that, if left unchecked, the Muslim rebellion, which had already affected Outer Mongolia, might spread to Inner Mongolia, thereby posing a direct threat to the imperial capital of Peking. The court opted for the continuation of Tso Tsung-t'ang's campaign for the recovery of Sinkiang, which would for the next several years claim the bulk of Ch'ing government revenues.[22]

In these strained circumstances, Li and a few like-minded provincial officials were denied funds necessary to launch a naval program on the scale they had hoped for. Li was left to deal with the situation surrounding Korea by means other than military. Although his objective of protecting Korea from Japanese encroachment was clear enough, the means and method by which to attain it were not readily available. Li's search for a new approach, if not a new policy, was to continue for several years.

Following the settlement of the Taiwan incident, the Japanese government took steps to consolidate its diplomatic gains. In early 1875, it ordered Liu-ch'iu to stop sending tributary envoys to China. Emboldened by their "success" in Taiwan, the Japanese decided to proceed to settle the Korean question. As the Japanese-Korean diplomatic feud—which had been going on ever since the Meiji Restoration in 1868, allegedly because of Korea's outright refusal to deal directly with the new Japanese regime—was heating up again, many in China voiced concern over the growing Japanese threat to China, as well as to Korea, a sentiment that was shared by Westerners as well. In May 1875, J. P. Cowless, an English instructor of the T'ung-wen Kuan (the Interpreters' College), submitted a letter to the Tsungli Yamen, in which he speculated on the possible consequences of Japanese encroachment on Korea: Japan might demand, he said, a territorial concession in Korea and force Korea to send tribute to Japan while cutting off its relations with China. Or, he continued, the Japanese might entice the Koreans with money; the latter, already fearful of Japanese power, might be persuaded to grant the Japanese the right to station troops or the right to free passage for them in Korea. The Japanese would then move to the Korean-Manchurian border surreptitiously and wait for an opportune moment to cross the Yalu River and move straight into Sheng-ching (Shenyang). The Japanese thereafter might ally themselves with the Westerners to threaten China.[23] Cowless presented a scenario too dreadful for any Ch'ing official to contemplate.

Meanwhile, the Japanese leaders, following the American example in opening Japan, resorted to gunboat diplomacy and deliberately provoked the so-called Kanghwa Island incident in September 1875. When Japanese minister Mori Arinori arrived in Peking in early January 1876 to ascertain the Chinese government's attitude toward the Japanese-Korean dispute, Li wrote a letter to the Tsungli Yamen on January 19 expressing fear that Korea would be no match against Japan in the event of war between the two countries. "Should that country [Korea] appeal to the superior country [China] in the future by citing the precedent set during the Ming period," Li asked almost in despair, "what are we going to do?" After speculating on the dreadful consequences to China of a Japanese invasion of Korea, Li asked the Yamen to devise a way to advise the Korean government to bury its minor grudges and treat the Japanese with courtesy, perhaps even to send an envoy to Japan to explain the Kanghwa Island incident.[24] The following day, Li wrote a letter to Yi Yu-won, the former Korean chief state councilor who had recently visited Peking as special envoy. Li subtly conveyed his concern about recent developments in Japanese-Korean relations. When Japanese minister Mori visited him in Pao-ting a few days later, Li warned that should Japan attack Korea, China and Russia would send forces to Korea and there would be no profit for anyone if peace were damaged.[25] It was apparently with relief, if not equanimity, that Li and the Tsungli Yamen received the news of the signing of the Japanese-Korean Treaty of Kanghwa on February 27, 1876, which averted, as Li hoped, an armed conflict between the two countries, at least for the time being.

Li's search for an effective solution to the Korean problem continued. Lacking any substantial means to check Japanese ambitions, Li relied mainly on his own power of persuasion and friendly gestures in diplomacy in his effort to secure Japanese goodwill. Following the signing of the Kanghwa treaty, in early October 1876, former Japanese foreign minister Soejima Taneomi, who passed through Tientsin, told Li that Japan feared Russian encroachment and wished to cooperate with China in resisting it.[26] A month later, in November, Japanese minister to China Mori again visited Li. He, too, informed Li that Japan wished to cooperate with China and Korea in resisting Russian aggression and did not want to quarrel with either country. Li welcomed this cooperation wholeheartedly, stressing that Korea was China's eastern tributary and was on Japan's northern frontier and that both China and Japan should help Korea in its isolation and not make unacceptable demands.[27] Although it is unlikely that Li was lulled into complacency by the professed Japanese desire for cooperation, he seems, at this time, not to have completely abandoned his old hope that Japan could be persuaded to remain friendly to China and to refrain from encroaching on Korea. In 1877, when the Satsuma Rebellion broke out in Japan, Li readily loaned a hundred thousand cartridges to the hard-pressed Japanese government—a friendly act apparently calculated to win Japanese goodwill.[28]

Meanwhile, what rendered the Korean situation increasingly urgent was the seemingly growing Russian threat from the north. Early in 1876, when the crisis touched off by the Kanghwa incident appeared to be heading for a full-scale military confrontation between Japan and Korea, a concerned Tsungli Yamen alerted the military governors of the three Manchurian provinces to be on guard against possible Russian military moves along the Russian-Korean border. The fear of Russian aggression was heightened by the rumor that Russia might grant free passage through its territory to Japanese troops operating against Korea.[29] Russophobia was no doubt behind the aforementioned Japanese desire for cooperation with China against Russia conveyed by Soejima and Mori. For his part, Li, at this time, probably believed that whereas Japan was too busy defending itself, with no time to entertain any scheme against others, Russia, pursuing its expansionist policy in East Asia, was looking for an opportunity to seize a harbor or port in Korea to build a naval base. Hence, between Russia and Japan, Li's sympathy in this period appears to have leaned toward the latter.[30]

As has been shown, the Japanese-Korean rapprochement, brought about by the signing of the Treaty of Kanghwa, averted war between the two countries and preserved the peace in East Asia. But the period from 1876 to 1878 that followed was at best a time of uncertain peace for China. In the face of the danger of Japanese and Russian aggression, which seemed to be gradually building, Li's primary foreign policy concern was how to protect Korea from this danger. During this period, however, Li clearly had not yet developed a precise and well-defined strategy to attain this objective. It was only after another external crisis, precipitated by the Russians and aggravated by the Japanese, had confronted China that Li and his associates developed an articulate policy aimed at protecting the strategic Korean peninsula from the Russian, as well as the Japanese, threat.

An international balance of power in Korea, 1879–1882

Having established its exclusive, de facto control over Liu-ch'iu, after the conclusion of the Taiwan expedition, Tokyo proceeded to strengthen its hold on the archipelagic kingdom, while spurning Peking's repeated demands for the restoration of Liu-ch'iu's tributary ties with China. Preoccupied with domestic crises, such as the Satsuma Rebellion of 1877 and the subsequent assassination of Ōkubo Toshimichi in 1878, Tokyo, however, did not formally annex the kingdom. The Japanese may have refrained from taking such action because, in fact, they wished to cooperate with China to check Russian aggression and did not wish needlessly to antagonize China further. In 1878, Tso Tsung-t'ang brought his campaign to a successful conclusion and reestablished Ch'ing imperial authority in Sinkiang, except for the small enclave of Ili under Russian occupation. The Russians, however, refused to honor their earlier promise to withdraw from the area, thereby touching off a major international crisis. Taking advantage of the situation, Tokyo finally abolished the kingdom of Liu-ch'iu, incorporated it into Japanese administration, and renamed it the prefecture of Okinawa. This unilateral Japanese action, taken without consultation with either the Chinese or the Liu-ch'iuans, naturally angered the Chinese. It also dashed whatever remained of Li's old hope for Sino-Japanese cooperation in resisting Western aggression. As recently as a year before, Li, in a letter to Korean elder statesman Yi Yu-won, advised that Korea should ally itself with Japan to ward off the Russian threat.[31] Never again would Li entertain such hope.

Shortly after Japan's formal annexation of Liu-ch'iu, Ting Jih-ch'ang, former governor of Fukien and also Li's close friend, memorialized the throne to recommend that the court order Korea to enter into treaty relations with Western powers. Ting explained: Because Korea has been forced to sign a treaty with Japan, Japan would be deterred from taking aggressive action against Korea, if Korea signed treaties with other countries as well, for then, if Japan did take action, it would be denounced by all the countries having treaty relationships with Korea. Thomas F. Wade, British minister in Peking, also made a similar recommendation to the Tsungli Yamen, warning that should Korea fail to establish treaty relations with Western powers, it would surely follow Liu-ch'iu's fate. On August 21, 1879, the Yamen memorialized the throne to request that the court order Li to undertake the task of persuading and guiding Korea to establish treaty relations with Western countries as recommended by Ting.[32] Li was so ordered the same day.

Based on the ideas put forward by his associates, Li formulated a new Ch'ing policy aiming at the protection of Korea, an area of principal diplomatic and strategic concern to him as governor-general of Chihli and imperial commissioner of trade for the Northern Ports. The strategy to attain this objective was to have Korea establish treaty relations, under the treaty system introduced by the West, with as many countries as possible, so that an international balance of power and interest would be created in Korea that would prevent any one power from taking over the country alone. The balance-of-power concept, on which Li's strategy was based, was not unlike the traditional Chinese stratagem of *i-i chih-i* (control barbarians with barbarians), which China had historically used to maintain its supremacy among the nomadic peoples in and beyond its Inner

Asian frontier. Under this stratagem, China used one or more groups of so-called barbarians of these regions to check other and stronger barbarians, or used a strong group of barbarians to control weaker ones.[33] In addition, Li was aware that contemporary European powers, such as Victorian England and Bismarckian Germany, were regular practitioners of balance-of-power diplomacy. More directly, Li was inspired by China's contemporary experience in dealing with Western powers. During the Anglo-Chinese negotiations that led to the settlement of the Margary affair in 1876, he had an opportunity to observe firsthand the restraint exercised upon such a powerful country as Britain by other Western nations. Because China itself was, at this time, the beneficiary of an existing international balance of power in China, Li hoped to create a similar situation in Korea by cultivating Western commercial interests in the Korean peninsula as a counterweight against Japan and Russia.[34]

Li approached his task cautiously. On August 26—five days after receiving his assignment—he sent off a letter to Yi Yu-won, the Korean elder statesman with whom he had been in correspondence since 1876. In his letter, Li cited the recent seizure of Liu-ch'iu as an example of Japanese perversity and cunning and warned that Korea must secretly build up its armaments to prepare itself against Japanese aggression. "Since your country already has been compelled to sign a treaty and open trade with Japan," he went on, "other countries will certainly follow Japan's example and desire the same deal as Japan. Japan, in turn, may consider that a rare opportunity to exploit. For the present, therefore, you should adopt the stratagem of using enemies to control enemies: Sign treaties with Western powers, one by one, and use them to check Japan." Li mentioned the effective British intervention in the recent Russo-Turkish War, which saved Turkey from total catastrophe. Extolling the efficacy of international law, he cited Belgium, Denmark, and Turkey as small or weak countries protected by it. Treaties with Britain, Germany, and the United States, he argued, would be the best guarantee for Korea's safety from Russian and Japanese aggression.[35] In a memorial a few days later, Li stated that because Korea was not familiar with Western customs, if it should decide to discuss treaties with Western powers, China must negotiate on its behalf and serve as mediator to forestall trouble.[36] He lamented that Korea, still imprisoned in tradition, could not appreciate careful plans made by China on its behalf. He further noted that leading Korea into the arena of international life was a task that could not be accomplished overnight.[37]

Li had his first opportunity to put into execution his new Korea policy a year later in late August 1880, when U.S. Navy Commodore Robert W. Shufeldt visited him in Tientsin. Shufeldt was on a mission to seek a treaty with Korea. The urgency of the international situation surrounding Korea, heightened by the Ili crisis between China and Russia and by Japan's continued refusal to discuss the Liu-ch'iu question, made Li apparently abandon his earlier caution and depart further from the tradition of mutual noninterference under the Sino-Korean tribute system. It was Li who invited Shufeldt to Tientsin, when the latter was trying to secure Japanese good offices in approaching the Korean government. Without prior consultation with the Korean government, Li told Shufeldt that he would use his influence with the Korean government to accede to the American request for a treaty. Pleased with Li's offer of help, Shufeldt left China the following month to seek new instructions from Washington.[38]

In his effort to persuade the Koreans, Li was aided materially by two Chinese diplomats stationed in Tokyo at that time: Minister Ho Ju-chang and Counselor Huang Tsun-hsien of the Chinese legation. Ho was closely associated with Li, both personally and professionally. Before he left for his Tokyo post in 1877 as China's first minister to Japan, Li asked him to keep Korea in mind and to take timely action to mediate, if necessary, between Japan and Korea.[39] Although they shared a common concern for the safety of Korea from Russian and Japanese encroachment, Li and Ho differed on certain points of approach and tactic. Ho took a not unfriendly but more uncompromising stand toward Japan; he repeatedly urged Li and the Tsungli Yamen to take a militant stand in the Liu-ch'iu dispute and to send a military expedition to Japan to settle it by force if necessary. He considered Japan not yet strong enough to defy China militarily. Ho accordingly argued that the greatest danger to China—and to Korea—was Russian aggression from the north, not Japanese aggression from the south, and he preferred Sino-Japanese cooperation against Russia to Sino-Russian cooperation against Japan.[40]

While in agreement with Ho that if the Japanese were unchecked in Liu-ch'iu, they would next take their aggression to Korea, Li took a more realistic position. He argued that Liu-ch'iu was a tiny kingdom whose tribute to China was merely a symbol; it would be vain for China to go to war over a symbol. Although he had entertained hope earlier for some sort of Sino-Japanese cooperation in international affairs, Li was thoroughly disillusioned with the Japanese by this time; he took the position that China should make concessions to Russia in Sinkiang and thereby secure Russian goodwill and cooperation in checking Japanese ambitions toward Korea. He argued that because the combined military strength of China and Japan still was not equal to that of Russia, a Sino-Japanese alliance would result in dual damage to China: concessions to Japan and losses to Russia. Opposing military action against Japan, Li advocated a strategy whereby China would simply delay the settlement of the Liu-ch'iu question until such time as it gained sufficient naval strength.[41]

During the summer of 1880, when Kim Hong-jip, a Korean goodwill envoy, visited Tokyo, Ho and Huang met with him frequently for long and cordial talks. They impressed upon Kim the urgent need for Korea to enter into treaty relations with Western countries, especially the United States, in order to create an international balance of power in Korea, which would prevent both Russia and Japan from independently seizing the peninsula. Huang wrote an essay for him, entitled "A Strategy for Korea" (Ch'ao-hsien ts'e-lueh). Opening his essay with a brief reference to Russia's eastward expansion, Huang expounded that because of its pivotal geographical position, Korea now was a prime target of Russian aggrandizement in East Asia. To meet this threat, Korea must "be intimate with China, unite with Japan, and ally itself with the United States." Japan and Korea, Huang explained, are so close to each other that if either were seized by Russia, the other would not be able to survive alone. Therefore, Korea must overcome minor misgivings about Japan and promote great plans with Japan. Huang praised the United States as the only Western power that "has always upheld justice" and "never permitted the European powers to perpetrate evil deeds freely." If the United States signed a treaty with Korea, Britain, Germany, France, and Italy would follow its lead; then, even if Russia attacked Korea, it would not be able to achieve its ambitions, for the other Western treaty powers would not permit it.[42]

Ho and Huang made a strong and positive impression on Kim, a talented official enjoying the confidence of King Kojong. Following his return home, Kim was instrumental in convincing Kojong and his ministers of the need for Korea to establish open intercourse with the outside world. Still, more than a year was to go by before Li received word from the Korean court asking him to conduct negotiations with the United States on its behalf. With this blanket request, Li proceeded to conduct negotiations with Shufeldt with full authority in the spring of 1882. Li's long and patient efforts finally culminated in the signing of a treaty between Korea and the United States on May 22, 1882. Within the next few weeks, Great Britain and Germany followed suit.[43] The first important, concrete steps were thus taken to achieve Li's objective: creation of an internal balance of power in the Korean peninsula by utilizing the modern treaty system introduced by the West.

Unfortunately, an event unforeseen by Li and his associates and collaborators intervened. In mid-July—less than a month after the last of the three treaties had been signed—a violent riot by disgruntled soldiers occurred in Seoul. The rioters stormed the royal palace, murdered several ministers, burned down the Japanese legation, and restored to power the xenophobic Taewon'gun and his conservative followers. It was feared that the Taewon'gun would abrogate the new treaties and again close the country to foreigners, thereby provoking a military confrontation with the Japanese. The riot also created a dangerous vacuum of military power in Korea, into which the Japanese could simply walk and conquer the country. To fill the vacuum and prevent the Taewon'gun from wrecking Li's carefully planned and laboriously executed Korea strategy, the Chinese authorities rushed three thousand troops of the Anhwei Army to Korea in August. At the same time, Japanese minister Hanabusa Yoshimoto, who had fled from Seoul during the riot, returned with four warships, three transports, and one infantry battalion. The preponderance of Chinese military power apparently prevented armed clash between the two sides.[44] A new treaty was signed between Japan and Korea at the end of August, thereby settling the crisis and restoring peace in the peninsula for the time being.

Conclusion

When he embarked on his career as China's leading diplomat and principal architect of policy toward Japan and Korea in 1870, Li Hung-chang was relatively free of biases and prejudices common among the contemporary Ch'ing officials and literati toward Japan and the Japanese—biases colored by the lingering memory of Japanese piracy during the Ming period and prejudices stemming from China's long imperial tradition and cultural superiority. If Li was not exactly filled with goodwill and not always inclined to be friendly toward the Japanese, he was at least open-minded. He praised the Japanese for their energetic and successful efforts in military modernization and self-strengthening and felt that China should emulate them in this respect. Though not fully trusting, Li did not regard the Japanese as hostile or aggressive in intent toward China. He did not question the professed Japanese desire for cooperation with China in resisting Western aggression. Nor did Li consider Japan at this time strong enough to be a direct threat by itself to China. He did, however, believe that a Japan controlled by or allied with a major Western power would become a dangerous Western base of aggression against China. This realistic appraisal and basically well-meaning and open-minded attitude toward Japan underlay Li's initial Japanese policy in the early 1870s, which was aimed at preventing Japan from allying itself with the West and at securing, if possible, Japanese cooperation in resisting Western aggression. This strategy, together with Li's pragmatism, enabled him readily to accommodate the Japanese demand for equality with China when he negotiated the first modern treaty between China and Japan in 1871.

The subsequent behavior of Japan, however, soon disabused Li of whatever notion he may have had of Sino-Japanese cooperation against the West and made him gradually change his attitude. The demand for revision of the new treaty with China before its ratification, the rise of the *sei-Kan* controversy, and the subsequent Taiwan expedition all seemed to reveal with stark clarity Japan's aggressive designs on Korea, which Li considered to be of more vital strategic importance for the survival of the Ch'ing state than China's own southern coastal provinces. Accordingly, Li's primary foreign policy concern during this and succeeding periods was how to protect Korea from Japanese and Russian aggression. To meet this threat from Japan and other maritime powers, Li repeatedly called for China's construction of a large Western-style navy.[45]

The need for a Western-style modern navy, made more urgent by the Japanese expedition to Taiwan in 1874, was recognized by virtually everyone. Yet, preoccupied with the task of recovering Sinkiang from the Muslim rebels, the Ch'ing government was unable to provide funds necessary for that purpose. In these circumstances, Li was compelled to rely on diplomacy rather than military power in protecting Korea. While Li's aim of warding off the Japanese and the Russian threats remained clear and, in fact, became more urgent, the means and method of attaining it were not readily available. This was especially true after a series of Japanese actions, including the Taiwan expedition and the Kanghwa Island incident, proved the treaty with Japan unreliable as a deterrent to aggressive Japanese action against China and Korea. During the mid-1870s—a period of uncertain peace—Li searched for an effective strategy for protecting Korea and China's suzerainty and strategic position in the peninsula while continuing the policy of caution and restraint toward Japan. Japan's ultimate seizure of Liu-ch'iu early in 1879—at a time when China was embroiled in a dangerous dispute with Russia over Ili—made it difficult for Li to continue that policy without some modification or change. It was in response to this international crisis that Li and his associates developed the new balance-of-power strategy for the protection of Korea from Japanese and Russian aggression.

Similar in concept to China's traditional stratagem of "controlling barbarians with barbarians," the new strategy was inspired more directly by China's contemporary experience as the beneficiary of an international balance of power among the Western treaty powers in China. Personally, Li was further inspired by his experience during the negotiations that led to the settlement of the Margary affair with Britain in 1876. Under this new strategy, Korea was to be encouraged and guided to enter into treaty relations with Western powers so that these countries would develop sufficient commercial interests in Korea to serve as counterweights to Japan and Russia. The balance of power thus created in Korea would prevent both Japan and Russia from independently seizing the peninsula.

The signing of Korea's first treaties with the United States, Britain, and Germany in the summer of 1882 appeared to have created an institutional framework in which the kind of balance of power Li envisioned could be created in the peninsula. But the events that quickly followed not only derailed Li's plan before it was firmly set on its course, they virtually wrecked it. Instead of a balance of power, what emerged in its wake in Korea was a situation in which China and Japan were pitted against each other in a duel not only for the control of the peninsula but also for hegemony in East Asia. The new situation forced Li to move in a direction that he had not originally contemplated. The result of all this was an imperialistic domination of Korea by China, which was alien in theory and spirit, if not always in practice, to the Confucian principles and rules that had basically governed Sino-Korean relations during most of the Ch'ing period. There followed Korea's rapid disillusionment with and progressive alienation from its traditional suzerain.

Notes

1. For Li's multiple roles, see Liu, chapter 3 above.

2. Li Hung-chang, *Li Wen-chung-kung ch'üan-chi* (Complete works of Li Hung-chang), 100 *ts'e*, (Nanking, 1908; hereafter cited as *LWCK*), *P'eng-liao han-kao* (Letters to friends and colleagues) (hereafter cited as *Letters*), 3:16b–17a. Also Liu, chapter 2 above.

3. Liu, chapter 2 above.

4. *Ch'ou-pan i-wu shih-mo* (The complete account of the management of barbarian affairs), 100 *chüan* (Peiping: Palace Museum, 1930; hereafter cited as *IWSM*), T'ung-chih, 77:35a.

5. Ibid., 78:23a–24b.

6. For Japan's alignment of its foreign policy with the West in this period, see Key-Hiuk Kim, *The Last Phase of the East Asian World Order: Korea, Japan, and the Chinese Empire, 1860–1882* (Berkeley and Los Angeles: The University of California Press, 1880), 155–69.

7. *IWSM*, T'ung-chih, 79:7b–8b. Kim, *The East Asian World Order*, 143.

8. *LWCK, Tsou-kao* (hereafter cited as *Memorials*), 17:53a–54b.

9. *LWCK, Tsungli yamen han-kao* (Letters to the Tsungli Yamen) (hereafter cited as *Tsungli Yamen Letters*), 1:13a–14a.

10. Kim, *The East Asian World Order*, 149–50.

11. *Nihon gaikō bunsho* (Diplomatic documents of Japan) (Japan: Gaimushō, comp., Tokyo: Nihon kokusai kyōkai, 1936– ; hereafter cited as *NGB*), 8:238, 245.

12. For Li's view on Korea's strategic importance, see *LWCK Tsungli Yamen Letters*, 1:49a–b.

13. For Japan's attempt at treaty revision, see Kim, *The East Asian World Order*, 166–68.

14. For details concerning the *sei-Kan* controversy, see ibid., 169–87.

15. *LWCK Tsungli Yamen Letters*, 2:20a–b.

16. Ibid., 2:30b.

17. Liu, chapter 3 above.

18. Ibid.

19. *LWCK Tsungli Yamen Letters*, 2:42a–b.

20. *LWCK Letters*, 13:3a.

21. *LWCK Tsungli Yamen Letters*, 1:49a–b.

22. For the details of the debate, see Immanuel C. Y. Hsu, "The Great Policy Debate in China, 1874: Maritime Defense vs. Frontier Defense," *Harvard Journal of Asiatic Studies*, vol. 25 (1964–65), 212–28.

23. *Ch'ing-chi Chung-Jih-Han kuan-hsi shih-liao* (Historical materials on Sino-Japanese-Korean relations during the late Ch'ing period), 11 vols. (Taipei: The Institute of Modern History, Academia Sinica, 1972; hereafter cited as *CJHSL*), 2:262b–63b.

24. *LWCK Tsungli Yamen Letters*, 4:30b–31a.

25. For Li's letter to Yi and the latter's reply, see ibid., 4:30a–32a. For Li's talk with Mori, see ibid., 4:33a–b.

26. Li Shou-k'ung, *Li Hung-chang chuan* (Biography of Li Hung-chang) (Taipei: Hsueh-sheng shu-chü, 1979), 226.

27. *LWCK Tsungli Yamen Letters*, 6:31a–b.

28. Ibid., 7:3b–4a.

29. For the letters to the governors and their replies, see *CJHSL*, 2:294, 2:297–98, 2:300–303.

30. Li, *Li Hung-chang chuan*, 226.

31. Ibid.

32. *Ch'ing Kuang-hsü ch'ao Chung-Jih chiao-she shih-liao* (Historical materials on Sino-Japanese relations during the Kuang-hsü reign), 88 *chüan* in two-volume reprint (Taipei: Wen-hai, 1970; hereafter cited as *CKCJ*), 1:31b–32b.

33. Ying-shih Yü, *Trade and Expansionism in Han China: A Study of Sino-Barbarian Economic Relations* (Berkeley: The University of California Press, 1967), 14–16.

34. Kim, *The East Asian World Order*, 342–43.

35. *CJHSL*, 2:366–69.
36. Ibid., 2:373–74. *LWCK Tsungli Yamen Letters*, 10:23a–b.
37. *CJHSL*, 2:397.
38. Kim, *The East Asian World Order*, 304–305.
39. Ibid., 277.
40. *CJHSL*, 2:403.
41. See Li's memorial on the Liu-ch'iu question in *CKCJ*, 2:14b–17a. See also E. Leung, chapter 8 below.
42. For the text of Huang's essay, see Kuksa p'yonch'an wiwonhoe, ed., *Susinsa Kirok* (Records of friendship envoys) (Seoul: T'amgudang, 1971), 160–71.
43. For the details of these treaties, including the negotiations that led to their signing, see Okudaira Takehiko, *Chōsen kaikoku kōshō shimatsu* (A complete account of negotiations leading to the opening of Korea) (Reprint) (Tokyo: Tōkō shoin, 1969).
44. For details, see Kim, *The East Asian World Order*, 316–25.
45. See Wang, chapter 12 below.

8

Li Hung-chang and the Liu-ch'iu (Ryūkyū) Controversy, 1871–1881

Edwin Pak-wah Leung

Li Hung-chang's role in China's foreign affairs during the late Ch'ing period has been a subject of much study. Little is known, however, about his role in the Sino-Japanese dispute over the Liu-ch'iu (Ryūkyū) Islands in the period between 1871 and 1881. What was Li's attitude toward the tributary states in general, and toward the ex-tributary state, Japan, in particular, during the period of controversy? What was Li's influence on China's foreign policy decision-making during this period? How did Li resolve (or not resolve) the seeming dilemma at a time when China was thrust into the modern nation-state system while maintaining the traditional tributary state system? Specifically, what was Li's policy toward Liu-ch'iu vis-à-vis Japan?

This chapter attempts to answer these questions by focusing on the Liu-ch'iu controversy. The controversy arose because of Liu-ch'iu's "dual-subordination" to both China and Japan, a status that was at best confusing in modern international law.[1] While the Liu-ch'iu king sought to preserve his kingdom in the face of Japanese annexation by turning to China for protection, the deteriorating Ch'ing monarchy obviously was incapable of sending a rescue mission to the faithful Liu-ch'iu. As this chapter will show, however, Li Hung-chang, during the period of the Liu-ch'iu controversy, contemplated the idea of forming an "alliance" between China and Japan against the encroaching Western powers. He considered this possible Sino-Japanese "alliance" as a policy priority over the "empty name" of Chinese suzerainty over the tributary state Liu-ch'iu. With pragmatism and care, he cultivated this idea with visiting Japanese leaders throughout the 1870s, only to learn, after Japan's annexation of Liu-ch'iu in 1879, that the Meiji government was actually not willing to go along. Li's miscalculation of the Japanese interest, in retrospect, weakened China's position vis-à-vis Japan in the protracted Liu-ch'iu dispute, even though his original design was to ally with Japan in order to strengthen China's position against the

162

Western imperialists. As this chapter will also show, many Japanese leaders showed reciprocal interest in Li's "alliance" idea, convincing Li that he was not alone in trying to achieve this goal. Japan's forceful actions in Liu-ch'iu, therefore, shocked Li Hung-chang into the realization that a Sino-Japanese alliance was not possible. Toward the end of the Liu-ch'iu controversy, Li quickly and pragmatically shifted his pro-Japan policy to counter the rise of Japanese power in the Asian world order.

Official Sino-Japanese relations had been held in abeyance for the three hundred years preceding 1871. Japan was also a tributary state of China for a time during the Ming period. The Japanese shogun, Ashikaga Yoshimitsu, accepted the tributary status in order to enrich his coffers from trade—from 1433 to 1549 eleven tribute and trade missions sailed to China. Subsequently, however, nationalistic Japanese statesmen found such relations humiliating, and discontinued the practice after the middle of the sixteenth century, thus ending official contact with the mainland.

The year 1871 marked a new change in Sino-Japanese diplomatic relations. Soon after the newly created Japanese Foreign Ministry came into being in 1870, Yanagiwara Sakimitsu was sent by his government to Peking to seek a commercial treaty similar to China's treaties with Western nations. He was instructed, in particular, to secure the most-favored-nation clause in the treaty. Although his mission was viewed by the ultra-conservative elements in the Chinese government as opportunistic and ill-timed, it was received with warmth by the more pragmatic and progressive leaders, like Li Hung-chang, newly appointed governor-general of Chihli and superintendent of trade for the Northern Ports. Li felt that:

> Japan, which was not a dependency of China, was totally different from Korea, Liu-ch'iu, and Annam. That she had come to request trade without first seeking support from any Western power showed her independence and good will. If China refused her this time, her friendship would be lost and she might even seek Western intervention on her behalf, in which case it would be difficult for China to refuse again. An antagonized Japan could be an even greater source of trouble than the Western nations because of her geographical proximity. It was therefore in China's interest to treat Japan on a friendly and equal basis and send commissioners to Japan who could look after the Chinese there, watch the movements of the Japanese government, and cultivate harmonious relations between the two states.[2]

Li Hung-chang toyed with the idea of a possible Sino-Japanese "alliance" in the wake of Western encroachments in Asia. His suggestion to "cultivate harmonious relations" with China's ex-tributary state was not out of love for Japan but out of a cold realization of the need to strengthen China's position in order to ward off the Western threat. Li was also aware that "an antagonized Japan could be an even greater source of trouble than the Western nations because of her geographical proximity."[3]

For these reasons, the Yanagiwara mission was well received. In fact, to show Chinese good will, a Sino-Japanese treaty with eighteen articles and a trade regulation of thirty-three articles was finally signed in 1871 by Li and Yanagiwara's successor, Date Munenari. Among other provisions, the treaty allowed for the exchange of envoys and consuls and the rendering of good offices to each other should a third party intimidate or threaten either of the contracting parties. By careful negotiation, Li Hung-chang purposely excluded from the treaty the most-favored-nation clause.[4]

Article One of the Treaty was an important provision: "In all that regards the territorial possessions of either country, the two governments shall treat each other with proper courtesy, without the slightest infringement or encroachment on the other side."[5] China took for granted that the term "territorial possessions" was meant to include those tributary states around China's frontiers. But this Chinese assumption was not to be shared by the Japanese. This ambiguity was not realized until the controversies over Liu-ch'iu and Korea arose in later years.

In 1874, Japan sent an expeditionary force to Taiwan to "punish" the aborigines there who had earlier maltreated the shipwrecked Liu-ch'iuans and Japanese. One incident occurred in 1871 concerning Liu-ch'iuan citizens; the other, in 1873, involved Japanese nationals. The Japanese government, on the pretext of these two incidents, decided to take action in an attempt to resolve Liu-ch'iu's "dual-subordination" problem. By sending forces to Taiwan in the name of "protecting its nationals [meant to include the Liu-ch'iuans]," the Japanese government would first challenge the Chinese suzerainty in Liu-ch'iu and then legitimize its claim by stating that it had already exercised sovereignty over Liu-ch'iu. The detailed story of Japan's Taiwan expedition, however, is beyond the scope of this study.[6] Suffice it to say, not only did the Japanese expeditionary forces sent to Taiwan fail to accomplish the objective of "punishing" the aborigines by being "trapped" there, but the episode also touched off a crisis between China and Japan—a development that worried Li Hung-chang, as well as many Japanese leaders. What followed was the dispatch of Ōkubo Toshimichi to China by the Japanese government to settle the crisis.

Ōkubo reached Peking on August 27, and immediately entered into negotiations. An agreement between Japan and China, with reference to the island of Taiwan, was finally signed on October 31, 1874; the Liu-ch'iu Islands, however, were never mentioned in the treaty.[7] As far as the Liu-ch'iu sovereignty problem is concerned, it is debatable as to whether or not China, by signing this agreement, had "accepted . . . the Japanese contention that the Lew Chews [Liu-ch'iuans] were Japanese subjects. . . ."[8] One historian has remarked that "the phraseology of the first article clearly affirmed the Japanese right to protect 'her subjects,' which was a clear recognition that the inhabitants of Lew Chews [Liu-ch'iu] were subjects of Japan."[9] The question stands: Was the treaty really a "clear recognition" that the Liu-ch'iuans were Japanese subjects? More specifically, had Ōkubo and the Chinese negotiators intended to find a solution to the Liu-ch'iu problem during the course of their negotiations? It is highly unlikely that either side, at least in 1874, had intended to clarify the ambiguous political status of the Liu-ch'iu Islands at the risk of directly opposing the other.

In retrospect, the later Japanese "distortion" of the 1874 treaty arose from the ambiguities of the treaty itself. Moreover, these ambiguities were tailored by the Meiji government in Japan's favor on the advice of Gustave Boissonade—a trusted legal advisor—in March 1875.[10] In 1874, however, Ōkubo Toshimichi himself, while in Peking, was unaware of the possible implication that China, by recognizing the Japanese Taiwan expedition as "righteous" and by paying the consolation money to the victims, was to recognize Japan's sovereignty over Liu-ch'iu. He made a frank confession on December 15, 1874, that the treaty he had just signed with China had *no* legal basis for Japan's sovereign claim over Liu-ch'iu.[11]

Earlier, in a letter to his friend Kuroda Kiyotaka, written on October 30—a day before the signing of the 1874 Sino-Japanese Treaty—Ōkubo had suggested that a good sum of the relief money be paid to those who displayed valor in battle. The remainder of the indemnity should be returned to China to be spent in Taiwan for the administration of the area inhabited by the aborigines and for the protection of navigators against future outrages.[12] Although his proposal was not acted on, it shows that Ōkubo did not consider the payment of consolation money an indication of China's agreement to abandon her suzerainty over the Liu-ch'iu Islands. What concerned the Japanese home minister at this point was not the Liu-ch'iu problem, but a quick conclusion of the Taiwan expedition. In fact, during the course of negotiations with the Chinese officials, Ōkubo even deliberately avoided raising the Liu-ch'iu issue in their discussions.[13]

Ōkubo's outward semblance of affecting a sense of humanity by remitting the relief money was not the real reason behind his gesture; rather, it was based on political considerations. By this unprecedented move, he hoped to dispel China's suspicions toward Japan, while at the same time revealing to the world Japan's magnanimity.[14] He was anxious to reach a *rapprochement* with China, a country with which Japan would have to cooperate to assure Japan's future prosperity.[15] Ōkubo's expression of good will toward China, conveyed in the course of his November 3 talk with Li Hung-chang in Tientsin, was not a mere formality but a genuine declaration of his feelings.[16] This undoubtedly impressed upon Li Japan's desire for a closer relationship with China. Li Hung-chang was receptive, yet equally aware of the rapidly rising power of Japan and its threat to China's security. But Li feared the Western maritime powers even more; initially Li had directed his schemes for self-strengthening against the West, not Japan. It was logical for him to think of Japan as a possible "ally" to ward off the Western threat, as China and Japan were geographically closer and culturally similar.

Throughout most of the 1870s, Li Hung-chang was relatively tolerant of Japanese expansionism. But, by 1879, when Liu-ch'iu was annexed against China's will, Li was forced to realize that a Sino-Japanese "alliance" was impossible.

After the settlement of the Taiwan crisis in 1875, Li Hung-chang remained convinced that his "alliance" idea would find supporters in Tokyo, even though the conditions in Liu-ch'iu deteriorated progressively. In his letter to the Tsungli Yamen on September 14, 1875, Li again pointed out the difference between Japan and the Western powers in their relations to China: Japan was close to China and an immediate source of anxiety and trouble for her, whereas the West was a long distance away.[17] Although fully aware of Japan's expansionist ambitions toward Liu-ch'iu, as well as toward Korea, Li still entertained the hope of Sino-Japanese cooperation against the Western powers throughout most of the 1870s. He believed that with its continuing unrest and huge financial deficits at home, Japan was in no position to undertake a new venture abroad. He was also aware of Japan's fear of Russia. In November 1876, Li was visited by Mori Arinori and Soejima Taneomi, two Japanese diplomats. Expressing concern over Russian expansionism, the visitors told him of Japan's desire for cooperation with China and Korea in warding off the Russian threat.[18] Ōkubo had expressed similar ideas to Li in 1874. Although it is unlikely that Li was lulled into complacency by Japan's professed desire for cooperation, he still hoped that Japan could be placated and would remain friendly to China in the latter's disputes with the Western powers. In 1877, when the Satsuma Rebellion broke out in Japan, Li readily loaned a hundred thousand cartridges to the Japanese government.[19] He could not have foreseen that the Japanese government, after the suppression of the Satsuma Rebellion, would annex Liu-ch'iu. In retrospect, Li's policy of tolerance toward Japan weakened China's position in the Liu-ch'iu dispute.

In Liu-ch'iu, drastic changes had taken place by 1877. The Japanese had steadily extended their authority over the Islands. All their efforts had been directed toward the establishment of a legal basis for Japan's claim, including the termination of Liu-ch'iu's tributary ties with China, as well as the creation of a Japanese Home Ministry office in Okinawa.[20] The pressure from Tokyo therefore constituted an unprecedented national crisis for the Liu-ch'iuan king Shō Tai. Consequently, he secretly sent two envoys, Kōchi Pechin (Hsiang Te-hung) and Lin Shih-kung, to China to seek aid.[21] They arrived in Fukien on April 12, 1877, and informed governor-general Ho Ching and governor Ting Jih-ch'ang that the tribute missions had been interrupted by the Japanese.[22] Ho and Ting, in a June 14 memorial to the throne, observed that a refusal to aid Liu-ch'iu might be construed by the Western powers as a sign that China was unable to protect her tributary states. They recommended that Ho Ju-chang, recently appointed minister to Japan, take up the matter with the Japanese.[23] This recommendation was acted on the same day that the memorial was received.[24] As will be seen later,

China, in actuality, was unable to resort to military means against Japan in defending Liu-ch'iu because of naval and financial reasons.

Ho Ju-chang's mission to Tokyo to open negotiation with the Japanese government regarding Liu-ch'iu admittedly did not produce any result. The Meiji government refused to negotiate on the grounds that the Liu-ch'iu affair was an internal matter of Japan, and that Ho Ju-chang was a foreign diplomat.[25] In April 1879, Japan finally annexed Liu-ch'iu, forcing the Liu-ch'iuan king to take up residence in Tokyo. The Liu-ch'iu Kingdom ceased to exist as a nation.[26]

News of the Japanese annexation of Liu-ch'iu came as a shock to Li Hung-chang, yet he still did not totally abandon the "alliance" idea. He reasoned that he could use the good offices of former U.S. president Ulysses S. Grant, who was scheduled to visit China at that time, to mediate in China's behalf. If the mediation were successful, Li thought, the "alliance" idea could still be viable.

Li met with Grant on May 28 in Tientsin. Grant's first impression of the governor-general was a favorable one; as he recollected some years later, he ranked Li first of the four great men whom he had met in his world tour.[27] This personal factor probably influenced the American ex-president on matters relating to the Liu-ch'iu affair during his visit to China.[28] Accepting Li's request to mediate in the Liu-ch'iu dispute, Grant went on to Japan to take up the case with the Japanese leaders.

Grant's mediation, as it turned out, also did not produce any concrete result.[29] It was difficult for him, as a Westerner, to be able to comprehend fully the concepts of tributary relationships. Furthermore, after hearing the Japanese side of the story, he simply could not make a judgment on the dispute. There were rumors that Grant had made a concrete suggestion to the Chinese and Japanese leaders for the peaceful settlement of the dispute: the partition of the Liu-ch'iu Islands between China and Japan.[30] Extant records do not support this claim. Grant, however, did suggest that China and Japan each should appoint a representative to meet and work out a solution to the Liu-ch'iu problem, a suggestion that was finally accepted by the Japanese government.[31] The Ch'ing government welcomed the suggestion, for it was Japan that had repeatedly refused to discuss the matter through diplomatic channels.

In 1880, the Japanese government decided to send Shishidō Tamaki to China, and this decision was considered, at least by Li Hung-chang, as a sign of Japan's willingness to negotiate directly with the Chinese government. Prince Kung, head of the Tsungli Yamen, was appointed by the Ch'ing government as its representative to negotiate with Shishidō. Negotiations began on August 15 and lasted for about two months. On October 21, a draft treaty was agreed on by the two representatives.[32] It appeared that, once ratified, the agreement would finally settle the Liu-ch'iu dispute between China and Japan.

As soon as the draft treaty was sent to the Peking court for ratification, however, it created a storm within Chinese officialdom. For, according to the terms of the draft treaty, China would grant Japan trading privileges and concessions (specifically the most-favored-nation clause) in exchange for keeping two southern islands of Liu-ch'iu, while Japan would keep the rest of the seventy-three islands permanently. The Liu-ch'iu Kingdom, the center of the controversy, would not be allowed to be restored. This agreement clearly represents unnecessary concessions made by Prince Kung to his Japanese counterpart. It was also inconsistent with China's policy toward Liu-ch'iu in terms of protecting the tributary states. On the other hand, it reflects Japan's ambition and aggressiveness, as well as its insincerity in dealing with China. This draft treaty shattered whatever hope Li Hung-chang still had toward Japan; he therefore strongly opposed its ratification.[33]

The timing of Li Hung-chang's rejection of the draft treaty is significant: China, in late 1880, was on the edge of settling a dispute with Russia over Ili in the northwest frontier.[34] With the Russian threat seemingly to be removed in the immediate future, and with his disillusionment over Japan's unwillingness to cooperate, Li now advocated peace with Russia instead of with Japan. He had learned from Commodore Robert Shufeldt of the U.S. navy that a Russian fleet of two ironclads and thirteen fast ships was already in Nagasaki and had purchased $500,000 worth of fuel.[35] Li believed Japan was ready to fish in the Sino-Russian troubled waters. Consequently, on September 30, 1880, he urged the Tsungli Yamen to adopt a conciliatory policy toward Russia, and to allow Marquis Tseng Chi-tse (the Chinese representative in St. Petersburg) greater power in negotiations with the Russians, so that a peaceful settlement over Ili might be reached.[36] Li also clarified his stand on the Liu-ch'iu issue: "I think China had better not receive the southern part of Liu-ch'iu and return it to the Liu-ch'iuans themselves. It seems to me Japan will never yield."[37] On November 11, at the request of the Grand Council (November 6), Li sent a powerful memorial to the throne which stated explicitly that because the two southern islands of Liu-ch'iu, to be retained by China, were of such little value, the granting of so broad a concession as the most-favored-nation clause to Japan was unwise.[38] Li feared that once the Japanese started to make trouble, other countries might follow suit. Li impressed upon the court:

> The whole situation hinges on whether the Russian question can be settled. If it can, Japan and all other countries will be hesitant [to move]; if it cannot, they will plot [against us]. Rather than make concessions to the Japanese who cannot help us resist Russia—thereby we lose to both Japan and Russia—would it not be preferable to make some concessions to Russia and secure her help in checking Japan? The strength and weakness of Russia and Japan differ by a hundred fold. Judging by the injustice of their claims, the Japanese also insulted us far more [than the Russians].[39]

An analysis of this statement reveals a basic change in Li Hung-chang's foreign policy: peace with Russia and resistance to Japanese aggression. The question arises: Why did Li's long-time "pro-Japan" policy change overnight? The answer has to be sought in light of both strategic and institutional considerations. First, Li did not consider the Liu-ch'iu problem a serious threat to China's security. From the very beginning, he regarded Liu-ch'iu's tribute as too insignificant an issue to cause China to go to war. He clearly expressed his view in a letter to Ho Ju-chang:

> Liu-ch'iu is a small place, beyond the seas and completely cut off from all other places . . . near to Japan and far away from China. . . . Even if China wished to assist and rescue her neighbors, the geographical situation prevents it. China receives no great benefit from the Liu-ch'iu tribute. Moreover, if China accepted tribute from Liu-ch'iu but could not protect it, then China would be looked down on by all countries. Japan would not listen to arguments. It would not only be a waste of time but also absurd for China to use force to fight for a small tribute from a small country, and for the sake of an empty name.[40]

It is here that Li first spoke of the tributary state system as an "empty name." In his letter to Tseng Chi-tse of October 19, 1879, Li also wrote that China's naval capacity and financial conditions crippled her ability to wage war against Japan. What concerned Li even more, therefore, was China's domestic effort for self-strengthening—a theme that had consistently been shared by a number of progressive officials: "Since we [China] cannot threaten war with Japan [over Liu-ch'iu], we have to adopt a soft policy, and at the same time to try our best effort for self-strengthening in order to strive for later strength and power."[41]

Li seems to have stressed the possibility that China's protest and Japan's fear of foreign intervention would restrain Japan from taking further action in Liu-ch'iu.[42] Accordingly, he instructed Ho Ju-chang to engage in diplomatic maneuvering, despite the latter's repeated suggestion for China to take military action. Another reason why Li did not advocate a show of force, as we have discussed, was his secret desire for a Sino-Japanese "alliance" to ward off the Western threat. But the news of Japan's annexation of Liu-ch'iu took him by surprise in 1879, and he was disillusioned by Tokyo's lack of cooperation. He also realized that he had underestimated Japan's strength. Nevertheless, he misconstrued the arrival of Shishidō Tamaki at Peking as a sign of Japan's willingness to negotiate directly with the Chinese government. He therefore ordered Ho Ju-chang to remain in Tokyo and continue to seek help from the various foreign ministers in Japan.[43]

Li was totally disillusioned, however, by the 1880 draft treaty negotiated by Shishidō Tamaki and Prince Kung. Why should China give Japan the pernicious most-favored-nation clause in exchange for the two small islands of Liu-ch'iu? Because Japan's annexation of the Liu-ch'iu Kingdom did not correspond to China's national interest, why should China sign the draft treaty, thus endorsing Japanese rule over the greater part of Liu-ch'iu?

For practical purposes, Li began to shift his policy, hoping that Russia could be appeased and thus support China in her disputes with foreign powers, especially with Japan. Li's concept appears similar to the traditional stratagem of "controlling barbarians with barbarians" (*i-i chih-i*), because both relied on the use of alien power to protect Chinese interest. This traditional policy was also akin to the European balance-of-power concept.

The balance of interest among several Western powers in China, as Li discovered in the summer of 1876 during his negotiations at Chefoo for the settlement of the Margary affair, might even serve to restrain the demands of so dominant a power as Britain.[44] He also knew that the combined interests of several Western powers in China helped stabilize China's position at this time. He was apparently acquainted with the European balance-of-power concept. In the summer of 1887, Ma Chien-chung, Li's protégé who had gone to France the previous year to study international politics with a group of Chinese naval cadets from the Foochow Shipyard, wrote from Paris expounding the balance-of-power principle and explaining that the Western nations had historically endeavored to maintain it in the conduct of international relations.[45] Li and Ma, along with other "progressive" Chinese (such as Huang Tsun-hsien, a councilor of the Chinese embassy at Tokyo),[46] were apparently impressed by the British intervention in the Russo-Turkish War and the Berlin Congress of that summer, which saved the Ottoman Empire from complete dismemberment and destruction, and helped preserve the existing balance of power in Europe.[47]

This "modern version" of the traditional Chinese stratagem of "using barbarians to control barbarians" provided Li Hung-chang with a rational basis for his new policy of peace with Russia and resistance against Japanese aggression. He was aware of Japan's fear of Russia and believed it was strategically more important to defend Korea in order to secure China from Japanese aggression.[48] This was a new variety of *i-i chih-i*, beyond traditional usage.

Another explanation for Li Hung-chang's opposition to the 1880 draft treaty seems to have been his rivalry with the Tsungli Yamen over foreign policy formulation. The Tsungli Yamen had been established after the Treaty of Peking in 1860 specifically to deal with foreign affairs. But, since its creation in 1861, its main policy had been to try to evade questions rather than face them.[49] As a result, issues were dealt with according to expediency, rather than well-conceived plans.

In contrast, Li Hung-chang by the late 1870s had become not only the implementer of policies but also their initiator. While the Tsungli Yamen was incapable of handling foreign affairs, Li had emerged as the most influential man of his time. His position as superintendent of trade for the Northern Ports, together with his right to handle foreign affairs, made him a one-man foreign office competing with the Tsungli Yamen.[50]

Li began acting as a powerful rival to the Tsungli Yamen. The official reports of Chinese ministers abroad were often addressed to both the Yamen and Li.[51] Li could directly issue orders to ministers abroad without the Yamen being informed.[52] The operation of the "two foreign offices" was an indication of the great trust Empress Dowager Tz'u-hsi placed in Li Hung-chang, but it constituted an anomaly in the administration of China's foreign policy. In actual practice, therefore, the superintendent of trade for the Northern Ports was in charge of the Ch'ing court's diplomatic activity in Sino-Japanese relations. The Chinese envoys abroad were directly under the command of the superintendent of trade for the Northern Ports, and the court's orders prepared by the Grand Council were sent to Li Hung-chang for transmission to ministers abroad. In effect, the Tsungli Yamen was bypassed.[53]

Li believed that he understood the Sino-Japanese problem and the Liu-ch'iu issue better than the Yamen ministers. It was Li Hung-chang, not the Yamen ministers, who signed the Sino-Japanese Treaty of Friendship (1871)—a treaty without the most-favored-nation clause, which he considered to be one of his greater diplomatic achievements. It was Li who advocated the importance of coastal defense against Japan, as illustrated in the great policy debate of maritime defense versus frontier defense in 1874.[54] It was also Li who initiated the idea of requesting the former American President Ulysses S. Grant to mediate the Liuch'iu dispute in the interest of China. Understandably, Li felt humiliated by not being given the power as special commissioner to work out the settlement with Shishidō Tamaki over Liu-ch'iu. The frustrated man might have decided to use his opposition to the 1880 draft treaty as a means to embarrass the Tsungli Yamen in their contest for power. In any event, because of strong opposition from Li, the Ch'ing court announced that it would not ratify the draft treaty.[55]

Because the Ch'ing court refused to ratify the draft treaty, Shishidō Tamaki decided to leave China as a protest in early 1881.[56] The Sino-Japanese dispute over Liu-ch'iu, therefore, remained unresolved legally. Although there were some further discussions and counter proposals at Peking, Tientsin, and Tokyo, this was the end of the Liu-ch'iu controversy.[57] From 1881 on, the Okinawa Prefecture of Liu-ch'iu, created by Japan after the annexation, has technically been an integral part of the Japanese empire. From the Chinese point of view, however, the Liu-ch'iu question was never settled.

The episode of the Sino-Japanese controversy over the fate of the Liu-ch'iu Kingdom significantly illustrates China's dilemma in juxtaposing the new modern nation-state with the old tributary state system. In reading the Chinese statements relating to the dispute, one cannot fail to observe the confusion in the minds of these statesmen as to the actual status of the Liu-ch'iu Islands. These islands were sometimes considered an independent state, at other times a part of China, or even worse, a "common dependency" of both China and Japan. This confusion, to be sure, reveals not only the ambiguous political status of Liuch'iu, as defined by Western international law, but also the incompatibility of the tributary state system with the modern nation-state system.

That the Chinese leaders had not comprehended in the 1870s that the tributary relationship had no status in Western international law may seem incredible. As a noted historian asserted: "By 1867 the Tsungli Yamen knew . . . that the tributary tie was a logical impossibility in the modern world."[58] As far as Liu-ch'iu's tributary relationship with China was concerned, Li Hung-chang believed it was not worth fighting for. As was cited above, in his letter to Ho Ju-chang in Tokyo, Li pointed out that "it would not only be a waste of time but also absurd for China to use force to fight for a small tribute from a small country . . . for the sake of an empty name."[59] Indeed, Li Hung-chang began to question China's moral obligation to defend the tributary system. It appears that the ideological structure of the Chinese Confucian universal empire had begun to crumble.

Li Hung-chang believed that a war with Japan over Liu-ch'iu would be detrimental to China's national security, as well as the self-strengthening movement. As was cited above, Li remarked, ". . . we have to adopt a soft policy, and at the same time to try our best effort for self-strengthening in order to strive for later strength and power."[60] From the very outset, he carefully and pragmatically tried to form a Sino-Japanese "alliance" against the West, for fear that "an antagonized Japan could be an even greater source of trouble than the Western nations because of her geographical proximity" to China. He hoped that the appeasement of Japan could better serve the Chinese interest. Li's design, therefore, must be understood in light of his pragmatism and his analysis of the international situation. And when it appeared that this goal could not be reached, as evidenced by Japan's decision to annex Liu-ch'iu against China's will and the subsequent draft treaty of 1880, Li began to shift pragmatically his "pro-Japan" policy by appeasing Japan's enemy (Russia) in order to counter the rise of Japanese power in Asia. This modern version of *i-i chih-i*, as explained in terms of balance of power, provided Li with the rationale for his foreign policy change. In retrospect, however, Li's abortive attempt to appease Japan in the 1870s weakened China's position vis-à-vis Japan in the Liu-ch'iu dispute. In the long run, China's "loss" of Liu-ch'iu to Japan contributed to the disintegration of the tributary state system in Asia.

Notes

Abbreviations

CKCJ   *Ch'ing Kuang-hsü ch'ao Chung-Jih chiao-she shih-liao* (Historical materials concerning Sino-Japanese negotiations during the Kuang-hsü period, 1875–1908) (Taipei, 1963).

CTSM   *T'ung-chih chia-hsü Jih-ping ch'in-T'ai shih-mo* (A complete account of the Japanese Formosan Expedition of 1874) (Taipei, 1959).

HA   *Hiratsuka Atsushi, Zoku Itō Hirobumi hiroku* (Supplement to the confidential records of Itō Hirobumi) (Tokyo, 1930).

IWSM   *Ch'ou-pan i-wu shih-mo* (The complete account of the management of barbarian affairs) (Peking, 1930).

KK   Kiyosawa Kiyoshi, *Gaiseika toshite no Ōkubo Toshimichi* (Okubo Toshimichi as a diplomat-politician) (Tokyo, 1942).

LWCK   *Li Wen-chung kung ch'üan-chi* (Complete works of Li Hung-chang) (Shanghai, 1921).

NGB   *Nihon gaikō bunsho* (including *Dai-Nihon gaiko bunsho*) (Diplomatic papers of Japan) (Tokyo, 1937–40, 1949–).

NGB:TH   *Nihon gaikō bunsho: Meiji nenkan tsuiho* (Diplomatic papers of Japan: Supplement to the Meiji period) (Tokyo, 1964).

OKSG   Ota Chōfu, *Okinawa kensei gojunen* (Fifty years of Okinawan prefectural administration) (Tokyo, 1932).

OTB   *Ōkubo Toshimichi bunsho* (The Ōkubo Toshimichi papers), 10 vols. (Tokyo, 1967–69).

RST   Endō Tatsu and Gotō Keishin, eds., *Ryūkyū shobun teiko* (Salient points in the disposition of Ryūkyū) (1879); reprinted in *Meiji bunka zenshu*, vol. 25.

THL   *Ch'ing Kuang-hsü ch'ao tung-hua lu* (The Tung-hua records of the Kuang-hsü period in the Ch'ing dynasty) (Taipei, 1963).

WCSL   *Ch'ing-chi wai-chiao shih-liao* (Historical materials of late Ch'ing diplomacy) (Peking, 1932–35).

1. Liu-ch'iu had not only acknowledged China's suzerainty since 1372, but, since 1609, also paid tribute to the Satsuma domain of Japan. This dual dependency on two overlords was the result of Liu-ch'iu's military and economic weaknesses. While China remained ignorant of Liu-ch'iu's dual subordination until the Sino-Japanese dispute arose, the Satsuma domain deliberately allowed Liu-ch'iu to continue the tribute missions to China so that it could reap the profits from Liu-ch'iu's trade with China.

2. *IWSM*, T'ung-chih, 77:35.

3. Ibid.

4. For details, see Wang Hsi, *Li Hung-chang yü Chung-Jih ting-yo* (Li Hung-chang and the Sino-Japanese Treaty of 1871) (Taipei, 1981).

5. *NGB:TH*, I:142; *IWSM*, T'ung-chih, 96:27–32.

6. For details, see Edwin Pak-wah Leung, "The Quasi-war in East Asia: Japan's Expedition to Taiwan and the Ryūkyū Controversy," *Modern Asian Studies* 17.2 (April 1983), 257–81.

7. *CTSM*, II, 141.

8. Shanti S. Gandhi, U.S. Diplomatic Relations with China, 1869–1882 (unpublished Ph.D. dissertation, Georgetown University, 1954), 308.

9. Ibid.

10. For Boissonade's advice to the Japanese government, see *HA*, 32–36.

11. *OTB*, VI, 237–39.

12. Ibid., VI, 152–61; *KK*, 237–41.

13. *OTB*, VI, 237.

14. Ibid., VI, 158–60.

15. *KK*, 243.

16. *Ōkubo Toshimichi nikki* (Diary of Ōkubo), last part, 339–42.

17. *LWCK Tsungli Yamen Letters*, 4:24–25.

18. Ibid., 6:31–32.

19. Ibid., 7:3–4.

20. For aspects of the "Disposition of Ryūkyū," see Endō Tatsu and Gotō Keishin, eds., *Ryūkyū shobun teiko* (Salient points in the disposition of Ryūkyū) (1879); reprinted in *Meiji bunka zenshu*, vol. 25.

21. Lin Shih-kung (Rin Seiko, 1841–80), *Pei-shang tsa-chi* (Miscellany of my northward trip) (1884).

22. *CKCJ*, I:21–22.

23. Ibid.

24. Ibid., I:22.

25. On October 7, 1878, the frustrated Ho Ju-chang sent the Japanese Foreign Ministry a note of strong protest. Although Ho's note was mentioned in *WCSL* 15:12, the full text of the note is nonexistent in Chinese documents. It can be found, however, in Japanese documents: *NGB*, XI, 271–72; Tada Komon, ed., *Iwakura Ko jikka* (A factual account of Iwakura Tomomi) (Tokyo, 1968), III, 578–79.

26. *RST*, 132–33; *OKSG*, 43–44.

27. Grant recalled, "I have met on this journey four great men, Bismarck, Beaconsfield, Gambetta, and Li Hung-chang. I am not sure, all things considered, but Li is the greatest of the four." In John Russell Young, *Men and Memories: Personal Reminiscences* (New York, 1901), II, 303.

28. According to Young, the relations between Grant and Li had almost the element of romance, ibid., 319; Liang Chung-ying, *Li Hung-chang tui Jih wai-chiao chueh-ts'e chih yen-chiu* (Studies on Li Hung-chang's foreign policy toward Japan) (Taipei, 1974), 79.

29. Edwin Pak-wah Leung, "General Ulysses S. Grant and the Sino-Japanese Dispute over the Ryūkyū (Liu-ch'iu) Islands," *Proceedings of the First International Symposium on Asian Studies* (Hong Kong, 1979), II, 421–49.

30. Richard T. Chang, "General Grant's 1879 Visit to Japan," *Monumenta Nipponica* XXIV.4 (Winter 1969), 381.

31. See Grant's identical letters of August 13, 1879, to Li Hung-chang and Iwakura Tomomi, in *Grant Papers* (in microfilm, Library of Congress), Reel 2, S.IB, 6312–15.

32. *CKCJ*, II, 8a–10b.

33. Ibid., II, 14b–17; *LWCK Memorials*, 39:1–15.

34. For details, see Immanuel C. Y. Hsu, *The Ili Crisis: A Study of Sino-Russian Diplomacy, 1871–1881* (Oxford, 1965).

35. *LWCK Tsungli Yamen Letters*, 11:26–28b.

36. September 30, 1880, ibid., 11:36b.

37. Ibid., 10:26a–27a.

38. *CKCJ*, II, 14.

39. Ibid., II, 14b–17; *LWCK Memorials*, 39:1–15.

40. *LWCK Tsungli Yamen Letters*, 8:5.

41. *LWCK Letters*, 9:1b–2b.

42. *LWCK Tsungli Yamen Letters*, 8:1–2.

43. *CKCJ*, no. 32.

44. See S. T. Wang, *The Margary Affair and the Chefoo Convention* (London, 1940).

45. Ch'en San-ching, "Lueh-lun Ma Chien-chung ti wai-chiao ssu-hsiang," (A brief discussion on the diplomatic thought of Ma Chien-chung), *Chung-yang yen-chiu-yuan chin-tai-shih yen-chiu-suo chi-k'an* III.2 (1972), 548.

46. Mai Chung-hua, comp., *Huang Ch'ao ching-shih wen hsin-pien* (A new compilation of writings of our imperial dynasty) (Taipei, 1972), 72:9a–13a.

47. Ch'en San-ching, "Lueh-lun Ma Chien-chung," III.2, 548.

48. *LWCK Tsungli Yamen Letters*, 8:1a, 4b–6a.

49. Ssu-ming Meng, *The Tsungli Yamen: Its Organization and Functions* (Cambridge, Mass., 1962), 3–4.

50. Liu Hsin-hsien, "Chung-kuo wai-chiao chih-tu ti yen-ke," (The evolution of Chinese diplomatic institutions), in *Chung-kuo chin-tai shih lun-tsung*, II.5, 23–28.

51. Tabohashi Kiyoshi, *Kindai Nissen kankei no kenkyū* (A study of Japanese-Korean relations in modern times) (Keijo, 1940), 13, 565.

52. *LWCK Memorials*, 1:23, 2:10, 6:26, 15:26.

53. *THL*, I.295 (November 1876) 45; I.319 (November 1876) 135; I.1037 (February 1881), 7.

54. See Immanuel C. Y. Hsu, "The Great Policy Debate in China, 1874: Maritime Defense vs. Frontier Defense," *Harvard Journal of Asiatic Studies* 25 (1964–65), 212–28.

55. *LWCK Memorials*, 39:1–5; *NGB*, XIII, 379–80.

56. Shishidō Tamaki's communications with the Chinese government are now collected in the *Shishidō Tamaki kankei bunsho* in the National Diet Library at Tokyo.

57. Liang Chia-pin, "Liu-ch'iu wang-kuo Chung-Jih cheng-ch'in kao-shih," (An investigation of the Sino-Japanese dispute over Liu-ch'iu and the fall of the Liu-ch'iu Kingdom), *Ta-lu tsa-chih* 48.5 (May 15, 1974), 193–218; 48.6 (June 15, 1974), 263–90.

58. Mary C. Wright, "The Adaptability of Ch'ing Diplomacy: The Case of Korea," *Journal of Asian Studies* 17.3 (May 1958), 381.

59. *LWCK Tsungli Yamen Letters* 8:5.

60. *LWCK Letters*, 9:1b–2b.

9

Li Hung-chang's Suzerain Policy toward Korea, 1882–1894

Ming-te Lin

From before the time of the Imo military riots (1882) to the eve of the Sino-Japanese War (1894), China abandoned her previous laissez-faire policy toward Korea and adopted a more active line. During the late nineteenth century, China's Korean policy was set by governor-general Li Hung-chang and was carried out by Yüan Shih-k'ai. The emergence of this policy and its evolutionary process were not only a crucial part of China's diplomatic history but also a key point in the development of Korea's political situation. The new policy had a profound impact on subsequent Sino-Japanese relations and the international situation in East Asia.

In this period, there were four important changes in the international situation of the Korean peninsula. First, Japan's expansionist mainland policy was aimed at the seizure of Korea to facilitate Japanese encroachment upon Manchuria. Second, the antagonism between Great Britain and Russia induced a British presence in an attempt to stop Russia's expansion southward. Third, the United States took steps to open the Korean market. Fourth, Ch'ing China struggled to sustain her vassal state and the security of her borders. In this international context, Li's Korean policy was to avail himself fully of diversionary tactics by taking a "wavering stance," expediently assembling power to ward off any threat to the traditional Chinese-Korean tributary relationship. Li's control of Korea from 1885 to 1894 through Yüan Shih-k'ai as resident official represented an anachronistic policy of intervention in Korea.

Li's Korean policy both responded to Japan's aggressive interference in Korean affairs since the early Meiji era and was designed to take advantage of other trends, especially the conflict between Britain and Russia for dominion in the area. Meanwhile, the policy was constrained by Ch'ing China's inferior political and economic capabilities. Under these circumstances, the relationship between China and Japan in this period became a prelude to the later confrontation between the two nations. The controversy over Korea's tributary status reflected the domestic and foreign conditions of China and Japan and their attitudes toward Korea and each other. Not until the Sino-Japanese War did this confrontation come to a temporary conclusion.

This chapter is an investigation of Li Hung-chang's Korean policy during the ten years before the Sino-Japanese War, and an exploration of the external circumstances effecting a radical change in China's policy from that of laissez-faire to one of active interference. In addition, this chapter deals with the impact of this change in policy on Korean affairs and its historical significance in modern Chinese history.

Li's Korean policy from laissez-faire to "check and balance"

After 1879, China's policy toward Korea changed from laissez-faire to interference, in part because of an increasing Western presence, as well as the conflicts and imbalance among the Western powers. Another reason for policy change was that traditional ties between Ch'ing China and her tributary, Korea, came to a crisis involving Japan. Japan's annexation of the Ryūkyū Kingdom, another of China's tributaries, made the Ch'ing government aware of the importance of the Korean peninsula to China's national defense.

Having inherited the traditional tributary system, China and Korea had maintained a special relationship since the early Ch'ing. In fact, the so-called vassal state was neither a colony nor a dependency. The ideology of the Chinese empire did not include the concept of a modern international community. The basic provisos of a suzerain-subordinate relationship were courtesy, tribute, investiture, and compliance with the Chinese calendar; but the Chinese suzerain did not manipulate or interfere in a tributary's internal and external affairs. Only when there were civil riots in a tributary did the suzerain have an obligation to dispatch troops for their suppression. A tributary was therefore still completely autonomous in its internal and external affairs, which was contradictory to modern international law regarding colonies or dependencies. Since the middle of the nineteenth century, however, with the rise of the Western powers' usage of "gunboat diplomacy," the Ch'ing government no longer could deal with increasingly complicated international affairs merely by resorting to exploitation of a tributary's autonomy.

The most noted result of China's Korean policy in the 1880s was the transformation from a traditional "vassal state system" to involvement in an imperialistic system in which the nominally subordinate relationship had to be modified to meet a new, modern international situation. Moreover, with the jolt of the Progressive Party's enlightenment and independence movement in Korea, the Ch'ing government, under the impact of external and domestic developments in Korea, was forced to alter its scheme in order to sustain and strengthen China's traditional suzerainty.

In addition, there was the problem of the Liu-ch'iu (Ryūkyū) Islands. The Chinese attitude toward Korea began to change in 1879, when Japan formally annexed the Liu-ch'iu Islands. At the same time, France was in the process of invading Annam, so the Ch'ing government was preoccupied with problems there. Furthermore, Russia menaced China from the northwest with threats of military action over the border dispute concerning the Ili valley. Under these circumstances, Japan's annexation of the Liu-ch'iu Islands aroused tremendous fear and bitter arguments within the Ch'ing government. Ting Jih-ch'ang, the high official in charge of defense in Southern China, and Ho Ju-chang, Chinese minister in Tokyo, espoused opening the Korean market to trade with Western nations in order to restrain Japan.[1] Liu K'un-i, governor-general of Liangkiang, also insisted on Korea's alliance with Western powers to curb the advances of Japan and Russia.[2]

In that year, 1879, the management of Korean affairs was transferred from the Board of Rites to the direct supervision and control of the commissioner for the Northern Ports, assisted by the minister to Japan.[3] In August, Li Hung-chang expressed his anxiety in his communications to the Tsungli Yamen: "Because the Liu-ch'iu Islands have been annexed, Korea is in a position of imminent danger; with the Western powers waiting around for intrusion, we can no longer refrain from devising ways and means for the security of Korea."[4] This comment reveals how profoundly Li was influenced by the loss of the Liu-ch'iu Islands. Li was not only concerned about Korea's isolation and helplessness, but he also feared that the Western powers' anticipated invasion of Korea was destined to threaten China.[5] China was dependent on Korea for the security of Manchuria, which, in turn, directly affected the security of Peking. At the end of the sixteenth century, Japan had attacked Korea, aiming to occupy Korea in an all-out effort. Although Japan did not succeed at that time, Ming China nevertheless lost control of Manchuria later on, and the Ming fall ensued. The Ch'ing government was fully aware of these events; therefore, the urgency of Ch'ing defense against Japan was in direct ratio to Japan's plans toward Korea. Li Hung-chang was especially concerned with the security of the Korean peninsula, regarding it as "the protective fence," the first line of defense for China.[6] Yüan Shih-k'ai, on the eve of the Kapsin coup, described the situation as follows: "Korea is the shield next to China, holding the key to the door of the Northeastern provinces. With threats from the alien powers around it, it is definitely something to worry about."[7] A small pamphlet entitled *Korean Strategy*, written by Huang Tsun-hsien, a Chinese official in Tokyo, and brought home from Japan by Kim Hong-jip, the second *susinsa* to Japan,[8] also immensely affected Korean policy-making.

In the summer of 1879, Li Hung-chang wrote a letter to Yi Yu-won in which he referred to both Japan's and Russia's ambitions toward Korea. In the letter, Li suggested that Korea, as a means of restraining the Japanese and the Russians, should reconstruct her armed forces, implement the "control barbarians with barbarians" strategy, and begin trading with the Western countries.[9] By the winter of 1880, China and Russia had a confrontation over the issue of the Ili district. Meanwhile, the Russians were building the Trans-Siberian Railroad in the vicinity of the Amur River and Vladivostok, which aroused anxiety in China and Korea. Soon Britain, concerned with the Russians' southbound expansion, sought to propose that the Tsungli Yamen persuade Korea to do business with the Western powers.[10] This resulted in the Ch'ing government assigning Li Hung-chang the task of arranging for treaties between Korea and the Western countries.[11] Faced with extremely unfavorable circumstances, the Kojong government had no choice but to accede reluctantly to concluding treaties with the Western powers. The eventual signing of the American-Korean treaty can be viewed as the commencement of the realization of Chinese "interventionist policy."

The United States, since concluding a treaty with Japan in 1854, had been paying attention to Korea. There had been negotiations between America and Korea brought about by several incidents, but they all ended up in failure and did not contribute to improved relations between the two countries.[12] It was not until the Japan-Korea treaty of Kanghwa in 1876 that America again began to show interest and offered to sign a treaty with Korea. In 1880, Commodore Robert W. Shufeldt, U.S.N., was sent to Korea for that purpose. But because he was introduced by Japan, the Kojong government rejected him.[13] Li's information on that event had convinced him that Japan had no intention of mediating for America, yet he still feared an alliance between Japan and the United States that would do harm to China's status in Korea. So he determined to compete for American interest. He invited Shufeldt to a meeting in Tientsin, to assure him that Li would promote the American-Korean treaty.[14] Li as mediator was doing two things. On the one hand, he attempted to prevent Japan from augmenting her power in Korea; on the other hand, he endeavored to maintain China's suzerain position by strengthening the tributary relationship with Korea.[15]

Ho Ju-chang was among those Chinese officials who argued that China should have the privilege of discussing with other powers how Korea would open her ports. Obviously, this idea reflected the position of "the superior nation's rights." But Li Hung-chang adopted a moderate view, choosing to follow the alternative position of "adjustment [regulation] behind the scenes." He instructed Ma Chien-chung and others to draft a set of regulations to be adopted by Korea.[16]

At the beginning of Article I of the draft, there is a definitive statement:

> Korea is the vassal state of China, but has always enjoyed autonomy in both its internal and external affairs. After the conclusion of this treaty, the King of Chosen [Korea] and the President of the United States shall deal with each other upon terms of perfect equality, and the subjects and citizens of the two nations shall maintain a perpetual relationship of friendship. If other powers deal unjustly or oppressively with either government, the other shall render assistance and protection or shall act as mediator in order to preserve perfect peace.[17]

The first half of Article I was meant to engender U.S. recognition of the tributary relationship that existed between China and Korea, in resistance to Japan's acknowledgment of an autonomous Korea by way of the Kanghwa Treaty. The second half of Article I provided mainly for the implementation of the "control barbarians with barbarians" strategy in a manner analogous to that of the preceding Sino-Japanese Amity Treaty of 1871; it was, however, these points that kept China and America from reaching an agreement on Article I. Shufeldt rejected this article on the basis of the Kanghwa Treaty, announcing that America would stay away from the Sino-Korean relationship and, instead, deal with Korea, the subject of the treaty, on equal terms. In addition, he refused to employ a term such as *Chinese tributary* in reference to Korea.[18]

In April 1882, Li Hung-chang sent Ma Chien-chung to visit Korea with Shufeldt. In Inchon, they held a meeting to discuss the treaty with two Korean representatives, Sin Hon and Kim Hong-jip. In effect, the treaty had been negotiated and agreed on mainly by Li and Shufeldt in Tientsin. As mentioned above, America persisted in the exclusion of Article I. Ma was therefore impelled to propose that the King of Korea proclaim Korea a tributary of China, but the proclamation was to be attached to the treaty instead of being formally incorporated within it.[19] Shufeldt believed that the proclamation lacked the effect of restraint because of its absence from the treaty itself, and this assessment finally eliminated the entangled wrangling over Article I between China and America. The Treaty of Peace, Amity, Commerce, and Navigation between the United States and Korea was signed by the Korean government on May 22, 1882.

Satisfied with the result, Li Hung-chang was naively convinced that his persistence in obtaining the formal statement by the King compelled other powers to recognize unequivocally China's sovereign position over Korea.[20] But, contrary to what he had hitherto believed, the United States government, after the conclusion of the treaty, still firmly sustained Korea's autonomy and denied China's suzerainty. In regard to the King's statement, the United States neither took responsibility for it nor formally proclaimed it.[21] This, indeed, dashed Li's hopes. In the words of Tyler Dennett, the treaty was "one of the great mistakes of his [Li's] career."[22] The treaty did not settle the legal status of Korea to the satisfaction of the parties concerned. Japan and the United States were foremost in upholding Korean independence, while China and Britain acted on the assumption that the traditional suzerain-dependency tie between China and Korea had not been altered in any way.[23]

For Korea, the aftermath brought the sequential advent of nations such as Britain, Germany, and others, and, with them, treaties whose provisions were similar to those of the pioneering American-Korean Treaty. With the exception of Austria, all of the nations accepted the King's statement to be a memorandum attached to their treaties.[24] By this time, the portal of Korea had been opened and, inextricably, Korea became a game in which the foreign powers contended. Because of the breakdown of Li's restraint policy, Korea inevitably entered the world of imperialism and suffered henceforth from the intrusion of foreign political and economic influences. Worst of all, the complexity of the Korean issue was aggravated.

Imo military mutiny and the changing attitude of China

In July 1882, the Imo military riot broke out. It was attributable to two critical factors: first, antipathy toward Japan's ambitions regarding Korea since the Kanghwa Treaty and, second, resentment against the Min clan's corruption. In addition, the *Zeitgeist* of xenophobia and anti-Japanese feelings among some Korean Confucian scholars helped set it off. As spontaneous as the eruption of a volcano, the riot exploded, involving as participants mostly poverty-ridden soldiers, lower-class people, and peasants. The riot was truly an accident, which coincided with Li Hung-chang's absence from his post while he was home in mourning for his mother's death. Chang Shu-sheng was then his deputy, and, accordingly, proceeded to deal with the riot by sending a Chinese force to Korea. Actually, however, Li and his staff in Tientsin were involved in decision-making.[25]

Regarding the suppression of the riot, Li's instructions laid special emphasis on two principles: the combination of arms and diplomacy and the repression of the "rebel party." The aim of the first principle was to prevent Japan from coercing Korea, and to bring China and Japan into an agreement; in reality, this measure would affirm China's suzerainty over Korea. The second principle was to sustain the sovereignty of the king of Korea as conferred by the Ch'ing emperor, in order to grasp more firmly China's control over Korean politics.

The arrest of the Taewon'gun, as proposed by Hsüeh Fu-ch'eng, was fully in accord with Li's long-term strategy.[26] Because of the Taewon'gun's arrest, China had won the first round. On the other hand, a good deal of advantage had also been taken by Japan. In this military mutiny, more than twenty Japanese, including Horimoto Reizo, were killed, and the Japanese legation was burned to the ground. The fire was actually set by Japanese Minister Hanabusa Yoshimoto just before his escape to Inchon.[27] Without hesitation, Japan sent troops to Korea and forced on Korea the conclusion of the insulting Chemulpo Treaty. For Japan, this was a delayed sequel to the Kanghwa Treaty which not only consolidated Japan's influence over Korean politics and economy but also expanded her military influence, especially by Japan's having been granted the right to station troops. As a result, both China and Japan had troops in Korea, which made military conflict between them inevitable; that was in the background of the Kapsin coup in 1884.[28]

After the Imo military mutiny, people in both Japan and China seethed with indignation. The Japanese were irritated by China's military intervention, and the mainstream of public opinion was in favor of an appeal to arms, which specifically was the Genyōsha position.[29] The government, however, remained in search of a peaceful solution and insisted on sustaining an autonomous Korea, rejecting China's involvement in negotiations between Japan and Korea and thus expressing Japan's denial of China's suzerainty over Korea. Worth noting is that Japan at this time presumed that it was not powerful enough to be China's rival; therefore, temporary compromise with Ch'ing China was considered appropriate, to avoid intrusion from the Western powers and disasters on both sides if any reckless military action was taken. But, from this time on, Japan began to regard Ch'ing China as a potential enemy and engage substantially in the expansion of Japan's armed forces.[30] In fact, this development was responsible for what took place later in the arena of Korean politics, namely, the vicissitudes of the impacts of China and Japan, the insolubility of the suzerainty issue, and Japan's eventual appeal to arms despite her seemingly inferior position.

As for the Chinese, a group of chauvinistic scholars and officials, collectively known as the Ch'ing-liu tang (Purist Party), was crying out for a more aggressive policy toward Korea. Suddenly, "the idea of conquering Japan" was enthusiastically upheld. Those in favor of this idea took it for granted that by no means could Japan compare in martial power with China. They also attributed the success of previous Japanese challenges to China's avoidance of warfare and constant forbearance. Consequently, they espoused a war with Japan, which they believed would solve the flagrant issues (Liu-ch'iu Islands, Korea, and so forth).[31] The stalwarts stationed in Korea, such as Yüan Shih-k'ai and particularly Chang Chien, echoed the radical views of the Purist Party. In his paper entitled "A Six-Point Policy on Korea," Chang argued that it would best serve the Chinese national interest if Korea were under the control of a Chinese royal supervisor.[32]

More thoughtfully, Li Hung-chang believed that any rash military action would be improper before China's superiority in armed forces was secure.[33] Besides, for the time being, China's most urgent issue was self-strengthening. Li never stopped keeping an eye on Japan, yet what he stood for was a more prudent wait-and-see attitude.[34]

The Imo military riot, however, gave China a great opportunity to interfere directly in Korean politics and to continue its suzerain policy over Korea. Li Hung-chang agreed with Chang P'ei-lun's proposal, also involving six points ("A Six-Point Program for the Solution of the Korean Problem"), except for the article about the occupation of Port Lazareff, which Li believed required further thought.[35] Moreover, the exertion of China's authority, according to Li, had to be secret and subtle, rather than open and direct. Toward this end, Li appointed Ch'en Shu-t'ang, a former Chinese consul in San Francisco, as the Chinese commissioner of commerce in Seoul. In the name of officiating in matters of trade, Ch'en was able to discuss any issue with the Korean government to ensure Chinese control over Korea. Meanwhile, in the arena of diplomacy, Li employed a foreign consul, P.G. von Möllendorff, to assist in maritime customs and foreign affairs in Korea and also sent a few other new officials, such as Ma Chien-ch'ang, to Korea to serve as political representatives. In regard to military matters, Li provided modern munitions and recommended Wu Ch'ang-ch'ing to organize and train modern Korean military units.[36] In the economic sphere, Li loaned money to Korea to preclude her turning to Japan for support, as well as to help in the exploitation of mines.[37] But surpassing all these actions was Li's most significant political measure—the conclusion, in October 1882, of an unequal treaty with the Korean government entitled "The Sino-Korean Regulations for Maritime and Overland Trade."

These regulations were distinguishable from ordinary trade regulations mainly because they were arranged exclusively for China and Korea and did not apply to other treaty powers. The treaty was actually a result of China's effort to express to the world, in the tone of modern treaties, the ambiguous traditional relationship between the two countries. No matter from what angle one considers the regulations—for example, the privileges in legal matters and in customs tariff or in other fields—they were all unequal, indicating to the world China's control over Korea, as well as her enjoyment of the privileges, even to the point of ranking the king of Korea no higher than China's commissioner of trade for the Northern Ports. The regulations shed more light on politics than on economics.[38]

The Kapsin coup and Li's interventionist policy

The Kapsin coup d'état was not merely a fight for hegemony between the Kaehwa tang (Party of Civilization, known as the Progressive Party) and the Sadae tang (Pro-China Party). Led by Kim Ok-kyun and Pak Yang-hyo, followers of the "Sirhak" thought that stressed the progressiveness and independence of Korea, the Kaehwa tang intended to overthrow the conservative government of the Min clan. The Mins sided with Ch'ing China, and the final aim of the opposition was to get rid of China's suzerainty and exercise Korea's autonomy and independence. Therefore, the Kapsin coup was regarded as a drastic reform movement among the *yangban* families.

After the Imo military mutiny, China had made every effort to strengthen her suzerainty over Korea and had patronized the Pro-China Party, so that the young independents were not powerful enough to influence major policies or carry out their programs of innovation. The situation forced them to risk breaking the law, while the interference and oppression of Chinese officials stationed in Korea generally aroused Korea's antipathy toward China.[39] The rumor that the Taewon'gun was being released also made the Korean government suspicious and fearful of Ch'ing China.[40] Meanwhile, the expansion of Chinese merchant activities created an unfavorable influence on the commerce of Korea.[41] Along with Ch'ing China's withdrawal of half its troops (1,500) from Korea and its preoccupation with the conflict with France over Annam, this was another stimulus for Korea to revolt. Moreover, the Japanese ruler and his subjects, particularly Takezoe Shin'ichirō, the Japanese minister in Korea, incited the Progressive Party to proceed to a political reformation. Thus, the Progressive Party, motivated and supported by Japan, started a coup d'état on December 4, 1884. They held King Kojong hostage and announced the "Reform Decrees of

Kapsin.''[42] In fact, they did not get substantial military support from Japan and, consequently, were attacked and defeated by Ch'ing troops.

This revolt failed, however, because the Progressive Party underestimated the strength of China's troops stationed in Seoul, and because it was overly dependent on foreign aid guaranteed by Takezoe Shin'ichirō. The failure also revealed its perfunctory plan for political reformation and its erroneous judgment of the status quo. Basically, the revolt failed because of Korea's unstable social and economic foundations, and because the enlightenment movement had not been embraced thoroughly by the masses.[43]

Soon after the revolt, the Ch'ing government made its first statement regarding the principle it would follow in handling the Korean problem, clearly indicating that it wished to resolve the problem in a peaceful way. Li Hung-chang previously had planned to restore the Taewon'gun to power, but his plan was rejected by the Ch'ing government.[44] Immediately afterward, according to the Japanese envoy's interpretation, the Ch'ing government concluded that Japan had no intention of provoking China and consented to adopt the proposition of Hsü Ch'eng-tsu, Chinese minister in Tokyo, to end the controversy by means of negotiation.[45] This plan resulted in the declaration of another new policy toward Korea: "The chief intent is the suppression of rebellion," according to the principle "to eliminate the delusion and to terminate the hostilities between China and Japan as the main theme."[46] Ch'ing China's inclination toward peace actually reflected China's preoccupation with the Annam problem. Li particularly dreaded Japan's alliance with France,[47] so he decided to build up military and naval strength (a battalion and two naval vessels) in Masan.[48]

On the Japanese side, the tendency toward peaceful resolution resulted from financial straits and deficient armaments. However, Japan still insisted on having Korea remain independent.[49] Inoue Kaoru, the minister plenipotentiary, was sent to Korea for negotiations, conducted in the presence of six hundred well-armed Japanese soldiers.[50] Inoue originally had two missions: first, Korean-Japanese negotiations; second, Sino-Japanese negotiations. The latter was then dropped by Japan on the grounds that the Chinese representative, Wu Ta-ch'eng, was not duly qualified as a plenipotentiary.[51] As for Korean-Japanese negotiations, the resulting agreement was the "Seoul Protocol" signed on January 9, 1885, which included an indemnity for Japanese victims, a formal letter of apology, and the maintenance of a thousand Japanese soldiers in Seoul.[52]

In April 1885, Itō Hirobumi was appointed ambassador plenipotentiary to China and undertook negotiations regarding the consequences of the Sino-Japanese clash in order to diminish the tension caused by the confrontation. He was also to address the dissatisfied mood within Japan aroused by China's forceful interference with Korean political affairs and the consequent weakening of the pro-Japanese party. Li Hung-chang represented the Ch'ing government when negotiations began in Tientsin on April 3, 1885. Japan demanded punishment of the Chinese commander, compensations to the Japanese, and the withdrawal of troops. Japan's principal aim was China's withdrawal; the other two demands were merely to alleviate the feelings of domestic hawkish Japanese and to screen Japan's main objective in the negotiations. Li and the Ch'ing government contested and argued adamantly on the issue of punishing the commander, but promised to withdraw troops quickly. The Ch'ing government had seemingly mistaken the means for the end, the result of being swayed by pride and the consideration of complaints from troops in Korea. Nevertheless, the main reason the Ch'ing government was ignorant of Japan's real intention was China's anxiety about Japan and France entering into a confederation.[53] Thus came about the Tientsin Convention on April 14. The Convention included the withdrawal of the troops of both signatories in four months, neither to have an appointed military official in Korea thereafter. The most important provision was that either signatory could dispatch troops to Korea in case of future uprisings or other serious disturbances there. In such an event, the signatories would notify Korea, as well as each other, and, upon settlement of the disturbance, any troops that had been dispatched were to be withdrawn completely.[54]

In truth, Japan's evident interference in Korean internal affairs, including her plot to incite and participate in the coup d'état, was never condemned or punished. Moreover, the Convention raised Japan to a position of importance equal to that of China in the Korean peninsula.[55] It was a great coup in Japanese diplomacy. On China's part, this diplomatic miscalculation notwithstanding, Li Hung-chang redoubled his effort to strengthen China's suzerainty over Korea.

Reassertion of China's suzerainty after the Kapsin coup

During the ten-year period from the Kapsin coup to the Sino-Japanese War, the Korean situation remained complex. The contest among Western nations in East Asia became increasingly acute and grave, with the British-Russian confrontation in the Middle East spreading to the Korean peninsula. Japan changed its attitude and policy toward Korea for fear that Russia's sphere of influence would extend southward. Adapting to the changing situation, Li Hung-chang turned to a more active policy toward Korea. Although Japan had as much right to dispatch troops to Korea as did China, as stated in the Tientsin Convention, this mechanism was of no avail in times of peace. Thus, through the official quartered in Korea, China could still stress the traditional tributary relations and reinforce its manipulation of Korea, if the official there was a person of sufficient sagacity and ability. Li found such a person in Yüan Shih-k'ai, a brash, forceful young man of twenty-six, well acquainted with Korea. As a result, in the next decade, Li and Yüan acted in coordination with each other from both within and outside of Korea, adopting a forceful policy in order to reassert China's suzerainty, and to make Korea live up to her role as a tributary of China.

Until the time of the Kapsin coup, Japan's Korean policy had been active and aggressive. After the Tientsin Convention, however, because of insufficient power and resources, Japan restrained her expansive intentions and waited for a chance to move later on. Besides, to prevent Russian influence from extending southward, Japan had to give tacit consent to China's reassertion of suzerainty, at least as a temporary expedient. Japan thought it far easier to cope with a big, but weak nation, such as China, than with Russia. At the Tientsin negotiations, Japan had agreed to take a more peaceful and passive line toward Korea. Previously, in March 1885, Enomoto Takeaki, the Japanese minister in Peking, had made a proposal to the Japanese government for the "joint protection of Korea by Japan and China,"[56] but the proposal was not adopted. Later on, after the consequent occurrence of the abortive secret Russo-Korean agreement and the British occupation of Port Hamilton, Japan was worried about Britain's and Russia's occupation of islands along the coast of Korea. Such occupation would definitely threaten Japan's national defense.[57] Japan therefore turned to collaboration with the Ch'ing government and encouraged China to interfere actively in Korean affairs. Inoue Kaoru, the foreign minister of Japan, suggested that China and Japan jointly intervene in Korean affairs,[58] which clearly revealed Japan's tacit recognition that Korea was a tributary of China. This was quite different from Japan's earlier policy toward Korea, which called on Japan to make every effort possible to incite Korea to shake off the yoke of China's suzerainty.

In an "Eight-Point Proposal to Control Korea," which Inoue Kaoru transmitted to Li Hung-chang through Enomoto in early July 1885, Inoue suggested that Li initiate the following measures as a guarantee against a possible Russo-Korean entente: (1) prohibit the Korean king and his coterie from dealing in state affairs or from advising some patriots and royalists on state affairs; (2) dismiss P. G. von Möllendorff and replace him with another foreigner, an American; and (3) send a competent diplomat to Korea to replace Ch'en Shu-t'ang. Inoue also suggested releasing the Taewon'gun to divert the pro-Russian party.[59] Li adopted some of Japan's suggestions but, because Li feared being restrained by Japan, he refused to adopt Inoue's original proposal for Sino-Japanese collaboration in controlling Korea.

Britain's attitude then gave a great prod to, and played a crucial role in, the reassertion of China's suzerainty over Korea. To check the expansion of Russia's influence in East Asia, and especially to impede Russia from encroaching on Korea, Britain tried her best to facilitate Ch'ing China's efforts to consolidate its suzerain role. Despite its defense of the system of unequal treaties with China, Britain was thus attempting to maintain friendly relations with China and strengthen China's position as a block to Russia's southern advance. Before the Kapsin coup, Britain had already expressed her attitude, but it became more evident when the existence of the Russo-Korean Secret Agreement became known. Specifically, the British minister to Japan, and Sir Robert Hart, Inspector General of the Imperial Maritime Customs, both urged Li Hung-chang to strengthen China's control over Korea.[60] The British government decided to have its minister to China serve jointly as envoy to Korea. This British position, with regard to Korea, can clearly be viewed in the light of the events surrounding the British occupation of Port Hamilton beginning in April 1885, and the ensuing diplomatic clash over that occupation. Britain agreed to withdraw on the condition that no other nation would occupy other ports. Instead of getting in touch with Korea, Britain negotiated with China exclusively. Accordingly, in October 1886, Britain agreed to withdraw from Port Hamilton in February 1887 upon China's assurance that Russia would not occupy Korea.[61] Britain also eagerly supported China's position as the suzerain power. Britain held to a policy of restraining Russia by maintaining an alliance with China until the eve of the Sino-Japanese War. This was clearly expressed in the British Foreign Office's letter, which set forth Britain's policy toward China for the minister in Peking, N. R. O'Conor. Therefore, O'Conor continued to regard China as "an ally" until the outbreak of the Sino-Japanese War.[62] That was the diplomatic basis of Li Hung-chang's ability to uphold China's suzerain position in Korea. On the other hand, Britain's later change of attitude in favor of Japan, her agreement to end unequal conventions with Japan, as well as her moving from a policy of restraining Russia by alliance with China to one of presenting a united front with Japan were actually crucial factors contributing to China's defeat in the Sino-Japanese War.[63]

As for Russia's attitude in this period, although China and powerful countries like Japan and Britain were fearful of Russia's intrusion into Korea, in fact in the second half of the nineteenth century, Russia seemed to have no intention of invading Korea. Russia just wished to keep the Korean status quo, not expecting Korea's relationships with other countries to threaten Russia's eastern borders. Therefore, Russia did not oppose China's policy of sustaining traditional tributary relations with Korea. Britain's occupation of Port Hamilton and the second "Russo-Korean Secret Agreement" initiated Russo-Chinese negotiations. N. F. Ladyzhenskii, the Russian chargé d'affaires in Peking, discussed Korean affairs with Li Hung-chang in September 1886. Russia indicated that she had no intention of intruding into Korea. Li then worked to design a policy to draw Russia to the Chinese side in order to deal with Japanese plans for invading Korea. This move revealed Li's policy of restraining Japan by alliance with Russia. Russia, for her part, was more threatened by China's intrusion into Korea than Japan's, so Russia went along with Li's proposal of a secret Russo-Chinese nonaggression agreement with regard to Korea. The preliminary agreement contained the following: "The two governments agree that there should be no change in the current situation in Korea and that neither has any intention ever to occupy any Korean territory."[64]

The Peking government, however, thought that the line "The two governments agree that there should be no change in the current situation in Korea" implied a guarantee for Korea; there was a fear that in the future, when dealing with the problem of Korea's vassal status, this clause might limit China's activities. The Chinese therefore insisted on removing that provision. In the end, the proposal was not included in the formal agreement but survived under the name of the Li-Ladyzhenskii verbal agreement (or the 1886 verbal agreement of Tientsin).[65]

In February 1887, Russia held a conference in St. Petersburg on the East Asian situation, to review and discuss Russia's policy toward Korea. Controversy was fostered over which country, Russia or China, was more likely to invade Korea. However, in principle Russia decided to have the Russian minister in Peking negotiate with China for a formal conclusion of the 1886 verbal agreement of Tientsin.[66] On May 8, 1888, Russia held a special conference to discuss its policy. In charge of the conference were A. N. Korf, governor-general of the Preamur Region, and I. A. Zinoviev, director of the Asian Department of the Ministry of Foreign Affairs. The conclusion reached by the conference provided the basis for Russian East Asian policy in the subsequent period. The main points were as follows:

1. Consensus that the occupation of Korea would not only be of no benefit to Russia but would spoil the relationship between Russia and China or between Russia and Great Britain.

2. Agreement on and support for China's sustaining the traditional tributary relationship with Korea.

3. Plans to bring up the 1886 verbal agreement of Tientsin and to make clear to China that Russia had no intention of encroaching upon Korea.[67]

Then Russia brought up the Tientsin verbal agreement for the third time and invited Japan and Britain to attend the conference, expecting a formal convention with China. This did not succeed,[68] however, as Russia emphasized preserving the integrity of Korean territory as the means of keeping Korea's status quo. On the other hand, China expected Russia's acknowledgement that Korea was one of China's tributaries. This was why China and Russia failed to arrive at an agreement. But Russia's passive attitude toward Korea and Britain's inciting China to strengthen its suzerainty actively were the main international factors allowing Li Hung-chang to adopt an aggressive policy toward Korea.

Although U.S. influence on Korea could not be compared with that of Russia and Japan, the United States always emphasized Korean autonomy and independence and supported the Progressive Party in its fight against China's suzerainty. Moreover, U.S. political thought and behavior had a positive impact on Korea. These factors, however, did not influence Li's Korean policy at the time.

In August 1890, Yüan Shih-k'ai accurately analyzed the international situation then facing Korea:

> Korea is on the verge of a breakdown—no power to count on inside, no help to depend on outside. America is fending for her own interests rather than having any further strategy. Similarly, Britain, France, and Germany have no ambitions to invade. Japan is concentrating on her own reforms and, therefore, she does not expect to see any change at all in the existing balance. With the Trans-Siberian Railroad still unfinished, Russia thinks only of the West, her own ambitions toward Korea now concealed.[69]

Under these advantageous international circumstances, China's aggressive Korean policy, the "Li-Yüan Line," was finally formed.

To be sure, Li's strategy of alliance with Russia and Britain to resist Japan did not go unquestioned. In addition to those who adhered to Korean neutralization and joint control, such stalwarts as Yüan Shih-k'ai and Chang Chien were eager to make Korea an "overseas province" of China or to place Korea under the control of a Chinese royal supervisor. Still, Li did not dare act exactly as these critics suggested. Worried about arousing Korean antipathy, on the one hand, and fearing restraints from the Powers, including Japan, on the other, Li had to respect the partial autonomy which traditional suzerainty normally allowed Korea.

During the decade from 1885 to 1894, with both internal and external conditions in his favor, Li Hung-chang formulated the aggressive interventionist policy toward Korea and directed that it be executed by Yüan Shih-k'ai, upon Yüan's assignment, in October 1885, as director-general of diplomatic and consular affairs, residing in Korea. Yüan successfully carried out his mission. Yüan worked hard in gratitude for Li's confidence in him, but the main reasons for the overwhelming success of the Chinese policy were as follows: first, as a suzerain power in Korea, China had already enjoyed exclusive institutional advantages; second, the other nations in treaty relations with Korea either acquiesced tacitly or supported China's policy toward Korea; finally, the Korean people blindly accepted China's high-handed policy out of their principle of "sadae" (serving the great). Yüan's interference in Korean politics was so complete that all matters concerning internal administration, foreign affairs, and finance were within his range.[70] Moreover, he despised King Kojong, as well as the queen, and on several occasions proposed to depose the king.[71] His ultimate aim was to enhance China's suzerainty over Korea.

Although the Korean people were inclined to respect China and honor the principle of "sadae," Yüan's domineering policy aroused their antipathy, especially after they became imbued with the idea of *kaehwa* (enlightenment) and began to look forward to Korea's independence and autonomy. Unfortunately, this expectation suffocated under the unrelenting repression of foreign powers. With regard to Korean modernization, there is no general agreement among scholars as to the meaning of this term. The only way to approach the history of the movement, therefore, is to discuss it in terms of "Westernization" and "industrialization."

Of interest here is whether the interventionist policy ever obstructed the Korean enlightenment movement and frustrated its modernization. In 1881, Li Hung-chang attempted to help Korea reorganize and modernize its military forces while, at the same time, attending to modernization efforts in China. Late Ch'ing China's self-strengthening movement had neither developed as a political and economic system nor reached an adequate cultural and ideological level; that is, it still remained at the material, technological level. Accordingly, Li saw Korean modernization as nothing but a military problem. Yüan Shih-k'ai, during the decade from 1885 to 1894 when he was in Korea, because of both his overemphasis on political control and his lack of knowledge about modernization, made the maintenance of China's suzerainty his first priority. Toward that end, he was inclined to discriminate against foreign countries and their call for reforms, which indisputably established a pattern of his resisting Korean modernization.[72]

Conclusion

The traditional attitude of Ch'ing China toward her tributary Korea was one of benevolent indifference. Stubbornly adhering to the "ceremony of sadae," in which the tributary was supposed to abide by the rites of being granted titles of nobility and offering tribute, China always emphasized Korean "emotional recognition," a relationship that was loose rather than rigid. Moreover, to adapt to the changed international situation, China at first allowed Korea to be "autonomous in both internal and external affairs," which indicated that China did not at all fulfill her obligations to her vassal state. Obviously, China's concept of suzerainty was immensely contradictory to that of modern international law.

This situation changed, however, after 1879, when Japan annexed the Liuch'iu Islands. At that time, the Ch'ing government sensed that East Asian affairs were undergoing a tremendous change. In addition to the threat that Japan posed, the threat of southbound Russian power was becoming serious. At long last, China began to realize the importance of Korea, the gateway to Manchuria. Japan no longer concealed her increasing ambition toward Korea, which gradually aroused China's wariness, pushing China to abandon her conventional indifferent attitude toward Korea, and eventually brought her to replace her policy of restraining Japan and Russia with efforts to persuade Korea to trade with Western powers.

This was the background to the promotion of an American-Korean treaty by Li Hung-chang, who was then in charge of Korean policy. In addition, this could be viewed as an implementation of the check-and-balance strategy. Ironically, in opposition to Li's original scheme, America insisted on not recognizing China's suzerainty over Korea. Nevertheless, the American-Korean treaty had greater impact on the Korean people than did Japan's Kanghwa Treaty, for it made the Koreans conscious of their need for an equal status in the international community, and brought to an end Korea's isolated status as a hermit nation.

Li Hung-chang remained the mastermind and chief executor of China's policies toward Korea throughout the turbulent years from 1879 to 1894. Soon after the beginning of her participation in the international order, Korea had to deal with the Imo military riots. China, acting as the suzerain in accordance with the custom of pacifying the tributary, immediately sent forces to suppress the rebellion on behalf of the Korean government, which mainly aimed at defending itself against Japan. This was indeed the most aggressive and visible behavior of

China's intervention in Korean politics since the Yüan dynasty (Ming China assisted Korea once but did not interfere with her politics), and it was the turning point in Ch'ing China's policy toward Korea.

China's overwhelming support of the Sadae Party made the distribution of the Korean political power unbalanced. Consequently, the pro-Japanese Progressive Party, influenced by international affairs such as the Sino-French War, initiated the Kapsin coup to overthrow the pro-Ch'ing government; but the coup ended in failure because of the Ch'ing army's intervention. From then on, China became more positive over the issue of asserting her suzerainty; yet the Korean independent and autonomous movement did not waver at any time. Then came the turbulent decade of 1885 to 1894, when Li Hung-chang took perfect advantage both of the antagonism between Britain and Russia and of Japan's temporary wait-and-see attitude. Through Yüan Shih-k'ai, the Chinese official stationed in Korea, Li's interventionist policy was heavily implemented, thereby solidifying China's suzerainty.

Yüan Shih-k'ai's assignment was to participate in Korean political and diplomatic affairs. In reality, however, his control over Korea was far more comprehensive, including further involvement in the areas of finance and economics. Inevitably, Yüan's activities aroused the Korean government's resentment and fear and failed to contribute to an improvement in the relationship between Korea and China. Most unfortunately, it produced friction and barriers between the two countries. This phenomenon could be ascribed to two sets of factors: for Korea, the flourishing sprouts of changed thinking, the high expectation of the reform movement, and the growing sentiment for autonomy; for China, the efforts at the maintenance of suzerainty, negligence toward Korean political and economic reforms, and the incapability of promoting Korean modernization. It is also true, however, that China's own self-strengthening movement was not greatly successful, indicating that there were always barricades on the road to modernization and that the limits of traditionalism could not be shattered. It is understandable, therefore, that China could not contribute to Korea's modernization. On the other hand, Japan made every effort to engage in her own modernization, both enriching the nation and strengthening the armed forces, in sharp contrast to what happened in China. Japan's success in modernization served both as a model for Korean reformers and as an excuse for Japanese intrusion into Korea.

Regardless of how obvious China's interventionist policy toward Korea had been, it is inaccurate, as well as unfair, to charge her with the kind of intrusion enacted by Japan. This is the consensus of several scholars. Professor Yi Son-gun criticizes China for high-handed policy yet still remarks that China's economic policy toward Korea was one of benevolence; he also acknowledges that China had no ambition of acquiring Korean territory nor any intentions other than the desire to turn Korea into her satellite state.[73] Professor Pak Chong-gun points out the difference between the anti-Japanese and the anti-Ch'ing China sentiments in Korea, and stresses that China's interventionist policy was aimed at restraining Japan; therefore, he refutes the notion of undue Ch'ing intrusion.[74]

The Sino-Japanese War of 1894–95 was initiated by Japan for the sake of encroachment, which cannot be said of Li Hung-chang's policy toward Korea. On the contrary, had he not taken advantage of the changed state of international affairs and decisively implemented China's positive policy toward Korea, the Sino-Japanese War might have occurred ten years earlier.

Notes

1. *Ch'ing Kuang-hsü ch'ao Chung-Jih chiao-she shih-liao* (Historical materials on Sino-Japanese relations during the Kuang-hsü reign, hereafter cited as *CKCJ*) (Peiping, 1932) 1:31–32, August 21, 1879.

2. *CKCJ*, 2:19–21, December 16, 1880.

3. *Ch'ing-chi wai-chiao shih-liao* (Diplomatic source materials of the end of the Ch'ing dynasty, hereafter cited as *WCSL*) (Peiping, 1932–35), 15:1–3, February 23, 1881.

4. Li Hung-chang, *Li Wen-chung-kung ch'üan-chi,I-shu han-kao* (The collected writings of Li Hung-chang, hereafter cited as *LWCK,* Tsungli Yamen Letters) (Nanking, 1908) 9:34, August 29, 1879.

5. Li Hung-chang, *Li Wen-chung-kung ch'üan-chi, Tsou-kao* (hereafter cited as *LWCK Memorials*), 34:4–14. July 31, 1879.

6. *LWCK Tsungli Yamen Letters*, 4:30, January 19, 1876; Tsiang T'ing-fu, *Chin-tai Chung-kuo wai-chiao-shih tzu-liao chi-yao* (The collected materials of the diplomatic history of modern China) (Shanghai, 1931), vol. 2, 364.

7. *LWCK Tsungli Yamen Letters*, 16:10–11, November 12, 1884.

8. *LWCK Memorials*, 38:24–27; *WCSL*, 2:32,42, October 7, 1880; Nihon gaiko bunsho (Diplomatic documents of Japan, hereafter cited as *NGB*) (Tokyo, 1936–) vol. 13, 389–90; Kim Hong-jip, *Susinsa ilgi* (Diary of a friendship envoy) in Kuksa p'yonch'an wiwonhoe, comp. *Susinsa kirok* (Records of friendship envoys) (Seoul, 1971), 160–70.

9. *WCSL*, 16:14–17, August 26, 1879; *LWCK Memorials*, 34:44–45, August 31, 1879; Hsüeh Fu-ch'eng, *Yung-an ch'üan-chi:wai-pien* (Complete works of Hsüeh Fu-ch'eng) (Shanghai, 1887–88), 3:60–61.

10. *CKCJ*, 2:31, February 19, 1881; *British Foreign Archives, F.O.* 17/559; T. Wade to Granville, telegram, January 27, 1881.

11. *Ch'ing-chi Chung-Jih-Han kuan-hsi shih-liao* (Historical materials on Sino-Japanese-Korean relations during the late Ch'ing period, hereafter cited as *CJHSL*) (Taipei, 1972), 2:461–62, February 27, 1881, March 2, 1881; *LWCK Tsungli Yamen Letters*, 12:6–7, March 1, 1881.

12. Tyler Dennett, *Americans in Eastern Asia: A Critical Study of the Policy of the United States in the Nineteenth Century* (New York, 1922), 453.

13. Ibid., 436.

14. *LWCK Tsungli Yamen Letters*, 13:7–10, March 25 and 27, 1882.

15. Kin Eisaku, *Kanmatsu nationalism no kenkyū* (A study of Korean nationalism during the late Yi dynasty) (Tokyo, 1975), 161.

16. *CJHSL*, 2:481–82, February 16, 1881.

17. Okudaira Takehiko, *Chōsen kaikoku kōshō shimatsu* (Negotiations on the opening of Korea from beginning to end) (Tokyo, 1935), 103.

18. *LWCK Tsungli Yamen Letters*, 13:31–32, April 20, 1882; *LWCK Memorials*, 43:34–35, April 23, 1882.

19. *CKCJ*, 3:13, May 15, 1885 (enclosure 2).

20. Ma Chien-chung, *Shih-k'o-tsai chi-yen chi-hsing* (Essays and travel accounts of Ma Chien-chung) (Taipei, reprint, 1968), 4:12.

21. Tyler Dennett, *Americans in Eastern Asia*, 464.

22. Ibid., 460–61; Melvin Frederick Nelson, *Korea and the Old Orders in Eastern Asia* (Baton Rouge: Louisiana State University Press, 1945), 149–56; 161–63.

23. C. I. Eugene Kim and Han-kyo Kim, *Korea and the Politics of Imperialism, 1876–1910* (Berkeley: University of California Press, 1968), 3.

24. Ibid., 31.

25. *CKCJ*, 3:32, August 7, 1882.

26. Hsüeh Fu-ch'eng, *Yung-an ch'üan-chi: wen-pien*, 2:56; Lin Ming-te, *Yüan Shih-k'ai yü Ch'ao-hsien* (Yüan Shih-k'ai and Korea) (Taipei, 1970), 33–35.

27. *NGB*, 15:217–21; Kin Seimei, *Nikkan gaikō shiryō shūsei* (Collection of sources of diplomatic relations between Japan and Korea) (Tokyo, 1963), vol. 7, 72.

28. P'eng Tse-chou (Hō Takushu), *Meiji shoki Nik-Kan-Shin kankei no kenkyū* (Studies on Japanese-Korean-Chinese relations in the early Meiji period) (Tokyo, 1969), 264–65.

29. Genyōsha shashi hensankai, *Genyōsha shi* (History of Genyōsha) (Tokyo, 1927), 239–40.

30. Tanaka Naokichi, "Nissen kankei no ichidanmen" (One aspect of Japanese-Korean relations) *Kokusai seiji*, August 1957, 89.

31. *CKCJ*, 4:16–17, October 3, 1882; *WCSL*, 29:22, October 13, 1882; Chang P'ei-lun, *Chien-yü-chi tsou-i* (Memorials of Chang P'ei-lun) (1918), 2:59–63.

32. Chang Hsiao-jo, *Nan-t'ung Chang Chi-chih hsien-sheng chuan-chi fu nien-p'u nien-piao* (A chronological autobiography of Chang Chi-chih) (Shanghai, 1931), 3:35–36.

33. *LWCK Memorials* 44:27–29, October 3, 1882; *CKCJ*, 4:28–29, October 13, 1882; 4:31–32, November 15, 1882; *CWSL*, 29:22–24, October 13, 1882; 30:5–10, November 17, 1882.

34. J.O.P. Bland, *Li Hung-chang* (London, 1917), 162–65.

35. *CKCJ*, 4:16–17, October 3, 1882.

36. *CKCJ*, 4:32–36, November 15, 1882; Wang Yün-sheng, *Liu-shih-nien-lai Chung-kuo yü Jih-pen* (Sino-Japanese relations of the last sixty years) (Tientsin, 1932), 1:184–85.

37. Wang Hsin-chung, *Chung-Jih chia-wu chan-cheng chih wai-chiao pei-ching* (Background of the diplomatic relations during the Sino-Japanese War) (Peiping, 1939), 57–60.

38. Wang Yün-sheng, *Liu-shih-nien-lai*, 1:210.

39. Kim Yun-sik, *Unyangjip* (Collective writings of Kim Yun-sik) (Seoul, 1913), 12:32–35.

40. Lin Ming-te, *Yüan Shih-k'ai*, 41.

41. Ibid.

42. Kin Eisaku, *Kanmatsu nationalism*, 168; Ito Hirobumi, comp. *Chōsen kōshō shiryo* (Materials on Japanese-Korean relations) (Tokyo, 1936), vol. 1, 462–63.

43. Pak Yin-sik, *Han-kuo tu-li yün-tung chih hsüeh-shih* (A lamentable history of the Korean independence movement) (Seoul, 1947), 4.

44. *CJHSL*, 3:1502, December 13, 1884; *CKCJ*, 5:26,32, December 12, 1884; *LWCK Tsungli Yamen Letters*, 16:12, December 14, 1884.

45. *CKCJ*, 5:29, December 14, 1884; 5:36, December 16, 1884; *WCSL*, 50:5, December 14, 1884.

46. *CKCJ*, 5:25–26, December 12, 1884; *WCSL*, 50:1, December 24, 1884.

47. Li Hung-chang, *Li Wen-chung-kung ch'üan-chi, Tien-Kao* (hereafter cited as *LWCK Telegrams*), 4:23, December 23, 1884; CKSL, 5:24, December 20, 1884.

48. *CKCJ*, 50:17–19, December 21, 1884; *LWCK Memorials*, 52:5–6; December 19, 1884.

49. Tabohashi Kiyoshi, *Kindai Nissen kankei no kenkyū* (Studies on modern Japanese-Korean relations) (Keijo, 1940), vol. 1, 1015–19.

50. Kin Seimei, *Nikkan gaikō*, vol. 3, 114.

51. Yoshida Sakuzō, comp. *Meiji bunka zenshū* (Collected works on Meiji culture) (Tokyo, 1928), vol. 6, 211–15.

52. *Nihon gaikō nenpyō narabi shuyo bunsho* (Chronology and main documents of Japanese foreign policy) (Tokyo, 1955), vol. 1., 101.

53. *LWCK Telegrams*, 4:28, December 16, 1884; 6:36, January 16, 1885; 7:9, February 10, 1885.

54. *Nihon gaikō nenpyō*, vol. 1, 103–4.

55. Tyler Dennett, *Americans in Eastern Asia*, 480; Tsiang T'ing-fu, "Sino-Japanese Diplomatic Relations, 1870–1894," *Chinese Social and Political Science Review*, XVII (April 1933), 106.

56. Kin Seimei, *Nikkan gaikō*, vol. 7, 583.

57. *Nihon gaikō bunsho: Meiji nenkan tsuiho* (Supplementary documents on Japan's diplomacy in Meiji period) (Tokyo, 1949), vol. 1, 357–58; *CKCJ*, 8:18, May 5, 1885; *LWCK Memorials*, 5:38, December 29, 1884.

58. *Nihon gaikō bunsho. Meiji nenkan tsuiho*, vol. 1, 356; *CKCJ*, 8:21–23. July 29, 1885.

59. *CKCJ*, 8:27, July 29, 1885; *LWCK Tsungli Yamen Letters*, 17:31, July 27, 1885.

60. Lin Ming-te, *Yüan Shih-k'ai*, 29–30.

61. Ibid., 296–97; Yo Sasaki, *The International Environment at the Time of the Sino-Japanese War (1894–1895)—Anglo-Russian Far Eastern Policy and the Beginning of the Sino-Japanese War, Memoirs of the Research Department of the Toyo Bunko*, no. 42 (1984), 26.

62. Yo Sasaki, *The International Environment*, 26–27.

63. Ibid., 27.

64. *LWCK Tsungli Yamen Letters*, 18:42, October 9, 1886; *WCSL*, 69:16–17, October 24, 1886; *CKCS*, 10:17–18, October 11 and 15, 1886; *LWCK Telegrams*, 7:47, October 25, 1886.

65. *CKCJ*, 10:17, October 11, 1886.

66. *WCSL*, 69:14, October 11, 1886; Yo Sasaki, *The International Environment*, 15.

67. Yo Sasaki, *The International Environment*, 16–17; Lin Ming-te, *Yüan Shih-k'ai*, 15.

68. Yo Sasaki, *The International Environment*, 56; *LWCK Tsungli Yamen Letters*, 19:20–22, October 14 and November 4, 1888.

69. *CJHSL*, 5:2810, August 27, 1890.

70. Young-ick Lew, "Yüan Shih-k'ai's Residence and the Korean Enlightenment Movement (1885–1894)," *The Journal of Korean Studies*, vol. 5 (1984), 78–106; Lin Ming-te, *Yüan Shih-k'ai*, 159–255.

71. *LWCK Tsungli Yamen Letters*, 16:10–11, November 12, 1884; Lin Ming-te, *Yüan Shih-k'ai*, 262.

72. Young-ick Lew, "Yüan Shih-k'ai's Residence," 78.

73. Yi Son-gun, *Han'guksa: ch'oegunse p'yon* (Recent Korean history) (Seoul, 1961), translated by Lin Ch'iu-shan, *Han-kuo chin-tai-shih* (Taipei, 1967), 625–26.

74. Pak Chong-gun, "Chōsen ni okeru kindaiteki kaikaku no suii" (Reform movement in modern Korea), *Rekishigaku kenkyū*, no. 300, 51.

Part V
Li as Modernizer

10

Li Hung-chang and the Kiangnan Arsenal, 1860–1895

Thomas L. Kennedy

The relationship of a single official, Li Hung-chang, to a single institution, the Kiangnan Arsenal, in the collapsing power structure of the late Ch'ing dynasty seems at first glance an extremely limited topic for historical inquiry, one unlikely to yield important conclusions. Students of nineteenth-century China know, however, that Li Hung-chang's many-sided career touched nearly every function of the Chinese state and every sector of the economy. The Kiangnan Arsenal, China's premier national defense industry, was at the forefront of economic and technological change and was involved in the redistribution of governing power.[1] Li's career intersected with Kiangnan's development in several ways that illustrate his role as China's leading statesman in the late nineteenth century. First, Li was present at the creation. It was largely his vision of industrialization that brought Kiangnan into existence and guided its initial operations. Second, Li's efforts to retain control over Kiangnan after his transfer to North China in 1870 cast him as a player on the national stage and tested his mettle in the arena of imperial politics. Finally, at Kiangnan, Li confronted directly the technology on which China's survival depended. The foreign technicians at Kiangnan and other arsenals were the purveyors of this technology. Li's dealings with them were a measure of his adaptability and acumen in the new art of transferring technology.

Establishment and early operation of Kiangnan

Though the Kiangnan Arsenal entered production in Shanghai in 1865, its establishment resulted from practical reform ideas advanced by scholars of the Confucian school of statecraft since the eighteenth century. In the nineteenth century, as pressures on the ruling Ch'ing dynasty from domestic rebellion and foreign aggression intensified, these ideas were expressed in specific government programs. China's humiliation in the first Opium War (1839–42) prompted the

197

statecraft scholar Wei Yuan (1794–1857), long an advocate of practical reforms in government operations, to call for a reappraisal of the basis for China's foreign relations. "Learn the superior techniques of the barbarians," wrote Wei Yuan "in order to control them." By foreign techniques he meant principally the superior ordnance and steamships of the Western powers and the skill Western commanders demonstrated in employing their armed forces.[2]

Wei Yuan's ideas did not gain immediate acceptance. By the fall of 1860, however, the crisis brought on by the Anglo-French occupation of Peking and the Taiping Army's advance on Shanghai crystallized the reform ideas of provincial military leaders campaigning against the Taipings in the Yangtze Valley. In the early 1860s two of these leaders, Tseng Kuo-fan and Li Hung-chang, were deeply influenced by the persuasive statecraft writings of Feng Kuei-fen, who served on Li's staff while he was governor of Kiangsu in 1864–65. Writing in 1860–61, Feng reiterated Wei Yuan's dictum that Chinese should learn the superior techniques of the barbarians in order to bring them under control. He went further than Wei Yuan, however, calling for China to strengthen itself through changes in the educational system and the distribution of political power, as well as modernization of the military industry. Feng's proposals marked the origins of the "Self-Strengthening Movement" in the 1860s.[3]

While such ideas were being considered by Li, he witnessed a graphic demonstration of the superiority of Western steamships and ordnance. In March 1862 Chinese gentry and merchants from the beleaguered city of Shanghai rented seven British steamships, which they dispatched upstream on the Yangtze to the province of Anhwei. There they embarked Li's Huai Army and transported it downstream through areas held by the Taipings to Shanghai. In Shanghai, Li saw the superiority of Western ordnance employed by forces defending the city: British, French, and Indian troops, as well as Chinese soldiers commanded by British officers of the Ever-Victorious Army.[4] Li followed the general policy lines laid down by his mentor, Tseng Kuo-fan, who was directing the overall strategy against the Taiping forces in the Lower Yangtze area—to minimize the intervention and influence of foreign forces in China while seeking to obtain and reproduce their superior armaments.[5]

Paralleling the efforts of Tseng Kuo-fan, who in 1862 established an arsenal and ammunition plant staffed by Chinese engineers at his headquarters at Anking, Li began explosive shell production in Shanghai in 1863 and in Soochow after the recapture of the city in December of that year. Production at Soochow was under the direction of a British medical doctor, Halliday Macartney, who had joined Li's staff. Shanghai Taotai Ting Jih-ch'ang directed production in Shanghai where, by 1864, small cannon were also produced. Macartney persuaded Li to purchase and employ China's first steam-powered production machinery.[6] Ting Jih-ch'ang probably discussed with Li Wang T'ao's *Huo-chi shuo-lueh* (A brief discussion of firearms), in which the ideas of statecraft scholar Feng Kuei-fen for the use of machinery to bring about broad changes in the economy were reiterated in the context of armaments production for suppression of rebellion and eventually for an anti-imperialist struggle.[7]

Li saw the urgent need for foreign ordnance and ammunition to be supplied to the provincial armies engaged in the suppression of the Taipings, but was wary of developing long-term reliance on foreign suppliers. This led him to call for changes in the economy and related sectors of the educational system designed not only to support current production in order to suppress rebellion but also to strengthen China in the long term against the unrelenting pressure of foreign imperialism. In the spring of 1864, Li reported to the Tsungli Yamen on the arsenals he had established in Soochow and Shanghai. He called on the government to acquire capital equipment and argued eloquently for educational changes to train needed technical and scientific personnel for ordnance production.

> I consider that if China wishes to make itself strong, then there is nothing more important than study and practice with the excellent weapons of the foreign nations. To learn about these foreign weapons, there is no better way than to seek the machines which make machines and learn their way [of making them] but not employ their personnel. If we wish to seek machinery for making machinery and the personnel to make machinery, then we should establish a special course and select scholars. The scholars for the rest of their life should have a goal through which they will become rich and famous; then this undertaking can be successful, the skill can be perfected and the talent [necessary to do it] also can be assembled.[8]

As a first step in solving the manpower problem, in 1864 Li opened a school in Shanghai for instruction in foreign languages (later to be known as Kuang Fang-yen-kuan).[9] Though the need for machine tools capable of turning out specialized equipment for production of heavy ordnance and marine engines was becoming clear, the high costs and uncertainties of purchasing equipment abroad led Li to commission Shanghai Taotai Ting Jih-ch'ang to explore the possibilities of purchasing one of the foreign machine shops already operating in Shanghai.[10]

The interest that Li evinced in the acquisition of capital equipment and the training of technical manpower reflected his awareness of the need for a broadly based approach of industrialization, an approach that went beyond the acquisition of foreign materiel and the employment of foreign technicians to produce urgently needed ordnance and ammunition. This awareness found concrete expression in the establishment of the Kiangnan Arsenal in Shanghai in 1865.

The *Chiang-nan chih-tsao tsung-chü*, literally the Kiangnan General Manufacturing Bureau, so named by Li Hung-chang, began operating under Chinese management in late May or June 1865 in a previously foreign-owned machine shop at a site that was later know as Hunt's wharf in the Hung-k'ou (Hong Kew) section of Shanghai. Though the name that Li gave it denoted that this was an agency in the official bureaucracy dedicated to general types of production, it became known to foreigners almost immediately as the Kiangnan Arsenal, a name that its successor institutions have borne to the present. In the late summer of 1865, Li submitted a memorial to the throne on the establishment of Kiangnan in which he noted that he had changed the name to "Kiangnan General Manufacturing Bureau" to clarify its mission. He cited a basic tenet of Confucian philosophy that things should bear names that denote their reality and distinguish them from other things (cheng-ming pien-wu).[11] His memorial went on to elaborate the mission that he foresaw for Kiangnan, explaining that for the present, given the urgent need for suppression of the Nien Rebellion in North China, it would be necessary to concentrate on military production:

> What we have is machinery-producing machinery; no matter what type of machinery, it can be reproduced step-by-step following the [right] method; then, it can be employed to make that type of product; there are no limits to what can be produced; all things can be mastered. At present we are unable to do everything at once; it is most important that we still produce iron ordnance to meet our military needs. . . . Foreign machinery can produce machinery for plowing, weaving, printing, ceramics and tile-making, which will benefit the daily needs of the people; originally it was not just for munitions. . . . I predit that in several decades there certainly will be wealthy Chinese farmers and great traders who will imitate foreign machine-manufacturing for their own profit.[12]

These views quite probably were influenced by the ideas of Ting Jih-ch'ang, who supervised Kiangnan from his post in Shanghai. In correspondence with Li, Ting advocated the establishment of large-scale plants to make machinery for use in textile manufacture, agriculture, and water conservancy, as well as a new policy in the awarding of official status and material emoluments to favor those who showed expertise in science and technology.[13]

Kiangnan's machinery was purchased with funds raised by Ting Jih-ch'ang and through other official channels. Later in 1865 the plant was augmented by machinery purchased in the United States by Yung Wing, a Yale-educated Chinese in the employ of Tseng Kuo-fan.[14] Kiangnan was under the general supervision of Li Hung-chang, who in the summer of 1865 was named acting governor-general of the Liangkiang provinces (Kiangsu, Kiangsi, and Anhwei), replacing Tseng Kuo-fan. Tseng had been ordered to lead Li's Huai Army against the Nien rebels on the plains of North China, where the imperial forces had suffered serious setbacks. Kiangnan's initial mission was to provide logistical support for these Huai Army units; the Huai Army budget provided Kiangnan's operating budget.[15] This necessitated the hasty conversion of much of Kiangnan's equipment, originally intended for marine production, to production of ordnance and ammunition.

Kiangnan's early operations were beset by technical and personnel problems. Not only were the Chinese managers lacking the technical know-how, the foreign foreman and technicians retained from the staff of the foreign machine shop proved unable to make the conversion to ordnance and ammunition production. By February 1866, technical and personnel problems necessitated a shutdown of all operations for more than a week while boilers were repaired. Though repairs were accomplished, small arms production could not be resumed because of a defective furnace. Several thousand rounds of gun ammunition were produced in the spring of 1866, but small-arms ammunition production never reached significant quantities, and artillery production was delayed awaiting the arrival of a British cannon to serve as a model.

Li was angered by Kiangnan's prolonged, costly, but unsuccessful efforts to produce small arms. He felt that Feng Chün-kuang, one of the managers, had relied excessively on foreign technicians who were shipwrights, not ordnance technicians. The foreign technicians, in turn, had dodged responsibility by pointing to the inadequacies of the equipment. Li gave the arsenal staff an ultimatum: the furnace, which was at the root of the problem of producing small arms, was to be rebuilt. If Kiangnan was not turning out foreign-style small arms within one month after the completion of the new furnace, Chinese officials at the arsenal would be deprived of their salaries and the foreign foreman would be paid off and deported, with a letter to his consul explaining the unsatisfactory nature of his employment.

Meanwhile, Li began purchasing foreign small arms for use by the Huai Army forces battling the Nien. In the summer of 1866 the arsenal turned out small cannon comparable to foreign-made pieces, but small-arms production was still lacking in quality and quantity.[16] Li moved to strengthen logistical support for Huai Army units in North China by removing the Soochow Arsenal to Nanking. There he reestablished it as the Nanking Arsenal (Chin-ling chih-tsao-chü). The new arsenal entered production in 1866 under Li's watchful observation from the Nanking headquarters of the Liangkiang governor-general.[17]

The struggle against the Nien was not going well. Before the end of 1866, Li was transferred to North China to command the anti-Nien campaign of the Huai Army. Tseng returned to his post as governor-general of the Liangkiang provinces with the mission of providing logistical support for the forces commanded by Li in North China. As the military situation in North China worsened in 1867, Li lent his support to the establishment of yet another arsenal in Tientsin, one that had been proposed earlier by the Tsungli Yamen and the commissioner of northern ports, Ch'ung-hou.[18]

Meanwhile, Tseng Kuo-fan's return to the post of governor-general of the Liangkiang provinces and concurrently commissioner of southern ports proved to be of brief duration but of enormous consequence for the Kiangnan Arsenal, which again came under his supervision. Discouraged by Kiangnan's failure to achieve satisfactory results in ordnance production, Li, before leaving for North China, had agreed to discontinue ordnance production temporarily and relocate Kiangnan at a site better suited for construction of small harbor-defense vessels.[19] Tseng, an enthusiastic advocate of shipbuilding, secured imperial approval in 1867 for allocation of 10 percent of the proceeds of the Shanghai maritime customs to support shipbuilding at Kiangnan and 10 percent for support of the forces battling the Nien. Subsequently, the latter 10 percent was also directed to production costs at Kiangnan. The arsenal was relocated at a new ten-acre site at Kao-ch'ang Miao, on the banks of the Huang-p'u south of the city of Shanghai. There, during the winter of 1867–68, new production facilities including a dry-dock were erected, new equipment for shipbuilding and ordnance production was purchased and installed, and a bureau for translation of technical and scientific works was opened. In the next few years these facilities were steadily augmented. Included were machinery for the production of Remington repeating rifles and a technical training institute.[20]

Following the defeat of the Nien in 1868, Tseng was called once again to North China, this time as governor-general of the metropolitan province of Chihli and commissioner of northern ports, posts he held until 1870 when the assassination of his successor in the Liangkiang provinces, Ma Hsin-i, returned Tseng once more to Nanking. Li served a brief stint as governor-general of Hunan and Hupei beginning in 1869. In 1870, however, as the likelihood of renewed hostilities with France mounted following an eruption of anti-imperialist violence and the loss of French lives and property in Tientsin, Li was summoned with his Huai Army to Chihli. In the aftermath of this incident, which became known as the Tientsin Massacre, Tseng was ordered back to the governor-generalship at Nanking to serve concurrently as commissioner of southern ports, and Li was named governor-general of Chihli and commissioner of northern ports, posts he held, with only a brief interruption in the early 1880s, until his dismissal in 1895 following China's humiliation in the Sino-Japanese War.

The Kiangnan shipbuilding program

Until Tseng's death in early 1872 and the adoption of a new maritime defense policy in 1875, the southern commissioners used Kiangnan's huge annual customs allocation principally for the construction of steamships. A total of seven large naval vessels, including an ironclad of the "monitor" class, as well as six harbor defense vessels and a sailing ship, were completed by 1875. Though the technological advances incorporated in these vessels were impressive, they were constructed with imported material under the supervision of foreign technicians at costs that far exceeded the purchase price.[21] The costs for maintenance and operation of these vessels grew far more rapidly than did the customs allocation from which they were defrayed.

Muted criticism of the shipbuilding program at Kiangnan began as early as 1869. In 1872 subchancellor of the Grand Secretariat Sung Chin leveled a withering attack at the high costs of operations at Kiangnan and other arsenals and called for a cessation of the most conspicuous and most costly program: shipbuilding.[22] This precipitated a heated argument over the merits of continuing

China's domestic shipbuilding program at Kiangnan and the Foochow Dockyard, an argument that became part of a larger debate over priorities and expenditures for strategic defense on the northwest frontier versus maritime defense along the east coast.

After 1870, as governor-general of Chihli and commissioner of northern ports, Li became increasingly absorbed in the affairs of North China. Because of the strategic importance and political sensitivity of his post, the court looked to him also for advice and counsel on national defense planning. Li himself seemed loath to relinquish influence over the military industries in the Yangtze Valley that he had worked to establish. When the court asked for his opinion on Sung Chin's recommendation to halt shipbuilding at Kiangnan, Li consulted his former protégé Feng Chun-kuang, then director of Kiangnan. Echoing Feng's arguments for a balanced scheme of industrial modernization of the extractive, refining, transportation, and textile industries,[23] Li called for continuation of Kiangnan's shipbuilding program as part of the scheme. Li's recommendations to continue shipbuilding at Kiangnan, however, were hedged with conditions. He questioned the cost effectiveness of shipbuilding and proposed reducing expenditures by further limiting vessels to the specifications of the fifth vessel then under construction, and deploying Kiangnan steamships to commercial users and provincial governments who would bear the cost of maintenance and operations.[24] By introducing conditions for continuation of shipbuilding, Li implicitly raised the alternative of using a greater share of Kiangnan's customs income for the production of ordnance and ammunition, types of production that he had favored at the Tientsin Arsenal since his arrival in North China.[25]

By 1874 it was clear that neither scheme proposed by Li to abate the costs of steamship maintenance and operation would provide prompt relief for the drain on Kiangnan's budget. Furthermore, the question of national strategic priorities, including the production of steamships and ordnance, was raised again in the context of a Muslim separatist movement in Northwest China and a struggle with Japan for control of Taiwan and the Ryūkyūs. In late 1874 the forces of Shensi/Kansu Governor-General Tso Tsung-t'ang, having subdued the Muslim uprising in those two provinces, stood poised to attack the Sinkiang region where the independent Muslim kingdom of Yakub Beg was gaining international recognition. Earlier in the year, on the advice of the British minister, China had avoided hostilities with Japan by conceding the right to defend the interests of Ryūkyūan fishermen attacked by Taiwan aborigines. With the benefit of historical hindsight, it seems uncertain that China was greatly outclassed by Japan's naval might. Nevertheless, in early November 1874 China signed a humiliating agreement with Japan that eventually led to the relinquishment of China's claim to suzerainty over the Ryūkyūs.[26]

Several days later, recoiling from the shock of this agreement, the court called for opinions from leading provincial officials on basic strategies and priorities in national defense proposed by the Tsungli Yamen. Though the matters discussed in memorials submitted by provincial officials dealt with many specific aspects of national defense, a basic difference on broad policy developed between those who favored giving higher priority to resources for frontier defense in the northwest and those who preferred defense efforts principally for the strengthening of maritime and coastal defense. Tso Tsung-t'ang was the leading protagonist of frontier defense, while Li championed maritime and coastal defense.[27]

Though the debate was resolved in favor of frontier defense in the northwest, opening the way for Tso Tsung-t'ang's forces to pacify the region that in 1884 became the province of Sinkiang, a new maritime defense policy was also adopted, one that reflected some of the strategic priorities Li had discussed in his memorial to the throne. Li had called for a cutback in what he regarded as costly and ineffective naval construction at Kiangnan in favor of a maritime-defense strategy based on coastal defense installations, small harbor-defense gunboats, and naval mines to guard strategic points on the coast such as the mouth of the Yangtze and the approaches to Peking. These would be backed up by mobile infantry to resist invasions. An outer defense line of battleships, also part of Li's scheme, would include few if any Kiangnan vessels. Purchase from foreign countries, Li advised, would ensure vessels suited for this mission.

Li also took the opportunity to advocate the concentration of military and fiscal authority in the hands of regional commanders to facilitate naval development and create a more effective command structure.[28] Such recommendations for broad organizational changes in imperial administration, coming as they did in the wake of his earlier advocacy of educational and economic restructuring, suggest that by the mid-1870s, if not earlier, Li was a strong proponent of institutional changes in concert with industrial development.

Though the concept of balanced industrial development and related institutional changes crystallized in Li's mind by the 1870s, actual change came slowly and in a piecemeal fashion. The reasons seem discernible. From the Tientsin Massacre in 1870 until the Sino-Japanese War of 1894–95, foreign threats to China's territory or dependencies created a series of military emergencies which required that available resources be focused on military production. Furthermore, imperial leadership showed little interest in effecting the infrastructural changes needed to support industrialization. Though individual projects, such as Kiangnan, initiated by Li and others were impressive, there was a lack of overall direction and leadership. These undertakings proved insufficient, in themselves, to bolster the dynasty against the intensifying onslaught of imperialism.

In the absence of strong imperial leadership after Tseng's death in early 1872, Li resumed a more influential role in the direction of Kiangnan, giving advice on technological matters and on matters concerning personnel and operations. Primary responsibility for Kiangnan resided, however, with the Liangkiang governor-general, the southern commissioner. The new maritime defense policy announced in May 1875 charged Northern Commissioner Li, with his headquarters at Tientsin, and Southern Commissioner Shen Pao-chen, with headquarters at Nanking, with the responsibility for coastal defense in their respective regions. A new fund of four million taels annually to be contributed by the provinces was established to support their efforts. The years immediately following the adoption of the new maritime defense policy, 1875–79, saw the concentration of the maritime defense funds, which fell far short of the projected four million taels annually, under the control of Northern Commissioner Li. This consolidation was proposed by Li and agreed to by Southern Commissioner Shen to hasten the buildup of a northern fleet through purchase from Europe. Another effect, however, was to cut off the flow of new financial resources for shipbuilding to Kiangnan.[29]

Though shipbuilding virtually ceased after 1875, the costs of steamship maintenance continued to drain customs funds;[30] the remaining funds allocated annually from the Shanghai Maritime Customs proceeds were used principally for the production of ordnance and ammunition to support the new policy. Li had made his priorities known both in his recommendations to the throne and in his development of the Tientsin Arsenal during the 1870s: he felt that the most appropriate mission for China's arsenals at this stage in their development was the production of powder and ammunition.[31] Kiangnan already had a plant for the production of small arms. In 1876 the arsenal acquired machinery and foreign technicians for the production of heavy coastal defense artillery. Ordnance as well as ammunition production would be increasingly important in the years ahead.

After the death of Southern Commissioner Shen Pao-chen in 1879, the post of southern commissioner was held by a series of distinguished officials of Hunanese origin: Liu Kun-i (1879–81, 1891–1902), Tso Tsung-t'ang (1881–84), and Tseng Kuo-ch'üan (1884–90). Similarly, the directorship of Kiangnan was held by Hunanese officials, the best known of whom were Nieh Ch'i-kuei (1883–90), Tseng Kuo-fan's son-in-law, and Liu Ch'i-hsiang (1890–95), son of the renowned Hunanese official Liu Jung. In the two decades prior to the Sino-Japanese War (1894–95), under supervision of these southern commissioners and the leadership of Nieh and Liu, Kiangnan evolved from a naval dockyard to an arsenal and ammunition plant. The changeover, however, was not immediate, and the lingering costs of steamship maintenance provided a fiscal reminder of the early emphasis on shipbuilding. Furthermore, by the end of the 1870s, the southern commissioner had regained control of the South's share of the maritime defense allocations, part of which was used for a brief but costly resumption of shipbuilding at Kiangnan in the early 1880s, while Li's influence at court was under attack by his political foes in the conservative Ch'ing-liu (Purity) faction.[32] The most significant result of this renewed effort was the steel-plated gunboat *Pao Min*, completed in 1885 at a cost overrun of more than 50,000 taels.[33]

In the discussions of naval reorganization following the destruction of the Foochow squadron in the Sino-French War (1884–85), Li memorialized the throne that Kiangnan vessels were unsuitable for use. Domestic construction, he advised, should be concentrated at the Foochow Naval Dockyard. Shortly thereafter, the new Navy Yamen was established and charged with the development of a northern fleet on a priority basis. Li was named an associate controller, and the maritime defense funds previously controlled by the northern and southern commissioners were centralized under the new yamen.[34] The extension of Li's authority over the naval budget sounded the death knell for what had been a marginal and cost-effective shipbuilding program at Kiangnan lopsidedly dependent on foreign technology and matériel.

The production of heavy ordnance

While the shipbuilding program sputtered to a halt, the decade following the adoption of the new maritime defense policy in 1875 proved crucial for the development of ordnance production in China's arsenals. After Li's transfer to North China in 1870, he discharged the British manager of the Tientsin Arsenal, Mr. Meadows, whose plans for the acquisition of new equipment Li regarded as premature and overly expansive. He replaced Meadows with Shen Pao-ching, a former director of the Kiangnan Arsenal whom Li recommended as one who could deal with foreigners without letting authority slip into their hands. When Meadows's successor as director of foreign technicians, a Mr. McIlwraith, became embroiled in a personnel dispute with one of the foreign technicians, it was ultimately referred to the British minister, Sir Thomas Wade. After more than a year's delay during which time the technician performed no duties and drew full salary, Wade approved McIlwraith's discharge of the technician but awarded him a generous severance payment from the arsenal.[35]

Li directed the new Chinese management at Tientsin to expand facilities for the production of small arms and ammunition. The production of Remington-type rifles began in 1876; by the late 1870s, Tientsin's output of powder, cartridges, and artillery ammunition outstripped Kiangnan's. Li acquired heavy artillery needed in North China from the Nanking Arsenal, which remained under the directorship of Dr. Halliday Macartney. In January 1875, however, two Nanking-built cast-iron coastal-defense guns blew up at the Taku forts near Tientsin, killing several Chinese members of the gun crews.

Arsenal operations had not gone well at Nanking since Li's departure in late 1866. The Nanking plant was an adjunct of Li's Huai Army, receiving most of its operating funds from the Huai Army budget and delivering most of its output to Huai Army units.[36] Macartney had been feuding with the Chinese manager, Liu Tso-yü. Liu complained to Li that the foreign technicians were not training the Chinese workmen in the techniques of ordnance production. Macartney countered that he lacked the control over the work force needed to conduct training. He charged that Chinese supervisors made personnel shifts without consulting him, more often than not on the basis of nepotism or cronyism. The result was a work force of hangers-on and favorites uninterested or slow to learn. The decline in product quality was clear to Li by 1872. He called Macartney to his headquarters in Tientsin but seems to have accepted Macartney's explanation that the Chinese staff was obstructing his efforts for, in 1873, Li relieved Liu of his duties.[37] Nevertheless, the situation continued to deteriorate.

In 1874 Macartney returned from a seven-month purchasing trip in Europe, only to be called again to Li's headquarters in Tientsin to explain the poor quality of Nanking products and his failure to train the Chinese staff. This time Li seemed less willing to accept Macartney's charges that the Chinese supervisors had frustrated his efforts. Li sanctioned personnel shifts that created several Chinese managers and reduced Macartney to the status of foreign instructor. Macartney promptly resigned to escape responsibility for the "wild, costly, and abortive attempts at manufacture" by the Chinese staff at the arsenal.

Li had not accepted Macartney's resignation when the two Nanking-built guns blew up at Taku on January 5, 1875. The investigation ordered by Li disclosed that the guns had burst because they were manufactured with poor-quality iron, iron actually brought to China as ballast rather than for industrial use. Macartney had sanctioned the production of ordnance from the inferior grade of iron as a stopgap measure while awaiting better iron. But then the guns had been sent to Taku without test firing at the Arsenal. Li could not excuse Macartney's actions; he ordered the Englishman to transfer all responsibilities to the Chinese staff and vacate his post.[38]

This incident raised doubts in Li's mind about the feasibility of domestic production of heavy coastal-defense artillery. Nevertheless, in late 1875, prompted by the need for naval and coastal-defense guns, he recommended the production of rifled, steel-barreled, muzzle-loading guns built up with wrought iron on the British Armstrong Company model. The following year, Kiangnan launched a crash program directed by John Mackenzie, superintendent of the Armstrong Company's Newcastle plant, to produce built-up, muzzle-loading coastal-defense guns. When Mackenzie arrived in China he found that Li Hung-chang and other high-ranking officials still had serious doubts that modern ordnance could be produced by Chinese artisans. One Western employee of the arsenal remembered that an atmosphere of crisis prevailed among the Chinese and the Western staff; they believed Li was about to recommend to the throne that Kiangnan be closed. Chinese and Western employees urged Mackenzie to show results in the production of the new guns as soon as possible. Even if the quality was not the best, as long as they did not blow up, concrete results would probably keep Kiangnan open and save jobs.[39]

Chinese officials at first were skeptical of Mackenzie's ability to deliver on his promise to produce the new guns at Kiangnan. But Mackenzie seems to have accepted this as a personal and professional challenge: he set to work resolutely directing the Chinese staff, determined to show results. Progress during 1877 was rapid. By late spring of that year, production facilities were complete and Chinese artisans were trained. Ten of the new guns were nearing completion. In 1878 Li threw his support behind the new production. In a memorial to the throne, he praised the stability and durability of the Armstrong and recommended its production at Kiangnan. The first two Armstrong-model coastal-defense guns were successfully test fired at Kiangnan in December 1878.[40]

In the wake of the Taku tragedy, Li influenced Kiangnan to produce the Armstrong-model coastal-defense gun, the strongest and the safest of the heavy ordnance produced in the West. But the Armstrongs were already obsolescent, lacking in firepower and more cumbersome than the breechloaders produced by other Western powers.[41] The tragedy of the explosion of the Nanking-built guns at Taku also forced Li to confront directly the complexities of modern industrial management in traditional Chinese society. He had relied on Macartney, a physician, for technical direction in ordnance production. Earlier Macartney had served Li well, but now he appeared to be beyond his depth. Li was wary of the influence of foreigners in his arsenals and wished to see production turned over to competent Chinese as soon as possible, as it had been at Tientsin. Still he was aware that Kiangnan's staff was not prepared for technological independence. The solution worked out at Kiangnan and accepted by Li was to restrict foreign participation in arsenal production to technical advice and instruction, while management authority was reserved for Chinese officials. This formula opened the way for successful Chinese-foreign cooperation to produce the Armstrong-model coastal-defense guns under the direction of Mackenzie's team of well-qualified foreign technicians and industrious and intelligent Chinese artisans. In the 1880s, however, the Chinese management came increasingly under the control of the Hunanese clique and was increasingly infected with nepotism, cronyism, and corruption.

Many, but not all, of the activities at Kiangnan simply drifted out of Li's control after 1880. There is no doubt that during these years peculation of official funds took place at Kiangnan, that appointments were made on the basis of personal and family connections rather than qualifications, and that administrative inefficiency was widely tolerated. Such abuses are rarely part of the official record, making it difficult to assign them a relative weight as factors inhibiting the arsenal in the fulfillment of its mission. Still, it is certain that inefficiency and waste hindered operations. Available sources point to the likelihood that the 1880s and early 1890s were the times when abuses were most widespread. Newspaper reports after the turn of the century charged that purchasing of materials at Kiangnan had been undermined by official corruption and ignorance.[42] The autobiography of Director Nieh Ch'i-kuei's wife reveals that Southern Commissioner Tso Tsung-t'ang was aware of malfeasance on the part of the director of Kiangnan and that he moved to correct it. But Tso himself appointed Nieh to the assistant directorship of Kiangnan in 1883 principally because he was the son-in-law of Tso's old Hunanese comrade-in-arms and cofounder of Kiangnan, Tseng Kuo-fan.[43] So strong was the Hunanese clique at Kiangnan that there was a temple on the arsenal grounds dedicated to Tseng Kuo-fan where arsenal officials gathered to pay respects before his tablet.[44] Liu Ch'i-hsiang followed

Nieh as director of Kiangnan. Liu's sister had married Tseng Kuo-fan's oldest son, Tseng Chi-tse, whom Liu had accompanied on a diplomatic assignment to St. Petersburg. Liu was also a relative of Li. Later reports charge that there was an unprecedented expansion of official staff, laborers, and servants and enormous inflation of salaries during Liu's tenure.[45]

There is little doubt that Li condoned a large-scale raid on the Shanghai customs proceeds by Nieh Ch'i-kuei, who in 1890 was named Shanghai Taotai. Part of these funds appear to have been used to purchase shares for Nieh in the New Hua-hsin Cotton Mill, a joint official-private enterprise in Shanghai that Li sponsored beginning in 1888.[46] It is impossible to quantify, however, the effect, if any, that this drain of customs revenue had on Kiangnan's income during the 1890s, or to show that Li was directly involved in the financial malpractices or the cronyism that infected Kiangnan in the 1880s and 1890s.

By the early 1880s, Kiangnan small arms and ammunition were no longer shipped to North China. Li regarded Kiangnan Remingtons as obsolete, and the Tientsin Arsenal's production of ammunition made supply from Kiangnan unnecessary. The obsolescence of the Remington rifle led to the conversion of equipment at Tientsin for the production of Mauser ammunition. Kiangnan also began turning out Mauser cartridges to supply the needs of provincial armies that had adopted the imported rifles as their weapons.[47]

The need to supply provincial armies increasingly influenced ammunition production at Kiangnan. In the decade between the Sino-French and the Sino-Japanese War, the arsenal turned out no less than six different types of cartridges, reflecting the demands created by the unregulated acquisition of small arms by provincial forces. The imperial government's efforts to adopt a national standard bore-diameter and to standardize cartridge-production equipment proved futile.[48] Earlier in the 1870s, Li had coordinated naval vessel acquisition and coastal-defense artillery production with the southern commissioner Shen Pao-chen. In the 1880s and 1890s, however, as Kiangnan came under the control of a tightly knit Hunanese clique, coordination became more the exception than the rule. Apart from several hundred experimental rifles developed at Kiangnan and shipped to Li in the early 1890s, Li's forces received no small arms or ammunition from Kiangnan before the Sino-Japanese War. The improved coastal-defense ordnance produced at Kiangnan during the interwar decade—including breechloaders and rapid-fire guns—was, however, shipped to installations under Li's command.[49]

Kiangnan's logistical contribution to the Chinese forces during the Sino-Japanese War, was therefore minimal. Units under Li's control, the Huai Army and the Peiyang Navy, opposed Japanese forces in Korea and the Gulf of Chihli, but neither received significant supply from Kiangnan. Some units under control of the southern commissioner that were equipped with Kiangnan ordnance and ammunition were transferred into the war zone, but their contribution was, at best, marginal.[50]

The simple fact is that the Kiangnan Arsenal had developed as the premier institution in China for the production of armaments, but during the 1880s and 1890s, as the self-perpetuating Hunanese clique tightened its control over Kiangnan, Li's influence over management and production policies diminished. This is not to suggest that the southern commissioners or the management at Kiangnan took measures to prevent supply of units under Li's control. On the contrary, it seems that Li's forces in North China either did not want or did not need the small arms and various types of ammuition turned out at Kiangnan. However, the huge coastal-defense guns produced there were in demand in North China, and they continued to be shipped to installations controlled by Li.

Conclusions

The foregoing resumé of Kiangnan's development before the Sino-Japanese War, brief as it is, discloses points at which the many-sided official career of Li Hung-chang intersected with Kiangnan's institutional development. Though Li's contact with Kiangnan in the prewar years was neither continuous nor intimate, it was Li's vision of the development a of machine industry in China together with that of Tseng Kuo-fan that, in the 1860s, brought Kiangnan into existence. The concept that Li evolved for the establishment and development of Kiangnan resulted from his familiarity with the ideas of the nineteenth-century School of Statecraft and from his personal observation of the efficacy of Western armaments and steamships. It is widely acknowledged that Li's early interest in military industrial modernization led him to advocate the introduction of machine production in nonmilitary sectors of the economy in the late 1870s and the 1880s and eventually to call for institutional reforms in education and armed forces organization. The record is clear, however: Li advocated drastic reform of China's economic and educational institutions in the early 1860s as the vision of Kiangnan began to take shape in his mind.[51] Even before he had gained extensive knowledge of Western societies, the influence of the practical, problem-solving School of Statecraft seems to have opened Li's eyes to the need for fundamental changes in Chinese civilization.

Five years after the establishment of Kiangnan, Li was transferred to North China, which remained the principal focus for his career for the next quarter century. Despite his new location, his role as a counselor to the court and his wide personal connections enabled him to retain an important voice in the affairs of Kiangnan during the 1870s: he helped Kiangnan to rid itself of a costly and ineffective shipbuilding program. In the 1880s and 1890s his direct influence seems to have waned, though it did not entirely disappear. Li's influence at Kiangnan clearly extended beyond the boundaries of the province in North China over which he held sway officially and cast him in the role of a national political figure. Though critics of his leadership elsewhere have leveled serious charges of nepotism, cronyism, and corruption,[52] these abuses at the arsenal occurred at a time when Li's influence in internal administration was not decisive. It is difficult to assign him a share in the responsibility for the retarding effect that they had on Kiangnan's development.

One of the most crucial aspects of the leadership of Kiangnan and other Chinese arsenals before the Sino-Japanese War was supervising the transfer of Western technology to China. Could machine industry develop employing Chinese resources alone or would periodic transfusions of technology and personnel continue to be required? The foreign technicians were, of course, crucial to the transfer of technology. If China were to achieve technological independence, much would depend on their role as instructors. The technicians with whom Li dealt were a mixed lot. Li became exasperated with the incompetence and procrastination of the first technicians at Kiangnan, shipwrights doubling as ordnance technicians. He dealt successfully with the problems caused by foreign management at Tientsin, though it cost the arsenal dearly. Macartney, the best-known foreigner in the Chinese arsenals, was an innovative and loyal employee of Li's, but he was a physician without qualifications or experience as an ordnance engineer. Ultimately, Macartney's ignorance caused disaster and Li had no choice but to cashier him. The tragic loss of life caused by faulty ordnance made under Macartney's guidance seems to have influenced Li to support production of safe, strong, but obsolescent Armstrong-model ordnance at Kiangnan. Thanks in part to the technical know-how and instructional skill of John Mackenzie and his men, production of the Armstrongs succeeded at Kiangnan, but it was not long before the model had to be replaced.

Li seems to have been aware of the shortcomings and strengths of the foreign technicians in his employ; however, his options were limited. Securing replacements from Europe was difficult if not impossible. The assessment of the technology itself was a bewildering task. Hindsight shows that Li's choices were sometimes farsighted, as in his introduction of steam machinery at Soochow and Kiangnan, and sometimes flawed, as in his selection of Armstrong ordnance for Kiangnan.

A host of problems beset Kiangnan in the 1880s and 1890s as it drifted from Li's control, problems that were endemic to China's early government industries. The annual operating income, derived from a percentage of the Shanghai customs proceeds, fluctuated wildly from year to year; high product costs resulted from prolonged reliance on foreign technicians, imported matériel, and imported equipment, high personnel costs and administrative inefficiency; high personnel and administrative costs stemmed from reliance on traditional administrative models and the persistence of institutionalized corruption; a weak central administration proved unable to effect product standardization; a state and society mired in the ways of the past and pressured by foreign aggression failed to change promptly the related infrastructure in the economy, the educational system, and government agencies needed to support industrialization. It is not that improvements in all these areas were not underway; they were. It was simply that the environment of virulent imperialism that brought Japan to challenge China's traditional suzerainty over Korea in 1894–95 imposed a timetable for military industrial change that the Chinese ordnance industry, and Kiangnan especially, could not meet.[53]

Be that as it may, the differences are clear between the way Kiangnan and the Tientsin Arsenal met the challenge of military industrial change necessitated by imperialist pressures. In North China, where Li influenced an early decision to narrow production to powder and ammunition and rely on foreign acquisition for most arms and naval vessels, the Tientsin Arsenal became a relatively efficient power and ammunition works. Its development was limited principally by its comparatively small and unstable income from the annual proceeds of the Tientsin Customs. The sources do not disclose the syndrome of waste, inefficiency, corruption, and reliance on foreign personnel and matériel comparable to that which beset the huge and diversified production facilities at Kiangnan.[54]

Notes

1. The principal studies on the Kiangnan Arsenal in this period include Wang Erhmin, *Ch'ing-chi ping-kung-yeh ti hsing-ch'i* (The growth of military industry in the late Ch'ing dynasty) (Taipei, 1963); Thomas L. Kennedy, *The Arms of Kiangnan: Modernization in the Chinese Ordnance Industry 1860–1895* (Boulder, 1978); Liao He-yung, *Wanch'ing tzu-ch'iang yun-tung chün-pei wen-t'i chih yen-chiu* (A study of military preparedness in the Self-Strengthening Movement of the late Ch'ing dynasty) (Taipei, 1987); Fan Kuang-tan, *Li Hung-chang chih hai-fang yun-tung chi ch'i-hou-kuo* (Li Hung-chang's maritime defense activities and their results), M.A. thesis, Chung-kuo wen-hua ta-hsueh (Chinese Cultural University), 1979; Chiang-nan tsao-ch'uan-ch'ang-shih pien-hsieh-tsu (Kiangnan Dockyard history editorial group), *Chiang-nan tsao-ch'uan-ch'ang shih 1865–1949* (History of the Kiangnan Dockyard 1865–1949) (Shanghai, 1975); Hou Fu-tung, ed., *Chiang-su chin-tai ping-kung shih-lueh* (Historical sketch of modern military industry in Kiangsu) (Nanking, 1989).

2. Hao Chang, *Liang Ch'i-ch'ao and Intellectual Transition in China 1890–1907*, (Cambridge, 1971), 26–34; Ssu-yu Teng and John K. Fairbank, *China's Response to the West* (New York, 1963), 30–35.

3. Lü Shih-ch'iang, "Feng Kuei-fen ti cheng-chih ssu-hsiang" (Feng Kuei-fen's political thought) *Chung-hua wen-hua fu-hsing yueh-kan* (Chinese cultural renaissance monthly) 4, 2 (February 1971) 1–8; Teng and Fairbank, *China's Response to the West*, 50–55; Kwang-Ching Liu, "The Confucian as Patriot and Pragmatist: Li Hung-chang's Formative Years, 1823–1866," *Harvard Journal of Asiatic Studies* 30 (1970): 5–45, chapter 2, this volume.

4. Liu, "The Confucian as Patriot and Pragmatist"; Li Hung-chang, *Li Wen-chung kung ch'üan-chi* (Complete works of Li Hung-chang) (reprint, Taipei, 1965), cited hereafter as *LWCK Letters* 1:11b, 54a.

5. Wang Erh-min, "China's Use of Foreign Military Assistance in the Lower Yangtze Valley, 1860–64," *Bulletin of the Institute of Modern History, Academia Sinica* 2 (June 1971): 535–83.

6. Sun Yü-t'ang ed., *Chung-kuo chin-tai kung-yeh-shih tzu-liao 1840–1895* (Materials on modern Chinese industrial history 1840–1895) (Peking, 1957), 2 vols., 1:249–63; Gideon Chen, *Tseng Kuo-fan: Pioneer Promoter of the Steamship in China* (Peiping,

1935), 82–92; Arthur W. Hummel, ed., *Eminent Chinese of the Ch'ing Dynasty* (Taipei, 1964 reprint), 479, 540; Wang, *Ch'ing-chi ping-kung-yeh*, 77–78, 105–106; Kennedy, *Arms of Kiangnan*, 34–45; Chou Shih-ch'eng, *Huai-chün p'ing-Nien-chi* (Record of the Huai Army's pacification of the Nien) (Shanghai, 1977), 12:2; Demetrius Boulger, *The Life of Sir Halliday Macartney* (London, 1908), 79, 123–32.

7. Wang T'ao, *T'ao-yuan wen-lu wai-pien* (Additional essays of Wang T'ao) (Hong Kong, 1882) 10 vols., 8:8–10.

8. Sun, *Kung-yeh-shih tzu-liao*, 1:257–62.

9. Knight Biggerstaff, *The Earliest Modern Government Schools in China* (Ithaca, 1961), 170–77.

10. Sun, *Kung-yeh-shih tzu-liao* 1:271–75; Kennedy, *Arms of Kiangnan*, 45–46; Kuo Ting-yee et al., eds., *Hai-fang tang* (Maritime defense archives) (Taipei, 1957), 5 vols., 3:13–26.

11. Fung Yu-lan, *A History of Chinese Philosophy* (Princeton, 1952), 2 vols., 1:305–306.

12. Sun, *Kung-yeh-shih tzu-liao*, 1:271–75.

13. Ting Jih-ch'ang, *Ting chung-cheng cheng-shu* (Political papers of Ting Jih-ch'ang) (Yale University, Sterling Library, manuscript), 26: 76–79.

14. Yung Wing, *My Life in China and America* (New York, 1909), 149–64.

15. Stanley Spector, *Li Hung-chang and the Huai Army* (Seattle, 1964), 117; Chou, *Huai-chün p'ing-Nien-chi*, 11:9, Sun, *Kung-yeh-shih tzu-liao*, 1:271–75.

16. *Yang-wu yun-tung wen-hsien hui-pien* (Collected documents on the Western Affairs movement) (Taipei edition, 1963), 8 vols., 4:127–29; *Hai-fang tang*, 3:27–28.

17. Boulger, *Macartney*, 145–72; *Yang-wu yun-tung*, 4:32, 39, 44, 46, 185; Sun, *Kung-yeh-shih tzu-liao*, 1:328–29.

18. Sun, *Kung-yeh-shih tzu-liao*, 346–50; *Yang-wu yun-tung*, 237–39; *Hai-fang tang*, 3:45–46.

19. *Hai-fang tang*, 3:27–28.

20. Sun, *Kung-yeh-shih tzu-liao*, 276–81, 313–17.

21. Kennedy, *Arms of Kiangnan*, 79.

22. *Yang-wu yun-tung*, 4:105–106.

23. *Hai-fang tang* 3:95–110, 2:367–72.

24. Ibid., 2:367–72.

25. *LWCK Memorials* 17:360, 20:12a–15b, 22:8, 50a–51a, 23:19–22, 24:10–25a, Tsungli Yamen letters 2:33–34a; *Tien-chin fu-chih* (Gazetteer of Tientsin) (1876), 27:7–8.

26. John L. Rawlinson, *China's Struggle for Naval Development 1839–1895* (Cambridge, 1967), 61; Kennedy, *Arms of Kiangnan*, 89.

27. Immanuel C. Y. Hsü, "The Great Policy Debate in China, 1874: Maritime Defense vs. Frontier Defense," *Harvard Journal of Asiatic Studies* 25 (1964–65): 212–28; *Yang-wu yun-tung*, 1:26–155.

28. *LWCK Memorials* 24:10–25.

29. *Yang-wu yun-tung*, 1:162–65, 2:378; Thomas L. Kennedy, "Industrial Metamorphosis in the Self-Strengthening Movement: Li Hung-chang and the Kiangnan Shipbuilding Program," *Journal of the Institute of Chinese Studies of the Chinese University of Hong Kong* 4, 1 (1971):207–28.

30. *LWCK Memorials* 32:5–9a; *Hai-fang tang* 3:147; *Yang-wu yun-tung* 2:379.

31. *LWCK Memorials* 17:36, 20:12–15, 23:19–22, 28:1–4, 22:8, 22:50–51a, 24:10–25, Tsungli Yamen letters 2:33–34a; British Parliamentary Papers, Foreign Office 233/85/3815.

32. Lloyd Eastman, "*Ch'ing-i* and Chinese Policy Formation during the Nineteenth Century." *The Journal of Asian Studies* 24, 4 (August 1965): 595–611.

33. *Yang-wu yun-tung*, 4:51–52, 62.

34. Ibid., 2:463, 467, 489–94.

35. British Parliamentary Papers, Foreign Office 17/656/233, Wade to Foreign Office, November 6, 1873.

36. *LWCK Memorials* 21:36, 25:45, 29:38, 37:50–52a, *Letters* 13:27–28; Sun, *Kung-yeh-shih tzu-liao* 1:327–329; *Yang-wu yun-tung* 4:32, 36, 39, 44, 46, 185; Boulger, *Macartney*, 145–88; Wang Erh-min, *Huai-chün chih* (History of the Huai Army) (Taipei, 1967), 297–98; British Parliamentary Papers, Admiralty 1/6262/2, memo submitted by Admiral Shadwell, February 5, 1873.

37. Boulger, *Macartney*, 198–212.

38. Ibid., 216–45.

39. *Yang-wu yun-tung*, 4:30–31; *Hai-fang tang*, 3:101; Kan Tso-lin, "Chiang-nan chih-tsao-chü chih chien-shih" (Brief history of the Kiangnan Arsenal), *Tung-fang tsa-chih* (Eastern miscellany) 11 (1914): 5:46–48, 6:21–24.

40. Kan Tso-lin, "Chiang-nan chih-tsao-chü chih chien-shih"; *LWCK Letters* 18:18, *Memorials* 32:5–9a, Feng Chün-kuang, *Hsi-hsing jih-chi* (Diary of Western travel) (1881), 4; Sun, *Kung-yeh-shih tzu-liao*, 1:300–301; *North-China Herald and Supreme Court and Consular Gazette).* (Shanghai): December 28, 1878, July 22, 1879.

41. Kan, "Chiang-nan chih-tsao-chü chih chien-shih."

42. Ch'en Chen, ed., *Chung-kuo chin-tai kung-yeh-shih tzu-liao* (Materials on modern Chinese industrial history), 3rd collection (Peking 1961), 2 vols., 1:73–81.

43. Tseng Pao-sun and Tseng Chi-fen, *Tseng Pao-sun hui-i-lu fu ch'ung-te lao-jen tzu-ting nien-p'u* (The memoirs of Tseng Pao-sun with the autobiography of Nieh Tseng Chi-fen) (Changsha, 1986), autobiography, 28–29.

44. Tang T'o, ed., *Ch'ieh-wan lao-jen ch'i-shih-sui tzu hsu* (Biography of Li Chung-chueh) held by Institute of Modern History, Academia Sinica, Taiwan, 272–75; *North China Herald*: November 12, 1902; Shen Yun-lung, ed., *Hsien-tai cheng-chih jen-wu shu-p'ing* (Critical appraisal of contemporary political personages) (Taipei, 1966) 2 vols., 2:51.

45. Liu K'un-i, *Liu Chung-ch'eng kung i-chi* (Collected papers of the late Liu K'un-i) (Taipei, 1966), *Memorials* 25:33; Hummel, *Eminent Chinese of the Ch'ing Period*, 855; Li En-han, *Tseng Chi-tse ti wai-chiao* (The diplomacy of Tseng Chi-tse) (Taipei, 1966), 6, 118–19, 226; Ch'en, *Kung-yeh-shih tzu-liao*, 3rd collection, 1:77–81.

46. Wellington K. K. Chan, *Merchants, Mandarins, and Modern Enterprise in Late Ch'ing China* (Cambridge, 1977), 89–92; Li Hsin and Sun Ssu-pai, eds., *Min-kuo jen-wu-chih* (Biographies of the Republican period) (Peking, 1980), 249, asserts Nieh was involved with the planning of the new Hua-hsin Mill while still at Kiangnan in 1888.

47. *LWCK Letters* 20:3b–5a, Memorials 16:16–18; Wei Yun-kung, *Chiang-nan chih-tsao-chü chi* (Records of the Kiangnan Arsenal) (Shanghai 1905), 10 vols., 3:10–12.

48. Wei, *Chiang-nan chih-tsao-chü chi*, 3:19–39; *LWCK Memorials* 22:5–9a.

49. *North China Herald*, June 9, 1893; Wei, *Chiang-nan chih-tsao-chü chi*, 3:29–57, 63–64.

50. Kennedy, *Arms of Kiangnan*, 136.

51. For further discussion of Li's early reform advocacies see Chang Ming-chiu, "Lun Li Hung-chang te pien-fa ssu-hsiang" (On the reform thought of Li Hung-chang), *Li-shih yen-chiu* (Historical research) (1989), 6:65–78; Liu, "The Confucian as Patriot and Pragmatist."

52. For an example of such charges, see John K. Fairbank, Edwin O. Reischauer, and Albert M. Craig, *East Asia, The Modern Transformation* (Boston, 1965), 381–82.

53. Kennedy, *Arms of Kiangnan*, 146–60.

54. Ibid., 142–47.

Ministers of the Navy Yamen. From left to right: Shan-ch'ing, Prince Ch'un, and Li Hung-chang. (From Mrs. Archibald Little, *Intimate China.* London: Hutchinson, 1899.)

Li Hung-chang in London, 1896. (From Mrs. Archibald Little, *Li Hung-chang: His Life and Time.* London: Cassell, 1903.)

11

Li Hung-chang and Modern Enterprise: The China Merchants' Company, 1872–1885

Chi-kong Lai

The role of Li Hung-chang (1823–1901) in the development of modern enterprises in late Ch'ing China has been one of the most important controversies in the study of modern Chinese history. Some scholars denounce Li as a traitor[1] and insist that Li's policies inflicted a serious wound on modern China.[2] Other scholars, conceding that Li's policies and practices were not above criticism, still argue that his policies did facilitate China's early industrialization.[3] Proper evaluation of Li's role thus requires further study of his involvement, over a period of many years, in the complex development of modern enterprise in China. This study will focus on a concrete case—the China Merchants' Steam Navigation Company (*Lun-ch'uan chao-shang chü*).[4]

The China Merchants' Company is a major example of the so-called *kuan-tu shang-pan* enterprises. From its history through two phases—1872–83, a period of marked success, and 1884–95, a period of decline—one can observe the problems modern enterprises faced in late Ch'ing China.[5] The first question raised here is the role of Li's policies in the success of the China Merchants' Company between 1872 and 1885. A second inquiry concerns Li's attempt and ultimate failure to maintain the administrative autonomy of the company. During his long tenure as governor-general of the metropolitan province of Chihli and as imperial commissioner of trade and foreign relations for the Northern Ports (1870–95), Li Hung-chang founded a number of modern enterprises as a defense against foreign economic encroachment.[6] Li was not slow in providing government funds for such undertakings, yet he realized that the resources of the state alone were inadequate to sustain industrialization. Private capital would have to be mobilized.

In the background of Li's policies lay the fact that in China's treaty ports, Chinese merchants with capital were unwilling to invest in modern enterprises

216

under their own names.[7] Li Hung-chang faced the problem of how to get merchants involved in such plans. The Chinese merchants in the treaty ports would invest in such enterprises only when they were guaranteed a large measure of independence, yet such enterprises needed government support to get started. The key questions are: (1) How did Li "invite merchants"(*chao-shang*) to invest in modern enterprise? (2) How did he secure government support for such enterprise? and (3) To what extent did such policies facilitate (or, as some contend, hinder) economic innovation?

The original design for the China Merchants' Company as conceived by Li was that capital in joint stock form would be owned by the merchants and that the company would be administered according to its own rules and regulations. Li suggested in a memorial to the throne the principle of *kuan-tu shang-pan*—that is, even though the project was under government supervision, profit and loss were entirely the responsibility of the merchants, and did not involve the government.[8] The policy Li initiated not only was applied to the China Merchants' Company but also set an example for other government-sponsored enterprises.

The China Merchants' Company was established primarily for the purpose of competing commercially with foreign companies that operated steamships in Chinese waters. To a large extent, the company did achieve the purpose of regaining "control of profits"(*li-ch'üan*) in the shipping business, and the company continued to grow for more than a decade until 1883. But despite the advantages that the China Merchants' Company once enjoyed, profits were not reinvested in technological improvement after the Sino-French War of 1884–85. Why?[9]

My thesis is that the early success of the China Merchants' Company was largely the result of Li's sponsorship; moreover, I contend that this success depended mostly on Li's ability not only to secure state support but also to keep bureaucratic interference in the company's affairs at a minimum. From 1877 on, many officials suggested that the court take over the ownership of the China Merchants' Company.[10] It was Li who protected the autonomy of the company's management and encouraged the merchants to invest in the enterprise. However, Li's policy could not be free of criticism and interference from conservative officials, both in Peking and in the Liangkiang area. The failure of the Empress Dowager Tz'u-hsi's court to provide for the increasing needs of China's defense efforts, as well as the financial crisis of Shanghai in 1883,[11] caused partly by the Sino-French tension over Vietnam,[12] made it very difficult to continue further support of the shipping company. Merchants who managed the company were removed, and the company's capacity for growth declined. Partly because of the example of the China Merchants' Company, businessmen's confidence in the policy of "inviting merchants" suffered. I would contend that the comparative success of the China Merchants' Company during its first decade was the result of a balance between government financial support and the autonomy of the company's merchant management. When government support was replaced by bureaucratic control, the balance was upset.

Government-merchant relations in mid-nineteenth-century China

The China Merchants' Company was established by the throne's approval of a memorial by governor-general Li.[13] In his memorandum to the Tsungli Yamen dated December 23, 1872, Li Hung-chang outlined the following formula:

> [The arrangement] should still be government supervision and merchant operation. The government will control the general plan and examine its merits and demerits, while the merchant directors [shang-tung] will be allowed to set up their own regulations so that the merchants will gladly submit to control.[14]

This system of organization became a model for other self-strengthening industries founded in the 1870s, including the Hupei Coal Mining Company (1875),[15] the Kaiping Mining Company (1877), and the Shanghai Cotton Cloth Mill (1878).[16] Under this system, enterprises were not government-owned; the ownership was rather vested in a joint-stock organization which made possible the mobilization of large amounts of Chinese merchant capital.

To appreciate the success of the China Merchants' Company in organizing a larger capital, it is necessary to discuss two related situations: (1) the patterns of Chinese merchants' investment behavior at the time; and (2) the role of the state in inducing merchant investment in the steamship business.

Institutional factors would affect merchants' attitudes toward modern enterprise, such as the steamship business. Gentry and merchants were potential investors in modern enterprises. Chung-li Chang estimates that the personal income of the "Chinese gentry," including merchants, was 645 million taels per annum in the late nineteenth century.[17] Some hong merchants in the Canton of the pretreaty days[18] and compradors of the treaty-port era earned very large profits from the expansion of foreign trade.[19] According to Yen-ping Hao, the total amount earned by the compradors in the period from 1842 to 1894 could be as high as 530.8 million taels.[20] Where did this capital go?

In Chinese society, the merchants were not important politically because they had no legal protection or means of political organization. As Balazs points out, "Official status allowed those who enjoyed it to enrich themselves by every means, legal or illegal, and to acquire new lands, or enlarge the family estate."[21] Thus, through their sons' passing the examination and becoming officials, merchants could gain the power to protect the family's interests.[22] Also, membership in a strong lineage would ensure official protection. To protect their interest, many merchants spent a huge amount of their capital on lineage-building, education, and buying official titles.[23] The rate of return on agricultural land was only around 2.5–5 percent per year but ownership of farmland was a safe investment and a source of prestige.[24]

In nineteenth-century China, ranks were still conferred on those who made large donations to help pay the cost of public works, famine relief, military campaigns, and the celebration of imperial birthdays. In the case of North China famine relief in 1878, Shen pao[25] reported that 100,000 taels were raised in less than a month. By mid-July 1878, the Chekiang governor reported that 20,000 taels had been mobilized in Hangchow, 25,000 in Ningpo and Shao-hsing, and 11,000 in Hu-chou. The silk merchant and famous banker Hu Kuang-yung alone donated at least 15,000 taels.[26] The total donations for relief during the North China famine are not known, but the Ningpo and Shao-hsing gentry contributed more than 300,000 taels.[27]

The high interest rates in mid-nineteenth century China affected merchants' investment behavior. The annual interest rate quoted by Shanghai native banks for loans was around 12–15 percent annually and was computed daily.[28] But many merchants invested their profits in moneylending in the rural sector because interest rates for loans there varied from 20 to 30 percent per year.[29] In the mid-nineteenth century, the generally regulated interest for pawnshops in Shanghai, for example, was 2–3 percent per month for loans made against pawned goods.[30] Tong King-sing in 1858 owned two pawnshops that yielded a net return of 40 percent per annum for the capital invested.[31] Investing in moneylending was risky, but the returns were high.[32]

Studies of foreign investment and economic development in modern China have shown that Chinese merchants were more willing to invest in foreign firms than in modern Chinese enterprises.[33] If Chinese merchants invested in a foreign firm, their capital would enjoy foreign protection.[34] This was more secure than putting funds in a Chinese firm because these firms did not have legal protection from the Ch'ing government.[35]

In his Chiu-shih chieh-yao (Important suggestions for the salvation of the age), Cheng Kuan-ying pointed out:

> In Shanghai and on the Yangtze River at present [c.1871–72] there are more than 17–18 steamships operating. The capital of these shipping companies must be 1,000,000 to 2,000,000 taels; all this is Chinese merchants' capital. Nine out of ten [Chinese merchants] have put their money in foreign companies' business.

Cheng also noted that "The Chinese merchants [who invested in foreign firms] were not happy about subordinating themselves to the foreign merchants."[36] But foreigners seemed more trustworthy than Chinese officials. Cheng wrote: "The merchants are afraid of the officials' power and officials are not worthy of trust."[37]

It was precisely Li Hung-chang's policy to tap Chinese capital that was invested in foreign firms. Li's problem was to make the conditions attractive enough to the Chinese merchants so that they would undertake a government-sponsored enterprise.

Li's support and the China Merchants' Company's success under merchant management

The China Merchants' Company was officially formed on January 14, 1873, in order to convey tribute rice from the southern provinces to Tientsin and to compete with foreign steamship lines for the freight service on the coast.[38] The suggestion of the employment of steamships for the transport of the tribute rice was not a new one. Tseng Kuo-fan, governor-general at Nanking, and Ting Jih-ch'ang, governor of Kiangsu, had encouraged the idea proposed by Yung Wing in 1867–68 that the steamships then being built for the government at Foochow and Shanghai might be profitably employed in the rice transport service.[39] The debate in 1872 on the question of whether the Foochow Navy Yard should be closed to save expenditure,[40] as well as the situation created by the declining number of Kiangsu and Chekiang seagoing junks,[41] drew the attention of government officials to the steamship project.

In founding the China Merchants' Company Li Hung-chang's principal motive was, as he put it, to "get a share of the foreigners' profits."[42] In his letter of December 11, 1872, to Chang Shu-sheng (the Liangkiang governor-general), Li stressed:

> The use of steamships for the transport of tribute rice by sea route is but a minor consideration. The project will open up new prospects for the dignity of the state, for commerce, for revenue, and for military strength for China for hundreds of years to come.[43]

Li decided that the company should be owned solely by Chinese merchants. At the same time, Li realized that "it is difficult to recruit merchants" to join modern Chinese enterprises. With his letter to the Tsungli Yamen dated June 2, 1872, Li enclosed a memorandum by Wu Ta-t'ing (who was identified as a former "Taiwan taotai"), which noted:

> In China wealthy and reliable merchants usually have their own businesses. They will not offer funds to a business that they do not know well. Merchants would refuse to join the project, perhaps even to consider it. Moreover, some merchants are in business with foreign firms; they have been dealing with foreigners for a long time. Knowing that government regulation cannot be enforced against the foreigners, they may not be pleased with this plan. . . . These are the difficulties.[44]

Crucial to the success of the company was Li's own commitment and his position in the politics of the empire.

Around August 1872, Li was assured by Chu Ch'i-ang, commissioner of sea transport for Chekiang Province,[45]

> that the wealthy merchants from various provinces have been investing in steamships or employing their capital in shipping or trading at the various

ports—but have always done so under the names of the foreign merchants. If the government should set up a "merchants bureau" and invite the merchants to participate [chao-lai], their share capital in [foreign] steamships would no doubt come gradually into the government bureau.[46]

In 1872 Li ordered Chu Ch'i-ang to establish a bureau (chü)in Shanghai. Chu was appointed commissioner (tsung-pan) in charge of the new bureau, the "Public Bureau for Inviting Merchants to Operate Steamships"(Lun-ch'uan chao-shang kung-chü).[47] Li himself is said to have invested 50,000 taels from the funds under his control as "share money" (ku-fen yin), but evidence on this point is not clear. He did arrange a government loan of 135,000 taels (200,000 strings of copper cash) to the company in late 1872, from Tientsin military funds.[48] As governor-general of Chihli, Li had enough influence to arrange the government freight of tribute rice to support the company.[49]

On November 24, 1872, Li submitted to the Tsungli Yamen the "Articles of the Merchant Steamship Bureau" (Lun-ch'uan chao-shang chü t'iao-kuei) drafted by Chu Ch'i-ang. The document clearly states:

> For those who own shares which they want to transfer to third parties, the head-office must be notified. . . . Shares can be sold only to Chinese merchants.[50]

Governor-general Li was inspired by a kind of economic nationalism—resistance to foreign economic domination. His patriotic sentiment[51] demanded that the shipping project not allow any foreign investors to join the company.[52] To attract native merchant capital, investors were guaranteed an annual "official dividend" (kuan-li) of 10 percent on their investment.[53] However, despite Li's policy of giving support and aid, the plan for " inviting merchants" was not successful until the summer of 1873.

In the beginning Chinese merchants were highly reluctant, if not altogether unwilling, to invest in the company.[54] As of April 1873, merchants were said to have pledged share capital totaling more that 100,000 taels, but only 10,000 taels in cash had been collected from Yü Hsi-sheng.[55] Two prominent figures of the Shanghai Chinese commercial community—the banker and silk trader Hu Kuang-yung, and the tea merchant Li Cheng-yü—had declined to take any subscriptions.[56] Chu Ch'i-ang was replaced in June 1873 because he proved to be totally incompetent in his effort to direct steamship operations and to raise capital. At the time, merchants had subscribed for shares totaling around 370,000 taels, but only 180,000 taels in cash had been collected.[57]

In the summer of 1873, two former comprador-merchants, T'ang T'ing-shu (1832–1892, known to foreigners as Tong King-sing) and Hsü Jun (1838–1911), took over the actual management of the company. Tong was comprador of Jardine Matheson & Company[58] and Hsü was formerly of Dent & Co. Both had long experience in the steamship business. Under the leadership of Tong and Hsü, the paid-up share capital had increased to 476,000 taels by the fall of 1873.[59]

Table 1

Tonnages of the China Merchants' Company's Fleet, 1872–1884

Year	Number of steamships	Net tonnage
1872	1	619
1873	4	2,319
1874	6	4,088
1875	9	7,834
1876	11	11,854
1877	29	30,526
1878	25	26,916
1879	25	26,916
1880	26	28,255
1881	26	27,827
1882	26	29,474
1883	26	33,378
1884	26	33,378

Sources: HYSTL, 1, 000; Liu, "British-Chinese Steamship Rivalry," 76–77.

A chronology of the growth under merchant management, 1874–83

Although the carriage of the tribute grain was very profitable, this service to the government was only a secondary purpose of the company. According to its original plan, conveyance of private merchandise was the first objective.[60] To develop the carrying trade and to compete with foreign firms in this business, the company needed to buy more steamships. In 1874 the company had only six ships (table 1). The dividend issued for that year was 10 percent. The company's fleet in the second year expanded to ten ships[61] (but one ship was lost in an accident[62]), while a dividend of 15 percent was given out. Tong King-sing and Hsü Jun then ordered six new steamships,[63] with the expectation of allotting more shares. Unfortunately, the Margary affair in Yunnan, famine in the south, and drought in the north all took place within the same year and caused a decline in trade.[64] As a result, the company was unable to get new shareholders, and some of the original shareholders were so alarmed that many sold their shares at 50 percent and 60 percent discounts.[65] Although a dividend of 10 percent was paid for the third year, the company's accounts showed a loss of 35,000 taels.

At the commencement of the fourth year (1876), two new river steamers arrived.[66] The new Chinese tonnage induced lower freight rates charged by Russell and Company and by Butterfield & Swire, resulting in a loss of several tens of thousands of taels on the part of the Chinese company. Payment of interest took a large slice out of the company's earnings. The company promised to pay the shareholders of a subsidiary insurance company 15 percent per year. Some of the working capital was borrowed temporarily from the native banks of Shanghai. Unfortunately, interest in Shanghai was very high between the third and eighth lunar months, and the debts in the banks were subject to the daily fluctuation of interest rates.[67] To overcome the insufficiency of private capital, the company from time to time had to borrow from the government.[68] It was thanks to this last resource that the short-term, high-interest loans the company owed to the native banks were repaid.[69]

In December 1876, the company was faced with the opportunity to buy out the entire fleet[70] and shore properties of the Shanghai Steam Navigation Company (managed by Russell and Company), for 2,200,000 taels.[71] Sheng Hsuan-huai suggested that the government order the salt transport merchants to buy 792,000 taels of the China Merchants' Company's shares and that provincial treasurers and customs taotais solicit wealthy merchants' subscriptions to the company's shares. Owing to the prior need for famine relief in the north, for which the salt merchants were making large donations, Li Hung-chang rejected Sheng's plan.[72] The purchase of the Shanghai Steam Navigation Company by the China Merchants' Company in January 1877 was made possible by government loans. Thanks to Shen Pao-chen, governor-general of Liangkiang, as well as the high authorities of Kiangsu, Chekiang, Kiangsi, and Hupei, public funds were deposited with the company totaling one million taels.[73] Li Hung-chang took part in arranging some of these loans.[74] With its purchase of the American fleet, the China Merchants' Company emerged as the leading steamship enterprise in Chinese waters.[75]

Although the company afterwards had to compete especially with the aggressive operations of Butterfield & Swire, the overall result of the year's work in 1877–78 was such that the company was able to pay a dividend of 10 percent in addition to replacing the losses it had previously sustained.[76] In 1877 Li memorialized that 40–50 percent of tribute rice and all other government cargo at the ports where the company operated should be consigned to its ships.[77]

Between 1877 and 1878, only 44,490 taels of new share capital was raised by the China Merchants' Company.[78] The company was engaged in an intense rate war with Butterfield & Swire.[79] The company again found it necessary to borrow from the native banks in Shanghai in order to meet its obligations. Its capital was then only three-quarters of a million taels, while the amount due native banks was 2,570,000 taels. The interest on the company's liabilities to native bankers amounted to no less than 360,000 taels per annum, and a government loan again was available. In December 1878, Li, who was fully aware of the fall of freight rates because of the competition with Butterfield & Swire,[80] authorized a loan of about 150,000 taels to the company.[81] The company was able to pay a dividend of 5 percent to the shareholders, carrying over another 5 percent to the reserve fund.

As the rate war progressed between the British steamship companies and the China Merchants' Company, all suffered great losses. To enable the company to continue the freight war, in 1877 Li had obtained imperial permission for the suspension of interest payments on the company's loans from the government for three years, and to allow the company five years to repay government loans thereafter.[82] The first freight rate agreement between British and Chinese companies was concluded in 1878.[83]

The Chinese company's managers instituted reform in 1879 with a view to increasing revenue.[84] They disposed of the company's foundry, where a large amount of capital was locked up, and they arranged a fixed allowance for the expenditures of each of the company's branches to reduce expenditures. The result was so satisfactory that in 1880, the company not only had reduced the interest account by more than 100,000 taels but also had declared a dividend of 10 percent and had written off 420,000 taels from the assets account for depreciation.

Overall, after early 1874, the growth of paid-up capital was slow (see table 2); nevertheless, the amount reached 1,000,000 taels (the authorized capital) seven years after the founding of the company. In 1880, new shares were subscribed by Chinese merchants in Siam, Honolulu, and San Francisco.[85] In 1882 stock capital expanded to 2,000,000 taels, the highest paid-up share capital before 1897.[86] The company's reports for the seventh and eighth years (1880–81) showed that the liabilities and interest account underwent a steady annual diminution. Not only was 400,000 taels written off in each of the two years but during that time the company also paid back to the government 775,598 taels of the previous loans.[87] The value of the company's shares rose.[88] Each original share of 100 taels had yielded a total dividend of 100 percent during the first nine years, and in 1882 each share was worth more than 220 taels in the market (see tables 3 and 4, page 226). During the first nine years the shareholders had thus enjoyed an average return of 20 percent per year.[89]

The company's achievements and Li's role

The China Merchants' Company was designed to compete commercially with foreign steamship companies in China; it did achieve the goal of "sharing the foreigners' control over profits" (*fen yang-shang li-ch'üan*).[90] During the several years before the founding of the China Merchants' Company, foreign shipping companies that operated in Chinese waters made total yearly earnings of an estimated 7,877,000 taels of silver.[91] After the China Merchants' Company was established, the total profits of foreign shipping companies declined. The conveyance of merchandise by steamship was no longer confined to foreign bottoms.[92]

The steady fall of freight rates since the company started was a benefit to the Chinese commercial community at large.[93] Ch'en Lan-pin, the chief minister of the Court of Imperial Sacrifices (*T'ai-ch'ang shih ch'ing*), estimated in 1876 that the total loss of earnings on the part of foreign shipping companies was 4,923,000 taels between 1873 and 1876. To contend with the China Merchants' Company, foreign shipping companies had to reduce their freight rates, incurring losses of more than 8,136,000 taels in the same period. Consequently, Chinese

Table 2

Share Capital of the China Merchants' Company, 1873–1884

(unit: Shanghai taels)

Year	Share capital	Net increases	Annual rate of growth (%)
Jan.–June 1873	60,000	60,000	100.00
1873–74*	476,000	416,000	694.00
1874–75	602,400	126,400	26.55
1875–76	685,510	83,110	13.80
1876–77	730,000	44,490	9.20
1877–78	751,000	20,900	2.86
1878–79	800,600	49,600	6.60
1879–80	830,300	29,700	3.70
1880–81	1,000,000	169,700	20.43
1881–82	1,000,000	0	0
1882–83	2,000,000	1,000,000	100.00
1883–84	2,000,000	0	0

Sources: Annual Reports of the China Merchants' Company (*HYSTL*, 972–78, 1, 000; *Shen Pao* [September 12, 1874; September 2, 1875; September 15, 1883]; *NCH* [April 12, 1877; November 1, 1877; October 17, 1878; October 3, 1879; September 30, 1880; September 27, 1881; October 18, 1882]).

*The reports and accounts of the China Merchants' Company are from the first day of the seventh moon to the end of the sixth moon (Chinese calendar) of the following year.

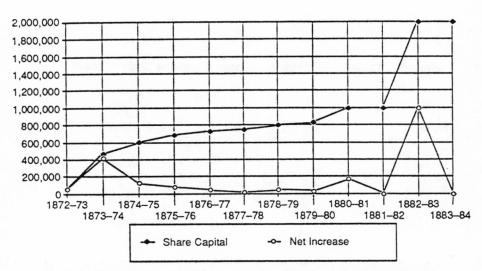

Figure 1. **Increase of the China Merchants' Company's Share Capital, 1873–1884** (in Shanghai taels)

Table 3

Dividends Paid by the China Merchants' Company, 1873–1883

	Official dividend (*kuan-li*) (%)	Extra dividend (*yu-li*) (%)
1873–74	10	—
1874–75	10	5
1875–76	10	—
1876–77	10	—
1877–78	10	—
1878–79	10	—
1879–80	10	—
1880–81	10	—
1881–82	10	10 *
1882–83	10	—

Source: Feuerwerker, *China's Early Industrialization*, 179.

*The China Merchants' Company's 1882 report. According to this report, "the item (extra dividend) should not be made because the Company is still in debt to other people; but as we have come to a resolution to call for another million taels of capital, and as this amount rightfully belongs to the shareholders, we have thought it advisable to make this dividend in order to lessen the call they have to pay by 10 percent" (see *NCH* [October 18, 1882], 418).

Table 4

The Market Value of the China Merchants' Company Share in 1882

Month in 1882	Price per share (in Shanghai taels)
Face value	100.0
February 1	220.0
June 12	250.0
August 15	248.0
August 28	242.5
September 26	253.0
December	231.0

Source: Chang Kuo-hui, *Yang-wu yun-tung yu chin-tai ch'i-yi* (Self-strengthening movement and modern Chinese enterprises) (Peking: Chung-kuo she-hui ke-hsueh chu-pan-she, 1979), 301.

Table 5

Gross Receipts of the China Merchants' Company between 1873 and 1884

Year	Gross receipts (in Shanghai taels)
1873–74	419,661
1874–75	583,758
1875–76	695,279
1876–77	1,542,091
1877–78	2,322,335
1878–79	2,203,312
1879–80	1,893,394
1880–81	2,026,374
1881–82	1,884,655
1882–83	1,643,536
1883–84	1,923,700

Source: Chang, *Yang-wu yun-tung*, 176.

merchants spent less for foreigners' services, perhaps saving a total of 13,000,000 taels in the three-year period from 1873 to 1876.[94] The Chinese company's business increased to a high plateau. The gross receipts of the company between 1873 and 1883 are given in table 5.

It will be noted that a peak of more than 2.3 million taels in 1877–78 was followed by a stabilization of around 1.9 million over the following years, but the lower figure reflects a number of external factors, including stepped-up competition, lower rates, and a decline in the tribute rice shipments. The company was performing well in a more demanding environment.

There were other ways in which the China Merchants' Company served China's interests. It contributed to the customs duties at China's maritime customs from year to year. The company performed an important function in maritime defense, at various times carrying troops to Korea, Taiwan, and Shanhaikuan.[95] Famine in North China (1876–79) was a serious disaster to the country; Li relied on the company to ship relief funds and supplies.[96] The donations to relief funds made by the company and its managers are shown in table 6 on page 228.

Government support for the company far outweighed what the state extracted from it in this early period. Li Hung-chang's policies were of crucial importance. Thanks to him, as well as to the high authorities of Kiangsu, Chekiang, Kiangsi, and Hupei, and the customs taotais of Tientsin and Shanghai, public loans totaling 1,908,000 taels were at various times deposited with the company.[97] At least nineteen official loans were arranged before 1885 (table 7, page 228).[98] Before 1882, the total government loans amounted to much more than the total paid-up share capital; these loans represented about 50–60 percent of the company's total

Table 6

Donations by the China Merchants' Company and Its Senior Officers for Famine Relief in North China, 1878

Name	Total donations (in Shanghai taels)
China Merchants' Company[a]	18,504.4
Tong King-sing[b]	500.0
Hsü Jun[b]	500.0
Chu Ch'i-ang[b]	1,390.0
Chu Ch'i-chao[b]	695.0

Sources: [a]Shen Pao (October 3, 1878), 4; [b]LWCK Memorials, 31: 5–6.

Table 7

Government Loans to the China Merchants' Company, 1872–1883

(in Shanghai taels)

Government loans	Year	Amount of loan	Annual interest rate (%)
Tientsin military funds	1872	120,000	7
Wood likin of Nanking	1875	100,000	8
Chekiang public funds	1875	100,000	8
Coastal defense funds	1876	100,000	8
Yangchou commissary	1876	100,000	8
Chihli military funds	1876	50,000	10
Pao-ting military funds	1876	50,000	8
Chefoo customs	1876	100,000	8
Nanking provincial treasury	1877	100,000	10
Kiangan commissary	1877	200,000	10
Shanghai customs	1877	200,000	10
Chekiang silk revenue	1877	200,000	10
Kiangsi treasury	1877	200,000	10
Hupei treasury	1877	100,000	10
Coastal defense funds	1878	150,000	
Coastal defense funds	1878–81	100,000	
Funds for diplomatic missions	1881	80,000	
Tientsin funds for coastal defense	1883	200,000	

Source: Lai, "The Proposal to Nationalize," 21.

Table 8

Capital Account of the China Merchants' Company, 1873–1891

(unit: Shanghai taels)

Year	Total $(1 = 2 + 3)$	Share capital (2)	Loans (3)	Government loans (4)	% of government loans $(4 / 1 \times 100)$
1873–74	599,023	476,000	123,023	123,023	20.54
1874–75	1,251,995	602,400	649,595	136,957	10.94
1875–76	2,123,457	685,100	1,438,357	353,499	16.65
1876–77	3,964,288	730,200	3,234,088	1,866,979	47.09
1877–78	4,570,702	751,000	3,819,702	1,928,868	42.20
1878–79	3,936,188	800,600	3,153,588	1,928,868	49.00
1879–80	3,887,046	830,300	3,056,746	1,903,868	48.98
1880–81	3,620,529	1,000,000	2,620,529	1,518,867	41.95
1881–82	4,537,512	1,000,000	3,537,512	1,217,967	26.84
1882–83	5,334,637	2,000,000	3,334,637	964,292	18.88
1883–84	4,270,852	2,000,000	2,270,852	1,192,565	27.92
1885	NA	NA	NA	NA	NA
1886	4,169,690	2,000,000	2,169,690	1,170,222	28.06
1887	3,882,232	2,000,000	1,882,232	1,065,254	27.44
1888	3,418,016	2,000,000	1,418,016	793,715	23.22
1889	3,260,535	2,000,000	1,260,535	688,241	21.11
1890	2,750,559	2,000,000	150,559	90,241	0.33
1891	2,685,490	2,000,000	685,490	0	0

Sources: Chang, *Yang-wu yun-tung*, 168–69; Lai, "The Proposal to Nationalize," 17.

debts, or 2.2 times more than the maximum paid-up capital between 1876 and 1889 (table 8; figure 2).[99]

These loans were guaranteed an interest of only 7–10 percent per annum.[100] The rate was lower than the shareholders' guaranteed annual dividend.[101] Actually, no interest was paid on these loans for the entire period between 1877 and 1885. The suspended interest totaled more than 900,000 taels for those eight years. This was as much as about half the maximum paid-up share capital. Thus, interest due the government, more than a hundred thousand taels every year, was used to subsidize the enterprise.

Government loans did not come easily. It was reported that Li's troops revolted in 1873 because they could not get their pay partly as the result of his using Tientsin army funds to support the company that year.[102] The government funds borrowed for the purchase of the Shanghai Steam Navigation Company's fleet amounted to 1,000,000 taels. To make this purchase possible, Li had memorialized the throne to transfer public funds from the Hupei provincial revenue office. The amount of 150,000 taels, sent for famine relief, was later transferred to the China Merchants' Company to yield interest, presumably for further fam-

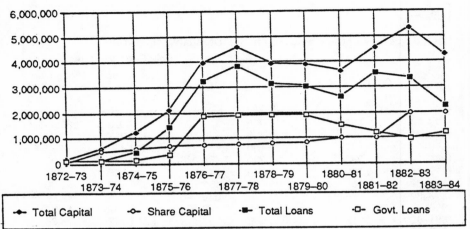

Figure 2. The China Merchants' Company's Capital Account, 1872–1884 (in Shanghai taels)

ine relief.[103] Famine was widespread in North China in 1877. Liu K'un-i later pointed out that "the funds would have been better spent at the time for disaster relief."[104]

In 1885, at a time when the China Merchants' Company was recovering its ships and other property from Russell and Company, to which they were fictitiously sold at the outbreak of the Sino-French War, Liu insisted that the company should repay the loan immediately. Li made a strong reply in a telegram dated December 16, 1885:

> We have just discussed how to recover all the property of the China Merchants' Company. Russell and Company is delaying the process and the terms of transfer have not been decided. Now, the freight transporting tribute rice must be given to Russell and Company, consequently China Merchants' Company cannot arrange for any advance of money. You [Liu] at this moment want to collect the public funds and spend them on the repair of the seashore dikes. . . . It is important to discuss the reduction of the company's debts later, after the ships of the China Merchants' Company are all received from Russell and Company. I do not want to hear of your mischief again.[105]

In addition to government loans, Governor-General Li helped to strengthen the company by arranging for a larger consignment of tribute rice. As we have seen, Li had enough influence on the provincial officials concerned to have them allot to the company a part of the annual shipment of tribute rice from their provinces. These officials, led by Li, memorialized the throne jointly in 1877. For shipping tribute rice, the company was paid at the same rate of freight as that enjoyed by the seagoing junks, as much as 0.6 taels per picul as of 1879,[106] and 0.531 taels per picul between 1880 and 1884.[107] These rates were

Table 9

Tribute Grain Shipped by the China Merchants' Company

(in Shanghai taels)

Year	Tribute grain shipped	Rate of freight	Total earning (Tribute grain shipped x rate of freight)
June 1873	170,000[a]	0.600[b]	102,000
1873–74	250,000	0.600	150,000
1874–75	300,000[c]	0.600	180,000
1875–76	450,000[d]	0.600	270,000
1876–77	290,000[d]	0.600	174,000
1877–78	523,000	0.600	313,800
1878–79	520,000	0.600	312,000
1879–80	570,000[d]	0.600	342,000
1880–81	475,415[d]	0.531[e]	252,445
1881–82	557,000[d]	0.531	295,767
1882–83	580,000[d]	0.531	307,980
1883–84	390,000[d]	0.531	207,090
1884–85	470,000[d]	0.531	249,570

Sources: [a]Shen Pao 4 (June 13, 1973); [b]Chin-tai ming-jen shou-cha, vol. 2, 863–64; Shen Pao 1 (March 16, 1875); [c]Kwang-Ching Liu, "Steamship Enterprise in Nineteenth-Century China," The Journal of Asian Studies 18, no. 4 (1959), 443; [d]CSCPKS, vol. 2, 21–34; [e]LWCK Memorials, 36: 32–34.

two or three times higher than the average rate charged by the foreign steamship companies.[108] For the tribute-rice freight, the company received an average of around 500,000 piculs per year (table 9). Li also arranged to use the company's steamers for shipping troops (table 10, next page), and he persuaded some provincial officials to employ the company's steamships for other government purposes.[109]

Overall, Li believed that the company should be managed by merchants even when it was financially supported by officials. The word support (fu-ch'ih) implied a fear that the merchants' capital might be insufficient to carry on the operation of the company for an extended period; for this reason the government consigned the shipment of the tribute rice to the company, and lent the company funds.

Li's efforts and ultimate failure to maintain the autonomy of the company's management

Although the China Merchants' Company enjoyed remarkable growth before 1885, the company did not continue to reinvest in capital equipment after the Sino-French War of 1884–85. In 1877 the company owned thirty steamships and could boast the highest tonnage among steamship companies in China.[110] In

Table 10

The China Merchants' Company's Earnings from Transporting Troops and Military Supplies

Year	Rate of freight	Total earnings (in Shanghai taels)
1873–74	—	29,087.4[a]
1874–75	—	2,625.4[b]
1881–82	5 tls./person	86,690.0[c]

Sources: *LWCK Memorials:* [a]27: 14; [b]29: 31,34; [c]46: 9.

Table 11

Changes in Shipping Tonnages of the China Merchants' Company and the China Navigation Company, 1877–1893

	The China Merchants' Company		The China Navigation Company	
	Ships	Net tonnage	Ships	Net tonnage
Fleet during 1877	30[a]	ca.30,526	5	8,361
Additions, 1877–93	16	15,378	34	36,630
Sold, 1877–93	3	2,174	—	—
Fleet during 1893	26	23,284	29	34,543

Sources: [a]*HYSTL*, 1, 000; Liu, "Steamship Enterprise," 452.

the period from 1878 to 1883, the company purchased nine new ships and completed a large investment in wharves and warehouses.[111] However, the company did not continue to expand after 1885. The China Merchants' Company had a fleet of only twenty-six ships in 1893.[112] Meanwhile, the tonnage of foreign steamship companies in Chinese waters grew rapidly (table 11). To understand more fully why the China Merchants' Company declined it is necessary to reconsider the relationship between government policy and Chinese merchant investment.

Before 1885, the administration of the China Merchants' Company was to a large extent on a strictly commercial footing. When Tong King-sing took charge and commenced the reorganization of the company in 1873, certain "rules" (*chü-kuei*) and "regulations" (*chang-ch'eng*) were drafted according to which the affairs of the company were to be carried out on mercantile principles.[113] Article 2 of the "regulations" states:

Since this undertaking has been put under merchant operation [*shih-kuei shang-pan*], it seems that the government should condescend to comply with the regular practices of business, so that these practices may be more easily followed.[114]

As large shareholders, the principal merchant directors invested personal funds in the enterprise and expected returns in the form of dividends. Article 3 of the "rules" provides for the following:

A merchant director shall be elected for each hundred shares; and from among the merchant directors a chief director [*tsung-tung*] shall be elected . . . [all] to serve for a period of three years.[115]

Article 4 of the "rules" states:

The merchant chief is the administrative head [*chü-cheng*] of the main office of the bureaus, and one or two merchant directors shall serve as his deputies. . . . The other merchant directors shall be assigned duties at the branches of the bureau by direction of the main office.[116]

According to Tong and Hsü, "Funds are to the China Merchants' Company like soldiers and horses to the military. As merchants, we should protect ourselves. None of the merchant-directors in the China Merchants' Company are allowed to be indebted to the company, or be on the account of the China Merchants' Company. This rule is laid down in accordance with the regulations."[117]

In 1873, it was agreed that the remuneration of the directors, agents, and servants of the company, including their expenses, should be defrayed from an allowance of only 5 percent of freight receipts.[118]

Tong and Hsü insisted that the company should not be run like a yamen. They proposed: "As to the accounts of receipts and expenditures, there will be a daily journal, a monthly statement, and an annual summary statement, which are to be checked by the merchant directors together with the staff members. Should a report be required, copies of the original books may be submitted. It is recommended that the compilation of formal reports on expenditures [*tsao-ts'e pao-hsiao*] not be required, so as to reduce clerical work."[119]

According to these "regulations," no officials were to be appointed to the company. No official clerks or runners were to be employed; the bureaucratic practice of making official reports and forwarding accounts for official inspection was not to be applied.

Inasmuch as these "rules" and "regulations" were approved by Li, they represented his policy. Li appointed the top administrators of the China Merchants' Company, but until 1885, as far as Li was concerned, the company was meant to be an enterprise operating strictly on a commercial footing. At the same time, Li appointed some government officials, including Sheng Hsuan-huai (who was on Li's staff before 1873) and Chu Ch'i-ang as managers of affairs regarding tribute-rice transport. From the beginning, Sheng wanted to be the principal supervisor of the company itself, and tried several times to persuade Li to appoint him to such a position.[120] However, Li was on the side of the merchants.[121] Not only did Li write often to other officials about the great contribution Tong and Hsü made to the company,[122] he even removed Sheng from his position in the company as tribute-rice manager.[123]

As governor-general of Chihli, Li reported to the Board in 1877 that he had transferred 100,000 taels to the China Merchants' Company as loans carrying interest; 50,000 taels were from the Tientsin circuit (*tao*) and 50,000 taels were from the Tientsin customs funds. In March 1880 Li memorialized the throne that beginning that year, the China Merchants' Company should repay its government loans over a period of five years in equal amounts; these were to be deducted from earnings for transporting tribute rice each year. In June 1880 Li memorialized to propose the purchase of two American ironclads for the Ch'ing navy. Because there were no other sources of funds, Li proposed allocating for this purpose the 1,000,000 taels expected from the China Merchants' Company over the next three years, to be deducted from the tribute-rice freight. Under the circumstances, the China Merchants' Company had to report to the Board about its procedure for repaying government loans, but it still did not have to report the details of its internal affairs.[124]

However, as the company expanded and continued to make profits, a number of officials proposed that the government take over the ownership of the company.[125] Such proposals were made in 1877 by Shen Pao-chen (governor-general of Liangkiang), in 1879 by Yeh T'ing-chüan (a tribute-grain manager of the company), and in 1881 by Liu K'un-i (then governor-general of Liangkiang). Liu's proposal posed an especially serious threat.

Yeh T'ing-chüan, who was the Shanghai taotai at one time, suggested in a letter to Li Hung-chang that the government should expend about 2,000,000 taels of public funds to take over the China Merchants' Company, although he did not use the modern term *nationalization* (*kuo-yu hua*). Yeh noted that the takeover would save interest totaling 200,000 taels from native banks, as well as dividends to the shareholders amounting to 70,000 taels annually. He believed that the government would get full returns from its 2,000,000-tael investment within ten years.[126] However, Li did not accept this proposal. In fact, he removed Yeh from the company's management.[127]

Liu K'un-i's proposal was to convert government loans into government shares, making the government the largest single shareholder. In his letter to Li Chao-t'ang, dated February 15, 1881, Liu K'un-i said: "The suspended interest [for government loans to the company] was more than 700,000 taels, so the total amount of the government loans was over 1,500,000 taels which I proposed to put in the China Merchants' Company as government shares."[128]

The company's shareholders immediately interpreted Liu's proposal as a means to introduce government control over the company's management. As described above, the company's directors were the largest shareholders, and the managers of branch offices were also shareholders. The total number of shares the China Merchants' Company had issued was 800,600 taels in 1878–79. Tong and his close relatives owned about 80,000 taels, and Tong's other relatives subscribed to 200,000 taels. Hsü Jun and his relatives controlled as many shares as Tong and his relatives. More than half the shares were thus under the control of the two merchant managers.[129] From the standpoint of the merchant managers, there was no need for official inspection. If the managers were to act dishonestly in any way, they reasoned, "How could the majority of the shareholders, who were friends or relations of the managers and who lived so near one another, fail to detect these acts?" It was thought that the merchants should thus be responsible for their own investments. At the time that the China Merchants' Company was under heavy criticism from the censors in Peking, Tong and Hsü had said in a letter:

> To repay the loans to the government, we could [if necessary] sell all the ships and wharves. We could also close the company and establish another one. Since the profit and loss are entirely the responsibility of the merchants and do not involve the government, the government does not need to investigate the company's accounts.[130]

Thanks to Li Hung-chang's protection, Liu's plan was not realized. In his letter to Wang Hsien-ch'ien, Liu ruefully acknowledged the success of Li's efforts:

> Li Hung-chang memorialized the court that the funds [which were borrowed from the public funds] should be returned in five years and that later all the profit would belong to the China Merchants' Company, and not to the government. In the future the administration of the company will belong to merchants, not the government![131]

Because Li's policy prevailed, the autonomy of the company's management was preserved, and merchant investments were encouraged. As a result, not only did the company expand its capital twofold but many merchants were also attracted to invest in other modern Chinese enterprises. A major example was the Shanghai Cotton Cloth Mill, which received a paid-up share capital of 400,000 taels, as planned, in 1881, and shares beyond that amount were enthusiastically subscribed before a quarrel developed between the merchant managers Cheng Kuan-ying and Ching Yuan-shan, on the one hand, and gentry activists, Kung Shou-t'u and Tai Heng, on the other.[132]

It is clear from Li Hung-chang's efforts up to the mid-1880s that the Ch'ing state did not always play a negative role in building up nonmilitary modern enterprises. In the aftermath of the financial crisis in Shanghai in 1883, Li, evidently bowing to irresistible political and financial pressures, ordered the reorganization of the company. In the end, Li appointed Sheng Hsuan-huai in 1885 as its director-general (*tu-pan*), partly because Sheng had become its largest shareholder in 1885. There is evidence that in 1885, in the aftermath of the financial crisis and the Sino-French war, Tong proposed to invite foreign capital to help finance the company under his continued management. This would have been a departure from the original policy of not allowing foreigners to own any share in the company.[133] The policy was not accepted and under Sheng the shares were owned by Chinese only.

During his directorship between 1885 and 1902, Sheng continued to hold regular official posts[134] and to control the company's affairs from Chefoo or Tientsin. He chose his favorites as top administrators of the company in Shanghai, regardless of the size of their shareholdings. Bureaucratic control in the company increased. Most of the top administrators were of official background, lacking experience in the operation of modern enterprises. The company's profits were not reinvested in expansion. This loss of mercantile control of the China Merchants' Company led to disenchantment among merchants who had been interested in government-sponsored enterprises and, in general, dampened the willingness of the Chinese merchants to put their capital in other modern enterprises.[135]

The early success story of the China Merchants' Company leaves us with the question of why government's positive role in modern Chinese enterprises faltered, and with what effect, after 1885.

In 1885, government loans to the China Merchants' Company still totaled more than 832,274 taels. The president of the Board of Revenue, insisting that it was his duty to keep track of all government loans to the company, wanted to check its accounts in detail. The Board president exaggerated: "For ten years, the China Merchants' Company has not increased its capital or dividends; the government loans and foreign debts have been innumerable. Is there any corruption?"

The Board president requested an imperial decree ordering high government officials to make a thorough investigation into the management of the company's affairs. He stressed that the "China Merchants' Company received appropriations of government funds, as well as assistance in earnings from the transport of tribute grains. Moreover, the government remits taxes from certain cargo carried by the China Merchants' Company. Therefore the company's annual expenditure and income should be checked by officials."

The Board president wanted full information on the government loans received by the China Merchants' Company—in which year, from which province, from which source, and in what amount were the loans originally made. The Board demanded to inspect

the official records on the amounts the company has repaid [and the amount the company still owed the provinces in 1885] . . . when the loans should begin to yield interest and at what rate per year. For auditing purposes, all such information should be listed in a memorial. As to repayment of government funds, more than 770,000 taels should be paid after the foreign debts are retired. All repayments should be reported to the Board of Revenue in order to clear the record.

The Board president insisted that the managers of the China Merchants' Company should be chosen after consultation with high officials. He also suggested that the throne order the company to submit a number of explicit financial statements on where it stood. From 1885 on, all information on the company's personnel, loans, income, expenditure, profit, daily operation, ownership and location of the ships and the wharves should be listed in the standard forms (*tsao-ts'e*) and submitted to the Board of Revenue for approval.[136]

Li Hung-chang and the early history of the China Merchants' Company

State policies can play an important role in promoting economic growth. Social scientists have presented a number of arguments regarding why state intervention is sometimes necessary for economic development.[137] The substitution model suggests that in a backward economy, a strong state may replace market forces by bureaucratic intervention in the economy.[138] In this chapter, I have explored how Li's policies helped the success of the China Merchants' Company between 1872 and 1885.

The Ch'ing state, as represented by Li Hung-chang, did play a part in economic development. Through his influence in government, Li was able to secure government loans and other subsidies to modern enterprises. To explain why Li could not help the China Merchants' Company after 1885, we may begin with a model of "state building" derived originally from European history.[139] The role of the state in the economy was growing in the China of the 1870s. The active self-strengthening movement, of which Li's efforts to promote modern enterprise were a part, can be considered as a process of modern state building in late Ch'ing China.[140]

Because Li's own political position changed, his ability to help the company declined. During the Sino-French conflict and the peace negotiations, Li was heavily criticized, especially by the Purist party (*ch'ing-liu tang*), for military setbacks and the proposed concessions to France. Li's options and power suffered as a result. The Sino-French War and Japan's threat to Korea placed urgent and heavy demands on government resources for defense needs. When available funds were largely allocated to military purposes, government support for private enterprise had to suffer. Gerschenkron's concept of substitution does not fully apply to this case. The Ch'ing government as a whole did play a positive role in laying a foundation for the China Merchants' Company, but by the 1880s the government no longer had enough funds to support similar enterprises. Later the government even took funds away from the company. After 1891, under the directorship of Sheng Hsuan-huai, the company contributed around 100,000 taels to the government each year.

The China Merchants' Company might have been able to sustain itself without further government support, assuming a favorable investment climate. But a combination of government extraction and loss of managerial autonomy under Sheng's supervision led the company to stagnation and a declining competitive position. When Li could no longer maintain the independence of the enterprise's management, merchants quickly lost their confidence in the company's future. The original policy of "inviting merchants" to invest in modern enterprise was no longer attractive.

To conclude, Li's founding of the China Merchants' Company in 1873 was an innovative achievement in Chinese history. The initial success of the company was a result of the combination of the government's financial support and the merchant managers' autonomy. Under such favorable circumstances, merchants were willing to commit their resources to the company. When government support led to direct bureaucratic control of the management, the latter's autonomy was undermined, and the balance was upset. Under bureaucratic control, the quality of management was severely impaired, performance suffered, and the company was exposed to state fiscal extractions—circumstances that severely discouraged investment in the China Merchants' Company and other modern enterprises.

I have emphasized in this chapter that the early success of the China Merchants' Company was to a large extent owing to Li's ability to provide government support for and, at the same time, maintain the autonomy of the company's merchant management. In this sense, Li Hung-chang had adopted in the 1870s a farsighted policy for industrialization. The system presided over by Sheng Hsuan-huai in 1885 and later was not an improvement. On the other hand, the importance of Li's personal role highlights the difficult question of stability and reliability. When under the pressure of crisis in foreign relations Li could not maintain his earlier policy of protecting the merchants, bureaucratic intervention increased and merchants quickly lost confidence in government-sponsored enterprises.[141]

The China Merchants' Company was an important experiment. The Chinese merchants' confidence in this particular type of government enterprise depended on whether the China Merchants' Company was successful. When government intervention increased, merchants reduced their support and, with that, the fate of this type of venture was sealed.

Notes

Abbreviations

CSCPKS *Ch'ing-ch'a cheng-li chao-shang chü wei-yuan hui, pao-kao shu* (A report on the investigation of the CMSN Company), compiled by a committee investigating the CMSN Company. Nanking, 1927.

CTSHCP   *Chiao-t'ung shih: hang-cheng pien* (History of communications; shipping), compiled by a committee jointly sponsored by the ministries of communications and railways. Nanking, 1931.

HFT   *Hai-fang tang* (Archives on maritime defense), photo-offset reproduction of Tsungli Yamen papers published by the Institute of Modern History of Academia Sinica. Taipei, 1957.

HYCNP   Hsü Jun, *Hsü Yü-chai tzu-hsü nien-p'u, fu Shang-hai tsa-chi* (Autobiographical chronicle by Hsü Yü-chai, together with miscellaneous notes on Shanghai), c.1927. Taipei reproduction, Shih-huo ch'u-pan she, 1977.

HYSTL   *Chung-kuo chin-tai hang-yun-shih tzu-liao* (Source materials on the history of shipping in modern China), ed. Nieh Pao-chang (Nie Baozhang). Shanghai: Jen-min ch'u-pan-she, 1983.

LHCC   *Li Hung-chang ch'üan-chi* (Complete works of Li Hung-chang), vol. 1, *Tien-kao* (Telegrams). Shanghai: Jen-min ch'u-pan-she. 1985.

LWCK   Li Hung-chang, *Li Wen-chung-kung ch'üan-chi* (The complete works of Li Hung-chang). Shanghai, 1921 (reproduction of the original edition, Nanking 1905). *P'eng-liao han-kao* (Letters to friends and colleagues, hereafter cited as *LWCK Letters*); *Tsou-kao* (Memorials, cited as *LWCK Memorials*); *I-shu han-kao* (Dispatches to the Tsungli Yamen, cited as *LWCK Tsungli Yamen Letters*).

NCH   *North China Herald.*

NYSTL   *Chung-kuo chin-tai nung-yeh shih tzu-liao ti-i chi, 1840–1911* (Source materials on the history of agriculture in modern China, first collection, 1840–1911), ed. Li Wen-chih. Peking: San-lien, 1957.

SHCCSL   *Shang-hai ch'ien-chuang shih-liao* (Historical material on Shanghai "native banks"). Shanghai: Chung-kuo jen-min yin-hang Shang-hai-shih fen-hang, 1960.

YWYT   *Yang-wu yun-tung* (The Western Affairs movement). ed. Chung-kuo k'o-hsueh yuan chin-tai-shih yen-chiu-so et al. Shanghai: Jen-min, 1961.

1. Juan Fang-chi (Juan Fangji) et al., *Yang-wu yun-tung shih lun-wen hsüan* (Selected articles on the history of the Western Affairs movement) (Peking: Jen-min, 1985), 56, 102.

2. Mou An-shih, *Yang-wu yun-tung* (The Western Affairs movement) (Shanghai: Jen-min ch'u-pan she, 1956), 1–2, 91–95, 113–22.

3. Ting-yee Kuo and Kwang-Ching Liu, "Self-strengthening: The Pursuit of Western Technology," in *The Cambridge History of China*, ed. John K. Fairbank, vol. 10, *Late Ch'ing, 1800–1911, Part 1* (Cambridge: Cambridge University Press, 1978), 507–11; Wellington K. K. Chan, "Government, Merchants, and Industry to 1911," in *The Cambridge History of China*, ed. John K. Fairbank and Kwang-Ching Liu, vol. 11, *Late Ch'ing, 1800–1911, Part 2* (Cambridge: Cambridge University Press, 1980), 422–29; Albert Feuerwerker, *China's Early Industrialization: Sheng Hsüan-huai (1844–1916) and Mandarin Enterprise* (Cambridge, Mass.: Harvard University Press, 1958), 8–15; Hu Pin (Hu Bin) and Li Shi-yü (Li Shiyue), "Li Hung-chang ho Lun-ch'uan chao-shang chü" (Li

Hung-chang and the China Merchants' Company), in *Yang-wu yun-tung shih lun-wen hsüan*, ed. Juan Fang-chi et al., 271–95. Feuerwerker (*China's Early Industrialization*, 250) notes that "while Li Hung-chang did not hesitate to profit personally from the enterprises that he sponsored, his support of modern-type industry was clearly part of a larger concern with diplomacy and national defense and with the development of his regional power." Whether Li derived personal profit from the enterprises has not been proven.

4. The literal meaning of this name is "Bureau for Inviting Merchants [to Operate] Steamships," hereafter cited as China Merchants' Company.

5. See Kwang-Ching Liu, Ts'ung lun-ch'uan chao-shang-chü tsao-ch'i li-shih k'an kuan-tu shang-pan ti liang-ko hsing-t'ai (The early history of the China Merchants' Company and the two different patterns of the *kuan-tu shang-pan* system) (manuscript).

6. "Beginning in 1862, he [Li Hung-chang] was for more than three decades the foremost champion of China's self-strengthening (*tzu-ch'iang*)—a policy for the building up of China's military and financial power, primarily through the adoption of Western technology, so as to enable her to cope with future aggression" (see Liu, chapter 2, above); also Ellsworth C. Carlson, *The Kaiping Mines, 1877–1912* (Cambridge, Mass.: Harvard East Asian Monographs, 1971), 2–5.

7. Some compradores accumulated capital and invested it in foreign firms or in traditional Chinese business, such as pawnshops. See Kwang-Ching Liu, "Tong King-sing: His Compradore Years," in *Tsing Hua Journal of Chinese Studies*, New Series (1961), 2:143–83; Yen-p'ing Hao, *The Compradore in Nineteenth Century China: Bridge between East and West* (Cambridge, Mass.: Harvard University Press, 1971); Yen-p'ing Hao, *The Commercial Revolution in Nineteenth-Century China: The Rise of Sino-Western Mercantile Capitalism* (Berkeley: University of California Press, 1986), 245–76; Wang Ching-yü (Wang Jingyu), "Shih-chiu shih-chi wai-kuo ch'in-hua ch'i-yeh chung ti hua-shang fu-ku huo-tung" (The activities of Chinese merchants in subscribing to capital shares in the aggressive foreign enterprises in China during the nineteenth century), in *Shih-chiu shih-chi hsi-fang tzu-pen-chu-i tui Chung-kuo ti ching-chi ch'in-lueh* (The encroachment of Western capitalism on the Chinese economy in the nineteenth century) (Peking: Jen-min, 1983), 483–526.

8. *LWCK Letters*, 20:33; 36:35.

9. Some scholars have insisted that the official extraction of funds seriously hindered the development of the China Merchants' Company. See Fan Pai-ch'uan (Fan Baichuan), *Chung-kuo lun-ch'uan hang-yun-yeh te hsing-ch'i* (The rise of steamship navigation in China) (Szechuan: Jen-min, 1981), 251–54; Wang Hsi (Wang Xi), "Lun wan-ch'ing kuan-tu shang-pan" (The system of government supervision and merchant operation in late Ch'ing China), in *Yang-wu yun-tung shih lun-wen hsüan* (Selected articles on the Western Affairs movement) (Peking: Jen-min, 1985), 221–70; Chang Wei-an, Cheng-chih yü ching-chi: Chung-kuo chin-shih liang-ko ching-chi tsu-chih chih fen-hsi (Politics and economy: An analysis of two economic organizations in late imperial China), Ph.D. dissertation, Tunghai University, 1987. Feuerwerker (*China's Early Industrialization*, 27) explains that "in the absence of any commercial code the shareholders had no legal appeal against these exactions. Their only protection was the power of one official or group of officials who might have a particular interest in the company against the demands of outsiders." This thesis opposing the state's interests to those of the merchants is important. Tuan Pen-luo (Duan Benluo) even contends that "when private capital was invested in an enterprise 'operated by merchants under government supervision,' it was as if it had fallen into a trap." See Tuan Pen-luo, "Chien-lun *kuan-tu shang-pan* tui min-tsu tzu-pen-chu-i fa-chan ti tsu-chih tso-yung" (The "government supervision and merchant operation" system as an obsta-

cle to the development of national capitalism), *Li-shih chiao-hsueh* 10 (1982): 14–18. But did the Ch'ing bureaucracy always suppress initiative in modern enterprises?

10. Chi-kong Lai, "Lun-ch'uan chao-shang chü kuo yu wen-t'i, 1878–1881" (The proposal to nationalize the China Merchants' Steam Navigation Company, 1878–1881), in *Bulletin of the Institute of Modern History, Academia Sinica* (Taipei: 1988), 17:15–40.

11. See Ch'üan Han-sheng, *Chung-kuo ching-chi shih lun-ts'ung* (Collected essays on Chinese economic history) (Hong Kong: Hsin ya yen-chiu so, 1972), 777–94; Kwang-Ching Liu, "1883 Shanghai chin-yung feng-ch'ao" (The financial crisis in Shanghai, 1883), *Journal of Fudan University* (Shanghai, 1983), 94–102; Hao, *Commercial Revolution*, 323–34.

12. Lloyd E. Eastman, *Throne and Mandarins: China's Search for a Policy during the Sino-French Controversy, 1880–1885* (Cambridge, Mass.: Harvard University Press, 1967).

13. *LWCK Memorials*, 20:31–33; *LWCK Tsungli Yamen Letters*, 1:38–40.

14. *LWCK Tsungli Yamen Letters*, 1:40.

15. For example, the "Regulations of Hupei Coal Mining Company" (1875) was based on the model of the China Merchants' Company. See Ch'en Hsü-lu (Chen Xulu) et al., *Sheng Hsüan-huai tang-an tzu-chiao hsüan-chi* (Compilation of selected materials from the Sheng Hsüan-huai Archives) (Shanghai: Jen-min, 1981), 2:24–27.

16. See Carlson, *The Kaiping Mines, 1877–1912*; Feuerwerker, *China's Early Industrialization;* Wellington K. K. Chan, *Merchants, Mandarins, and Modern Enterprise in Late Ch'ing China* (Cambridge, Mass.: Harvard University Press, 1977); Kwang-Ching Liu, "A Chinese Entrepreneur," in *The Thistle and the Jade: A Celebration of 150 Years of Jardine, Matheson and Co.*, ed. Maggie Keswick (London: Octopus Books, 1982), 102–27; Chang Kuo-hui (Zhang Guohui), *Yang-wu yun-tung yü chin-tai ch'i-yeh* (The Western Affairs movement and modern Chinese enterprises) (Peking: Chung-kuo she-hui k'o-hsueh ch'u-pan-she, 1979); Fan Chen-kan, Ch'ing-chi kuan-tu shang-pan ch'i-yeh chi-ch'i kuan-shang kuan-hsi (Official-merchant relationships in the *Kuan-tu shang-pan* enterprises, 1873–1911), Ph.D. dissertation, National Taiwan University, 1986.

17. Chung-li Chang, *The Income of the Chinese Gentry* (Seattle: University of Washington Press, 1962), 197.

18. The Wu family was the richest of the Hong merchants. H. B. Morse reports that Howqua (of the famous Wu family) had twenty-six million Mexican dollars in 1834. Morse believes that Howqua had "probably the largest mercantile fortune in the world." See H. B. Morse, *The International Relations of the Chinese Empire* (London, 1910), 1:86.

19. On the rise of mercantile capitalism in China, see Hao, *Commercial Revolution*.

20. Hao, *Compradore*, 104–5.

21. Etienne Balazs, *Chinese Civilization and Bureaucracy* (New Haven: Yale University Press, 1964), 154.

22. See Ping-ti Ho, *The Ladder of Success in Imperial China: Aspects of Social Mobility, 1368–1911* (New York: Columbia University Press, 1962).

23. According to Hilary Beattie, Yeh Hsien-en (Ye Xianen), Li Wen-chih (Li Wenzhi), and Mary Rankin, a large amount of the Chekiang and Anhwei (Hui-chou and T'ung-ch'eng) merchants' capital was spent on lineage-building and buying official titles. See Hilary Beattie, *Land and the Lineage in China: A Study of T'ung-ch'eng County, Anhwei, in the Ming and Ch'ing Dynasties* (Cambridge: Cambridge University Press, 1979); Yeh Hsien-en, *Ming-Ch'ing hui-chou nung-ts'un she-hui yü tien-p'u chih* (Ming-Ch'ing peasant society and tenant system) (Anhui: Jen-min, 1983); Li Wen-chih, "Lun Ming Ch'ing shih tai ti tsung-tsu chih" (The lineage system in the Ming and Ch'ing

period), *Chung-kuo she-hui k'o-hsueh yuan ching-chi yen-chiu so chi-k'an* (Peking: 1983), 4:278–338, Mary B. Rankin, *Elite Activism and Political Transformation in China* (Stanford: Stanford University Press, 1986).

24. Chung-li Chang, *The Income of the Chinese Gentry*, 139–41; Dwight H. Perkins, *Agricultural Development in China, 1368–1968* (Chicago: Aldine, 1969), 93–95.

25. *Shen pao*, May 21, 1878, 2.

26. See *LWCK Memorials*, 31:5–6. Rankin's recent work notes that Hu donated around 30,000 taels in 1878. See Rankin, *Elite Activism*, 143.

27. Rankin, *Elite Activism*, 153.

28. Yen-p'ing Hao's recent work (*Commercial Revolution*, 345) points out that the annual interest rate was about 12 percent between 1820 and 1880. Hao notes: "This rate [12 percent] was somewhat higher than that in contemporary Europe (6–8 percent), but was substantially lower than the prevailing rate in both traditional China (usually 40 percent or more) and the interior in modern time (35–50 percent or more)." On the other hand, Rankin (*Elite Activism*, 149) provides a case that "some small Ning-po banks failed because they had to pay up to 0.145 percent interest a day (53 percent a year) to keep accounts." The 53 percent interest rate in Ning-po was certainly an extreme case because the interest rate fluctuated daily (see *SHCCSL*, 39, 628–42). But even at 12 percent the interest rate was still high compared to that in Europe. According to Sidney Homer, the short-term interest rates of English banks varied from 2.49 percent to 4.81 percent between 1872 and 1885. See Homer, *A History of Interest Rates* (New Brunswick: Rutgers University Press, 1977), 209.

29. *NYSTL*, 563–66. The highest rate was more than 100 percent per year in some remote regions (see *NYSTL*, 574–76).

30. Ibid., 571–73. In inscriptions concerning pawnshops on stone tablets in Shanghai in 1906, the regulated interest rate was 2 percent per month for loans secured on pawned goods. See *Shang-hai pei-k'o tzu-liao hsuan-chi* (Selected epigraphic materials from Shanghai) (Shanghai: Jen-min, 1980), 410. According to Lien-sheng Yang, "Rates of interest in pawnbroking were fixed by regulations promulgated by various local governments. In general, the ceiling rate was 3 percent per month in the eighteenth century, and 2 percent after the nineteenth century. The rate, however, varied with the size of the loan." See Lien-sheng Yang, *Money and Credit in China: A Short History* (Cambridge, Mass.: Harvard University Press, 1952), 98.

31. Kwang-Ching Liu, "Tong King-sing: His Compradore Years," 156–57.

32. There were 9,904 pawnshops in all of China in 1723, 19,000 by the mid-eighteenth century, and by the early 1800s around 25,000. See T. S. Whelan, *The Pawnshop in China* (Ann Arbor: Center for Chinese Studies, University of Michigan, 1979), 1, 10.

33. Wang Ching-yü, "The activities of Chinese merchants in foreign enterprises"; Chi-ming Hou, *Foreign Investment and Economic Development 1840–1937* (Cambridge, Mass.: Harvard University Press, 1965).

34. As William T. Rowe has written, "It became common practice for Chinese businessmen to set up bogus 'foreign firms' (*Yang-hang*), in which a Western front man was registered as principal owner when in fact he was merely a salaried clerk employed for the sole purpose of signing Transit Pass (*yang-p'iao*) applications." See William Rowe, *Hankow: Commerce and Society in a Chinese City: 1706–1889* (Stanford: Stanford University Press, 1984), 84.

35. Hao (*Commercial Revolution*, 355) estimates that "by the last decade of the Ch'ing period the Chinese capital in foreign firms totaled more than 16,000,000 taels." Wang Ching-yü ("The activities of Chinese merchants in foreign enterprises," 528) estimates that Chinese merchants invested 40,000,000 taels in foreign firms by the end of the nineteenth century.

36. *Chiu-shih chieh yao*, in Cheng Kuan-ying, *Cheng Kuan-ying chi* (Collected works of Cheng Kuan-ying) (Shanghai: Jen-min, 1982), 1:54.

37. Ibid. In his letter to the Expectant Taotai Yeh T'ing-chüan written around 1880, Cheng stated, "I have heard the reason why the Chinese merchants' companies could not bring about prosperity: because the state only oppressed merchants and did not protect them." See Cheng Kuan-ying, *Sheng-shih wei-yen hou-pien* (Warnings to a prosperous age, a sequel) (Shanghai: 1920), 8:3b.

38. In his memorial to the throne dated July 26, 1873, Li stressed, "At present, along the several thousand li of our coasts are to be found numerous foreign ships. This is unprecedented in all of our history. Since it is no longer possible for us to tend to our affairs behind closed doors, we ought to take advantage of the sea-route transport facilities and expand them by degrees, so as to open new channels of commerce and increase the stock of military supplies. At present, the tribute rice of Kiangsu and Chekiang is entirely transported by sea. Your servant invited Chinese merchants to participate in this transport; the result has been successful." See *LWCK Memorials*, 22:14.

39. See *HFT*, 1:870–81, 3:925; *LWCK Memorials*, 20:31, Yung Wing, *My Life in China and America* (New York: Henry Holt, 1909), 171–72. Also see Lü Shih-ch'iang, *Chung-kuo tsao-ch'i ti lun-ch'uan ching-ying* (Early steamship projects in China) (Taipei: Institute of Modern History, Academia Sinica, 1962), 184–224.

40. *YWYT*, 5: 105–28. Also see David Pong, "Keeping the Foochow Navy Yard Afloat: Government Finance and China's Early Modern Defense Industry, 1866–75," *Modern Asian Studies*, 21, 1 (1987): 135–42.

41. In the reign of Emperor Tao-kuang (1820–1850), the native junks numbered more than three thousand, but there were two thousand between 1850 and 1860 and only four hundred remaining around 1873. See *LWCK Letters*, 12:29; *British Parliamentary Papers, China 6 (1874): Embassy and Consular Commercial Reports* (Ireland: Irish University Press, n.d.), 134; *HYSTL*, 1317.

42. As the British consul, Chaloner Alabaster, remarked in his report on the trade in Ning-po in 1873: "The establishment of a Chinese line of steamers I have noticed elsewhere, but it is of political as well as commercial importance, the chief avowed object of the Viceroy of Chihli in establishing it having been the diminution of foreign influence and interest on the coast." See *British Parliamentary Papers, China 6 (1874): Embassy and Consular Commercial Reports*, 87.

43. *LWCK Letters*, 12:31 (December 11, 1872). For the English translation of this letter, see Liu, chapter 3 above, 62.

44. *HFT*, 1:904.

45. *LWCK Memorials*, 20:32b. Also See Wang Ching-yü (Wang Jingyu), "Birth of the Chinese Bourgeoisie," *Chinese Studies in History* 17,4 (1984): 38–39.

46. *LWCK Memorials*, 20:32b. Also see *LWCK Letters* 12:29.

47. *CTSHCP*, I, chapter 2, 140; *LWCK Letters*, 12:28–30, 36, 13:1; *HFT*, 1:910. Also see Kwang-Ching Liu, "British-Chinese Steamship Rivalry in China, 1873–1885," in *Economic Development of China and Japan: Studies in Economic History and Political Economy*, ed. C. D. Cowan (London: George Allen & Unwin, 1964), 53.

48. *CTSHCP*, I, chapter 2, 140; *HYSTL*, 789; *CSCPKS*, 2:18.

49. In December 1872, Li had secured the agreement of the Kiangsu and Chekiang authorities to have 20 percent of their annual shipment of tribute rice transported by the China Merchants' Company. See *LWCK Letters*, 12:29, 34; *HFT*, 3:926.

50. *HFT*, 1:923.

51. See Liu, chapters 2 and 3, above.

52. The prospectus of the China Merchants' Company issued by Tong and Hsu in 1879 also says: "For each share a scrip certificate will be issued, on which, to prevent

foreigners from borrowing a Chinese name in order to possess a share, will be clearly written the name and birthplace of the owners. . . . Transfer to third parties is only allowed with sanction by the head-office and never in any case to foreigners." *CTSHCP*, I, chapter 2, 144; *NCH*, April 21, 1877, 390. According to Hsü Jun, "The original regulations were: if someone wanted to transfer the ownership of shares to another person, he should give priority to transferring them to the China Merchants' Company itself; this would have the effect of preventing shareholders from selling the shares to foreigners and from returning the shares whenever they like. It means that the shares will be sold and registered by the China Merchants' Company." See *HYSTL*, 1156.

53. Article 4 of the "Regulations" of the China Merchants' Company mentioned an annual dividend [*li-yin*] of 10 percent, and stated that the amount of extra dividends would be decided by the shareholders.

54. *LWCK Letters*, 13:2, 13; *British Parliamentary Papers, China 6 (1874): Embassy and Consular Commercial Reports*, 85.

55. *CTSHCP*, I, chapter 2, 140.

56. *LWCK Letters*, 12:36–37.

57. *CSCPKS*, 2:19.

58. Tong became the chief compradore of Jardine, Matheson and Company in 1863 and also served as a director of three shipping companies and as director of the Canton guild of the tea and silk trades. See Liu, "Tong King-sing: His Compradore Years"; Wang Ching-yü, *T'ang T'ing-shu yen-chiu* (Studies on T'ang T'ing-shu) (Peking: Chung-kuo she-hui k'o-hsueh, 1981).

59. *Shen pao*, September 17, 1874. Hsü Jun's appointment was doubtless related to the fact that he was one of the largest shareholders.

60. Tseng Kuo-fan had approved such an idea. See *NCH*, April 12, 1877, 371.

61. The company's fleet that year included *I-tun* (507 net tons), *Yung-ch'ing* (661), *Fu-hsing* (532), *Li-yün* (734), *Yung-ning* (324), *Tung-t'ing* (315), *Ho-chung* (849), *Fu-yu* (920), and *Li-hang* (131). Liu, "British-Chinese Steamship Rivalry," 76.

62. *Fu-hsing* was lost in an accident.

63. These six new ships were *Han-yang* (404), *Ta-yu* (419), *Jih-hsin* (754), *Hou-sheng* (795), *Pao-ta* (870), and *Feng-shun* (863). See Liu, "British-Chinese Steamship Rivalry," 76–77.

64. The company's report for 1877 stated, "The prolongation of the Yunnan disagreement over the spring and winter of last year; the famine in the South and drought in the North during the spring and summer of this year causing a stagnation in trade; and the reduction of freights by foreigners, and the heavy rate of interest prevailing this year." See *NCH*, April 12, 1987, 371.

65. *HYSTL*, 1157.

66. These two river steamers were *Chiang-k'uan* (1,030 net tons) and *Han-kuang* (838). In the same year, *I-tun* was dismantled.

67. According to the Annual Report and Accounts of the company for the year ended on August 8, 1877, "there [was] a marked element of danger in the use of borrowed capital where loans [were] made, as in China, not on debentures having a fixed term to run, with a fixed rate of interest, but on day-to-day terms with fluctuating interest." *NCH*, November 1, 1877, 392.

68. In his memorial to the throne dated May 5, 1880, Li noted: "The China Merchants' Company is different from government agencies which are provided for by public funds. But the founding of the company is very important to the purpose of recovering economic control (*li-chüan*), and would help state finance and people's livelihood. Therefore, the company needs the government's support. To make up for the inadequacy of merchant funding, the company needs to borrow money from the govern-

ment." See *LWCK Memorials*, 36:35.

69. *LWCK Tsungli Yamen Letters*, 7: 21; *HFT*, 3:975f; *NCH*, April 12, 187, 372.

70. The steamships purchased from the Shanghai Steam Navigation were *Chiang-hui* (1,172 net tons), *Chiang-piao* (879), *Chiang-t'en* (1,079), *Chiang-ching* (1,084), *Chiang-yüan* (768), *Chen-hsi* (561), *Chen-tung* (724), *Hai-ch'en* (763), *Hai-yen* (710), *Huai-yüan* (1,115), *Hai-san* (574), *Hai-ting* (649), *Chiang-ch'ang* (806), *Mei-li* (181), *Chiang-t'ung* (339), and *Chiang-fu* (857). *HFT*, 3:946–47; also see Liu, "British-Chinese Steamship Rivalry," 77.

71. *HFT*, 3:946–47; Lai. "The Proposal to Nationalize," 22.

72. *LWCK Memorials*, 40:23; also see Feuerwerker, *China's Early Industrialization*, 125.

73. *LWCK Letters*, 17:13; *HFT*, 3:939–82.

74. *LWCK Letters*, 16:37–38.

75. Liu, "British-Chinese Steamship Rivalry," 60.

76. Two ships, *Hou-sheng* and *Chiang-ch'ang*, were lost in 1878.

77. *LWCK Memorials*, 30:33.

78. Ibid., *LWCK Memorials*, 40:23b.

79. *LWCK Letters*, 17:27; *HFT*, 3:981. Also see Liu, "British-Chinese Steamship Rivalry," 60–66.

80. *LWCK Letters*, 17:27; *LWCK Memorials*, 30:30, 36:32, *HFT*, 3:975.

81. *HYSTL*, 921–23.

82. *LWCK Memorials*, 30:31; 36:32–34.

83. Hsia Tung-yuan (Xia Dongyuan), *Wan-Ch'ing yang-wu yun-tung yen-chiu* (Studies on the Western Affairs movement in late Ch'ing China) (Szechwan: Jen-min, 1985), 182–84.

84. *NCH*, October 3, 1879, 331.

85. *NCH*, September 30, 1880, 302. Sources indicate that 50,000 taels were subscribed by Chinese in Siam and 65,200 taels by those in other Southeast Asian ports as well. See *HYSTL*, 982–88.

86. Feuerwerker, *China's Early Industrialization*, 124.

87. Lai, "The Proposal to Nationalize," 35.

88. *NCH*, October 18, 1882, 418–20.

89. Feuerwerker, *China's Early Industrialization*, 124.

90. See *LWCK Memorials*, 19:48; *LWCK Letters*, 12:31 (December 11, 1872); Kwang-Ching Liu, The Creation of the China Merchants' Steam Navigation Company, 1872–1874 (manuscript), 5–6.

91. *YWYT*, 6:9–10.

92. *NCH*, April 12, 1877, 370.

93. The decline of freight rates from Shanghai to the other treaty ports in the mid-1870s were, for example, as follows: Ning-po, from $2.5 to $0.50; Yangtze freights (to Hankow), from 5 taels to 2 taels; Tientsin freights, from 8 taels to 5 taels. Passenger fares were reduced by 50 percent and even by 70 percent of former rates. See *NCH*, April 12, 1877, 370.

94. *YWYT*, 6:9–10.

95. *LWCK Letters*, 14:7, 18–19.

96. Ibid., 18:4–5; *LWCK Memorials*, 27:29–30; 30:32; 31:5–6.

97. *LWCK Memorials*, 30:31, 36:32–33.

98. *HFT*, 3:979–82; *HYSTL*, 923–35. Also see Lai, "The Proposal to Nationalize," 23.

99. Lai, "The Proposal to Nationalize," 19.

100. Ibid., 23; *HYSTL*, 914–19.

101. The company's report published in April 1877 reveals an ambiguous aspect of the government deposit: "It is not stated what rate of interest is paid on the public monies;

the total amount is 20,820 taels, which, taking the average of deposits, would be about 8 percent. The report states, however, that at one time the government advanced 700,000 taels; the rate of interest, therefore, must have been lower; so that it would seem the Chinese government borrows money from foreigners at 10 percent or more, in order to lend to this company at a loss." *NCH*, April 21, 1877, 389.

102. Ibid.

103. Liu K'un-i, *Liu Chung-ch'eng kung i-chi* (Collected papers of the late Liu K'un-i) (c.1909; Taipei: Wen-hai reprints) *Letters*, 6:45.

104. Ibid.

105. *LHCCC*, 525.

106. Wang Erh-min and Chan Sin-wai, comps., *Chin-tai ming-jen shou-cha chen chi: Sheng Hsüan-huai chen ts'ang shu-tu ch'u-pien* (Authentic letters from the hands of eminent men in modern China: The first selections from Sheng Hsüan-huai's own archive) (Hong Kong: Chinese University Press, 1987), 2:863–64, *Shen pao*, March 16, 1875, 1.

107. *LWCK Memorials*, 36:33.

108. *HYSTL*, 909–11.

109. *LWCK Letters*, 15:11.

110. *HYSTL*, 1000; Kwang-Ching Liu, "Steamship Enterprise in Nineteenth-Century China," *Journal of Asian Studies, 18 (1959), 440.* These nine new ships were *Chiang-p'ing* (392 net tons), *Mei-fu* (793), *Chih-yuan* (1,177), *P'u-ch'i* (631), *Kung-pe* (692), *T'u-nan* (942), *Chiang-yü* (2,270), *Fu-shun* (1,504), and *Kuang-li* (1,508). See Liu, "British-Chinese Steamship Rivalry," 77.

111. *HYCNP*, 87–88; Liu, "British-Chinese Steamship Rivalry," 69.

112. Kwang-Ching Liu, "Steamship Enterprise in Nineteenth-Century China," 452.

113. *CTSHCP*, I, chapter 2, 143–46. English translation of both documents is from Liu, The Creation.

114. *CTSHCP*, I, chapter 2, 145.

115. Ibid., 143.

116. Ibid.

117. *HYSTL*, 1156.

118. *CTSHCP*, I, chapter 2, 145.

119. Ibid.

120. *Sheng Hsüan-huai Archives*, cited in Liu, The Early History of the China Merchants' Company.

121. Hsia Tung-yuan's *Wan-Ch'ing yang-wu yun-tung yen-chiu*, 250–76; also see *Sheng Hsüan-huai tang-an tzu-chiao hsüan-chi* (Compilation of selected materials from the Sheng Hsüan-huai Archives), 2:456.

122. *LWCK Letters*, 17:41–42.

123. Liu, "The Early Hitory of the China Merchants' Company."

124. Shen T'ung-sheng et al., eds., *Kuang-hsü cheng-yao* (Important policies of the Kuang-hsü reign) (Shanghai: Nan-yang kuan shu chü, 1909; Taipei reproduction, Wen-hai, 1969), 12:1–4.

125. *Shen pao*, July 9, 1877, 1.

126. Ibid., 854–55.

127. Lai, "The Proposal to Nationalize."

128. *Liu Chung-ch'eng kung i-chi: Letters*, 8:17.

129. *HYCNP*, 86; *Sheng Hsüan-huai Archives*, cited in Liu, The Early History of the China Merchants' Company.

130. *Sheng Hsüan-huai Archives*, cited in Liu, The Early History of the China Merchants' Company.

131. *Liu Chung-ch'eng kung i-chi: Letters*, 7:64–65 (letter dated October 3, 1880).

132. Ching Yuan-shan, *Chu-i ch'u-chi* (The works of Ching Yuan-shan) (Macau, 1901), 2:38.

133. *Chin-tai ming-jen shou-cha chen chi*, 6:2711–12.

134. *Shan-tung t'ung-chih* (Shantung provincial gazetteer) (Taipei: Hua-wen reprint of 1915 edition), 1812–13.

135. Chin Yuan-shan, *Chu-i ch'u-chi*, 1:31.

136. *Kuang-hsü cheng-yao*, 12:1–4.

137. The state in the modern era is treated by Weber as a rationalized bureaucratic organization operating according to legal and procedural guidelines. Douglass North has pointed out that the state could reduce transaction costs in order to foster maximum output of the economy and provide a legal framework for commercial development, such as property rights. See Douglass C. North, *Structure and Change in Economic History* (New York, W. W. Norton, 1981), 24; North "Government and the Cost of Exchange in History," *Journal of Economic History*, 44, 2 (1984): 255–64.

138. In his *Economic Backwardness in Historical Perspective*, Alexander Gerschenkron argues that economic development in backward countries substantially benefits from a strong state that intervenes in economic activities. He notes, "Economic development in a backward country such as Russia can be viewed as a series of attempts to find—or to create—substitutes for those factors which in more advanced countries had substantially facilitated economic development, but which were lacking in conditions of Russian backwardness,. Such substitutions are the key to an understanding of the way in which the original disabilities were overcome and a process of sustained industrial growth was started. It is these acts of substitution that came to determine the specific pattern of industrial development in Russia." See Gerschenkron, *Economic Backwardness in Historical Perspective* (Cambridge, Mass.: Harvard University Press, 1962), 123.

139. To explain the interrelationship between state making and capitalist development in modern Europe, Charles Tilly points out that modern national states have taken on tasks ranging from state making, war making, and protection to extraction, and that the state makers and their policies have purposefully or unintentionally reshaped many aspects of capitalist development. Tilly reduces the process of state making to the operation of state economic interest. When the national states began to grow, the state makers always extracted the resources from the subject population and therefore created the tension between expanding states and capitalists' interest. See Charles Tilly, ed., *Formation of National States in Western Europe* (Princeton, N.J.: Princeton University Press, 1975); Tilly, "Space for Capital, Space for States," *Theory and Society* 15 (1986): 301–309.

140. For recent works using Charles Tilly's state-making model, see Rankin, *Elite Activism*; Susan Mann, *Local Merchants and Chinese Bureaucracy, 1750–1950* (Stanford: Stanford University Press, 1987); and Prasenjit Duara, *Culture, Power, and the State: Rural North China, 1900–1942* (Stanford: Stanford University Press, 1988).

141. *Cheng Kuan-ying chi*, 1:611. Also see Chan, *Merchants, Mandarins, and Modern Enterprise*; Hsia Tung-yuan, *Cheng Kuan-ying chuan* (A biography of Chen Kuan-ying) (Shanghai: Hua-tung shih-fan ta-hsueh, 1985); and Yen-p'ing Hao, *Commercial Revolution*.

12

Li Hung-chang and the Peiyang Navy

Chia-chien Wang

After the Opium War (1839–42), the Chinese literati-officials began to realize that it was impossible for China to defend herself against the Western maritime powers without a strong and effective navy. The establishment of a modern navy became an urgent and persistent concern in China's struggle to Westernize. Lin Tse-hsü (1785–1850) was the prominent Chinese official who recognized the importance of having such a navy during his painful encounter with the British over the opium issue. He once proposed to use the excise tax revenue of Kwangtung province to purchase Western guns and ships as a first step toward modernizing the Chinese navy.[1] Unfortunately, his proposal was rejected by Emperor Hsuan-tsung and was of no avail. Wei Yuan (1794–1857), Lin's good friend, brought up the issue in his *Hai-kuo t'u-chih* (Illustrated gazetteer of the maritime countries) and urged the authorities concerned to build state-run ship-yards and arsenals to make guns, cannon, and vessels at Sand Point (Sha-chiao) and Big Point (Ta-chiao) in Kwangtung province. Wei's plan was to overhaul and reorganize the water force of the Green Standard Army (Lü-ying) as a new and powerful navy, under the control of the provinces of Kiangsu, Chekiang, Fukien, and Kwangtung.[2] But without the government's support, the whole plan was little more than empty talk, a proposal that came to nothing.

A new opportunity arose in the first year of the T'ung-chih reign, 1862. Minister Wen-hsiang of the Tsungli Yamen sought the help of Horatio Nelson Lay, who was head of the Imperial Maritime Customs service. Through Lay's good offices, the Ch'ing government purchased seven warships from England, and established a small "Anglo-Chinese fleet." The Tsungli Yamen appointed Sherard Osborn, a British captain, as head of the fleet. To their mutual disappointment,

---

The Chinese version of this article appeared in *Li-shih hsueh-pao* (Bulletin of historical research), no. 16 (June 1988): 91–105.

248

however, the British and the Chinese could not agree over the allocation of authority. The plan ended in failure.[3] Subsequently, Ting Jih-ch'ang (1823–1872), governor of Kiangsu, proposed, in 1868 and 1870, respectively, a Water Force under Three Commands (*San-yang shui-shih*) and a River and High Seas Water Force (*Nei-chiang wai-hai shui-shih*). In the same period, new arsenals and shipyards had been set up in Shanghai (1865) and Foochow (1866). However, owing to the lukewarm support of the government and the poor leadership of the high officials concerned, no substantial progress was made. It was not until 1874, the year the Japanese invaded Taiwan, that the Ch'ing government resolved to reform and consolidate its coastal defense forces. Coastal defense was then divided into two commands, the Nanyang and the Peiyang. The governor-general of Liangkiang was appointed imperial commissioner in charge of the coastal defense of the four provinces of Kiangsu, Chekiang, Fukien, and Kwangtung; the governor-general of Chihli province was made imperial commissioner in charge of the defense of Shantung, Chihli, and the southern area of Manchuria.[4] Even so, the Chinese navy had not been strengthened significantly. According to the report of Thomas Wade, the British minister to China in 1878, the Chinese navy was composed only of small local fleets stationed in Shanghai and Foochow. Its facilities and training were by no means comparable to those of European navies.[5] There was, in fact, no unified navy for the empire, and it was in this condition that China entered the Sino-French War, during which the Chinese navy in the South was totally lost.

Eventually, however, under the leadership of Li Hung-chang, the Peiyang command was modernized and came to be regarded as the new navy of the Ch'ing Empire in the later 1880s. It was known as the Peiyang Fleet or the Northern Naval Squadron. The historical background of the Peiyang Navy was complex. Its success or failure not only was crucial to Chinese coastal defense but also affected the balance of seapower between China and Japan. This modernization effort is worthy of historians' close attention. As the founder of the Peiyang Navy, Li was responsible for its success in more ways than one. His objectives and his experience in establishing the navy, the frustration and hardship he encountered, were all intertwined with the squadron's destiny. This chapter will attempt to analyze the various factors involved.

Li's perception of a modern navy and his objectives

Li Hung-chang, born in Hofei, Anhwei province, in 1823, was the leader of the self-strengthening movement. He was statesman and diplomat, as well as a military strategist. Remarkably versatile, Li had a hand in almost every aspect of China's modernization and his influence was considerable in the government of the period. This chapter, however, will focus only on Li's role in the building of the navy.

The origins of the modern Chinese navy can be traced to the period when Li was an assistant to Tseng Kuo-fan in the military operations against the Taipings.

Li became an expert in military affairs and realized the importance of having a navy. He was recommended by Tseng to be Commissioner of the Salt Administration at Lianghuai, in charge of the naval unit at Huai-yang.[6] Li's knowledge of naval affairs was limited in this period to the traditional Chinese water force; as yet, he knew little about the navies of modern Western powers. It was not until the spring of 1862, when he was ordered to come to the aid of Kiangsu province in the struggle against the Taipings, that he came to realize the challenge of the European navies. It fell upon Li to lead the Anhwei troops, as well as the Huai-yang sailors, on a journey by hired British steamers from Anking down the river to Shanghai. Subsequently, Li fought in collaboration with British and French troops in Shanghai and was assisted by the Ever-Victorious Army. He was very impressed by the excellence of Western cannon, the precision of the rifles, and the pomp of the Western drill formation. He felt deeply that China was much inferior to the Western powers in military capability.[7]

The Huai-yang navy that Li commanded was composed of sampans and junks. He was profoundly aware that these were obsolete as naval vessels. He said: "It makes no difference whether you have these junks or not."[8] Li was determined to learn from other nations; he advised his subordinates "to be humble and patient and learn one or two secrets from foreigners."[9] In his discussion with his superior, Tseng Kuo-fan, Li presented the same point of view: "If our weapons can compete with foreigners, we will not only be able to suppress internal rebellion but will also be strong enough to fight against foreign aggressors. . . . If we have howitzers and steamships, the foreign countries might as well give up." Li urged Tseng to "follow Japan and Russia as models, to take strong leadership and be humble in order to learn secrets from the foreigners. Only when we do that can China become truly independent a hundred years from now."[10]

In October 1864, when the Taipings were about to be completely subdued, Chinese officials and commoners were congratulating themselves on the prospect of peace and prosperity after years of internal turmoil and external menace. Li thought otherwise. He had deep worries. In a letter to a friend, he wrote that "the foreign weapons and soldiers are a hundred times better than ours. . . . We will not be able to stop their arrogance." Li felt that "Our army might be capable of putting down domestic rebellion, but it will not be able to fight the enemy from outside. If we cannot strengthen ourselves in time, reform our military system, and improve our weapons, if we still follow the practice of using the army of the Green Standard, it will be like placing wood near a furnace; the situation will be extremely dangerous." In Li's opinion, military capability was part of "the foundations of a country, and it is crucial to our control of the barbarians. The current situation is very different from that of the past; we should not be confined to our ancestors' methods." Regarding the army, Li felt the old and the weak should be dismissed, the soldiers' pay and rations should be amply provided for, the troops should be given strict discipline, and the small outposts of the Green Standard Army should be reorganized and consolidated. Only then might the Green Standard Army be dependable. As for the navy, all the old-fashioned ships had to be replaced. Moreover, China had to have modern dockyards and purchase shipbuilding machinery from foreigners. Steamships had to be built first, "then steamships carrying artillery. Only then would the navy be dependable."[11] From the sources cited above, we can see that Li already had a picture in mind of a new army and navy for China. His idea of a Chinese navy included the reform of the Green Standard water force, the adoption of Western-style equipment, and the establishment of modern shipyards and arsenals that could produce modern ships and cannon. Li's ideas were analogous to Wei Yuan's idea of "learning from the barbarians' special techniques in order to control the barbarians." Subsequently, the shipyard at Foochow and the arsenal at Kiangnan were maintained with Li's support. He deserves credit for his role in the modernization efforts of the 1860s and 1870s. (See above, chapters 4 and 10.)

After Li Hung-chang became governor-general of Chihli in 1870 and concurrently the commissioner of trade for the Northern Ports, his thinking about the navy underwent further changes. He realized even more clearly than before that China was surrounded by fierce enemies. The country was in danger. He felt deeply that China was confronted with "the greatest change in its situation in three thousand years."[12] Moreover, the Japanese invasion of Taiwan in 1874 led him to believe that Japanese militarist ambitions toward China were more threatening than the menace of the Western countries. Western countries were aggressive but they were far away, whereas Japan was right at China's doorstep and would take advantage of any opportunity for aggression. Li believed that Japan was to be "a great threat to China sometime in the future."[13] After he received the imperial commission to superintend the coastal defenses of the Northern Ports, he set it as his goal to cope with the challenge of Japan. The development of a navy was a top priority in Li's policy regarding foreign relations and self-strengthening.[14] In his opinion, guns, ships, and navies were the great strengths of Western powers. It would take a long time for China to catch up with the West. Japan had learned from the Western countries only recently, so it would be easier for China to compete with Japan.

Li's policy for a navy that would defend China against the Japanese is of great historical significance. Of course, among the leaders of the self-strengthening movement, Li was not the only one with such insight. Wen-hsiang, Shen Pao-chen, and others also held the same view. Li's idea of establishing a Chinese navy with Japan as the assumed enemy was shared by at least a few statesmen of the time.[15]

It must, however, be observed that Li's idea of a navy was limited by the strategy of self-defense. Li did not have an aggressive view of seapower. Although he had the vision of training a powerful navy, including ironclads, to dominate the seas south of China and to confront Japan and Korea, his main purpose was defense rather than offense; indeed he saw military strength chiefly as a deterrent.[16] He was still under the influence of the traditional Chinese concept of China as a land power. Japan, however, was different. In the beginning, Japan, like China, paid attention only to coastal defense. Subsequently, partly owing to the influence of Alfred Mahan, the American naval strategist, the Japanese concept of seapower underwent a tremendous change. The Japanese government instilled in the people the appreciation of seapower. At the same time, urgent plans were made for overseas expansion. China, on the other hand, had been using the book *On New Coastal Defense*, by a Prussian author, as the guide for its naval strategy. In the end, Li was satisfied with the defense of a few ports, guarding Peking in the north and the fiscally rich areas in the south, without the ambition of extending naval power to the high seas. The geographical and historical differences between China and Japan could account for the difference in attitudes. Different concepts led to divergent development of the navies in China and Japan.[17]

**Purchasing warships and cannon—
the founding of the Peiyang Navy**

The Northern Naval Squadron was founded later than the Southern Naval Squadron. When Li Hung-chang was appointed governor-general of Chihli in September 1870, there were no modern warships in the three important ports in the North Seas. It was not until October 1872 that Li, as commissioner of trade for the Northern Ports, arranged to have two ships, the *Ts'ao-chiang* and *Chen-hai*, transferred from the Nanyang command to Tientsin to patrol the seas.[18] In May 1874, the Japanese invaded Taiwan. Li was greatly aroused and strongly urged buying ironclads to strengthen coastal defense. Yet his suggestion could not be put into practice immediately.[19] Li did not take aggressive action until May 1875, when he was authorized, as superintendent of coastal defense of the Northern Ports, to inaugurate formation of a new navy. During the period of more than a decade that followed, several millions of taels were expended on procuring various types of warships, including ironclads, cruisers, and torpedo boats, for the Peiyang Navy.

The Peiyang Navy was to consist of twenty-six warships which could be divided into two categories: those built in China and those bought from foreign countries. The former category was smaller in number and less important. These warships accounted for 34.6 percent of the total, and there were nine of these in all: *K'ang-chi, Wei-yüan, T'ai-an, Chen-hai, Ts'ao-chiang, Mei-yün, Li-yün, Hai-ching*, and *P'ing-yüan. P'ing-yüan* was an ironclad built by the Foochow shipyard; the other eight were support ships, training ships, and freighters. The other category of warships was considered the main squadron. There were seventeen of these, including *Ting-yüan, Chen-yüan, Chi-yüan, Chih-yüan, Ching-yüan, Lai-yüan, Tsing-yüan, Chen-an, Ch'ao-yung, Yang-wei, Chen-tung, Chen-hsi, Chen-nan, Chen-pei, Chen-chung, Chen-pien*, and *Min-chieh*. Comprising 65.4

percent of the entire fleet, the seventeen ships were built abroad, thirteen in England and four in Germany. They were either battleships, cruisers, or other warships, except for one, *Min-chieh*, which was a motor junk used for drill. *Chen-yüan* and *Ting-yüan* were built by the Vulcan shipyards in Germany and were each 298 feet, 5 inches long; 60 feet, 4 inches wide; and 19 feet, 6 inches in draft. The reinforced middle part of the hull was 144 feet long and 14 inches thick, the shielding of the gun deck was 12 inches thick, and that of the commander's deck, 8 inches thick. Both ships had 6,000 horsepower and a speed of 14.5 nautical miles per hour. They each carried ten cannon, including four heavy ones with a caliber of 12 inches installed front and back. Other artillery on each of these ships included ten five-barrel Gatling guns, 525 breechloading Gatling guns, and torpedoes. The two warships were very powerful and were considered of superior quality by international standards.[20]

Apart from the two battleships, at least a number of the vessels were well equipped and battle worthy. *Chih-yüan* and *Tsing-yüan* were purchased from England, as were *Ch'ao-yung* and *Yang-wei*, built by Armstrong & Co.; *Chi-yüan* and *Ching-yüan* were built in Germany. Six Chinese-built ironclads were also fit for battle. The founding of the Northern Naval Squadron was the result of considerable painstaking effort on Li's part.

Li was also interested in fast torpedo boats. He believed that defense and offense could be effective only when torpedo boats and ironclads were used at the same time. He purchased in 1881 ten torpedo boats from Vulcan of Germany;[21] in 1887 his representative signed a contract with a naval yard in England for a first-class, high-seas torpedo boat of the latest style (125 feet long, 13 feet wide, 1,000 horsepower, drawing 6 feet and 6 inches, with a speed of 25 miles per hour), at a cost of 2,500 pounds (more than 85,700 taels).[22] The torpedo boats were put under the torpedo-boat commands in Weihaiwei and Port Arthur, respectively, and the crews were trained by British and German experts. The two groups of torpedo boats were an integral part of the Peiyang Navy, although they did not prove useful in the Sino-Japanese War of 1894. Among the ships in the Peiyang Navy, twelve mosquito gunboats bought from Britain through Robert Hart proved to be a disappointment and incurred much criticism. Not only did the twelve gunboats cost a great deal but the guns were too large for the small ships, resulting in instability. They were of little use on the high seas. Li shook his head in regret when he talked about them.[23]

Naval schools and training

A modern navy is the product of Western technology, and it involves many fields of knowledge. It is more difficult to establish a navy than an army, because of the highly technical requirements of navigation, training, and deployment. Li knew this well and often exhorted the naval officers and men to learn from Western methods and to specialize. He urged them to "study with care and train properly" and to keep up their practicing and be ready for battle.[24] When a newly bought warship arrived, Li would go to the harbor and examine it personally, in order to gain an understanding of the capabilities of the ship and its artillery.

Li retained a number of foreign officers to help in training personnel, and he wanted the pilots, engineers, firemen, and crews to be experienced men. Li went about the building of the navy systematically and carefully. He spared no expense in sending hundreds of naval officers and men to England and Germany to man the newly purchased men-of-war on their voyages to China, so as to give them practice.

Li was convinced that naval academies were of fundamental importance.[25] To the Foochow shipyard, established in 1866, was affiliated an academy for the training of naval officers. Li utilized many graduates of this academy in the Peiyang Squadron. However, the Foochow Academy could not actually meet the new squadron's needs. Moreover, there was an imbalance between southern and northern native-place origins within the Peiyang Navy, the majority of the personnel being from Foochow. In 1880, Li founded the Northern Naval College in Tientsin to train northern students. Up to the Sino-Japanese War of 1894, some 300 cadets graduated from the Tientsin Naval College and other northern academies. During the same period, there were 630 cadets who graduated from the Foochow Academy, twice the number of those from the north. Students from the Foochow shipyard continued to be employed not only by the Peiyang Squadron but also by the Nanyang Squadron. Because of their history and larger numbers, those from Fukien comprised the majority of the Peiyang Navy officers.[26]

Chinese naval academies provided only basic and general training. Li was insistent on sending naval students abroad, especially for studies relating to navigation. From 1877 to 1890, three groups totaling thirty-five naval cadets were sent to England. Some went to the Royal Naval College in Greenwich, some to the Royal Artillery Academy in Woolwich, and still others had experience serving in the British Navy. These cadets returned to occupy superior positions in the Peiyang Navy, and came to be entrusted with important responsibilities. Foremost among them were Liu Pu-ch'an and Lin T'ai-tseng. Of the thirty-five students sent to England, 89 percent (thirty-one) were from the Foochow Shipyard Academy. The other four were from Tientsin Naval Academy, but even among them one was a Cantonese. Clearly Southerners formed the vast majority of the Peiyang officer corps.[27]

Selecting senior officers and organizing the fleet

Besides purchasing ships and guns and arranging training of naval personnel, Li Hung-chang paid much attention to the selection of commanding officers. This, however, was a difficult task, because in China naval matters had not been assigned to a specialized profession as in Western countries. As seen above, a number of students from the Foochow Shipyard had studied abroad. But because of their relative youth and lack of experience, they were not qualified to be the commanding officer. It seems that Li had no choice but to designate Ting Ju-ch'ang, a Huai Army veteran, commanding admiral. Ting was a strong, honest, and courageous officer, experienced in the army but lacking the necessary qualifications in naval affairs.[28] Li found it necessary to employ foreign experts to assist Ting, creating a fundamental problem for the Peiyang Squadron. In 1879, Li appointed three Englishmen, captains Clayson, Cocker, and Johnstone, as instructors for the Peiyang Navy, with Clayson as chief instructor. The three captains proved to be unsuitable, because their experience had been entirely on merchant ships and not on naval vessels.

Subsequently, Li replaced them with William M. Lang, another Englishman. A graduate of the Royal Naval Academy, Lang had served as a captain in the British Navy. He was a dedicated and responsible officer with considerable experience. He was the logical first choice as chief inspector of the Peiyang fleet, and was appointed twice, in 1882 and again in 1885, serving a total of six years. Under his careful planning and direction, the Peiyang Navy made great progress, and won considerable foreign and domestic attention. Lang was forced to leave Peiyang in 1890, when he was outmaneuvered by some of the Chinese officers in the notorious "Flag-hoisting controversy."[29] After Lang's departure, other foreign officers were hired by Li for the Peiyang Navy: two from Britain, two from the United States, and four from Germany. None of them, however, had Lang's talent and skills, nor were they given equivalent power and authority to correct the problems and attitude within the fleet. The Peiyang Navy deteriorated after 1890.[30]

The formal establishment of the Peiyang Squadron did not come until 1888. There were several reasons for this delay. The ships purchased from foreign countries took some time to arrive. Li initially was not certain how the fleet should be organized and deployed. Since the 1860s, three separate naval plans had been proposed: the "River and High Seas" (Nei-chiang wai-hai) plan, drawn up by Tseng Kuo-fan; the Three Coasts Command (San-yang) plan, devised by Ting Jih-ch'ang; and the Peiyang Navy plan, drafted by Li's advisor Hsueh Fu-ch'eng.[31] All three plans were insufficiently concrete, so the formal organization of Li's Peiyang fleet was much delayed. In March 1888, after being urged by the court to take action, Li ordered his subordinates—Tientsin customs official Chou Fu, Peiyang Admiral Ting Ju-ch'ang, captains Liu Pu-ch'an and Lin T'ai-tseng, and the Peiyang Navy's managing circuit-intendant Lo Feng-lu—to consult with William Lang. The document establishing the structure of the Peiyang Navy was drawn up three months later. Finally, after Li had discussed the proposal with the president of the Board of the Navy, Prince Ch'un, the document was approved by the throne and promulgated in August 1888.[32] The plan followed the structure of the traditional Green Standard water force and that of the Yangtze Navy (Ch'ang-chiang shui-shih), but it also borrowed selectively from the naval organizations of Britain, France, and Germany.

According to the system worked out, the Peiyang Navy was divided into a front squadron and a rear squadron. The former was the main battle unit of the fleet. It was made up of nine battalions (each battalion consisting of one ship) divided into the middle, the right, and the left wings. The rear squadron provided logistic support and was responsible for the training and supply of the entire fleet. It was made up of 16 torpedo units. The Peiyang Navy had by then more than 30 warships, aggregating more than 41,000 tons, 120 guns, and more than 4,000 crew members.[33] Apart from foreign experts, there were eighty-seven superior officers, including engineers. Forty-three of them, nearly half the total, were formally trained: thirty-five graduated from the Foochow Shipyard Academy (40 percent) and eight from the Tientsin Naval College (9 percent). Twenty-four of these studied abroad: thirteen in Britain, ten in the United States, and one in Germany. Among those not formally trained abroad, several had been to England, France, or Germany on short tours for observation, helping to superintend shipbuilding or sailing back to China with the ships. It is obvious that as a group, the officers were more qualified than their peers in the Green Standard water force or in the Yangtze Navy.[34]

Initially the Peiyang fleet did not have a standard training procedure. Only with the publication of the *Pei-yang hai-chün chang-ch'eng* (Regulations of the Peiyang Navy) were there regulations for the following eight procedures: *hsiao-ts'ao* (small exercises), *ta-ts'ao* (large exercises), *hui-ts'ao* (joint exercises), *hui-shao* (joint cruising), *ho-ts'ao* (joint drill), *ts'ao-hsun* (cruising drill), *hsun-li* (parade inspections), and *chiao-yueh* (great parade inspections).[35] On each occasion, merits and demerits were recorded, and rewards and punishments dealt out accordingly. Not only were regular exercises stressed, the fleet was regularly dispatched on cruises along the entire China coast. In addition, it visited Vladivostok and Korean ports and went as far south as Singapore and Southeast Asian waters.

The Peiyang Navy succeeded for a time in maintaining Chinese seapower in northeast Asia. But with the departure of Lang in 1890, there was no one to supervise the training of the force and it deteriorated. Li Hung-chang was aging. He was kept busy with other pressing matters, and he did not have time to spare for the details of naval affairs.[36]

Fortifying naval bases

A modern navy must have bases, fortified for protection, with docks and shipyards for the maintenance and repair of ships. The line of defense of Peiyang (the North Sea) runs from the mouth of the Yalu River to Kiaochow Bay, encompassing a considerable range of coastal waters. The ports therein, including Tsingtao, Yentai (Chefoo), Weihaiwei, Talien, Port Arthur, Yingkou, Shanhaikuan, Peitang, and Taku, needed to be fortified. Because of budgetary limitations, however, Li Hung-chang could build fortifications only selectively: Taku, Weihaiwei, and Port Arthur received the lion's share of his attention. Let us look at each of these cases.

Taku

This base served as the port of Tientsin, where the Peiyang Navy's headquarters were located. Therefore, Tientsin and Taku were of special importance to the navy. Many important naval institutions were situated there, such as the Taku Shipyard, the Tientsin Arsenal, the Tientsin Naval College, and the Peiyang Military Academy, as well as the headquarters of the torpedo and mining battalions, the telegraph office and academy, the coal storage facility, and the naval hospital and medical academy. Taku and Tientsin, then, formed the base area of the Peiyang Navy.[37]

Weihaiwei

Located at the northern edge of the Shantung Peninsula, Weihaiwei, together with Talien and Port Arthur, controls the entrance to Po-hai Bay, the approach to the metropolitan area around Peking. Within the spacious Weihaiwei harbor lies Liukung Island and its adjacent deep waters, forming an excellent shipyard site. Li Hung-chang, because of budgetary constraints, did not turn his full attention to Weihaiwei until February 1887, when he sent Tai Tsung-ch'ien and Liu Han-fang there to make a survey. In Weihaiwei fortifications were built, as well as an arsenal, a torpedo factory and academy, an ammunition depot, and coal storage facilities. A metal wharf for loading coal was built under the direction of a German engineer.[38] The following year, a headquarters of the Peiyang Squadron was established on Liukung Island. Subsequently, under Admiral Ting Ju-ch'ang, the Peiyang Naval Academy and a naval hospital were set up in Weihaiwei, further enhancing its importance.

Port Arthur

This strategic base, long nicknamed the "Gibraltar of the East," is at the very tip of the Liaotung Peninsula. Li had long been aware of its importance. Large units of the Huai Army were stationed in the region. The base was fortified and torpedo and mining battalions were installed, but the dockyards involved very difficult engineering. Yuan Pao-ling was appointed initially to head the Port Arthur engineering bureau. Then it was taken over by a French syndicate. The entire project was finally completed in 1890, after ten years and at a cost of some three million taels. Especially impressive was the stone wharf, of larger than usual dimensions. The importance of Port Arthur can be seen by the stipulation in *Regulations of the Peiyang Navy* requiring senior officers of the fleet to spend six months a year there. Port Arthur was the most important base in the iron triangle of Port Arthur, Weihaiwei, and Taku.[39]

It has been a subject of controversy ever since the late Ch'ing whether a naval port should indeed have been developed at Port Arthur. Some have claimed that Tsingtao would have been a better location for a naval port. Others have blamed Li Hung-chang for choosing Port Arthur because of personal considerations. I believe that building a naval port at Port Arthur was not a mistake. It is reasonable to surmise that it was primarily because of budget limitations that Li did not also build a fortified port at Tsingtao. Such an inference is strongly supported by Li's own statement at the time: "Tsingtao is one of the first-rate deep-water bays in north China . . . yet because of financial limitations we have no way to develop it for the time being."[40]

Insuperable difficulties and the inevitable collapse

The Peiyang Navy was planned in 1875 and formally established in 1888. Unfortunately, it was destroyed completely by the Japanese navy in the first Sino-Japanese War (1894–95). Li's efforts were completely in vain. The Peiyang Navy's defeat resulted in China losing her seapower. The military situation on the Liaotung Peninsula was also changed, and China's situation for the ensuing decades was adversely affected. How did all this happen?

The destruction of the Peiyang fleet can be attributed in part to the strategy of passive defense adopted by the Ch'ing government.[41] However, the Peiyang Navy itself had several serious defects. First, there was the matter of institutional ambiguity. The Peiyang Navy was nominally subordinate to the Naval Yamen at Peking. Because the president of the Yamen, Prince Ch'un, was completely ignorant of naval matters, the fleet was actually under Li Hung-chang's management. Li was a loyal official, but he was responsible for many pressing matters. These included diplomatic relations and defense both on land and the high seas, as well as his domestic duty of being the governor-general of Chihli and, in fact, the leader of the governors and governors-general. With political problems arising daily, he was too busy in the late 1880s and early 1890s to pay more than peripheral attention to the Peiyang Navy.

Second, there was an unclear chain of command. Because Li could not always pay attention to it, the Peiyang Navy was managed by Ting Ju-ch'ang. Ting had no formal training in naval affairs. Consequently, he was generally looked down on by his subordinate officers, most of whom were graduates of Chinese naval academies. Some of the foreign officers whom Ting relied on were arrogant and overly demanding. There was constant, unpleasant tension between these foreign officers and the Chinese officers; the "Flag-hoisting controversy" was symptomatic of this.[42] The resultant dismissal of Lang led to further deterioration and corruption within the Peiyang Navy.[43]

Third, insufficient finances were a serious problem. Initially, 2 million taels were budgeted annually for coastal defense, but the amount was never completely forthcoming. Pursuant to the subordination of the Peiyang Navy to the Naval Yamen, the fleet's annual budget was reduced to less than 1.3 million taels.[44] Worse still, in April 1891, the Board of Revenue (Hu-pu) recommended against the purchasing of large guns for the battleships and for the reduction of naval personnel. These proposals were approved by the throne.[45] This made it virtually impossible to renovate the fleet and its equipment.[46] Those who were aware of the situation at the time worried about the viability of the Peiyang Navy itself.[47] During the Sino-Japanese War, the Peiyang Navy suffered defeat and indeed total disaster. Lack of discipline led some units to desert in the heat of battle.[48] The Peiyang Navy's shortcomings were completely revealed.[49] Li, fully cognizant of these shortcomings, consistently sought to avoid war and confrontation with the enemy fleet. For this he has been castigated by many historians. In light of the Peiyang Navy's weaknesses, however, it is doubtful whether a more courageous policy or strategy would have made a difference.[50]

Conclusion

In response to the rising seapower of Western nations, and provoked especially by the growing threat of Japan, China decided to build a navy. Li Hung-chang was the right man in the right place, and he took this monumental responsibility on himself. A number of scholars have contended that Li established the Peiyang Navy primarily to solidify his own power base and, under the pretext of dealing with external aggression, actually to enhance the power of the Huai Army.[51] From the historical perspective, I find this interpretation highly speculative and lacking sufficient evidence.

The modern navy was an innovation of the nineteenth century. Naval development required sophisticated equipment and highly specialized technical and scientific knowledge. Considering all aspects—industry, science and technology, personnel, and finance—China at the time was quite unqualified to support a modern navy. It was only through the almost single-handed efforts of Li Hung-chang that the Peiyang Navy even came into existence. With ten years of continuous effort, he had created a fleet of 30 warships, 120 guns, and 4,000 officers and men, superior, at least numerically, to Japan's naval forces.[52]

Li's task was far more difficult than one can imagine today, for he faced the multiple tasks of seeking funds from the government in Peking and persuading other provincial officials to cooperate, while warding off a constant stream of criticism from several sources. The weakness of the central government in Peking is well known. The Ch'ing government, as a whole, saddled Li with many obstacles. It was riddled with bureaucratic abuse, provincialism, and factional infighting. The Peiyang Navy itself suffered from inadequate organization and obsolete equipment. Under the circumstances, Li's naval efforts should be judged not against an impossible ideal but rather within the entire context of the internal situation at the time.

Notes

1. See Lin Tse-hsü, *Lin Wen-chung kung cheng-shu* (Political papers of Lin Tse-hsü) (Taipei: Wen-hai, 1967), part 2, 4:20.
2. Wei Yuan, *Hai-kuo t'u-chih* (Illustrated gazetteer of the maritime countries) (Taipei: Ch'eng-wen, 1966, reprint of 1847 edition), 2:35–52.
3. John L. Rawlinson, "The Lay-Osborn Flotilla, Its Development and Significance," *Papers on China* (Harvard University), 4 (1950): 58–93.

4. *Ch'ing Te-chung ching huang-ti shih-lu* (Veritable records of the Kuang-hsü reign) (Taipei: Hua-wen, 1964), 8–9. Edict of 4/26.

5. Public Record Office F.O. 17/782, 152: 172–73. Wade to Salisbury, August 27, 1878.

6. Tseng Kuo-fan, *Tseng Wen-chung kung ch'üan-chi* (Collected papers of Tseng Kuo-fan) (Taipei: Wen-hai, 1974), *Tsou-kao* (*Memorials*), 11:82–83b.

7. Li Hung-chang, *Li Wen-chung-kung ch'üan-chi* (Collected papers of Li Hung-chang) (Nanking, 1905), *P'eng-liao han-kao* (Letters to friends and colleagues, hereafter cited as *LWCK Letters*), 2:46b.

8. Ibid., 2:1.

9. Ibid., 2:47.

10. Ibid., 3:17, 19.

11. Ibid., 5:34.

12. Li Hung-chang, *Li Wen-chung-kung ch'üan-chi, Tsou-kao* (*Memorials*, hereafter cited as *LWCK Memorials*), 19:45.

13. Ibid., 24:26.

14. Ibid., 39:33.

15. On Wen-hsiang's views, see Chou Chia-mei, *Chi pu-fu chai ch'üan-chi* (Collected writings of Chou Chia-mei) (Taipei reprint: Kuang-wen, 1972), 40–45; on Shen Pao-chen's views, see Ch'ih Chung-yu, *Hai-chün ta-shih-chi* (Major naval events) (Taipei reprint: Wen-hai, 1975), entry for 1874, 4.

16. *LWCK Letters*, 20:33.

17. On the transformation of Japanese naval thinking, see Ogasawara Nasei, *Teikoku kaigun shiron* (Historical essays on the Imperial Navy, 2d printing, Tokyo 1899), preface. Chinese naval thinking was influenced by a German work rendered into Chinese as *Fang-hai hsin-lun* (New treatise on maritime defense); see *LWCK Memorials*, 24:16. The Chinese were also influenced by a British parliamentarian who argued that small gunboats were most effective for such defense. See Wang T'ao, *T'ao-yuan wen-lu wai-pien* (Essays of Wang T'ao: A supplementary collection) (Shanghai, 1897), 3:16–18.

18. *LWCK Memorials*, 20:7.

19. Ibid., 24:16.

20. Ibid., 55:16.

21. Ibid., 56:18.

22. Ibid., 62:40.

23. Liu K'un-i, *Liu Chung-ch'eng kung shu-tu* (Letters of Liu K'un-i) (Taipei: Wen-hai, 1968), 17:2–3.

24. *LWCK Memorials*, 55:18.

25. *LWCK Memorials*, 52:9.

26. Sources available in Archives of the former Naval Ministry. See especially Military Science category, *P'ien-i* division, vol. 320, *Chiao-lien*, no. 31: *Ma-wei hai-chün hsueh-hsiao* (Foochow Naval Academy), ed. Liang T'ung-i, including an annual list of graduates. See also ibid., vol. 361, no. 32: *T'ien-tsin shui-shih hsueh-t'ang shih-lueh* (Brief history of the Tientsin Naval Academy), ed. Li Chao-t'ang. The last source includes not only data on the graduates of the naval academy in Tientsin but also on those of the academy at Kunming Lake in Peking, of the Torpedo School in Lushun, and of the Weihaiwei Naval Academy. Cadets from these academies, because of their junior status, enjoyed only the lower ranks in the Peiyang Navy.

27. See Wang Chia-chien, *Chung-kuo chin-tai hai-chün shih lun-chi* (Studies on the history of the modern Chinese Navy) (Taipei: Wen-shih-che, 1984), 27–59. In addition to cadets sent to England, some were sent to France and specialized in shipbuilding; among them a few were to enter the service of the Peiyang Navy.

28. *LWCK Memorials*, 25:24.

29. The "Flag-hoisting" controversy occurred on March 6, 1890, when the Peiyang squadron was in Hong Kong. Admiral Ting Ju-ch'ang, commanding four naval ships, was on an expedition to Hainan. Lang was in charge of the other ships in Hong Kong and, as usual, the admiral's flag was hoisted. Captain Liu Pu-ch'an and other officers took down the flag on the grounds that Lang was not an admiral. The conflict between Lang and the younger officers of the Peiyang Navy thus came to the surface. Lang failed to obtain Li's support on this matter and resigned indignantly. See Wang, *Chung-kuo chin-tai hai-chün*, 75–82.

30. For the Peiyang Navy's history after Lang's resignation, see ibid., 82–86.

31. Hsueh Fu-ch'eng, *Yung-an wen-chi wai-pien* (Hsueh Fu-ch'eng's writings, a supplementary collection) (Shanghai, 1893), 1:24–30.

32. See inter alia Chou Fu, *Tzu-ting nien-p'u* (Chou Fu's chronological autobiography) (Taipei: Kuang-wen, 1971), 1:24; *Kuang-hsü ch'ao Tung-hua hsü lu* (Tung-hua record of the Kuang-hsü period, 1875–1908) (Taipei: Ta-tung, 1968), 27:22.

33. Chang Hsia et al., *Ch'ing-mo hai-chün shih-liao* (Sources on the history of the late Ch'ing navy) (Peking: Hai-yang, 1982), 472–503: "Pei-yang hai-chün chang-ch'eng" (Regulations of the Peiyang Navy). According to the estimates of Kuo T'ing-i (Kuo Ting-yee), the Peiyang Navy comprised several types of warships totaling 40,000 tons, more than 120 artillery guns, and officers and men more than 4,000 strong. See Kuo T'ing-i, *Chin-tai Chung-kuo shih-kang* (Outline of modern Chinese history) (Hong Kong: The Chinese University Press, 1979), 256.

34. I will discuss this in my *Pei-yang hai-chün shih-kao* (Draft history of the Peiyang Navy), manuscript.

35. See "Pei-yang hai-chün chang-ch'eng," cited in note 33.

36. Liu Pu-ch'an and Lin T'ai-tseng both belonged to the first group of graduates of the Foochow Naval Academy sent to England. Liu became captain of the right wing (*yu-i tsung-ping*) and Lin captain of the left wing (*tso-i tsung-ping*) of the Peiyang Navy, both occupying a position in the hierarchy outranked only by Admiral Ting. Because Ting was not versed in naval matters, power gravitated to Liu and Lin.

37. *LWCK Memorials*, 17:16–27, 36; 18:20–21, 38:16–17, 32–33; 40:46–47, 50; 42:10; 44:22–23; 46:39–40; 48:33–35; 53:29, 42–43; 67:11–12.

38. Ibid., 57:34; 60:9–10; 71:35; 72:9–14.

39. Ibid., 66:3; 69:31–34; Wang, *Chung-kuo chin-tai hai-chün*, 95–146.

40. *LWCK Memorials*, 71:45. Critics of the policy at the time included Hsü Hsueh-ch'eng, who was minister to Germany, and Chu I-hsin, censor of the Shensi circuit; see Wang *Chung-kuo chin-tai hai-chün*, 128–33. The modern scholar Ma Yu-yuan believes that Li was selfish in building a base in Lushun; see my forthcoming work cited in note 34.

41. See inter alia Wu Ju-sung and Wang Chao-ch'un, "Shih-t'an chia-wu chan-cheng Pei-yang hai chün ti shih-yung wen t'i" (A tentative appraisal of the utilization of the Peiyang Navy in the War of 1894), in *Chung-Jih kuan-hsi shih lun-ts'ung* (Articles on Sino-Japanese relations) (Liao-ning: Jen-min, 1982), 110–21.

42. Ch'i Ch'i-chang, "Kuan-yü Pei-yang chien-tui ti chi-ko wen-t'i" (On a few problems regarding the Peiyang squadron), ibid., 99–109.

43. Yao Hsi-kuang, *Tung-fang ping-shih chi-lueh* (A brief record of the war in the East) (Shanghai, 1894), 4:4b; Kuo T'ing-i, *Chung-kuo chin-tai shih-kang*, 257.

44. Li Hung-chang, *Li Wen-chung kung ch'üan-chi, Hai-chün han-kao* (Letters to the Navy Yamen), 10–11.

45. *LWCK Memorials*, 72:5–36.

46. Ibid., 78:1.

47. Yao Hsi-kuang, *Tung-fang ping-shih*, 4:4b.

48. *LWCK Memorials*, 78:52–53, 61.

49. See Sun K'e-fu, "Ting Ju-ch'ang yü Chung-Jih chia-wu chan-cheng" (Ting Ju-ch'ang and the Sino-Japanese War of 1894), in *Chung-Jih kuan-hsi shih lun-ts'ung*, esp. 51.

50. See Wu Ju-sung and Wang Chao-ch'un, "Shih-t'an chia-wu," 114, referring to the desertion during the battle of Ta-tung-kou of *Chi-yuan*'s Fang Po-ch'ien, *Ming-chieh*'s Wu Ching-yung, and others.

51. See inter alia Wang Ch'eng-jen and Liu T'ieh-chün, "Lun yang-wu p'ai hsing-chien hai-chün ti mu-ti ho tso-yung" (On the goals and consequences of the Western Affairs clique's naval buildup), *Wu-han ta-hsueh hsueh-pao: She-hui k'o-hsueh pan* (Journal of Wuhan University: Social Sciences edition), no.3 (1986), esp. 109.

52. See above, note 34.

Part VI
Conclusion and Bibliography

13

Li Hung-chang: An Assessment

Samuel C. Chu

China in the year 1775 was a great empire. Under the long and dynamic reigns of the K'ang-hsi and Ch'ien-lung emperors the country had expanded its boundaries in all directions. It had a long and illustrious history. Its population, largest by far among all other peoples for centuries, enjoyed a relatively high standard of living. China was powerful, rich, and the cynosure of all the world, or so it seemed. Yet by 1900 the nation had been utterly humiliated, her sacred capital of Peking defiled under the boots of the eight "barbarian" nations in the wake of the Boxer debacle. By then, world opinion regarded China as another fading empire like that of the Persians, the Romans, and the Ottomans; the self-assurance of the Chinese themselves was severely shaken. The nineteenth century was a tragic period in Chinese history.

Twentieth-century China had seen a decided turnaround in her fortune and reputation. Nevertheless historians of China, especially those in the People's Republic, still have difficulty explaining China's near-collapse during the previous century. There is a tendency to assign blame—to the imperialist Western powers, to the "feudal" system, to the Manchu overlords of the Ch'ing dynasty, and to the class of Confucian scholar-officials who loyally supported the traditional system under the dynasty. Among these scholar-officials none served longer, or had more impact on the early stages of the transformation of China, than did Li Hung-chang. Yet precisely because of his prominence in Chinese politics from the decade of the 1860s to his death in 1901, Li has been judged harshly by historians ever since. Why has this largely negative assessment lasted so long? What accounts for the relative neglect of one of the key individuals in modern Chinese history?

One of the reasons is that, for any scholar studying Li and his times, the relevant source materials are overwhelming. A second reason is that, since Li's death, the vicissitudes of Chinese history have not been conducive to a more sympathetic assessment of his career.

Sources relating to Li are readily available, but they are not easy to use. All who work in nineteenth-century Chinese history recognize that the *Li Wen-chung kung ch'üan-chi* (*LWKC*), the collected papers of Li Hung-chang, though by no means complete, represents a formidable corpus of primary sources. This basic collection is currently being enlarged in a more accessible version from the People's Republic of China under the title *Li Hung-chang ch'üan-chi*. As important as *LWKC* is, there are many other primary sources from Li himself and from those with whom he dealt. To name just a few, there are his correspondence with Pan Ting-hsing (*Li Hung-chang chih P'an Ting-hsing shu-cha*), his correspondence relevant to the navy (*Li Wen-chung kung hai-chun han-kao*), and such other selected collections of Li documents as *Li Hung-chang chuan-chi tzu-liao*. Substantial portions of his writings can be found in the major historical source compendia, *Yang-wu yun-tung* (The Westernization movement) and *Chung-Jih chan-cheng* (The Sino-Japanese War). There is also a large number of documents on persons who interacted with Li throughout his long career, from his original benefactor Tseng Kuo-fan to such protégés as Sheng Hsuan-huai and Ma Chien-chung. Because of the vast and varied body of sources pertaining to Li, few scholars can claim to have mastered the relevant materials completely.

Research aids on Li are still inadequate, but we do have a few basic research tools. In 1977, Lei Lu-ch'ing published a chronology of Li in his edition of *Li Hung-chang nien-p'u*, which supplements but by no means replaces the much more detailed chronology edited nearly a decade earlier by Tou Tsung-yi (*Li Hung-chang nien-jih-p'u*). Even the 1955 aid to Li memorials, *Li Hung-chang tsou-yi mu-lu*, compiled at Tokyo from limited sources, can still be referred to for certain purposes.

The second reason why historians have long held a jaundiced view of Li Hung-chang is related to the major changes that have taken place in China since his time. From the twentieth century point of view, he was a man who supported the discredited Manchus; indeed he was instrumental in prolonging the life of the Ch'ing dynasty. He shared some of the less savory characteristics of nineteenth-century high officials. He was involved in unsuccessful negotiations with Western imperialist powers and Japan. For these reasons, among historians since the establishment of the Republic in 1911, and even more so after the founding of the People's Republic in 1949, Li acquired the reputation of a corrupt feudal reactionary and an abject "surrenderist" to the imperialists. Only in the decade of the 1980s has Li's reputation been partially restored. It seems few comparable historical figures have been so controversial.

We believe it is high time to take another look at Li Hung-chang. In the preceding chapters, Kwang-Ching Liu has led off our study by first locating Li within the broad context of China's nineteenth-century efforts at change. He then analyzes Li's early career, to the time of Li's successful suppression of the Nien Rebellion. This is followed by his evaluation of Li in the beginning of a long tenure as governor-general of Chihli province. Liu shows clearly the astonishing range of Li's activities, and the vigor and determination with which Li carried them out. From his "regional" base, Li increasingly was serving in the capacity of an official of the central government. As such, Li had frequent dealings with a number of powerful fellow officials. David Pong examines Li's long relationship with one of them, Shen Pao-chen, and rightly reminds us that credit for Li's success in the self-strengthening movement should be shared by Shen and others. One important advantage Li had was his continuing influence over the lower Yangtze valley, his home region and his earlier area of jurisdiction. The elements of Li's influence are analyzed by Yuen-sang Leung. In turn, Richard Smith shows Li's early willingness to learn from the West, first in military expertise.

As a diplomat, Li Hung-chang, even though he became involved in China's relationships with a number of nations, concentrated on his special assignment of dealing with Japan and Korea. Key-Hiuk Kim scrutinizes Li's policies and actions up to the conclusion of the U.S.-Korea treaty of 1882, and Ming-te Lin carries on the analysis from that time to the outbreak of the Sino-Japanese War in 1894. Although the two scholars do not always agree in their treatment of Li, together they demonstrate how Li, while faced by changing circumstances which dictated his taking up different policy options, maintained a consistent policy goal through the entire period. Edwin Leung's examination of the Liu-ch'iu controversy takes up Li's Japan policy in a specific dispute, rendering concrete some of the issues that characterized the larger Chinese-Japanese relationships.

As a modernizer, Li was heavily involved in many projects of the self-strengthening movement, which spanned the decades of the 1860s to the 1890s. Thomas Kennedy analyzes Li's first important enterprise, the Kiangnan Arsenal. One of his longer-lasting successes was the China Merchants' Steam Navigation Company. Chi-kong Lai reexamines in detail the nature of this enterprise and Li's key role in attracting private participation in its operations. The military counterpart to the China Merchants' Company was the Peiyang Navy. Chia-chien Wang examines Li's contributions to its origin and maintenance, and suggests that a modern navy's technical demands required Li to adopt Western methods in a more thoroughgoing manner. Together the two institutions, one civilian and one military, constitute case studies of Li's major modernizing endeavors. Their successes and failures are symptomatic of the successes and failures of the entire self-strengthening movement. They also delineate the parameters of Li's achievements and limitations.

Because our study is focused primarily on Li's dual role as modernizer and diplomat, let us first examine him in these two roles separately. I shall then place Li in the larger perspective of his entire career, confronting directly some of the charges that have been made against him.

Li as modernizer

Li Hung-chang was the single most important Ch'ing official in the self-strengthening movement. He was among its earliest leaders and did far more for it than any of his peers. To the extent that the self-strengthening movement can be regarded as an early phase of China's modernization, Li has a strong claim to being China's leading modernizer of his time.

In social science research, the concept of modernization has gone through a full cycle of acceptance and neglect. It had a high period of currency in the 1950s, when political scientists, economists, and anthropologists first became excited about studying the process of nation-building. This was a time when a number of former colonies in Asia and Africa achieved their independence following World War II. The term *modernization* was initially applied primarily to newly emerging independent nations, such as Burma and Ghana. It was later extended to the study of established Asian countries, such as China, which had previously undergone similar processes. Because the historical experience of these nations encompassed many different and interlinked aspects, narrower terms such as *industrial growth* seemed inadequate to explain the entire historical phenomenon. At the time even scholars in the so-called harder social sciences, such as economics, considered modernization a useful concept.

Now, more than thirty years later, the term *modernization* and the related term *modernizer* are in ill repute, abandoned by the economists and other social scientists on the grounds that they are too imprecise. Many historians also have come to avoid them. Instead, more limited terms, such as *economic change, industrialization,* and the like, are preferred. We have, however, found the terms *modernization,* and *modernizer* especially appropriate for the historical approach to Li Hung-chang. He is more than just an advocate of economic change, an industrialist, or a political reformer. He is all of these, and more. A subject such as Li requires an attempt at synthesis. Li is truly nineteenth-century China's modernizer par excellence. He was involved in every aspect of the self-strengthening efforts. He initiated most of them, pleaded for them with the throne, obtained early funding, provided legal and political protection, brought in needed technologies, and linked up all these components. Thus, as a modernizer, Li served the necessary catalytic function of an entrepreneur, in the classic Schumpeterian sense.

As shown by Kwang-Ching Liu, Li Hung-chang's modernizing efforts covered a wide spectrum of activities. He, with Tseng and Tso, founded virtually all of China's early arsenals and shipyards. He also modernized mines. Later he set up a shipping company, telegraph lines, and textile mills. He went beyond manufacturing and communications into educational concerns. Although he was committed to the inherited system of education, he suggested that the testing of Western technical knowledge be added to the civil service examinations. Together with Tseng, he sponsored students who traveled to the United States. Although these educational efforts did not go far enough, Li's work in promoting manufacturing and transportation enterprises did achieve solid results. In Chi-kong Lai's closer examination of the China Merchants' Company, Li is shown to be instrumental in setting up the *kuan-tu shang-pan* format for joint government-private enterprises. Li understood, as few other officials did, the investment patterns that attracted private investors. He protected the merchant managers of the company from the interference of bureaucratic officials. The company's subsequent decline can be traced directly to the time when Li, because of his preoccupation with other pressing duties, had to play a lesser role in company affairs. This pattern of the China Merchants' Company's growth and decline was repeated in other Li-initiated enterprises, underscoring the importance of Li as a modernizer.

Li as diplomat

Li Hung-chang has long been recognized as having played a large role in formulating and implementing nineteenth-century China's foreign policy. And it is to a great extent because of his diplomatic record that he is sharply condemned by many historians. Just as Li's modernizing role needs to be reexamined, a reassessment of Li as diplomat is long overdue.

As we have seen, from 1860 on, China's relations with foreign nations were handled by a new agency, the Tsungli Yamen. It, however, was not an autonomous government office, remaining functionally a suboffice of the Grand Council. Moreover, from its very establishment the Tsungli Yamen never had the complete power of a modern foreign ministry. That power was shared with the many governors and governors-general of the coastal provinces. A particularly apt example was Liu K'un-i, who from 1875 to 1902 served several terms as the governor-general of Liangkiang. Liu, who dealt most of the time with problems of internal administration, was not especially interested in foreign affairs. His jurisdiction, however, extended over the coastal region of the lower Yangtze valley, which necessarily required Liu to take charge of the foreign relations of his region. Other high regional officials of coastal provinces (Kwangtung, Fukien, and Shantung) did likewise. To this extent they shared the power of the Tsungli Yamen in the formulation and execution of China's foreign policy.

More important than mere regional officials, however, were the two new offices created at the same time as the Tsungli Yamen, namely, the commissioners of trade for the Northern and Southern Ports, respectively. These two commissioners, given wide latitude in handling China's foreign trading relationships, not only were designated specifically to share in the Tsungli Yamen's prerogatives but were actually thought of as more important in carrying out foreign policy. The above-mentioned Liu K'un-i, while serving as the governor-general of Liangkiang, held also the office of Commissioner of Trade for the Southern Ports. Li Hung-chang, with his Northern commissioner's office located in the strategic city of Tientsin, played an increasingly crucial role in diplomatic affairs. While he worked in tandem with the Tsungli Yamen for years, in time he superseded it in importance. This was as much the result of Li's personal qualities as of his official position. After the Tsungli Yamen had lost the service of the able Wen-hsiang (1818–1876) through death and that of Prince Kung (1833–1898) through political disgrace, foreign emissaries found Li more open and decisive than the Yamen officials. It became customary for foreign emissaries to tarry for a few days in Tientsin to see Li, before proceeding on to Peking. Not only did they realize that the Court would inevitably ask for Li's opinion at some stage of the deliberations but their very initial success in approaching the Ch'ing Court depended on their being able to get a sense of China's sentiments by the substance and tenor of Li's statements. Geography, politics, and personal qualities combined to make Li the indispensable figure in China's diplomacy.

Because Li played such a key role as a diplomat, his actions should be judged within the context of China's global posture as a whole. For China to join the "family of nations" in the latter nineteenth century was a daunting task. At the very time when China was abandoning her tributary system (except toward Korea), the West was entering the most competitive period of imperialism. As William Langer's classic book, *The Diplomacy of Imperialism*, well points out, it was not enough for China to learn the Western system of diplomacy (by the 1880s it had done that), but China had to operate from a position of weakness against powerful Western adversaries. Therefore, China's relationship with Western nations could not be that of equal partners. Li Hung-chang had to act within these severe constraints.

At various times Li served either in an advisory or a direct diplomatic capacity. The indirect role is evident in his dealings with France at the time of the Sino-French War. As is shown by Lloyd Eastman in his *Throne and Mandarins*, Li, although not directly involved in the war, tried to end it through the proposed Li-Fournier Convention. The Court, however, rejected this compromise in 1884, only to see it serve as the basis for the final Paris Treaty ending the war in 1885. Another example of Li playing an advisory role in foreign policy is in the 1881 settlement of the Ili dispute, where Tso Tsung-t'ang's bellicose policy was balanced by the Court with Li's more conciliatory one. Li, however, played a more direct role in dealing with Korea and Japan. Matters relating to Korea, as a former Chinese tributary state, had been handled traditionally by the Board of Rites. In 1879 the Court officially assigned Li to take charge of Korean affairs. Even though Li agreed strongly with Peking in wishing to maintain the tributary format with Korea, he came to realize that relations between China and Korea now had to be a part of the larger relationships involving China, Japan, and the powers. Following the suggestions of Ting Jih-ch'ang and others, Li strongly urged Korea to sign treaties with the United States and the European nations to resist Japan's newly aggressive policies. He further carried out this shift in China's Korean policy by sending Yuan Shih-k'ai as China's officially designated resident in Korea, a new post. He sent others to Korea as additional advisers to the Korean court. In all these decisions Li was the primary policymaker.

Nor did he limit his direct diplomatic role to China's close neighbors. On many occasions he initiated discussions with representatives from Britain, France, Russia, and other countries. One of his most intriguing relationships was with the United States. Li had sought American mediation as early as 1874. Later he was to repeat such initiatives several times. Michael Hunt, in his *Making of a Special Relationship*, emphasizes that the United States was one of Li's favorite diplomatic recourses. Li sought America's good offices thrice during the period of 1880 to 1894: During the Liu-ch'iu dispute with his overture to former President U.S. Grant, during the Sino-French War, and on the eve of the War of 1894. Unfortunately, all these initiatives failed.

Inasmuch as Li was given the specific charge of dealing with Korea and Japan, other high Court officials, especially Li's rivals, seized on this as an area of Li's vulnerability. He had scores of rivals at Court and among the regional officials. Especially troublesome was the group of young traditionalist officials known collectively as the *ch'ing-liu* or purist faction, who were engaged in *ch'ing-i* or "highminded discussion." They managed to stymie Li at several critical junctures during those decades. So while Li had a strong influence on China's foreign policy, by no means did he have a complete free hand when specific policies were being decided.

Li in the larger perspective

As stated earlier, the discussion of Li Hung-chang in this volume has been confined largely to his roles as a diplomat and as a modernizer. But even an assessment of Li serving in these two roles requires us to take into account the many other facets of Li's overall career. The present focus of this study precludes analyzing Li's other facets in detail, but a summary recapitulation of his life will provide us a larger perspective.

Born twenty-four years after the great Ch'ien-lung emperor's death, and nineteen years before the Treaty of Nanking, Li had an early education not significantly different from those of other young scholars. Kwang-Ching Liu has suggested, however, that Li was strongly inclined toward the statecraft tradition, one that departed from purely scholarly pursuits to deal with practical problems. As it turned out, the times were especially suitable for a person with Li's proclivities. He matured at a time when the empire was facing unprecedented change. Early success in the examinations opened for Li the door to an official career, but the Taiping uprising changed his prospect of a steady but slow climb up the official ladder. The exigencies of the civil war turned him into a military commander. Catching the eye of Tseng Kuo-fan, Li found his Anhwei ancestry an unexpected asset. The Hunanese in Tseng's entourage were absorbed into the Hsiang (Hunan) Army. Li was given the assignment of establishing an independent command with recruits mostly from Anhwei. This was the origin of the Huai Army. Li's early military experience proved decisive. Even after the Taipings had been pacified, military concerns were never far from his mind. The bulk of his modernizing activities later related directly or indirectly to China's security problems. Li, although primarily a civilian official, retained his concern for military affairs throughout his life.

Following the suppression of the several great rebellions, Li's talent as a politician also came into full play. First as governor of Kiangsu province, then as Liangkiang governor-general, and finally as Chihli governor-general, Li was called on to deal extensively with the Court. But because of the rapidly changing situation of the times, these positions also required him to deal directly with his fellow high officials in many parts of the country. As shown by David Pong, this required Li to demonstrate a high degree of political expertise.

Throughout, Li's championing of the self-strengthening movement involved him frequently with a number of foreign advisers. As commissioner of trade at first in Kiangsu and later in Chihli, he also met and dealt with a large number of foreign officials. Li became China's foremost "foreign affairs" expert, a role in which he continued even after 1894, the effective termination date of the present study.

While we have focused on the period before the Sino-Japanese War of 1894–95, the war can be seen as the culminating event in Li's long stewardship in masterminding Chinese policies toward Korea and Japan. The war also served as the final test of the success or failure of the self-strengthening movement. Reference to Li's involvement in the 1894 War and beyond is therefore relevant to our assessment of Li.

He was actually involved in every aspect of the war. He was still in charge of handling China's relationships with Korea and Japan when they reached the crisis stage. In the last-minute diplomatic maneuverings before the opening of hostilities, Li represented China in dealing not only with Japan but also with the major Western powers. He knew well that should war break out over Korea, his Huai Army units stationed in north China and the Peiyang Fleet, both under his command, would bear the brunt of the fighting. When hostilities commenced, these forces indeed constituted China's main combat units. Japan's attacks on a number of Chinese strong points, including Port Arthur and Weihaiwei, tested the worth of Li's decades-long efforts in fortifying them, at great cost. Such supporting facilities as telegraph lines and transport links, all established through Li's efforts, were vital to China's conduct of the war. Consequently, when China lost the war decisively, Li was judged by his contemporaries as chiefly responsible for the disaster. Nor has the passage of time changed this evaluation. There is general recognition that Li was slow in realizing Japan's determination to create a casus belli. He relied excessively on the intervention of the Western powers, and did not make adequate preparations for the contingencies of war until too late. Once the fighting began, he was unable to deploy his units effectively. Japanese forces prevailed by coordinating their attacks against loosely linked Chinese forces. Li made other questionable decisions. Chia-chien Wang emphasizes that the Peiyang Fleet, China's mobile offensive force on the high seas, was specifically enjoined by Li to adopt a defensive posture. Other scholars have argued that even after being defeated by the Japanese fleet at the Battle of the Yellow Sea, the Peiyang Fleet retained sufficient strength to serve as a potentially disruptive force against Japan's sea supply line. Li's orders, however, confined the fleet to Weihaiwei, which led to its surrender and destruction when the Japanese took the harbor by a combined land-sea siege.

Historians ever since the war, echoing the contemporary drumfire of calumny heaped on Li, have placed the major blame for China's shoddy performance on him. It is hard to argue against history. Even recognizing the extenuating circumstance of the general weakness of the Chinese empire in the 1890s, Li Hung-chang's conduct of the war is open to criticism at many points. Li's failure as a commander, however, should not obscure his performance as the main architect of China's defenses before the war, and his role in the history of China's modernization. The events of 1894 proved that ultimately Li's efforts were inadequate, and that the domestic political situation he had to contend with was intractable. Whatever the generalization, the fact remains that, without Li, China would have been even more vulnerable at the time of the Sino-Japanese War.

Following the humiliating Treaty of Shimonoseki in 1895, which Li had to negotiate on China's behalf, his power was drastically reduced. His role as a modernizer was ended, but because he remained China's most experienced diplomat, the Court continued to call on him to discharge a series of difficult assignments. To Li's legion of critics and rivals, this provided opportunities to embarrass him further. He was sent to St. Petersburg on the occasion of the coronation of Tsar Nicholas II in 1896, with secret instructions to conclude a treaty with Russia, for support against other rapacious Western powers and resurgent Japan. Whatever the presumed merits of this policy, it did not work. Within three years, German aggression in Shantung led to the creation in China of competing spheres of influence among the powers. Shortly afterward, the Boxer uprising occurred as a result. During that imbroglio Li joined other southern governors and governors-general in tacitly defying the Court, his action helping to serve to limit the areas of Boxer activities. This notwithstanding, the final humiliating assignment in 1901 of representing China at the Boxer settlement was thrust on him. On none of those occasions in Li's declining years did he particularly distinguish himself. Worn out by his labors, Li died within months of the Boxer settlement.

The issue of corruption

Implications have already been raised that Li Hung-chang's personal integrity was questioned. We must now address this issue. Did he acquire his wealth through legitimate means or was he incorrigibly corrupt, as his critics have charged? Obviously this is an important issue in assessing Li. Unfortunately, the relevant data at our disposal are not absolutely conclusive. Nevertheless, enough aspersions have been cast on Li that the issue should not be avoided. Let me begin by discussing factors that bear on the question of Li's probity.

One factor is the value system under which Li and his contemporaries operated. Early in Li's career he had come to terms with the prevailing system of his day. In 1862–63 Li made a strenuous effort to reform the Kiangsu likin system to produce more revenue for his Anhwei Army. Kwang-Ching Liu shows that Li sought men of integrity for likin collection duties, but where there were already men in place of questionable reputation who were proven fund-raisers, Li did not remove them. No proof exists that Li ever benefited personally from the corrupt likin officials, but that there were such men under his administration is indisputable.

Later in his career, that same willingness of Li to bow to practical necessity led historians to impugn his own ethical standards. In Li's later years the question of whether he was or was not personally implicated became much more difficult to resolve. Even then, however, his personal circumstances should be taken into account. Li held high office longer than most officials. Compared to Tseng Kuo-fan (1811–1872), for example, he served nearly three decades longer. He was involved in more large-scale military, naval, and industrial undertakings than any other official of his time. For Li to engage in this broad range of activities, he was in constant need of substantial sums of money. Neither imperial allocations, provincial tax revenue, nor private investors provided sufficient funds. Therefore he had to raise them through nontraditional means, such as the transfer of funds from one bank account to another. In time he became conditioned to fiscal manipulations. Li knew full well that his power did not rest solely on his control of revenue in his areas of jurisdiction or on his network of protégés and former subordinates or even on his continued control of the Huai Army and the Peiyang Navy. His power was based also on his ability to remain in the good graces of her Imperial Majesty, Tz'u-hsi. The vanity and venality of the Empress Dowager are well known. Under her virtual domination of the Court from the 1860s to her death in 1908, the Ch'ing Court became even more effete and corrupt. Li had to operate in that milieu. He had to please his imperial patroness, or risk political decline or impotence. With his highly tuned sense of political survival, Li became expert in playing up to Tz'u-hsi's vanity and greed. The full extent of funds channeled by Li to Tz'u-hsi and her functionaries remains a matter for further investigation, but of the existence of such funds there appears to be little doubt.

By the 1880s the pattern had been set. When in 1887 Prince Ch'un, acting with Tz'u-hsi's tacit approval, requested that Li forward funds earmarked for the navy to pay for the rebuilding of the Yuan-ming Yuan, Li readily lent his financial expertise for this purpose. Initially the transfer was supposedly temporary, but the funds were never returned to the original account. Instead, additional transfers followed. Li complained privately to friends that this effectively crippled the Peiyang Fleet, but it is noteworthy that Li never protested publicly until years later. His complicity in this notorious case seems beyond dispute.

A more damning case against Li arose out of the accusation that he had accepted illegal financial inducement from a foreign government. The case concerns the bribe that Russia allegedly offered to facilitate his signing a secret treaty in Russia's favor. If the allegation is true, then we are faced with a most serious charge, that of the high plenipotentiary of one sovereign state taking payments from another sovereign state on the eve of concluding a delicate diplomatic agreement. The case remains controversial. Charges stemming from Russian sources have not been fully corroborated from the Chinese side. We can be certain only of the circumstances of this episode. In 1896 Li Hung-chang was seventy-four *sui* of age. He had been in political disgrace since the Sino-Japanese War. Faced with bouts of ill health, Li was excessively concerned about his physical condition on his trip abroad. In short, Li was definitely in a period of physical decline. Perhaps even more important, Li by then had concluded that China had little recourse except to rely on Russian intervention in the face of mounting pressures from other European powers and Japan. He went to St. Petersburg with the Court's instruction to sign a treaty favorable to the Russians. While there can be no defense of Li if he indeed took the alleged bribe, it probably had no influence on his basic decision.

Was Li a mere politician?

Critics of Li's ethical shortcomings at least concede that he was a skilled politician, in the best and worst sense of the term. Li demonstrated his political skills early. Even before he left Anhwei, he had begun to build his political support. He acquired, especially from his native city of Ho-fei, the circle of protégés and friends that in later years served him well. As his fortunes rose, theirs rose with him, many of them entering his *mu-yu* system. Outside Anhwei he enlarged his circle of political contacts to the national level, but his earliest associates remained his closest supporters. In time they formed a powerful faction in national politics, exceeding in influence similar factions formed among the *mu-yu* of Tseng Kuo-fan, Tso Tsung-t'ang, and other high officials.

Li Hung-chang's success as a politician reached full fruition during the twenty-five years he held the concurrent positions of governor-general of Chihli and commissioner of trade for the Northern Ports, combining the dual roles of a key regional official and a national official. To operate successfully, Li had to involve himself even more in national politics. More than anything else, he astutely attached himself to the Empress Dowager Tz'u-hsi and her circle of sycophants at Court. Tz'u-hsi, moreover, governed by the principle of divide and rule. That, as well as his advocacy of policies of innovation, made him many powerful enemies at Court, not the least being the *ch'ing-i* group. Although the Empress Dowager often used *ch'ing-i* criticisms to chastise officials who were potential threats to her prerogatives, until the Sino-Japanese War Li never lost his tenure as Chihli governor-general. He was criticized on numerous occasions, but he managed to retain his important post for a quarter of a century. No better testimony can be found to Li as an exceptionally successful politician.

It is one thing to regard Li Hung-chang as an able politician; it is quite another to raise the question of whether he demonstrated noble qualities. As we have mentioned earlier, Li's reputation has gone through many ups and downs. It reached its nadir in the People's Republic in the decades of the 1950s through the 1970s. Marxist historians damned Li for his help in suppressing the Taipings, who they saw as peasant heroes. Li and his fellow ethnic Chinese officials were considered especially odious, because they were on the side of the Manchu oppressors of the Chinese people. Li was further condemned for being a defender of the old monarchical order, which was built on the Confucian value system. Worse yet, Marxist historians charged Li with being the greatest of all "surrenderists," consistently toadying to the Western imperialists by buying Western products and by signing a series of humiliating treaties. In short, these critics regarded Li Hung-chang as being the archetype of those who connived with enemies of the people within and without, thereby perpetuating the "semifeudal, semicolonial" conditions in nineteenth-century China. It should be pointed out, however, that this harsh assessment of Li has been modified of late. Since the beginning of the 1980s, even historians in the People's Republic have revised their previous extreme judgments. Nevertheless, there still remain, even among historians who are not Marxist, many who have serious reservations about Li.

Scholars who are loath to regard Li as anything more than a politician have generally faulted him along the following three lines: first, that Li suffers in comparison with his two prominent contemporaries, Tseng Kuo-fan and Tso Tsung-t'ang; second, that in his appointments he practiced gross nepotism favoring his own relatives and protégés; third, that the *ch'ing-i* criticisms of Li are warranted and damning. Let me address these charges specifically.

It is Li's misfortune in terms of his reputation to be a contemporary of Tseng and Tso. By most measures Tso's reputation has remained consistently the highest, while Tseng was considered in his lifetime and afterward a model Confucian scholar-official. We have already raised the issue of Li's personal wealth. Tseng, though never poor, and Tso, who was exceptional in his disdain for wealth, have had much higher historical reputations, in part because of their personal probity. In contrast, Li's wealth, and the question of how he acquired it, made him suspect.

That factor aside, there is little to choose between Li and the other two. All three established their loyalty to the Ch'ing dynasty by suppressing the Taipings. All three pioneered in advocating self-strengthening, and all three learned to cope with foreigners. Li happened to outlive his two contemporaries by several decades. Thus he actually made greater contributions than Tseng and Tso in what all three were trying to do regarding Westernized innovations. But Li had the misfortune of living through the decades of the 1880s and 1890s. No one who was in a position of responsibility in that period could have escaped criticism. Therefore there is the aura of the "surrenderist" about Li that is not attached to the other two. Moreover, Tso had the added advantage of being credited with the recovery of Sinkiang, and being willing to go to war with Russia over Ili. These accomplishments have endeared Tso to the Chinese ever since. Li was less fortunate.

On the charge of Li's excessive nepotism, extending even to his favoring his fellow provincials and friends, he cannot evade serious criticism. Many of his failures were the result of his appointment of ill-suited or even incompetent subordinates, whose chief claims were their personal ties to Li. Even on this issue, however, there were extenuating circumstances. Y. S. Leung has reminded us that high officials traditionally built up their personal network of supporters on the basis of three relationships: fellow provincials, colleagues, or fellow examination graduates. In making recommendations for appointments, high officials were not only permitted to favor nominees on the basis of these relationships, they were expected to do so. What Li did, therefore, was within the bounds of prevailing practices. In those instances where malfeasance was committed by officials whom Li recommended solely because of personal relationships, he cannot escape criticism. But he should not be subject to blanket condemnation.

Ch'ing-i charges against Li should be evaluated in the context of those making these charges. The *ch'ing-i* group, as is shown by a number of studies, argued largely from the rigid Classics-based ideological frame of reference. They were woefully ignorant of the realities of "barbarian" strength, and their alternative courses of action were seldom viable. By assuming that China had the choice of numerous options, or that honor and integrity demanded that China stand firm even if the consequences might be disastrous, they were more than ignorant, they were irresponsible. While Li made his share of questionable decisions, the *ch'ing-i* charges were not based solely on the merits of specific policies. Such charges arose in part because of the *ch'ing-i* insistence on adhering strictly to orthodox positions on righteous policies, and in part as a result of the pervasive pique of the younger traditionalists toward a powerful and unconventional political rival.

The Li Hung-chang that the *ch'ing-i* critics perceived was one who, because he lacked patriotism, consistently sold out China's national interests to her external enemies. Previous chapters in our study have demonstrated conclusively that this is entirely erroneous. Li was distrustful of foreign intentions throughout his life. He insisted on defending China's interests in all his dealings with foreigners. While he employed many foreign individuals, he made sure that they were under his control. In his voluminous writings he never ceased to avow that the motivating goal of his life was to build up China so that it could successfully resist foreign aggression. While the *ch'ing-i* group cloaked themselves in a rigid patriotic stance, Li preferred a nuanced approach. Such an approach called for China giving way in specific instances, one example being the dispute over the Liu-ch'iu Islands. His ultimate goal remained the rapid strengthening of China so that it could be free from foreign domination.

In the final analysis, Li deserves to be judged on his overall record. Beginning in the early 1860s, he was involved in nearly all major new and risky undertakings of the Ch'ing dynasty. Along with Tseng Kuo-fan, Tso Tsung-t'ang, Shen Paochen, and not many others, he bent his energy to the pressing problems of national regeneration. He saw that the solution to China's weaknesses was to adopt certain selected aspects in which the West was superior. Like other advocates of self-strengthening, Li had no doubt that the Confucian values, infusing all basic aspects of the Chinese way of life, had to be preserved. Thus he was pursuing what C. E. Black has termed *defensive modernization,* that is, adoption of certain innovative means intended not to change the traditional core but to preserve it. In this respect Li was different in degree, but not in kind, from the Meiji restoration leaders of Japan.

In his effort at self-strengthening, Li found that it was impossible not to become involved in foreign relations. Because for all practical purposes new technical knowledge could come only from abroad, he had to rely on foreigners, so he hired foreign advisers, instructors, and technicians. And while he was so engaged, China's security could only be preserved through negotiations. Li became involved in diplomacy out of necessity. Until such time as China became strong enough to take a firm stand, compromises and concessions were unavoidable. He proved a master at the diplomacy of the weak, standing firm in the few instances when it was possible to do so, and when it was not, making minimal concessions. He thought he could buy time by playing on the rivalries among the Western powers. Events ultimately proved him wrong, but what alternatives were there in his time?

Li Hung-chang deserves a more positive assessment for other reasons. He showed personal courage throughout his life. His energy and persistence stood out among an officialdom not noted for daring or dedication. His success in carrying out the bulk of the self-strengthening projects was remarkable, when unreliable funding and the constant drumfire of criticism might have discouraged a lesser man. Li remained steadfast in placing his loyalty at the disposal of the legitimate dynasty, yet he transcended that loyalty to work for the good of the nation and the Chinese people as a whole. While he had his share of personal weaknesses and public failures, his overall record was one of significant achievements, accomplished at a time of great difficulties for him and his nation. His was a record of innovation, beginning in the early 1860s after more than two decades of Chinese inaction after the defeat in the Opium War—and this record was sustained for three more decades. For all these reasons, it is submitted here that the question of whether Li's reputation should be revised substantially upward deserves to be raised. With all the reservations one must still make, the historian must consider whether Li can be, as many lesser men have been, justly described as a statesman.

Bibliographical Essay

In accordance with the nature of this concluding chapter, which differs from all preceding chapters, this general supplementary essay provides, in lieu of notes, selective bibliographical and historiographical references.

Basic sources

As stated by all contributors to this work, the indispensable basic source is *Li Wen-chung kung ch'üan-chi* (The complete works of Li Hung-chang) (Nanking,

1905). It has been reprinted in Taiwan by two publishers. The first three volumes of a new mainland edition of this work have been published under the title *Li Hung-chang ch'üan-chi* (Shanghai, 1985, 1986, 1987). The three volumes (all of telegrams) are valuable, and when subsequent volumes appear, they should further facilitate the use of as yet unpublished sources in the Shanghai Library.

Bibliographical information on other Li sources cited is as follows: *Li Hung-chang chih P'an Ting-hsin shu-cha* (Letters from Li Hung-chang to P'an Ting-hsin) (Taipei edition, 1960); *Li Wen-chung kung hai-chün han-kao* (Li Hung-chang's letters to the Navy Yamen) (Taipei reprint, 1972); *Li Hung-chang chuan-chi tzu-liao* (Materials for a biography of Li Hung-chang) (Taipei, 1978). The most recent discovery of more of Li's letters is in "Li Hung-chang chih Ting Jih-ch'ang han" (Li's letters to Ting), *Feng-shun wen shih* (1989), 2:47–167.

The two "chronicles" mentioned are *Li Hung-chang nien-(jih-)p'u* (Chronicles of Li Hung-chang), comp. Tou (Dou) Tsung-yi (Hong Kong, 1968), and *Li Hung-chang nien-p'u* (Chronicle of Li Hung-chang), comp. Lei Lu-ch'ing (Taipei, 1977). Selected memorials can be checked in *Li Hung-chang tsou-i mu-lu* (Index of Li Hung-chang memorials) (Tokyo, 1955), issued by the Toyo Bunko.

Documentary sources on key individuals with whom Li dealt are plentiful. I cite only the basic source for each selected key person as examples: on Tseng Kuo-fan, *Tseng Wen-cheng kung ch'üan-chi* (The complete works of Tseng Kuo-fan) (published beginning in 1876, reprinted in Taiwan, 1974); on Tso Tsung-t'ang, *Tso Wen-hsiang kung ch'üan-chi)* (The complete works of Tso Tsung-t'ang) (Changsha, published beginning in 1890, reprinted in Taiwan, 1964); on Kuo Sung-tao, *Yang-chih shu-wu wen-chi* (Collection of essays of Kuo Sung-tao) (N.p., 1892); on Shen Pao-chen, *Shen Wen-su kung cheng-shu* (The political papers of Shen Pao-chen) (Soochow, 1880); on Liu K'un-i, *Liu Chung-ch'eng kung i-chi* (The collected papers of the late Liu K'un-i) (1909, reprinted in Taiwan, 1968), also published under the title *Liu K'un-i i-chi* (Peking, 1959); on Weng T'ung-ho, *Weng T'ung-ho jih-chi* (The diary of Weng Tung-ho) (Shanghai, 1925, reprinted in Taiwan, 1970).

Modernization and the self-strengthening movement

The use of the concept of modernization in history is well discussed in C. E. Black, *The Dynamics of Modernization: A Study in Comparative History* (New York, 1966). In it China is placed with other nations on a scale of comparative modernization. A much more focused use of the concept is found in *Political Modernization in Japan and Turkey*, ed. Robert Ward and Dankwart Rustow (Princeton, 1964). More specifically, the concept is a useful analytical tool as applied primarily to twentieth-century China, in Gilbert Rozman, *The Modernization of China* (New York, 1981). A good discussion of the criticism and defense of the use of the concept of modernization as pertaining to China can be found in Paul A. Cohen, *Discovering History in China* (New York, 1984), chapter 2.

In the study of modernization in nineteenth-century China, historians have found the period of self-strengthening especially important. The literature on this period (called *tzu-ch'iang yun-tung* in Taiwan and *yang-wu yun-tung* in the PRC) has grown in recent years. A selective sampling is as follows.

In Taiwan, an early collection of existing studies was issued under the title *Tzu-ch'iang yun-tung* (The self-strengthening movement) (Taipei, 1956), in the series *Chung-kuo chin-tai shih lun-ts'ung* (Compendium on modern Chinese history), edited by Pao Tsun-p'eng et al. In the United States, interest in the topic received a great impetus with the publication of Ssu-yu Teng and John Fairbank, *China's Response to the West* (Cambridge, Mass., 1954). Another important work, Mary C. Wright's *The Last Stand of Chinese Conservatism: The T'ung-chih Restoration, 1862–1874* (Stanford, 1957) situated the movement in the larger context of a basically conservative revival. With the stimulus of these two seminal works came a small number of solid monographs, two of which were Ellsworth C. Carlson, *The Kaiping Mines, 1877–1912: A Case Study of Early Chinese Industrialization* (Cambridge, Mass., 1957; 2d ed., Cambridge, Mass., 1971) and Albert Feuerwerker, *China's Early Industrialization, Sheng Hsuan-huai (1844–1916) and Mandarin Enterprises* (Cambridge, Mass., 1958).

The publication of the eight-volume source compendium entitled *Yang-wu yun-tung* (The Westernization movement) (Shanghai, 1961), part of the series entitled *Chung-kuo chin-tai shih tzu-liao ts'ung-k'an* (Collections of source materials in modern Chinese history), rendered much of the rare and scattered basic sources conveniently available. Although compiled by Marxist scholars in the People's Republic of China, the *Yang-wu yun-tung* compendium shows no discernible political bias. In contrast, the monograph bearing the same title of *Yang-wu yun-tung* (Shanghai, 1956), written by the senior editor of the previous work, Mou An-shih, is much more ideologically oriented. Another monograph of Marxist orientation is Chang Kuo-hui, *Yang-wu yun-tung yü Chung-kuo chin-tai ch'i-yeh* (The Westernization movement and China's modern industrial enterprise) (Peking, 1979), but this is a much more analytical book and deserves careful attention. Equally deserving of careful consideration is Hsia Tung-yuan, *Yang-wu yun-tung shih* (History of the Western Affairs movement) (Shanghai 1992). Hsia is the author of two invaluable biographies of two men who worked for the enterprises Li founded: *Cheng Kuan-ying chuan* (life of Cheng Kuanying), rev. ed. (Shanghai, 1985) and *Sheng Hsuan-huai chuan* (Life of Sheng Hsuan-huai) (Shanghai, 1988).

For earlier and often Marxist views of Japanese scholarship on China's early modernization, see K. H. Kim (Key-Hiuk Kim), *Japanese Perspectives on China's Early Modernization, The Self-strengthening movement: A bibliographical survey* (Ann Arbor, Michigan, 1974).

For a judicious and authoritative non-Marxist overview of the self-strengthening movement, see "Self-strengthening: The Pursuit of Western Technology," by Ting-yee Kuo and Kwang-Ching Liu in *The Cambridge History of China*, vol. 10

(Cambridge, 1978), chapter 10. Also relevant is Kwang-Ching Liu, "The Ch'ing Restoration," in ibid., chapter 9. See also Liu's book, *Ching-shih ssu-hsiang yü hsin-hsing ch'i-yeh* (Statecraft thought and the newly arisen enterprises) (Taipei, 1990).

Among studies of enterprises in which Li Hung-chang was involved, the largest number, both monographs and articles, deal with the military. An early work is Wang Erh-min's *Ch'ing-chi ping-kung-yeh ti hsing-ch'i* (The rise of the armament industry during the Late Ch'ing) (Taipei, 1963), followed a few years later by the same author's authoritative *Huai-chün chih* (The Huai Army) (Taipei, 1967). On the navy, a major source is *Pei-yang hai-chün chang-ch'eng* (Regulations of the Pei-yang Navy) (1888 edition, also found in *Yang-wu yun-tung*, vol. 3). The standard survey of the navy in Chinese history remains Pao Tsun-p'eng, *Chung-kuo hai-chün shih* (History of the Chinese navy) (Taipei, 1951, enlarged edition in 1970). The latter edition of this work incorporates in part, but does not totally replace, Pao's *Ch'ing-chi hai-chün chiao-yü shih* (History of naval education during the Ch'ing dynasty) (Taipei, 1969). On the modern navy, however, John Rawlinson's, *China's Struggle for Naval Development, 1829–1895* (Cambridge, Mass., 1967) is better than the several Pao works. The author of chapter 9 in this study, Wang Chia-chien, has done extensive work on the Chinese navy and is currently the leading authority. Many of his relevant articles are now available in book form under the title *Chung-kuo chin-tai hai-chün shih lun-chi* (Collected studies on the modern Chinese navy) (Taipei, 1984). The latest study available is *Chung-kuo chin-tai hai-chün shih* (History of the modern Chinese navy) edited by Hu Li-jen et al. (Talien, 1990).

Two other documentary sources are particularly useful for military reforms. One is *Hai-fang tang* (Archives on maritime defense) (Taipei, 1957), which provides a standard reference for official actions proposed and enacted. The other is *Ch'ing-mo hai-chün shih-liao* (Historical documents on the navy in late Ch'ing times) (Peking, 1982), indispensable for the study of China's early modern navy.

For the Foochow Shipyard, the basic documents are found in *Ch'uan-cheng tsou-i hui-pien* (Collection of memorials regarding naval policies) (1888 edition, reprinted in Taipei, 1975). Recently available materials on Prosper Giquel, the chief foreign expert at the shipyard, have enabled Steven Leibo to publish *Transferring Technology to China: Prosper Giquel and the Self-strengthening Movement* (Berkeley, 1985). The latest books on the Foochow Shipyard are Lin Ch'ing-yuan, *Fu-chien ch'uan-cheng chü shih-kao* (Draft history of the Foochow Shipyard) (Fu-chou, 1986), and Lin Ch'ung-yung, *Shen Pao-chen yü Fu-chou ch'uan-cheng* (Shen Pao-chen and the Foochow Shipyard) (Taipei, 1987). For the Kiangnan Arsenal, the basic documents are found in *Chiang-nan chih-tsao chü ch'üan-an* (The complete documents of the Kiangnan Arsenal) (Shanghai, n.d.). For a fine analytical account of Kiangnan and other contemporary military enterprises, see Thomas L. Kennedy, *Arms of Kiangnan: Modernization in the Chinese Ordnance Industry, 1860–1895* (Boulder, Colo., 1978). Kennedy has also written a number of articles expanding on his main theme in this book.

Regarding these military aspects of the movement, certain chapters in *The Cambridge History of China* (Cambridge, 1978 and after) are very useful. See relevant portions of "Self-strengthening: The Pursuit of Western Technology" already referred to above. Equally valuable is "The Military Challenge: The Northwest and the Coast" by Kwang-Ching Liu and Richard J. Smith (*CHC*, vol. 11, chapter 4). The latter chapter is based, in part, on Smith's earlier articles, notably "Foreign-training and China's Self-strengthening: The Case of Feng-huang-shan, 1864–1873," *Modern Asian Studies*, vol. 10, no. 1 (1976), and "The Reform of Military Education in Late Ch'ing China, 1842–1895," *Journal of the Hong Kong Branch of the Royal Asiatic Society*, vol. 18 (1978).

On the nonmilitary side, one of the most successful enterprises was the China Merchants' Steam Navigation Company. Two pathbreaking studies of the early history of the CMSNC are Lü Shih-ch'iang, *Chung-kuo tsao-ch'i ti lun-ch'uan ching-ying* (Early steamship projects in China) (Taipei, 1962), and Kwang-Ching Liu, "British-Chinese Steamship Rivalry in China, 1873–1885," in *Economic Development of China and Japan*, ed. C. D. Cowan (London, 1964). A major survey of CMSNC up to 1949 is *Chao-shang chü shih: Chin-tai pu-fen* (History of the China Merchants' Steam Navigation Company: The modern period), ed. Chang Hou-ch'üan (Shanghai, 1988). The latest scholarship on this enterprise is represented by the chapter written by Chi-kong Lai in this study. A major source of self-strengthening enterprises is the serial *Sheng Hsuan-huai tang-an tzu-liao hsuan-chi* (Selected documentary sources of Sheng Hsuan-huai) (Shanghai, 1978 and after), which has separate volumes on the Hupei Coal Mining Company, on the Han-Yeh-P'ing iron and coal complex, on the Sino-Japanese War of 1894, and on the 1911 Revolution. Unfortunately, the publication of the volume on CMSNC, long projected, has been delayed and, as of mid-1993, has not yet appeared.

Until recently few overall assessments of the self-strengthening movement were available (other than the largely negative Marxist works already mentioned). In the 1970s Thomas Kennedy, in his "Self-strengthening: An Analysis Based on Some Recent Writings," *Ch'ing-shih wen-t'i*, vol. 3, no. 1 (November, 1974), initiated a positive view of the movement. In 1987 a conference on the subject was held by the Institute of Modern History of the Academia Sinica in Taiwan, resulting in *Ch'ing-chi tzu-ch'iang yun-tung yen-t'ao hui lun-wen-chi* (Proceedings of the conference on the self-strengthening movement in late Ch'ing China, 1860–1894) (Taipei, 1988). This conference, through its general theoretical and comparative papers, and other specific papers dealing with the movement's leadership, finances, and individual enterprises, has contributed further toward a comprehensive assessment of the movement.

Diplomacy

Even before the Chinese diplomatic archives were opened and made available to scholars abroad, solid books had been written based entirely on Western archives. Two examples are Hosea B. Morse, *The International Relations of the*

Chinese Empire (London, 1910 and after) and William L. Langer, *The Diplomacy of Imperialism, 1890–1902* (New York, 1935; 2d ed., New York, 1951). They remain useful. The opening of the archives made it possible to publish the most important sources on Chinese-Western relations: *Ch'ing-tai ch'ou-pan i-wu shih-mo* (The complete record of the management of barbarian affairs in Ch'ing times) (Peiping, 1930) covering the years before 1875, and *Ch'ing-chi wai-chiao shih-liao* (Historical materials on foreign relations in the latter part of the Ch'ing dynasty) (Peiping, 1932 and after) for the period after 1875. Two other basic sources are *Ch'ing Kuang-hsü ch'ao Chung-Jih chiao-she shih-liao* (Historical materials concerning Sino-Japanese negotiations during the Kuang-hsü period) (Peiping, 1932) and *Ch'ing Kuang-hsü ch'ao Chung-Fa chiao-she shih-liao* (Historical materials concerning Sino-French negotiations during the Kuang-hsü period) (Peiping, 1933). From these newly available documents, T. F. Tsiang published his pioneering article "Sino-Japanese Diplomatic Relations, 1870–1894," *Chinese Social and Political Science Review*, vol. 17 (1933), and his book *Chung-kuo wai-chiao shih tzu-liao chi-yao* (Selected materials for the history of China's foreign relations), 2 vols. (Shanghai, 1931, 1934). On Sino-Japanese relations, a major multivolume work is Wang Yün-sheng, *Liu-shih-nien lai Chung-kuo yü Jih-pen* (China and Japan in the last sixty years) (Tientsin, 1932 and after); the work has gone through major revisions, the latest in 1979, and must be used with caution. A reliable basic source is *Ch'ing-chi Chung-Jih-Han kuan-hsi shih-liao* (Historical sources on Sino-Japanese-Korean relations during the late Ch'ing period) (Taipei, 1972).

On the Tsungli Yamen, the forerunner of the Chinese foreign office, see Ssu-ming Meng, *The Tsungli Yamen: Its Organization and Functions* (Cambridge, Mass., 1962). Early Chinese efforts in modern diplomacy are well treated in two monographs: Immanuel Hsü, *China's Entrance into the Family of Nations: The Diplomatic Phase 1858–1880* (Cambridge, Mass., 1960) and Masataka Banno, *China and the West, 1858–1861: The Origins of the Tsungli Yamen* (Cambridge, Mass., 1964).

K. H. Kim, Edwin Leung, and Ming-te Lin, in chapters 7 through 9 of this study, have cited the basic sources for delineating Li's special responsibility for China's Japan and Korean policies. I need only highlight a few of them. An early classic using primarily Japanese sources is Tabohashi Kiyoshi's *Kindai Nissen kankei no kenkyu* (A study of Japanese-Korean relations in modern times) (Keijo, 1940). The same author wrote *Nisshin sen'eki qaikoshi no kenkyu* (A study of the diplomatic history of the Sino-Japanese War) (Tokyo, 1951, reprinted in 1965). These can still be consulted but should be used together with works of later scholarship. Two examples are Frederick F. Chien's *The Opening of Korea: A Study of Chinese Diplomacy, 1876–1885* (New Haven, Conn., 1967) and Ming-te Lin's *Yuan Shih-k'ai yü Ch'ao-hsien* (Yuan Shih-k'ai and Korea) (Taipei, 1970), one of the first books by a Chinese scholar using Korean in addition to Chinese and Japanese sources. An equally comprehensive book dealing with the period before Yuan's playing a part in Korea is Key-Hiuk Kim's *The Last Phase of the East Asian World Order: Korea, Japan, and the Chinese Empire, 1860–1882* (Berkeley, 1980).

On the Sino-French War of 1884–85, in which Li was also involved, I should mention, in addition to the *Ch'ing Kuang-hsü ch'ao Chung-Fa chiao-she shih-liao* already cited, *Chung-Fa chan-cheng* (The Sino-French War), ed. Shao Hsun-cheng et al. (Shanghai, 1955), a multivolume companion source collection to *Yang-wu yun-tung*. An especially useful monograph is Lloyd Eastman's *Throne and Mandarins: China's Search for a Policy during the Sino-French Controversy, 1880–1885* (Cambridge, Mass., 1967).

Li's involvement in the Sino-Japanese War of 1894–95 is outside the direct focus of this study, but the diplomatic background leading to it is not. Two titles merit special attention. Many diplomatic sources are to be found in *Chung-Jih chan-cheng* (The Sino-Japanese War), also edited by Shao Hsun-cheng et al. (Shanghai, 1956). This multivolume work is another in the series comprising *Yang-wu yun-tung* and *Chung-fa chan-cheng* already mentioned. The second work is Wang Hsing-chung's earlier pioneering monograph *Chung-Jih chia-wu chan-cheng chih wai-chiao pei-ching* (The diplomatic background of the Sino-Japanese War of 1894) (Peiping, 1937).

Li Hung-chang's diplomatic policies were especially subjected to sharp attacks by the *ch'ing-i* (pure discussion) group (also referred to as the *ch'ing-liu p'ai* or *ch'ing-liu tang*, the purist faction). One of the earliest studies of the *ch'ing-i* is Yen-p'ing Hao's "A Study of the Ch'ing-liu Tang: The Disinterested Scholar-Official Group, 1875–1884," *Harvard Papers on China*, vol. 15 (1961). This was followed by Lloyd Eastman's "Ch'ing-i and Chinese Policy Formation during the Nineteenth Century," *Journal of Asian Studies*, vol. 24, no. 24 (1965), which was expanded and incorporated in his *Throne and Mandarins*, mentioned above. The latest article on the *ch'ing-i* is by Marianne Bastid, "Ch'ing-i and the Self-strengthening Movement," *Proceedings of the Conference on the Self-strengthening Movement*, cited above.

Li's relationships with foreigners can be followed in a number of selected sources and monographs. The single most important foreigner in China at the time was Robert Hart. The classic study on Hart remains Stanley F. Wright, *Hart and the Chinese Customs* (Belfast, 1950). Valuable sources include *The I. G. in Peking: Letters of Robert Hart, Chinese Maritime Customs, 1868–1907*, ed John Fairbank et al. (Cambridge, Mass., 1975) and *Entering China's Service: Robert Hart's Journals, 1854–1863*, ed. Katherine Bruner et al. (Cambridge, Mass., 1986). Especially relevant is *Robert Hart and China's Early Modernization: His Journals, 1863–1866*, ed. Richard J. Smith et al. (Cambridge, Mass., 1991). Books have appeared recently on two other foreigners with connections to Li. On Robert Shufeldt, see Frederick C. Drake, *The Empire of the Seas* (Honolulu, 1984). On P. G. von Möllendorff, see Yur-Bok Lee, *West Goes East* (Honolulu, 1988). These and other sources show that foreigners were ambivalent toward Li.

Many English diplomats disliked Li intensely, as shown in P. D. Coates, *The China Consuls: British Consular Officers, 1843–1943* (Hong Kong, 1988). Shufeldt also came to dislike Li, but other Americans were more positive; for example, see John W. Foster, *Diplomatic Memoirs* (Boston, 1909) and John R. Young, *Men and Memories: Personal Reminiscences* (New York, 1901). The diplomatic historian Michael Hunt considers Li's handling of Americans sufficiently instructive to devote a separate chapter to the topic in his book, *The Making of a Special Relationship, The United States and China to 1914* (New York, 1983).

For a good view of late Ch'ing diplomacy, see Immanuel Hsü's chapter, "Late Ch'ing Foreign Relations, 1866–1905" in *The Cambridge History of China*, vol. 11, chapter 2.

The corruption issue

This is one of the more controversial aspects of Li Hung-chang. Here I limit myself to documentary and monographic evidence on two important cases: the 1888 transfer of naval funds for the reconstruction of the Summer Palace and the alleged Russian bribe to Li in 1896.

The episode of the naval funds transfer is discussed in both Pao Tsun-peng's first edition of his *Chung-kuo hai-chün shih* and Rawlinson's *China's Struggle for Naval Development* (both cited above), but the best detailed study of this issue is in Pao's article, "Ch'ing-chi hai-chün ching-fei k'ao-shih" (The truth about late Ch'ing naval funds), *Chung-kuo li-shih hsüeh-hui chi-k'an* (Journal of the Chinese historical society), vol. 1 (1969), 17–55. Much of this article is incorporated in Pao's second and much expanded edition of his *Hai-chün shih*. Another early article on this episode, published by Wu Hsiang-hsiang in *Chin-tai shih-shih lun-ts'ung* (Collected articles on recent historical events) in 1964, has been translated as "The Construction of the Summer Palace and Naval Funds in the Late Ch'ing Dynasty" in *Chinese Studies in History*, vol. 12, no. 1 (1978). A balanced discussion of this episode is found in the previously cited Liu and Smith chapter, "The Military Challenge" in *The Cambridge History of China*, vol. 11, 254–56.

The Russian bribe to Li, even more controversial, has been accepted as plausible by some senior scholars. Immanuel Hsü in his chapter on late Ch'ing foreign relations in *The Cambridge History of China* accepts it with minor reservations (vol. 11, 112). Hsü adds the proviso that the chief Russian official involved, Count S. I. Witte, denied the matter. In the earlier English translations of Witte's *Memoirs* (London, 1921), Witte did say he gave such a bribe, but this version of Witte's original memoirs is not accepted by all scholars. This charge is repeated in an annotated edition of Witte's three-volume Russian language *Memoirs* (Moscow, 1960) certifying that Witte stated that he authorized half a million rubles specifically for Li. The most recent account of this matter is found in George A. Lensen's posthumous work, *Balance of Intrigue: International Rivalry in Korea and Manchuria, 1884–1899* (Tallahassee, Fla., 1982), vol. 2,

510–12. Lensen's detailed information on the complicated machinations of this bribery is derived from the article "Likhunchangskii fond" by B. A. Romanov (*Bor'ba klassov*, 1924). Lensen adds that Li never received the full amount.

Studies of Li

The first Chinese critical work devoted to Li was Liang Ch'i-ch'ao's *Li Hung-chang* (1902 edition, republished in 1936, Taiwan reprint, 1963). It set the tone for all negative assessment of Li afterward. From its publication to 1949 there was only Wei Hsi-yü's short account, *Li Hung-chang* (Shanghai, 1931). Since the establishment of the People's Republic, Li had been thoroughly castigated as the chief culprit of the self-strengthening movement, itself condemned as anti-masses and pro-imperialists. Li was denounced in such books as Liang Ssu-ch'eng's *Li Hung-chang mai-kuo shih* (The history of Li Hung-chang's treasons) (Tientsin, 1951) and Hu Ping's *Mai-kuo tsei Li Hung-chang* (The traitor Li Hung-chang) (Shanghai, 1955). As late as the early 1980s, the leading party historian Hu Sheng, in his influential book *Tsung ya-p'ien chan-cheng tao wu-ssu yun-tung* (From the Opium War to the May Fourth Movement) (Peking, 1981), still regarded Li Hung-chang very negatively (chapter 10).

At the very time (1980–81) the Hu book appeared, there was a serious debate on Li and the entire self-strengthening movement in mainland journals and newspapers, resulting in a partial restoration of Li's reputation. The debate on Li is well summarized in *Chung-kuo li-shih-hsüeh nien-chien* (Annals of the Chinese historical profession), 1983 ed., 693–94. A recent reevaluation of Li is *Li Hung-chang yü Chung-kuo chin-tai hua* (Li Hung-chang and Chinese modernization) ed. Chou Chün and Yang Yü-jun (Hefei, Anhui, 1989). Yuan Shu-yi, professor of history at Hopei Normal College, is author of the recent *Li Hung-chang chuan* (Biography of Li Hung-chang), a work of 421 pages (Peking, 1991).

In contrast to the situation on the mainland, the reappraisal of Li in Taiwan has been gradual and cumulative. First came the reprinting of basic documents on the self-strengthening movement, already indicated. Then there appeared a number of solid articles and monographs by Li Kuo-ch'i, Li Shou-k'ung, Wang Chia-chien, and others. Li Shou-k'ung has written the first scholarly biography of Li: *Li Hung-chang chuan* (Biography of Li Hung-chang) (Taipei, 1978). Recent major contributions to the study of Li are to be found in the previously cited *Proceedings of the Conference on the Self-strengthening Movement* (1988). For an excellent study of the early phase of Li Hung-chang's career, see Li Kuo-ch'i's long article cited above, this volume, in Liu, "Introduction," note 29.

In English, several uncritical biographies were published in Li's lifetime and shortly afterward. They include Robert Douglas, *Li Hungchang* (London, 1895), Mrs. Archibald Little, *Li Hung-chang, His Life and Times* (London, n.d.), and J.O.P. Bland, *Li Hung-chang* (London and New York, 1917). A purported *Memoir of Li Hung-chang* (Boston and New York, 1913), edited by a certain William Mannix, turned out to be a complete forgery (so stated in the 1923 edition). The first reliable account of Li is William Hail's entry in *Eminent Chinese of the Ch'ing Period* (Washington, 1943), ed. Arthur Hummel. Of greater value is Stanley Spector's *Li Hung-chang and the Huai Army: A Study in Nineteenth-Century Chinese Regionalism* (Seattle, Wash., 1964). This book provides us with a wealth of information on Li's mature years, but its account of Li is placed within an analytic framework of regionalism, a framework that has been challenged by later studies. A more specialized study is Kenneth Folsom's *Friends, Guests, and Colleagues: The Mu-fu System in the late Ch'ing Period* (Berkeley, 1968), which deals with Li's network of "personal associates." An adequate biography of Li in a Western language remains to be written.

Glossary

Anking	安慶
Ashikaga Yoshimitsu	足利義滿
Chang Chien	張謇
Chang Hao	張灝
Chang Ming-chiu	章鳴九
Chang P'ei-lun	張佩綸
Chang Shu-sheng	張樹聲
chang-ch'eng	章程
chao-lai	招徠
chao-shang	招商
Ch'ao-hsien ts'e-lueh	朝鮮策略
Ch'ao-yung	超勇
Chemulpo	濟物浦
Chen-hai	鎮海
Ch'en Lan-pin	陳蘭彬
Ch'en Shu-t'ang	陳樹棠
Cheng Ju-ch'eng	鄭汝成
Cheng Kuan-ying	鄭觀應
cheng-ming pien-wu	正名辨物
Ch'eng Hsueh-ch'i	程學啟

Chi-yuan	濟遠
Chia yang-kuei-tzu	假洋鬼子
Chiang-nan chih-tsao-chü chi	<江南製造局記>
Chiang-nan chih-tsao-chü chien-shih	<江南製造局簡史>
Chiang-nan chih-tsao tsung-chü	江南製造總局
Chiang-nan tsao-ch'uan-ch'ang shih	<江南造船廠史>
Chiang-nan tsao-ch'uan-ch'ang shih pien-hsieh-tsu	江南造船廠史編寫組
Chiang-su chin-tai ping-kung shih lueh	<江蘇近代兵工史略>
chiao-yueh	校閱
chien-fang	簡放
chien-lin	監臨
chien-yueh	檢閱
chih-fu hsien	知府銜
Chih-yuan	致遠
Chihli	直隸
Chin-ling chih-tsao-chü	金陵製造局
Ch'in-t'ien chien	欽天監
Ch'ing-chi ping-kung-yeh ti hsing-ch'i	<清季兵工業的興起>
ch'ing-i	清議
ch'ing-liu	清流
Ch'ing-shih	<清史>
Ching Yuan-shan	經元善
Chiu-shih chieh-yao	救時揭要
Chou Sheng-ch'uan	周盛傳
Chou Shih-ch'eng	周世澄
Chu Ch'i-ang	朱其昂
chü-chang	局章
chü-kuei	局規

ch'u-hai yü-lei k'uai-t'ing	出海魚雷快艇
ch'u-yang hsueh-sheng Hu-chü	出洋學生滬局
chüan-chü	捐局
Chung-hua wen-hua fu-hsing yueh-k'an	<中華文化復興月刊>
Chung-kuo chin-tai kung-yeh-shih tzu-liao	<中國近代工業史資料>
Chung-kuo wen-hua ta-hsueh	中國文化大學
Ch'ung-hou	崇厚
Date Munenari	伊達宗城
Enomoto Takeaki	榎本武揚
Fang-hai hsin-lun	<防海新論>
fen yang-shang li-ch'üan	分洋商利權
Feng Chün-kuang	馮焌光
Feng Kuei-fen	馮桂芬
Feng Kuei-fen ti cheng-chih ssu-hsiang	<馮桂芬的政治思想>
Feng-huang shan	鳳凰山
feng-tien	封典
Fu-chi	福濟
fu-ch'ih	扶持
Fung Yu-lan	馮友蘭
Hai-fang tang	<海防檔>
hai-kuan tao	海關道
Hanabusa Yoshimoto	花房義質
hang	行
Ho Ching	何璟
Ho Ju-chang	何如璋
ho-ts'ao	合操
Horimoto Reizo	堀本禮造
Hsi-hsing jih-chi	<西行日記>
hsiang-hua	向化

hsiao-ts'ao	小操
Hsien-tai cheng-chih jen-wu shu-p'ing	＜現代政治人物述評＞
Hsu Ch'eng-tsu	徐承祖
Hsu Jun	徐潤
Hsueh Fu-ch'eng	薛福成
Hsueh Huan	薛煥
Hu Kuang-yung	胡光墉
Hu Lin-i	胡林翼
Hu-chou	湖州
Hua-hsin	華新
Huai-chün chih	＜淮軍志＞
Huai-chün p'ing-Nien-chi	＜淮軍平捻記＞
Huang Fang	黃芳
Huang T'i-fang	黃體芳
Huang Tsun-hsien	黃遵憲
Huang-p'u	黃浦
hui-ts'ao	會操
Hung-k'ou	虹口
hung-tan	紅單
Huo-ch'i shuo-lueh	＜火器說略＞
i-i chih-i	以夷制夷
i-tao	驛道
i-tzu erh-liu	一咨二留
Ili	伊犁
imsin	壬申
Inchon	仁川
Inoue Kaoru	井上馨
jo	弱
Kaihwa	開化

Kan Tso-lin	甘作霖
Kanghwa	江華
Kao-ch'ang Miao	高昌廟
kapsin	甲申
<u>Kiang-an</u>	江安
Kim Hong-jip	金宏集
Kim Ok-kyun	金玉均
Kojong (king)	高宗
ku-fen yin	股分銀
kuan-li	官利
kuan-tu shang-pan	官督商辦
Kuang Fang-yen-kuan	廣方言館
k'uang-chi ling-ch'i	匡濟令器
Kung Shou-t'u	龔壽圖
kung-so	公所
Kuo Ting-yee	郭廷以
kuo-yu hua	國有化
Kuroda Kiyotaka	黑田清隆
Li Chen-yü	李振玉
Li Chung-chueh	李鍾玨
Li En-han	李恩涵
Li Han-chang	李瀚章
Li Heng-sung	李恆嵩
Li Hsin	李新
Li Hsiu-ch'eng	李秀成
Li Huan	李桓
Li Hung-chang	李鴻章

<u>Li Hung-chang chih hai-fang yun-tung chi ch'i hou-kuo</u>

<李鴻章之海防運動及其後果>

Li Tsung-hsi	李宗羲
Li Wen-chung kung ch'üan-chi	＜李文忠公全集＞
li-ch'üan	利權
Li-shih yen-chiu	＜歷史研究＞
Liang Ch'i-ch'ao	梁啟超
Liao Ho-yung	廖和永
Lin Ch'ang-i	林昌彝
Lin Shih-kung	林世功
Lin T'ai-tseng	林泰曾
Liu Ch'i-hsiang	劉麒祥
Liu Chung-ch'eng kung i-chi	＜劉忠誠公遺集＞
Liu Han-fang	劉含芳
Liu Hsun-kao	劉郇膏
Liu Jung	劉蓉
Liu Kwang-Ching	劉廣京
Liu K'un-i	劉坤一
Liu Ping-chang	劉秉璋
Liu Pu-ch'an	劉步蟾
Liu Tso-yü	劉佐禹
Lo Feng-lu	羅豐祿
Lü Shih-ch'iang	呂實強
Lu-chou	盧州
Lü-yin	綠營
"Lun Li Hung-chang ti pien-fa ssu-hsiang"	"論李鴻章的變法思想"
Lun-ch'uan chao-shang chü	輪船招商局
Ma Chien-ch'ang	馬建常
Ma Chien-chung	馬建忠
Ma Hsin-i	馬新貽

Min	閩
Min-kuo jen-wu-chih	<民國人物志>
mu-chüan	畝捐
Mori Arinori	森有禮
Nieh Ch'i-kuei	聶緝椝
Nieh Tseng Chi-fen	聶曾紀芬
Nien	捻
Okinawa	沖繩
Pa-t'u-lu	巴圖魯
Pak Yong-hyo	朴泳孝
P'an Ting-hsin	潘鼎新
pang-t'u	邦土
pao-lan	包攬
pao min	保民
Pao-ting	保定
Peiyang (navy)	北洋（水師）
p'in	貧
ping-pei tao	兵備道
pu-hsuan	部選
Ryūkyū	琉球
sadae	事大
san-yang	三洋
Satsuma	薩摩
sei-Kan	征韓
sha-ch'uan	沙船
shan-hou fu-hsu chü	善後撫卹局
shang-tung	商董
Shao-hsing	紹興

Shen Pao	申報
Shen Pao-chen	沈保楨
Shen Yun-lung	沈雲龍
Sheng Hsuan-huai	盛宣懷
Sheng-chün	盛軍
Shishido Tamaki	突戶磯
Sho T'ai	尚泰
shu-chi-shih	庶吉士
Sin Hong	申宏
Soejima Taneomi	副島種臣
Sun Ch'iang-ming	孫鏘鳴
Sun Ssu-pai	孫思白
Sun Yü-t'ang	孫毓棠
Sung Chin	宋晉
ta-ts'ao	大操
Tai Heng	戴恆
Tai Tsung-ch'ien	戴宗騫
t'ai-ch'ang ssu ch'ing	太常寺卿
Takezoe Simichiro	竹添進一郎
Taku	大沽
T'ang Ching-hsing (Tong King-sing)	唐景星
T'ang T'ing-shu	唐廷樞
tao-t'ai	道台
T'ao-yuan wen-lu wai-pien	<韜園文錄外編>
Teng Ssu-yü	鄧嗣禹
t'iao-kuei	條規
T'ien-chin fu-chih	<天津府志>
tien-pao chü	電報局

Ting chung-ch'eng cheng-shu	<丁中丞政書>
Ting Jih-ch'ang	丁日昌
Ting Ju-ch'ang	丁汝昌
Ting Kung-ch'en	丁拱辰
ting-wei t'ung-nien	丁未同年
Ts'ao-chiang	操江
tsao-ts'e pao-hsiao	造冊報銷
Tseng Chi-tse	曾紀澤
Tseng chi-tse ti wai-chiao	<曾紀澤的外交>
Tseng Kuo-ch'üan	曾國荃
Tseng Kuo-fan	曾國藩
Tseng Pao-sun	曾寶蓀
Tseng Pao-sun hui-i-lu fu Ch'ung-te lao-jen tzu-ting nien-p'u	<曾寶蓀回憶錄附崇德老人自訂年譜>
Tso Tsung-t'ang	左宗棠
tsou-che	奏摺
tsung-pan	總辦
tsung-ping	總兵
tsung-tung	總董
Tsungli Yamen	總理衙門
tu-pan	督辦
Tung-fang tsa-chih	<東方雜誌>
t'ung-hsiang	同鄉
t'ung-liao	同僚
t'ung-ling	統領
t'ung-nien	同年
T'ung-wen-kuan	同文館
tzu-chih	自治

Tz'u-hsi	慈禧
wai-pu	外補
Wan-ch'ing tzu-ch'iang yun-tung chün-pei wen-t'i chih yen-chiu	<晚清自強運動軍備問題之研究>
Wang Erh-min	王爾敏
Wang K'ai-t'ai	王凱泰
Wang T'ao	王韜
Wei Yuan	魏源
Wei Yuan	威遠
Wei Yun-kung	魏允恭
Wen-hsiang	文祥
Wen-pao chü	文報局
Wu Ch'ang-ch'ing	吳長慶
Wu Hsu	吳煦
Wu Kuang-chien	吳光建
Wu Ta-ch'eng	吳大澂
Wu Ta-t'ing	吳大廷
Wu T'ang	吳棠
wu-li k'o-hsun	無例可循
wu-pei yuan	武備院
Yakub Beg	阿古柏伯克
Yanagiwara Sakimitsu	柳原前光
Yang Chia-lo	楊家駱
Yang Fang	楊坊
yang-ch'iang tui	洋槍隊
yang-p'ao ying	洋炮營
yang-wu wei-yuan	洋務委員
Yang-wu yun-tung wen-hsien hui-pien	<洋務運動文獻匯編>

Yeh T'ing-chüan	葉廷眷
yen-yun-shih	鹽運使
Yi Son-gun	李瑄根
Yi Yu-won	李裕元
Yin Chao-yung	殷兆鏞
ying kuei	營規
Ying-han	英翰
ying-kuan	營官
Yü Tsai-pang	余在榜
Yuan Chiu-kao	袁九皋
Yuan Shih-k'ai	袁世凱
Yung Wing	容閎
yung-i pien-hsia	用夷變夏

Index